Winds of Life
The Destinies of a Young Viennese Jew
1938-1958

In Memory of Our Parents

Gershon Evan

Winds of Life
The Destinies of a Young Viennese Jew
1938-1958

ARIADNE PRESS
Riverside, California

Library of Congress Cataloging-in-Publication Data

Evan, Gershon.
    Winds of life: the destinies of a young Viennese Jew, 1938-1958 / Gershon
Evan
        p.   cm. – (Biography, Autobiography, Memoirs Series)
    ISBN 1-57241-086-8
    1. Evan, Gershon. 2. Jews–Austria–Vienna Biography. 3. Jewish children
in the Holocaust–Austria–Vienna Biography. 4. Holocaust, Jewish (1939-
1945)–Austria–Vienna Personal narratives. 5. Holocaust survivors–Israel
Biography. 6. Holocaust survivors–California–San Francisco Biography. 7.
Vienna (Austria)–Biography. 8. Israel Biography. 9. San Francisco (Calif.)
Biography. I. Title. II. Series.
DS135.A93E93 2000
943.6' 13004924'0092–dc21
[B]

                                                                99-40508
                                                                CIP

Copyright ©2000 by Ariadne Press
270 Goins Court
Riverside, CA 92507

Contents

Foreword

Waiting to be seated in one of the busy restaurants in San Francisco, I struck up a conversation with a young gentleman who spoke with an unmistakable French accent. As after more than half a century away from the country of my birth, my spoken English has a German tinge, I was a little surprised when the man asked me about my place of origin. "Vienna," I said. Whereupon he, without the slightest hint of irony or a smile, exclaimed: "Let me guess, you were in music." I had to laugh and told him he was wrong.

It was, of course, the wildest of guesses, but the mention of Vienna will conjure up waltzes, an array of celebrated composers, and their equally famous compositions. Less important, although widely recognized, are Vienna's delectable cuisine and torten. The city's name will also bring to mind, in persons of a more advanced age, a number of distinguished doctors who practiced there, the most famous, of course, being Sigmund Freud.

Less familiar to people who have never been to Vienna are its beautiful parks with their abundance of lilacs in springtime, its museums, the Ring boulevard circling the central district, and the fancier shopping areas of Kärntnerstrasse and Graben. The beautiful Hofburg, Emperor Franz Joseph's castle in the Inner City, and his summer palace, and the extensive garden, called Schönbrunn, also mean little to people who have never visited them.

After recounting the story of my Viennese childhood to a New Yorker, I was told by him: "No different from growing up in Brooklyn."

Perhaps. Perhaps with some differences.

*   *

*

My life up to my early teens was so different from the one that followed, it might just as well have belonged to people on two different planets. The style of the following chronicle may mirror this contrast. I also found that life is a chain of episodes that, like pearls on a string, succeed each other. If life was placid, the pearls are uniform and nice in appearance, but they will lack the luster of natural pearls. If life was filled with excitement, then the pearls on the string are not little round balls, but uneven and different from each other like the events life had offered.

Childhood in Vienna

Memory is elusive. For most of us our earliest recollections are a succession of glimpses puncturing a big void. They are like mountain peaks emerging from a carpet of clouds, as viewed from a high-flying jet. We remember moments of our early life clearly, yet events before or after those moments are missing.

My earliest recollection is that of a darkened room illuminated by four Sabbath candles on a table covered by a white tablecloth. In retrospect, this memory is still so vivid because it captured facets of my childhood that have remained important all my life.

In the semi-darkness of the room was also a baby carriage. In it slept my infant sister Berta. I was three years old.

Our parents came from Galicia, which before World War I was part of the Austro-Hungarian Empire. Many of the Jews in this part of the country were poor, but "blessed" with many children, so they sent some of their offspring to relatives in distant countries, mainly the United States. America, in the late 19th and early 20th century was a magnet for impoverished people from Europe, primarily Italians and Irish, as well as Jews from Russia and Galicia. This early immigration of Jews to the United States saved the lives of thousands of other Jews half a century later.

After the Central Powers lost the war of 1914-18, oil-rich Galicia became a province of the newly created Poland. When the Germans overran Poland in 1939, the country was divided between Germany and the Soviet Union and Galicia fell to the USSR. It was captured by the Germans in 1941 but incorporated into Soviet Union again at the end of World War II.

Father came from a little town not far from Kolomea where he was born on October 8, 1893. As a teenager he was sent to a relative in Germany where he worked in the man's toy store to earn his keep. When World War I broke out in 1914 he traveled to Vienna to join the Austrian Army at the Rennweg barracks. Assigned to the Russian front, he was wounded and eventually fell into enemy hands.

Mother was born in a village called Peczeniczyn (pronounce Petshenitshin) on April 26, 1900. At the age of 14 she moved with her widowed mother to Vienna. She spoke, read, and wrote German fluently and studied at a business college. She often attended performances at the Vienna Opera House and like many other students who could not afford the price of a seat bought inexpensive tickets for the uppermost tier, where a section was reserved for standing-room-only. She told me she had to see every performance at least twice. Once to watch the proceedings on stage and the second time to follow the libretto. After marriage she no longer went to the opera.

1

We lived at 26 Brigittenauer Lände in one of the old apartment buildings strung out along the left bank of the Danube Canal. Our home consisted of the conventional one room and kitchen and, in our case, a grocery shop with a large storage room. The Canal, more like a stream, branches off the Danube in the northern part of the capital, and re-enters the big river about ten miles downstream. The island thus created consists of the Second and Twentieth Districts of the city and, because of its large Jewish population, was called by the Viennese derogatorily *die Matzesinsel* (matzos island).

The embankment of the canal, still uncultivated in those days, was the meeting place of Indians, cowboys, and bandits who lived in the vicinity. Adventure was on every boy's mind and in our games everyone wanted to be the movie hero Tom Mix whom we cheered on in silent movies on Sunday afternoons in the local theater. I did not realize then that my life would have more adventures than Tom Mix's ever had.

I loved my neighborhood and could have shouted with joy as the sun-flooded Lände stretched out in front of me. The Danube canal wound its way in a gentle curve toward the Inner City and the tall, single spire of St. Stephen's Cathedral raised its spire up through Vienna's rooftops to reach the sky.

Vienna has always suffered from a housing shortage. Most working class apartments in Vienna consisted of a single room and a kitchen. To flee the small and crowded quarters, where sometimes families of six or seven lived together, Viennese found their comfort and entertainment in the numerous cafés and neighborhood taverns. Those institutions were an essential part of city life. They were warm and friendly places for people to meet when they wanted to find relief from the dingy surroundings of their homes.

Jews frequenting cafés in the evening, sipped coffee, played cards and chess, talked politics or gossiped about those not present. Non-Jews sought companionship in taverns where they enjoyed wine and beer, played billiards and tarock, a popular card game, at the time, in Vienna.

As dictated by Austrian law, our store was closed on Sundays and all official Christian holidays. The only Jewish holidays on which our business was closed were *Rosh Hashana* (the New Year), and *Yom Kippur* (the Day of Atonement). On those high holidays my parents joined thousands of other Viennese Jews in places of prayer. Because many Jews were not members of synagogues, refusing to pay the high prices demanded for tickets, they rented restaurants and cafés and held services there.

2

Our parents fasted on Yom Kippur and during the eight days of Passover the four of us ate no bread or food containing yeast. Kitchen utensils used during that holiday had to be different from those in use the rest of the year. The plates, pots, and silver were stored in a wooden crate in the corner of the room until the appropriate time arrived. The use of this precious space in our home for Passover dishes reflected the high value mother placed on our faith. She also kept a strictly kosher kitchen, and we had different sets of kitchen utensils for milk and meat dishes. She would not eat anything *trefe* (non-kosher), but in contrast to her, my father, my sister, and I even ate pork.

Mother cooked and baked Viennese style, yet many of the meals served in our home originated from grandma's Jewish-Galician recipes. The main meal of the day in Vienna was served at midday, which made supper uninteresting. The exception to this routine in many Jewish households was the Friday night dinner.

On Thursdays mother and grandma went shopping for meat, poultry, and fish. Since everything had to be kosher, the prices for beef and chicken were triple the amount charged by regular stores. Each of the shops held its own fascination for me, so I joined them often when they made their purchases. On the visit to the fishmonger I learned of a Jewish legend that very few people knew about.

Rather disgustedly and yet captivated I watched a man use a mallet to kill a fish with a blow to its head. In the beginning it frightened me to see the carp or pike sliced open and cleaned out while it still seemed alive and twitched convulsively. When I told the fishmonger of my concern, he assured me the animal was dead. A fish's nerves were so strong, he explained that its body moved even though it was no longer alive.

Not trusting the man, I went to my father who confirmed the fact. He then asked me, "Have you heard of the fish that cried "Shmah Ysroel" (the prayer: Hear Israel's call) when he received the deadly blow to its head?" I hadn't. And father said that according to legend this wondrous event took place in Vienna a long time ago. At the next opportunity he promised to take me to the grave of that fish; it had been buried as if it were a human being.

One day father took me to a big building somewhere in Vienna. We entered a dark and musty hallway, passed a staircase leading to the upper floors, and exited through a door in the rear. This led to a spacious backyard and a Jewish cemetery of indeterminate age. Weather-beaten tombstones, atilt where the soil had given way to their weight, grew out of the ground like decaying teeth of a giant centenarian. Their inscriptions and dates were in Hebrew but my father, unfamiliar with the numbers the ancient letters represented, could not even guess their age.

(A friend told me years later that this Jewish cemetery originated in the Middle Ages and was the only one left in Vienna from that bygone era.)

Weeds grew in wild abundance, and the rather intimidating atmosphere of the graveyard instilled in me the feeling that I was looking at a haunted dreamscape. At any moment I expected the dybbuk[1] to transcend the invisible border between the living and the dead, to rise from one of the flattened mounds and materialize just where we wanted to walk. I clung to my father's hand while we made our way among the graves to look for the burial spot of the fish.

The little monument was an obelisk made up of rocks, which showed a plump, short fish at the top. His head, turned toward the sky, had its big mouth wide open as if to cry out its woe to an unfeeling deity. The whole setting was a splendid and neglected relic of Jewish life in the Vienna of old.

Though it looked uninspiring when we found it, I felt awed just standing at the foot of this grave. What or who had this creature been that was said to have called out to God the Hebrew words "Shmah Ysroel". But the deadly blow had struck and, as so many times in the history of the Jewish people, the appeal to God for rescue had been in vain.

Maybe this legend is just a metaphor for the Jewish people's relation to their God. People beg God to hear them, but He does not. Jews were forever on the losing side, a fate that goes back to their encounters with the Babylonians, the Greeks, the Romans, the Spanish Inquisition, and the innumerable kings, chiefs, and underlings who had it in for "the Chosen People." It really is a miracle that Jews still exist, particularly after the Germans' display of murderous efficiency.

I often asked father to tell me about the Great War, especially after I had seen a notebook of his filled with funny characters. He eventually told me that they were his memoirs but, to my sorrow, as they were written in the Cyrillic alphabet of Russian, I could not read them. From time to time he promised to translate those notes for me, but never got around to it. He did, however, during our rather short life together, talk about the horrors of war.

He recounted the frightening high-pitched scream of the attacking Russian soldiers with their round, needle-like bayonets. He spoke of death and destruction everywhere. He was silent about his wounds but told of his eventual capture and deportation to Siberia. He recalled that while he was in a POW camp near Krasnoyarsk, Cossacks would ride

---

[1] In Jewish folklore a dybbuk is believed to be a wandering soul that enters and possesses a person.

their horses into the assembled prisoners and in vicious attacks strike at anybody within their reach. They used the feared *nagaikas*, short-handled whips made from leather straps and braided like a pigtail. The situation became so unbearable that father and a friend tried to escape. They hid under railroad cars but were apprehended. For their unsuccessful attempt to flee, they were sentenced to be shot. For reasons unknown, the American Consul at Krasnoyarsk intervening on their behalf, saved them.

Summers were benign; they were quite warm. Winter was feared by all prisoners. Their clothing was no match for the bitter cold, and father said, that water pouring outside seemed to freeze in midair.

We had at home large prints showing scenes of the First World War, and though I was simultaneously fascinated and shocked by what I saw, I leafed through those pages again and again.

I looked at grotesquely distorted faces of soldiers hit by exploding grenades. The flying shrapnel showed in white lines fanning out from a dark spot on the ground. Wounded horses lay in the dirt and kicked the air in despair and pain. The animals' eyes were bulging in horror and fear, and I felt ashamed when my compassion was greater for the suffering of the beasts than that of the dying men with their twisted features.

The war came to an end in 1918. The turbulent times that followed the communist revolution postponed the return of thousands of POWs to their homeland. Three years passed before their hopes were realized and they returned to Vienna. In 1921, a lady matchmaker introduced father to mother and they were married the same year.

Seasons came and went, each supplying its own pleasures, but that kaleidoscope of changes never left a lasting impression on my mind. This lack of close relationship with the different cycles of the year changed one spring.

In one of my schoolbooks I had read the description of how the first spring flower, a delicate snowdrop, forced its little bell-shaped head through the snow. I was so impressed by this uneven contest of forces and the successful overcoming of odds that I felt as if I had been present in that snow-covered field, and had watched the little flower defy the unrelenting winter. And the snow that had enraptured me a few months ago, suddenly became the icy fist of the season that kept spring away.

Even today, while writing about this time of my life, I can still feel a love for this particular spring. Winter was on the wane, the snow melted, and the air had turned caressingly mellow. When I ran down the street the light breeze touching my cheeks felt good. The snow that had been cleared off the road and heaped onto the edge of the sidewalks created miniature mountain ranges. The balmy weather made the snow piles soft and mushy, and they collapsed into themselves like soap bubbles exposed to air. Winter had had its pleasures, but a 10-year-old looked ahead to the new season and the varied pleasures it brought with it. Life and life's joys were simple in those days, and wants more easily satisfied.

And when I was young, an hour was much longer than it is today. It might sound foolish; yet many readers will agree that more can be crammed into sixty minutes in one's youth than can be in my age. An hour, a week, or any other measurement of time was like a drop of ink on blotting paper. It spread way beyond its first spot. A clock's pendulum swung slower, and the sand in an hourglass needed longer to get through the aperture. But perhaps this seeming elasticity of time may be traced to the impatience of youth. It took so very long for birthdays, holidays, or summer vacations to arrive; and to become older seemed an endless wait.

Nonetheless, life ran its course, and I was usually content with the days and seasons and what they brought. There was always the morrow when I would be grown up and able to follow my dreams of travel, adventure, and excitement. And though the days, weeks, and months passed in a rather orderly and peaceful fashion, I can't remember a moment of boredom. With no friends around, I ordered my stamp collection and read.

Many Jewish families employed young girls as domestics. They came from villages not far from Vienna. The young women were not paid much, but had room and board and, most important, learned to cook and run a household. With the acquired experience of a few years of service the girls returning to their villages became desirable brides.

We too had a domestic at different times, the last one being Julie. She, more than any of the other girls, became almost a part of the family. Sundays were her days off, but she never went out, nor did she have a boyfriend. Julie quit after two years in our employ. An older sister had persuaded her not to work for Jews. Mother, unaware of the cause, offered her a raise in pay. However, this made no difference. When mother found out the real reason behind her leaving she was very upset. On the day Julie left, the girl cried. But leave she did.

This episode, several years before the Nazis took over, reflected the prevalent, though concealed sentiment of a great part of the Austrian population toward its Jews. We never again employed a domestic.

In 1930, we moved. Our parents sold the place on the Lände and acquired another store on Klosterneuburgerstrasse and an apartment on nearby Othmargasse.

On Klosterneuburgerstrasse, a busy street, our parents' dry goods store did well. After three years they returned to a grocery and delicatessen business, perhaps because it was more like their original business.

The living quarters now were a room and kitchen and also should have included a "Kabinett" or additional small room. However, the owner of the apartment building had rented it to a couple and their baby. I slept on a foldaway bed that was put up at night at the foot of my parents' bed. A live-in domestic, if we had had one, would have had a foldaway bed in the kitchen. Berta's bed was in a corner of the living room near the window.

Summer days in Vienna could be sweltering. *Hundstage*, they were called, or dog days. But what that poor animal had to do with the high temperature I never found out. Evenings that followed hot days would lose some of their intensity yet were still uncomfortable if one stayed home or lingered in the street to chatter with an acquaintance. Relief from the oppressive heat was to be found in a walk along the embankment of the Danube Canal, or a visit and light supper in the open-air restaurant of the nearby Augarten.

If one did stroll along the dirt lane above the grassy slope that slanted toward the water's edge, he had to contend with *Gelsen*, the pesky, blood-sucking mosquitos that, except for the itch after the bite, were harmless. Nevertheless we tried to swat them before they bit. Berta and I chased cockchafers, big beetles, which, after capture and in their effort to escape our cupped hands, tickled pleasantly against the skin and made us laugh.

In the Augarten at night one missed the beauty of the park but was compensated by the silence, the cooler air, and the fragrant aroma of the vegetation that was so much more profound in the dark.

At the restaurant, father and mother ordered yogurt, which our father loved, slices of dark farmers' bread and butter. Berta and I had a glass of milk each as well as bread and butter, and for dessert, of all things, a large pretzel sprinkled with coarse salt.

And then a real adventure happened.

Not to me, but to grandma. She visited her two daughters whom she had not seen since 1906 when in their early teens they had been sent from Galicia to America.

It was almost enough to satisfy my *Wanderlust* to know somebody in my family who had taken a trip to a place as far from my neighborhood as the moon.

Grandma's journey to New York took forever, and when she returned, she had a difficult time answering all of my questions. In front of me was a lady who had traveled an impressively great distance on a train and journeyed on a ship as big as several tall apartment buildings connected to each other. My excitement was no less, even after she explained how she had hated the ocean voyage. She was seasick the whole time and thought she was going to die. Her continued ringing for the nurse failed to alleviate her misery, for all that Florence Nightingale dispensed was the promise that our grandma would live.

I listened enthralled to her stories of New York and felt envious when she told of a visit to a huge amusement park called Coney Island that was so much bigger than our amusement park, the Prater. She had seen buildings that reached the clouds and streets where endless streams of cars and of people moved. Regretfully, though, she had not gone to those wide, flat prairies where buffaloes galloped, and cowboys chased bad guys. She even missed my beloved comedians, Charlie Chaplin and Laurel and Hardy. She did not even know who they were. But then, grandma never went to the movies as we did.

Grandpa and his three sons, Max, Jakob and Markus Seidler, owned Brüder Seidler, a factory in the Inner District. While the old gentleman was alive (he was grandma's second husband who had married her before I was born), grandma got up every Friday at 5 A.M. She worked all day to prepare the Sabbath dinner for her husband, his three sons, their spouses and five children. She did everything from scratch and also cleaned up after dinner. Grandfather presided at the head of the table and grandma sat at the other end, the place closest to the kitchen.

Being a Jewish homemaker of the old school, she never entertained the thought of rebellion against this kind of slavery.

Grandpa, who was mother's stepfather, died in 1933 without leaving a will. His death came as a shock to mother who for a long time recounted the death scene over and over. She insisted that he had desperately tried to tell her something before he died and she described the helpless look in his face as his mouth opened and closed emitting no sound. She believed that had he been able to speak, grandma's economic situation would have been far better than the one her stepsons provided.

The brothers gave grandma the choice of keeping her husband's savings book or giving it to them, in which case they would grant her a monthly allowance. Evidently unaware of the amount of money in their father's account – the sum was small – grandma choose the monthly pension, and the brothers got the inferior deal for their pettiness.

When I turned eleven, Vienna was in turmoil. Although I could not fully comprehend the things that were going on, it did affect me. Political violence shook the city I loved as the long-standing antagonism between the Conservatives and Social Democrats turned violent. Skirmishes took place between the private armies of the *Heimwehr*, fascist home guard, and the *Schutzbund*, defense league of the Social Democrats. In late 1933,

8

Chancellor Dollfuss suspended the parliamentary government and Austria became a dictatorship. The Social Democrats revolted in February 1934, but their uprising was crushed when, in bloody retaliation, government troops fired canons point-blank into buildings where workers lived and were entrenched.

On a walk with my family to the Inner City a few days later, we found barbed-wire fences closing off streets that led from the center of town and the government buildings to the Danube Canal embankment. Behind those obstacles police officers with machine guns had taken up positions, and the situation looked menacing enough to interrupt our peaceful walk and send us home.

After the failed revolt an authoritarian dictatorship under Chancellor Engelbert Dollfuss was created. All political parties and their respective private armies were banned.

In July of 1934, the Nazis, illegal then, tried unsuccessfully to overthrow the government and in the attempt, murdered Chancellor Dollfuss.

Kurt von Schuschnigg became the new chancellor of Austria.

So that our widowed grandma wouldn't be alone, mother asked me to move in with her. I had no objections, and in early 1935, at age 12, I did what my mother asked.

Grandma had a four-room apartment and I thought her furniture was luxurious. She put a narrow two-section china closet at my disposal and I thought I had attained the best of what life had to offer. I placed my clothing in the lower section and arranged the items closest to my heart, like books, school materials, and adventure novelettes, behind the glass doors of the upper shelves.

The daily four-mile round-trip walk between school, which I continued to attend in the Twentieth District, and grandma's apartment building in the Ninth, was no bother. I loved to walk and neither rain nor snow failed to dampen my spirit. Most of my free time I continued to spend in the old neighborhood where my friends lived.

Zionist Activities

When one was asked on the street in Vienna if one was a Jew, it was mostly meant as an insult. But the teenager who put the question to me not far from grandma's home looked like a nice fellow with no sinister motives. Curious to find the reason for his direct approach, I said yes.

"Do you belong to a Zionist youth group?" he inquired. When I said, no, he invited me to the "clubhouse," a two-room apartment in a nearby building. He belonged to Betar, a right-wing Zionist organization whose actual aims I did not know. In fact, I knew very little about Zionism, only that it was a movement to make Palestine a country for Jews.

My new acquaintance showed me his place. On the walls of both rooms were posters with Zionist slogans. Along with the printed words were pictorial views of different parts of Palestine and photographs of people important to the Zionist cause. For the first time I saw pictures of Jabotinsky, the guide and leader of the Revisionist party. Of Trumpeldor who had died a hero's death in the defense of a tiny outpost called *Tel Hai* (hill of life), in northern Palestine, and of Theodor Herzl[2], the major activist of modern political Zionism. My guide pointed to a map on the wall that showed a Jewish homeland on both sides of the Jordan and, in a voice that took on the quality of oratory and passion, he said: "The Land of the Bible was ours once. It has to be returned to us, if not in peace then in war. It will happen, and it must happen, for so it was promised."

I was impressed by the young man's account, but somewhat startled by the fervor of his last remarks. He appeared to be a different person than the one who had addressed me a short time earlier on the street.

Returning to a reasonable tone of voice, he explained how fellows like myself met on certain evenings during the week at the club to socialize, listen to lectures about *Erez Ysroel* (Land of Israel), sing Hebrew songs, dance the Hora, and go on occasional Sunday outings to the Vienna Woods.

It sounded like fun, and I was impressed by his description of the comradeship that bound the group together. His invitation to join them was exciting; yet I felt that I needed my parents' permission.

My father had no objection, but suggested I join the youth group of the party he belonged to, namely, the *Judenstaatspartei* (Party for a Jewish State).

Following his advice, I became a member of this youth group, whose outlook was not much different from that of Betar. I learned in detail about the efforts of Herzl, which were inspired by the virulent anti-Semitism he observed during the Dreyfus trial in Paris in 1894.

Herzl had lived, studied and worked in Vienna, which led me to assume that our city was the hub of the Zionist movement.

The young members of my group joined in the club's activities,

---

[2] Herzl, "Father of modern Zionism" was an assimilated Viennese Jew of Hungarian extraction. He was as much Viennese as any native, and at least as Austrian as any true-blue Austrian. When he died in 1904 at the early age of 44 he was buried in Vienna. During the early thirties thousands of Jews regularly marched to his grave on the anniversary of his death. The dream of a Jewish homeland, as promised by the Balfour Declaration, was then remote indeed.

though not always for reasons one might expect. Of all the political areas discussed at meetings only one stayed with me: Zionism called on people to go to Palestine and build a country for Jews. Everybody showed interest in the concept, yet nobody wanted to move there. Life in our city was too pleasant to be exchanged for the life Herzl described in his visionary book titled OLDNEWLAND. One thing that might have enticed me to go there was missing: the kind of adventures so temptingly described in the adventure dime novels I read. Palestine, not exotic enough, lacked the wild animals I wanted to hunt when I grew up. But even assuming the right features had been there, I still would not have wanted to live in Palestine permanently. I did not want to stay in any foreign place for long, but always to return to Vienna. It was my home... until I was taught differently.

Meanwhile, however, blissfully unaware of what the future held, we enjoyed the club's programs. On trips to the Vienna Woods we proudly wore shirts of dark blue, buttoned by silvery studs in front and at the breast pockets. And, to accentuate their military appearance, square patches of blue velvet, like those on army uniforms, embellished collar ends. We played soccer and I was the team's goalie. We listened to colorful stories about Eretz Ysrael, Land of Israel, and through them, and the sense of belonging, life became more meaningful.

Yet it wasn't only Herzl's idea that the Jews should go to Palestine. The same advice appeared written in chalk on the sidewalks of Vienna. I was bothered when loutish youths or even adults sometimes shouted in the Viennese vernacular after some of us on the street, "*Jud' fohr nach Palästina*" (Jew, go to Palestine). Nobody shouted after me, although, had someone done so, it would have made no difference. I had no intention of telling my father to move us all to the Holy Land just because some unsavory types wanted us to go there. I loved Vienna, and my life there, and nothing could ever dislodge me from my place of birth. I was proud of the city, and sang with fervor a song learned in school:

> Jedem Wiener glänzt das Auge,
> pocht das Herz, die Wange glüht,
> wenn nach jahrelanger Trennung
> er Sankt Stephan wiedersieht.

> Every Viennese's eye sparkles,
> cheek's aglow, his heart beats higher,
> when he, after years of absence,
> sees again St. Stephen's spire.[3]

---

[3] Vienna's famous landmark cathedral.

In the mind of a thirteen-year-old, causes and ideas have their own interpretations. They may contradict reality, therefore, be rejected as illogical by adults with more awareness of the real situation, yet, in the world of a child everything he believes in is real enough. Although, in retrospect, the naiveté of my love for the city becomes apparent, at the time my deep feelings for Vienna were real.

Despite my desire to see the world as pictured in my adventure novels, I regarded Vienna the center of the universe. My joy and sadness, the pleasures and emotions common to a youngster were inextricably bound to this city. In my youthful enthusiasm, I never thought that anybody would think differently, including the Jews who lived here. This belief seemed born out by the fact that at the time nearly 180,000 Jews resided in Vienna, and, though many were barely eking out a living, they stayed on. Had they been sufficiently unhappy they would have looked for new horizons, as did my friend Otto and his family, who had moved to Palestine a few years earlier.

Although his family had no permit to remain in the country (they entered on visitors visas) they stayed on. It was relatively simple to disappear among the Jewish population that had dramatically increased because of the influx of German Jews fleeing Nazi terror since 1933.

Even most idealists who went to Palestine during the very last part of the 19th and the early 20th century were dedicated to the Zionist idea primarily because of the persecution and pogroms they had suffered. Those people came from Eastern Europe, especially Russia, where the devout Christian population was indoctrinated and incited to violence by a virulently anti-Jewish clergy. Oppression of Jews took place daily. Pogroms and murder were tolerated under the Czarist monarchy of Holy Russia. Zionism and emigration developed and grew best in the fertile ground of rabid anti-Semitism.

Having been assigned the mandate of Palestine by the League of Nations in 1922, Great Britain issued a series of "White Papers" in the years that followed. The first of those infamous documents, called the Churchill White Paper, divided the land in a most disproportionate way. Of the original area of 45,000 square miles, 37,000 became today's Jordan, while only about 8,000 square miles were called Palestine[4]. The White Papers also restricted Jewish immigration according to the "economic capacity" of the country, which consisted mostly of arid tracts

---

[4] In 1917, Lord Balfour, then foreign secretary of Great Britain, declared in an official letter: "With respect to Palestine the British government expresses 'sympathy' with 'Jewish Zionist aspiration' and a favorable attitude toward 'the establishment in Palestine of a national home for the Jewish people.'" — Germany was trying to reach a similar agreement with its Turkish war ally.

of land and unhealthy swamps.

In spite of hardship and danger the development of the barren land by the first Jewish settlers progressed. Their agricultural pioneering spirit and success was complemented by the influx of enterprising German Jews. Cities expanded and commerce grew. Despite or perhaps because of this, subsequent White Papers curtailed immigration of Jews to Palestine even more. The last of those papers in 1939 reduced it to a trickle. As no restrictions were ever placed on the entry of Arabs, they came from neighboring states in an unending stream, seeking and finding work in the dynamic Oldnewland envisioned by Herzl. But Jews also kept immigration alive. The stricter British regulations became, the more the Jews relied on Aliya Beth (illegal entry into the country).

But if people did not themselves go to Eretz Israel, many of them all over the world collected coins in little cans for Keren Kayemet le Israel (the Jewish National Fund). The money was used to buy land from Arabs, Turks, and whoever was ready to sell. The pennies collected and sent to that arid little country were a steady transfusion of lifeblood that played an important role in the rather utopian project, the creation of a Jewish State.

A steady though small trickle of immigrants had been migrating to Palestine since the Diaspora of two thousand years ago. It consisted mainly of old people who went in search of a shortcut to heaven, which they hoped to find in the Promised Land when they died.

I have touched on the subject of memory before. How curious it is that minor events of the past stay alive in one's mind while greater ones vanish. The following episode is just such a minor event that I remember, potentially due to the unpleasant consequences it could have had a few years later.

A customer in our store, a ladies' dressmaker who lived in an apartment in the same building, came one day to the store accompanied by a slim, pretty girl my age. After attending to her purchases she asked our mother if my sister and I could come upstairs to keep her visiting niece company. The woman too lived in an apartment with one room and a kitchen, a big area of the room being taken up by a large bed near the far end wall. Preparing dinner in the kitchen, the lady left us to ourselves.

There were no toys and after a few futile attempts to invent games, Hansi, our new friend, suggested we play theater. She sat my sister in a chair near the window, and then led me across the room to the narrow space behind the bed. It was to be our dressing room. Sitting on the floor across from each other, she fumbled with her blouse, as if changing into something different, and then went out to do a few pirouettes and dance

13

steps in front of my sister. Having thus "performed," she informed the audience of more to come.

Taking her place again opposite me, she decided it was my turn to perform. First, however, I had to be prepared. She touched my shirt here and there and sliding her hands from below into my shorts to rearrange them triggered forbidden thoughts and pleasures in me. Having displayed my acting skills, I eagerly retired to our dressing room.

To get Hansi ready for the next act I moved her blouse slightly to the left and right and then tried to smooth out the waves of her skirt. As this met with little success and the folds stubbornly reappeared, I reached under the garment to make a better job of it. The back of my hand could feel the firm abdomen.

When she returned, we stopped pretending and went straight to passionate adolescent exploration.

Three years later, after the Nazis had assumed power, Hansi and I passed on the street. She had become a beautiful girl, but the uniform she wore was less appealing. She was walking with two other girls, and the three of them were dressed in the uniform of the BDM, *Bund Deutscher Mädel* (the girl's division of the Hitler Youth).

No doubt she recognized me, and, for a moment, I wondered if she was indoctrinated enough to wish me harm. Had she been so inclined, it was in her power to hurt me. At the time her word would have been accepted against anything a Jew may have said.

But they walked by me. Once the danger had passed, I was vain enough to feel affronted by her open disregard of me instead of being glad that nothing worse had happened.

Dreams of Adventure

One of my prized possessions was the Kozzen World Atlas. Its array of maps promised a world of travel and adventure to a young man addicted to dime novels. It filled my mind with desires that only real experiences, I thought, would satisfy. The printed word acquainted me with exotic peoples, their habits and habitats. It took me to regions near and far and to rivers and mountains with odd sounding names. The world became as familiar to me as the streets of my neighborhood. Fictitious characters in narratives brought Manaus, Timbuktu, Popocatepetl, French Foreign Legionnaires in Hanoi, and the twisted streets of Sidi-bel-Abbes and Oran, as near to me as the Soho and Limehouse underworld of Edgar Wallace's mystery stories. The world was a mosaic. It stretched like a many-colored fabric over a round sphere or flooded the pages of my atlas with dots, spots, twisted lines, and blotches in a spectrum of asymmetrical forms. As the far-away places of this enticing world were out of reach, I sought my excitement in Vienna.

My imagination helped.

Leo, a cousin seven years my senior, had escaped recently from Nazi Germany and was also living now in grandma's apartment. He owned a shiny black raincoat I yearned for. When he finally gave it to me, the thin rubber coating had become porous in places and was especially leaking around the pockets. Still, the coat created for me the illusion of being a tough character in a novel.

This fantasy was fostered by evening strolls in the inner city where dark tunnels of side streets leading off brightly-lit thoroughfares were filled with threats and danger. The visor of my cap low over my eyes and the corduroy-covered collar of the raincoat raised around my neck provided feelings of warmth, comfort, and daring. For some reason a light rain or misty drizzle caressing my cheeks intensified my illusory sense of boldness. I would see a dark netherworld just below the surface as the many-colored lights of advertisements reflected in the glistening asphalt. I enjoyed listening to the soft hiss of cars rolling over wet roads and loved watching the throngs of people on their way to and from entertainments. Pulsating nightlife beyond my reach, yet so alluring.

At times, a friend kept me company when I roamed the down town area. Like bobbing corks in flowing water we moved with the crowd or resisted their invisible pull to direct our steps toward our own destinations. We both dreamed of adventures, which we thought to find in the narrow, centuries-old alleys and streets of Vienna's center.

After the excursions we took the long way home. We walked the Ring, passing the Opera House, the Palace Garden, and the Heroes' Square. While strolling along the tall fence of the Volksgarten we often heard strains of waltz music through the greenery. I promised myself I would visit that invisible Garden Café as a grown-up, sit at a table, and order coffee and chocolate torte.

But real life was not sparing with adventures. I would experience more than my share of situations I rather would have read about sitting in a comfortable chair.

At the age of thirteen I had my Bar Mitzvah at the Seitenstetten Synagogue in the Inner City. It was a quiet event that only grandma, my parents and sister attended. Leo and Hugo, another cousin, fulfilled my dream when they bought me a wristwatch. Both were traveling salesmen for Brüder Seidler and were away on business. I received ten schillings (two dollars, perhaps, not too bad in 1936) each from Uncle Marcus and Uncle Jacob. Uncle Max and his wife bought me a book that sold in discount bookstores for less than two schillings.

After the religious ceremony, the uncles and their families were invited to grandma's apartment for an afternoon of coffee and cake. Only Aunt Anna, Jacob's wife, came. She brought the gifts... and the excuses of the others that they were too busy.

The Seidler clan had started out as a small business and had become one of the biggest manufacturers of women and men's undergarments, aprons, men's shirts, and work coats in Austria. The factory produced goods on the premises and had subcontractors working out of their homes. Though the Seidlers were stepbrothers and stepfather to my mother, there was no feeling of kinship between them and us. Only grandpa had a close relationship with mother. Our father was rather cold toward all four of them, a feeling that was mutual. He may have envied them their extraordinary success.

After the eighth grade, at the age of 14, I quit school and started to work for the Seidlers. Work at the factory was not the entertainment it had seemed on previous short visits.

My first job was in the apron and work-coat section of Frau Schmidt. At my introduction she commented sarcastically: "Another relative." What a beginning! To some employees I was to remain the relative of the owners, to the Seidlers I represented just another apprentice who addressed them as Herr or Frau Seidler.

Here I met Erich, another apprentice and one year my senior. In a short while we became inseparable friends. After work we walked one another home, that is, he walked me home and then I accompanied him over the two miles to his house. Half of our conversations dealt with soccer, movies, stamps and the like and the other half with girls, and especially with two of the three Jewish apprentice girls who worked at the factory.

My friend had his eyes set on slim, olive-skinned, dark-haired Selma, but somehow they never got together. I had mine on Gretl, a blond, blue-eyed pretty maiden, with whom I never had a chance. She was almost sixteen and a woman, while I was fourteen and, in her eyes, still a boy.

On Sundays my friend and I roamed the *Prater*, the amusement park, or took long walks in the Inner City. We attended soccer games of Hakoah, the Jewish soccer club, and usually ended the day with a visit to a movie theater.

We eventually worked together in the shipping department of the company.

Pre-Nazi Austria

During the turmoil of the pre-Nazi era in Germany, the Austrian Nazis of the early thirties tried to stir up discontent among the Viennese. Because they were too weak to bring about political changes by democratic means, and far too few to take the fight into the streets, they resorted to terror tactics. For an extended period, the city lived in fear. Nazis placed bombs in public places, often in telephone booths. The bombings only stopped when the new Austrian government, a Christian-Conservative dictatorship, arrested Nazis, and placed them in detention camps. The Nazis then turned to non-violent methods. Perhaps they were ordered by Hitler not to alienate the Austrians. The reverse side of the Austrian five groschen coin displayed the "crutched" cross. By flattening half of each of the four surrounding outside bars with a punch, this symbol became a swastika. The Nazis prepared coins in this way and dropped them in the streets, where people, believing to have found a coin, picked them up. Since it was against the law to use such altered coins, they were saved to be shown to friends as curiosity and, unintentionally, spread Nazi propaganda.

In January 1938, our parents sold their store on Klosterneuburgerstrasse and were looking for another place in the neighborhood. During the following two months, I frequently spent my after-work hours and Sunday mornings with them.

The situation in Austria was tense. The feeling of sitting atop a powder keg was widespread. Still, many people, especially the Jews, clung to the hope that no change in government or its political structure was imminent or likely. Germany was noisy and powerful, but Catholic Italy certainly would let no harm come to Catholic Austria, its little neighbor to the north. After all, Germany was perceived to be mostly Protestant.

Even Italy's policy toward its Jews was reassuring. It was in stark contrast to that of Germany. Das kleine Blatt, an Austrian newspaper in Vienna quoted the official Informazione Diplomatica of Rome, on February 18, 1938: "The Fascist Government (of Italy) has no intention of conforming to an anti-Semitic policy as some foreign circles are trying to suggest."

Austria's population was unevenly distributed. Of its six million inhabitants, two million lived in the capital, the other four million in the provinces. Until the dictatorship in 1933, most of the people of Vienna leaned toward the left of the political spectrum while the rest of the country's rural and mostly agricultural population favored the right.

Because of these political preferences, so the Jews reasoned, rural

17

Austrians were reactionary and anti-Semitic, the left-leaning Viennese, on the other hand, were socialist and more tolerant. That dreadful misconception was set right by the actions of Vienna's population toward its Jews the moment the Nazis took over.

One day, in early February of 1938, I suggested to my parents: "We sold our store and have plenty of money to emigrate to South Africa or America." And to stress the importance of my suggestion I added the dire prediction: "You'll see, Hitler will come to Vienna."

Why did I conjure up such a frightening picture when, in my heart, I did not believe in this prophecy? Was it a premonition or, as my mother smilingly implied, just my yearning for adventure? Those fateful words, unconvincingly expressed, became reality only too soon.

I repeated my suggestion several times during the next few weeks, but to no avail.

When my parents bought another store in February I quit pestering them. The exchange brought a profit as the previous change had, and father said it was in a safe place.

The new store on Jägerstrasse was in a quieter neighborhood. It would have been successful had the Anschluss not taken place.

My troubled evaluation of the future was partly influenced by the Austrian Chancellor's visit, or rather the results of his visit, to Hitler at Berchtesgaden in February of 1938. Upon his return to Vienna, a crypto-Nazi, Seiss-Inquart (after the war hanged for war crimes) became a member of the Austrian government. It proved that Chancellor Schuschnigg's attempt to reach an amicable agreement with the Führer had failed. The dictator's persuasive arguments, interspersed with tantrums and open threats, convinced our chancellor of the futility of his mission. The weak position of Austria vis-à-vis its powerful neighbor became obvious. With no outside help, the future of the little country looked bleak.

Not only Hitler's warning that the German army might advance should Herr Schuschnigg refuse his demands, but Schuschnigg's awareness that a great many Austrians wanted unification with Germany led him to give in. Hitler's first demand was the legalization of the Austrian Nazi party whose goal was the *Anschluss* (the union with Germany).

By the beginning of March, political parties outlawed for years were allowed to function again. The city stirred fitfully, like a bear awakened from hibernation before its time. Some, especially the Jewish population, clung to the foolish hope that Red Vienna, the bastion of the Social Democrats (comparable to England's Labor party), might rise again. This was a vain wish when it was obvious that the swastika dominated the streets of the city. Wherever one turned, there was the swastika. Small ones on coat lapels and in giant displays on walls and fences. It outshone and outdid the catchy slogan of Schuschnigg's party painted on walls or printed on posters all over Vienna, *"Rot, Weiss, Rot, bis in den Tod"* (Red, White, Red, unto death). It referred to the colors of the Austrian flag.

And yet, except for the Nazis and their sympathizers, some still hoped that no major changes of Europe's borders were imminent.

In the days before our new store was to open in the middle of March, our parents, with the help of a cleaning woman, were busy getting everything ready. The store had a room in the back that was to become a useful addition to our eventual living quarters.

Because I worked in the factory, I had little opportunity to help my parents refurbish the new place. Everything was scrubbed, cleaned, and wooden shelves painted and lined with white paper.

It was a Friday evening when I stopped by our store after work. I wanted to find out how preparations for the opening progressed and also to ask my mother's permission (father was always more agreeable) to go to a movie that night. It was not so much her consent I needed, but the excuse I would use when confronting a worried and upset grandma after coming home late. I could then say that I had had mom's permission to visit a theater. The streets of our city had been far from calm lately and this compelled me to use the ruse.

During those early days of March, Vienna was as peaceful as a disturbed anthill. People were agitated but hesitated to talk politics in the open. It was not the government they feared, but the multitude of *Hakenkreuzler* (swastika bearers), who appeared everywhere like maggots on a carcass. One did well to be careful of what one said and where one went, especially at night.

"The Hurricane" had been the film shown in the cinema on Währingerstrasse. A storm of equal intensity, but much more frightening because it was real, was taking place outside when I left the theater.

A singing and cheering mass of men and women flowed toward the Inner City. They appeared possessed by frenzy, delirious and enraptured on a high that no drug could produce. Never had I been forced to watch such total surrender to madness as the whooping and howling of that hysterical mob. Their arms outstretched in the stiff Hitler salute, they sang raucously about the blood of Jews that would gush from their knives[5]. That horror evoked the impression of a witch's cauldron filled with raging, raving devils.

---

[5] Song of the SA, Brown Shirts,: "Wenn das Judenblut vom Messer spritzt…"

19

Beside the unending stream of marchers on the roadway, the sidewalk was packed with people, all drifting toward downtown. Having to move in the opposite direction, I dodged many a suspicious glance, and shivers ran down my spine at the thought of being found to be a Jew. Red Vienna had gone under and a Vienna of the Brown Shirts had risen, fraught with danger for the Jews. As time would show, it was not so good for the "Ostmärker" either, as the Austrians would be called by the grace of Hitler.

March 11 was a black Friday indeed.

Fewer people passed me on Nussdorferstrasse and relieved I finally turned into Pulverturmgasse. In ordinary times the walk from the movie theater to grandma's house would have taken me about 15 minutes. On this night, however, time could not be measured in normal chronological terms. It seemed to stretch endlessly.

Pulverturmgasse, always quiet and peaceful, appeared lonelier than usual. As I climbed the stairs my scraping soles sounded terribly loud and I tried to step more softly. I ascended slowly but my thoughts raced ahead to the unavoidable moment when I would confront an agitated lady. I felt guilty and reproached myself for having created an intolerable worry for my parents and grandmother. Yet, on seeing me unharmed, grandma just heaved a sigh of relief and informed me of two phone calls by my parents to Dr. Herschmann, a Jewish physician on the floor below. Phones in homes or small businesses were a rarity in Vienna and neither grandma nor my parents owned one. As my parents had to walk to a public phone some distance from where they lived, I regretted my irresponsible behavior even more, for it had exposed them to the dangers of that night.

Because we could not get in touch with my family, we waited at the doctor's place for their call. When it finally came, I was glad to calm their fears about my safety.

In early March, a desperate Schuschnigg had proposed a plebiscite in the country. Hitler had no intention of leaving it up to the entire Austrian population to decide on its political future. It might have left him with only part of the cake and he wanted it all. When Schuschnigg called for a direct vote of the people on the question of independence, Hitler ordered the German army to cross into Austria and the Anschluss became fact. The plebiscite Hitler then called for was an obvious sham. After the votes were counted, a government communiqué announced that almost 100 percent of the Austrians, or rather Ostmärker had voted for him. Austria had become the Ostmark, an eastern province of the Third Reich.

Vienna, a city in Germany

The unmentionable happened overnight. None of those present at that time and place will ever forget the takeover by the Nazis. Early next morning, Saturday, March 12, 1938, German troops crossed the frontier into Austria, and a Nazi government, under the leadership of Seiss-Inquart, was formed. That same afternoon Hitler entered the country of his birth and was received by garlanded streets and cheering crowds. The documented enthusiastic reception he received by tens of thousands of citizens waiting impatiently left no doubt with whom their allegiance lay.

Vienna, once capital of the vast Austro-Hungarian empire, then the capital of the small but independent state of Austria, had been humbled to the capital of an eastern province of Germany.

When I got up that fateful Saturday morning, I was still unaware of what had taken place in the short time between my returning home last night and my breakfast this morning. As always on this day of the week, I turned on the radio with special anticipation. Radio Wien transmitted one of my favorite programs between 7:10 A.M. and 8:00 A.M., musical hits from the movies. Though Saturday was only a slightly shortened workday, the popular music before I left for work was a pleasant prelude to the expected weekend. This time, however, the staccato sounds of military music poured forth from the speaker. At first, I paid little attention to the change of pace, only when the voice coming over the air announced the next song, *Marschlied der SA* (Marching song of the SA) – (SA = Storm Troopers, Brown Shirts) I almost fell off my chair. "Grandma," I exclaimed in panic, "I believe Hitler is in Vienna." – To say 'Hitler' did not necessarily mean the man in person, it was a synonym for Nazism and its horrors.

I stayed home that day, and later my parents and sister arrived, only to confirm the dreadful news. The Nazis had taken over the government, and we wondered what the future had in store for us.

Sunday, my cousin Leo cut short his sales tour at Innsbruck and returned to Vienna. On the way back, he stopped at a gas station and was treated with great courtesy, thanks to his rather heavy German accent.

Monday morning, Leo and I went to work. Just a few people hurried past us on the street. I felt as if I was naked and running a gauntlet of peering eyes, though the only eyes watching were shiny windowpanes twinkling in the early sunshine.

As we crossed a street near the factory, four youths, between the ages of 10 and 16, passed us. The oldest carried a rifle, a shocking sight considering the bearer's age. It was not long before we learned that, with the blessing of the new government, age in some cases was of minor importance. It gave certain groups, at least in the beginning, carte

21

blanche for their actions. Many used the newly found freedom to their personal advantage. They hunted down people at will, and nobody dared to resist when accosted or attacked. A lad wearing a red armband with a black swastika on a white background became the ultimate power.

The pack took no notice of us and we continued unmolested.

Because the bright sun outside our eyes had to adjust to the dimness of the salesroom when we entered. The solid steel shutters on the windows were still closed, and the dim lights gave the long room an eerie atmosphere. The few employees who had turned up stood in little groups and talked in whispers. Some drifted to their sections in the back and upstairs, others remained up front, uncertain about their first day at work after the Anschluss. No one started working.

Suddenly the front door flew open, and a short, stocky man stormed in. He wore civilian clothes, but his left upper arm was adorned by that telltale armband. "Where is Markus Seidler?" he screamed in apparent rage.

Everybody shrank back, and only one man in the rear ran to get Willi Seidler, a nephew of the brothers. Markus Seidler was the mind and mover of the company; Willi assisted him in an administrative capacity.

Obviously intimidated and frightened by the man's aggressive behavior, the young Seidler asked what he wanted of Markus. The following story came to light.

The man had been a driver for the company and at one time while talking to Markus Seidler, a discussion about Nazis had taken place. During their talk, Seidler called Horst Wessel[6] a pimp who was killed by another pimp. The driver had warned his boss: "Herr Seidler, don't ever forget what you have said." The man had never forgotten the incident and I don't know if he later left his employ or was fired. Now the stage was set to avenge the insult to his hero, and retribution was what he had come for.

Willi Seidler led the former driver to the privacy of an office where a substantial sum of money (it was whispered) changed hands. After that, the insulted member of the party left, and nothing more was heard of the accuser or the accusation.

In time the rest of the employees drifted reluctantly to their stations, and Erich and I returned to wrap packages. Slowly the factory took on the appearance of work as usual; but of course, it was not so.

Despite the incident, we felt relatively safe inside the store. The

---

[6] Horst Wessel, a member of the German Nazi party in the late twenties, was, like most brownshirts, a street bully. After his death, Goebbels made him out to be a martyr, and the song, "Das Horst Wessel Lied," became the anthem of the Nazi brownshirts.

danger seemed to be lurking outside the door. More than the others, the Jewish employees dreaded the thought of leaving the security of the factory when the time came to go home.

Though the situation was bad for now, most of us, especially those with little chance to emigrate hoped that life would eventually return to normal. After all, five years after the Nazi takeover in Germany, Jews still lived there. Maybe once the street rabble in Austria had exhausted their fury, Jews would be accepted, or at least tolerated again by those who had been their neighbors for years. Jews had fought and bled alongside the Christian Germans and Austrians in the First World War. They had shared their misfortunes and triumphs, had enriched both countries with an unproportionat high number of scientists, doctors, writers and experts in many fields. Jews called themselves Germans and Austrians and were proud of it. The Nazis would not, and could not forget all this. Things would calm down, and violence would abate.

What misguided hope, what a terrible mistake not to see the Nazis for what they really were. Eventually everybody found out, but for many, it was too late. The Nazis did not give a damn what the Jews had done for Germany or Austria.

For the moment I did not want to think of the time when I would have to go home. I felt content that the unavoidable was still hours away. The ugliness outside seemed farther away than it really was.

Just before lunch, our boss, Frau Vankert, unexpectedly robbed us of our secure feeling. Addressing no one in particular, she said: "A few days ago a customer placed a small order that has to be delivered right now."

She waited for a comment and as no one volunteered, she continued: "It's only a ten-minute walk."

In normal times Erich and I would have jumped at the opportunity to leave the factory for a while and escape the tedium of packing. In normal times, however, Frau Vankert hardly would have asked for a volunteer; my friend would have been chosen for that enjoyable task. But the last two days had changed the world. She still had no problem. "Gustav," she told me, "you go."

My attempts to convince her of the dangers outside fell on deaf ears. To stop any further arguments she settled the matter with a myth. "You go," the lovely lady said. "You don't look Jewish." If she hoped to allay my fears, she failed. Nonetheless, I went.

This part of the Inner City consisted mainly of four-storied apartment buildings, containing also offices, small factories, and workshops. Stores on street level sold wholesale drygoods. When on earlier occasions I passed through this section on a Sunday, the lifeless

23

surroundings of this area were normal. But now, walking toward my destination, the same stillness in the streets produced an eerie effect. The few people I met moved at a fast pace. They kept close to the front of the buildings, hastening along as if they were late for an appointment.

I found our customer's store closed and was about to turn back when I spotted a faint light behind the wavy window curtain of the main door. Hoping to get rid of my package, I knocked. After a while the curtain was drawn slightly and a face appeared.

"Delivery from Brüder Seidler," I told the face. It seemed to study me for a while, then shook its head. "We can't take anything," the face announced through the glass. "We don't know what's going to happen."

On the way back I contemplated the fact that "the face" had confided in me a very dangerous thought. "We don't know what's going to happen." It had also destroyed the cover so generously bestowed upon me by Frau Vankert, "I did not look Jewish." No doubt "the face" had been of my faith, and had also recognized me as such. It, otherwise, never would have dared to express doubt about the great future the Nazis were preparing for all the believers and for those who still had to be convinced.

I was glad to have made it back to our place unscathed, and to have had no unusual event take place. My first day of work in the new *Gross Deutschland* (Greater Germany) came to a close. As it ended on a tranquil note, I hoped against hope that the days of the future might turn out to be equally calm. Perhaps things really would remain almost the way they had been. But life did not unfold according to my wishes. Not at all.

First came restrictions.

Intermarriage was prohibited, and sex between a Jew and a gentile meant a ticket to a concentration camp. Jews were not allowed to visit cinemas, theaters, bathing facilities, parks, or any place of entertainment. Stores displaying signs: "Jews forbidden," sprang up like weeds after a rain. The coffee house at the Hotel Metropol, where the Gestapo headquarters eventually was located, outdid the others by placing a large hand-painted sign in the window: "JEWS, DOGS, AND PRIESTS ARE FORBIDDEN TO ENTER." Imitators followed suit. Hakoah, the only Jewish soccer club, was disbanded. More than anything else I missed visits to movie theaters and the trade school I attended every Friday as an apprentice of Brüder Seidler.

Excesses against Jews took place everywhere. They were stopped in the streets or picked up at home. They were beaten, ridiculed, and humiliated. They were recruited at random to scrub off slogans of opposition parties painted before the Anschluss. They were handed toothbrushes to clean the graffiti from walls, houses and, on their knees, from sidewalks.

They were spat on, kicked, and taunted while doing it. They were hunted animals at the mercy of their tormentors whether they were young punks or adults. Yet despite what they were put through, the victims kept their sanity. There was always the hope that one day all of this would be like a horrible dream. That's what one lived for. — Six millions didn't.

Also, something strange happened to our name. I was born Gustav Ziegler. Went to Treustrasse elementary school, middle school and trade school under this name and suddenly, with the Nazi take-over, I became Gustav Pimselstein oder Pimsler[7]. Furthermore, every Jewish male or female whose first name was not of Hebrew origin had to add, not as an initial but in full, the middle name Israel or Sara. Anti-Semites had always used both names contemptuously when talking about Jews. My full name therefore suddenly read Gustav Israel Pimselstein oder Pimsler. How the addition, "oder (or) Pimsler," got there, I have no idea[8]. But when signing documents and my passport it certainly seemed a lengthy signature.

Events had not stopped our planet from turning, and life continued. It cannot be said that existence returned to normal for everything of value, not just in the financial sense, had radically changed. People were classified either subordinate or superior. They were either euphoric or dejected, depending on their past. For Jews, it made no difference. But even during those terrible times Jews, as always, tried to find comfort in humor. A sardonic saying made the rounds among them in Vienna: It took the Germans five years to inflict on their Jews what the Viennese accomplished in five days.

For Austrians, if they were not known Socialists or Communists, a golden era seemed to be dawning. Businesses prospered as never before. Germans came like locusts to the newly created Ostmark and bought everything they could lay their hands on. It wasn't surprising. They had a surplus of Reichsmarks and found goods and food here not seen for years in Hitler's paradise. And Hitler, to show that he had forgiven the Viennese for the bad times he had experienced in this city as a young fellow, created *Gross Wien* (Greater Vienna). He incorporated a few

---

[7] Until the beginning of the twentieth century many Jews in Galicia just married in a synagogue, neglecting to register their union with the government. Apparently no problems arose because of this carelessness until the Nazis came. People suddenly had to go by the name of their father's mother.

[8] Before I left Vienna, father told me of second cousin by the name of Pimsler on the island of Curacao in the Dutch East Indies.

suburbs into the original city and the Viennese were grateful and proud. Their city was not a capital any more, but it was bigger in size than Berlin.

Pictures of Hitler appeared everywhere. Walking one day past the *Urania*, the observatory, I saw that the front of the building covered by an immense likeness of Hitler's head. It was perhaps four stories high and was flanked by Nazi flags of equal length.

To our surprise, the Nazi government of Vienna permitted my parents to open their store. I assume the permission to establish this business was granted because the request had been submitted before the new rules for Jews were implemented. Bureaucracy had just continued in its old routine. When the new rulers perceived their "mistake," they speedily closed our business. It came about in a characteristic way.

A few weeks after the opening of the shop, three men in civilian clothes appeared at our store and, raising their right arms, screamed: "Heil Hitler." One of them rudely addressed our father: "Are you Pimselstein?" When father said yes, the man ordered: "Hand over the keys to the store and then you and your family get out of here."

Father gave him the keys and, after picking up their coats, my parents and sister left. — It was as simple as that.

They stayed at grandma's place for a few days, fearing the Nazis might follow up the seizure of our store by arresting father.

The first night after the business had been taken from them, our parents entered the store by using duplicate keys. They collected some flour and sugar, while Berta, still just a young girl of twelve took candies.

Sooner or later, most other Jewish retail stores shared our fate. They were either ransacked by Nazi troopers or taken over by their collaborators. All without compensation to the owners. Our place was cleaned out and only the recently painted wooden shelves were left. Bigger Jewish establishments received a token payment that did not come close to the real value of the business or property.

By May all Jewish employees had been dismissed from Brüder Seidler and the factory was taken over by an "Aryan."

Motivated by my insatiable yearning for adventure, I interested my friend Erich in an unrealistic journey to Palestine on foot. With the help of my Kozzen atlas we decided that the best course of travel was to follow the Danube River for most of the time and at some point turn south. From there we intended to use carefully selected roads, bypass cities and try to guess which border points would be easiest to cross without pertinent documents. But in all the preparations we never reflected on the impracticability of the task or the true chance of ever reaching our goal. We did not know any of the many languages spoken in

26

the countries we intended to cross, had no money for the trip, and never took into account the mountainous terrain in Turkey which had to be traversed on our way. With luck we might have landed in some jail and been forgotten by those arresting us. If we had bad luck, we might have been forced back to Germany. Many Jews fled to the West. None that I heard of tried to escape across Eastern Europe and the Levant on foot.

But what was just a dream I discussed with Erich eventually became reality later in my life. For now, while still together, we enthusiastically recorded the intended travel scheme in a little notebook.

Inactive in my Zionist party for some time, I agreed to join Erich's Zionist club. Group meetings, pleasant breaks in our otherwise aimless life, convened Saturday nights. They took place, of course, with the permission of the Gestapo, as any assembly of people had to be sanctioned by the Nazi secret police.

The first get-together in the cellar of an old apartment building ended in a bad scare for us. As we tried to leave the meeting, a policeman barred our exit. A tenant in the building had reported a suspicious assembly of teenagers in the basement, assuming no doubt he had uncovered an underground conspiracy. A police phone call to the Gestapo cleared us, and we were permitted to go home. What a disappointment we must have been to the patriotic informer.

On another occasion a more disturbing incident was forestalled.

We had met to listen to a special report about the latest happenings in Palestine. As the presentation was about to begin, a fellow burst into the room and announced excitedly that the place had to be vacated forthwith. The party council had been warned of an imminent raid on our club by the much-feared HJ or Hitler Youth.

We found ourselves trapped in a precarious situation. The house where we met was in the middle of an uninterrupted row of buildings that stretched for almost one third of a mile on our side of the street. On the other side was a narrow curved strip of park, running parallel to the Danube Canal. There were no side streets nearby into which we could escape. The only way to avoid an encounter with the notorious Hitler Youth was to leave and disappear as inconspicuously as circumstances permitted.

Expecting the worst, we climbed the stairs to the main floor and left at short intervals in groups of twos and threes. The dimly lit street and the bushes of the park on the other side of the road facilitated our escape. — In order not to worry our parents, we left close calls like these unmentioned, and luck was with me at all times.

During our get-togethers we were taught Hebrew songs. As most of us read Hebrew only haltingly, the foreign words were transcribed into

Latin letters on leaflets. The hora was danced in high spirits, and talks and lectures about Eretz Israel were received with rapt attention. Life in Palestine was made vivid to us. The emphasis was placed on the early settlers and the influence they had on the modern-day Kibbutzniks, the people living in kibbutzes. We were told of their arduous work, their primitive lifestyle and the physical dangers confronting them in times past and present. But it was hard not to feel a great pride when we learned how the mortally wounded Trumpeldor cried out: "*Tov lamut be at arzenu*" (it is good to die for our country). Trumpeldor had died just 18 years before at the defense of Tel Hai.

There were more people like him in the Eretz Israel of our time and more people were needed in the country's future. People dedicated and faithful to life in a kibbutz, people proud to farm the land, work in sheds and stand guard at night in defense of the Old-New country Herzl had envisioned and written about. The fighting Jew, who had been dormant for nearly two millennia, began to resurrect.

We became so enthralled by those accounts that, even I, who only wanted to go to America, was carried away by the enthusiasm of the lecturers. The meetings always culminated with the singing of Hatikva, the song named "Hope," Israel's national anthem today. I enjoyed the meetings, the animated stories and the thrilling prospects the country had to offer. Yet, once home with my parents and sister, my long-lasting fascination with the United States returned and the magical influence of our get-togethers faded. This was the summer of 1938. We were unaware of the tribulations in our future, the roads we would have to travel and the events awaiting us.

One day, the rise and fall of many voices on the street below our window attracted our attention. The sounds seemed to come directly from the bakery underneath our apartment. Carefully peeking outside, we found the cause of excitement in the building two doors away. Storm troopers were looting a Jewish haberdashery business. The store, just below street level, was reached by descending a few steps. It was broad daylight, and the wave-like rising and falling of the voices came from upright citizens who cheered the looting of the store. Their endorsement did not go unrewarded. From time to time, the storm troopers that carried stacks of merchandise to a waiting truck generously threw shirts, underwear, socks, aprons and other things to the cheering onlookers. Each successful catch was greeted by an approving howl.

Less fearful now of being detected by the preoccupied mob, I leaned out the window and watched the scene. Just another Jewish store liquidated. Not everybody participated in that open thievery. Some people stood at a distance and stared dispassionately at the spectacle of robbery condoned by the government. In time, people became deaf and blind to all that went on. Their eyes stared right through the outrages committed. Those opposed to the general excesses against Jews were afraid to express their feelings. Nobody could have been unaware of the tentacles of hate, greed, and sadism that stretched in our direction. Many participated in those crimes and everybody knew about them.

One evening in June of 1938, my cousin Leo came to us to say good-by. He intended to cross illegally into Switzerland. I envied him his adventure. He had converted his savings into a small diamond ring, which he hoped to sell on the other side of the border. The money thus acquired was to help him through the period when he would be without a livelihood. I knew I would miss him as a big brother and friend.

Anxiously, we waited for news hoping he had succeeded in his endeavor. When his first letter arrived from Switzerland, we celebrated the event like a holiday. He was permitted to stay just six weeks in Zurich, and, like so many other refugees, had to leave "friendly" Switzerland under threat of being deported back to Germany. Again he crossed borders without permission, ending up at Antwerp, Belgium. With an affidavit[9] he emigrated to the United States in December 1939; five months before the Germans captured Belgium.

Shortly after Leo's escape, grandma's apartment was claimed by an "Aryan." She too had to leave her furniture and most of her possessions behind without compensation. The only things she was permitted to keep were her bed, bedding, and strictly personal belongings. She and another Jewish woman who had lived on the floor above her now had to share a one-room-and-kitchen apartment. This apartment was on the fifth floor in the sister building behind a backyard and had no elevator. With the permission of Frau Bondy, the other lady, I stayed with them and slept nights on a folding bed. Both women were over 70 years old.

My days were spent mostly away from the apartment. Evenings, when I came home to sleep, I'd see petite Frau Bondy retire to the kitchen to get dressed for bed behind the closed door. When she reappeared she wore a faded dressing gown. Her thin, gray hair was covered by a flimsy fabric and around her mouth flickered that slightly embarrassed smile she displayed whenever I had to see her in that intimate get-up. Before the light was turned off and she removed her dressing gown, I had to turn my face to the wall.

---

[9] A written deed of a financially sound U.S. citizen to sponsor immigrants. Financially sound was important, for it was his responsibility to insure that the newcomers did not become a burden of the state.

I was a movie buff, a fan, a nut, and movies could have been my downfall in Nazi Germany. At least, I could have had the hell beaten out of me, for, even though Jews were forbidden to visit a theater, I went to the movies anyway. I don't know how many Jews visited cinemas, which was a dangerous and really stupid thing to do, but I did. It was known that occasionally storm troopers conducted inspections or some Nazi would stand up in the middle of a performance and scream: "It stinks of Jews." Then lights were turned on in the theater and the papers of those present checked. Woe to any Jew present.

It was not an easy decision to make. I thought about it for a long time before going through with it. When I think of it today, I wonder whether it had just been my wish to see a movie or an immature expression of revolt against that hateful discriminatory measure. When I left the theater after the performance, I felt ecstatic. I had broken a Nazi law and gotten away with it. Yet I knew I was tempting fate and was scared every time I did it.

Mother was terrified for my life and tried to dissuade me from my folly, but it was an addiction I could not break. At first I wanted to visit a theater only once, which I did. After a while, I tried it again and told myself it was for the last time. As time went by, and temptation grew, I attended yet another performance. In all, I went to the movies seven times between March 13, 1938, the date of the German takeover, and September 9, 1939. On this second date something happened that changed the direction of my life.

Having swallowed Austria with such ease, Hitler's demands on Czechoslovakia during the rest of 1938 became increasingly belligerent. The issue was the Sudetenland. In this part of the country, Hitler's protégé Konrad Henlein had begun agitation along Nazi lines, relying on Germany to back him. The worried Czech government mobilized part of its armed forces.

German newspapers piously reported that Czechoslovakia was trying to make the Western Powers believe that Germany was about to invade their state. They mocked their neighbor's panic while Germany put more men in uniform and France was mobilizing too.

The infamous Munich Pact of September 29, 1938 postponed, but failed to avert, World War II. The Western Powers, obviously afraid of Germany, succumbed to Hitler's blackmail and so forced Czechoslovakia to give up the Sudeten region. As with the law of the jungle (only the strong survive) the destruction of that unfortunate country continued. Poland occupied the Teschen area a few days later. Slovakia and Ruthenia broke away from the mother country. Germany, actually dissatisfied with the peaceful outcome of the pact, declared "Bohemia and Moravia" a German protectorate and occupied it outright. Hungary too demanded part of dismembered Czechoslovakia and received a large strip of southern Slovakia and the region they called "Carpato-Ukraine" which had been Ruthenia. Czechoslovakia ceased to exist. It disappeared from the world like a sea creature torn apart by sharks.

Jews read about those terrifying events in the newspapers. I followed the developments by watching German newsreels in movie theaters.

The World Shuts its Doors

In the same month of September 1938, a Nazi claimed my parents' home. Under conditions similar to that of grandma's eviction, my family moved out. They received permission to live in their empty store on Jägerstrasse.

The drama of the *Kristallnacht* (the night of broken glass), November 9th to the 10th, 1938, represented the greatest excess of Nazi viciousness up to that date. The killing of a German diplomat by a young Jew in Paris set in motion an unprecedented outburst of "spontaneous" violence by the German people. This mass savagery and havoc was instigated by the Nazi government. Jewish homes and shops not yet looted were broken into and pillaged. Synagogues were set ablaze though care was taken that the conflagration not put Christian neighbors in danger.

The Klucky temple, where grandpa had been one of the elders, had its inside pillars blasted and was then put to the torch. Outside, fire engines stood by in case adjacent buildings should be threatened by fire. Jews caught on streets or arrested at home were beaten, unlucky ones were sent to concentration camps. No insurance company had to pay compensation for the destruction of Jewish properties. To add insult to injury, German Jews, including those of the newly annexed Austria, had to cover the cost of repairs to buildings adjacent to destroyed synagogues. Jews were also held responsible for the "violent though righteous" expression of wrath by the German people and were fined additionally one billion marks punitive damages. This enormous amount was collected or confiscated without granting the victims any recourse.

"The Nazis won't harm Jews like you," Frau Schönbauer, a fanatical member of the then illegal Nazi party under the Schuschnigg regime had promised, trying to set my mother's mind at ease. But that was before the Germans marched into Austria. When our father was arrested for the first time in the aftermath of the 'Kristallnacht,' I came to her begging for help to free him. The terrified woman replied: "How can I? I can't help you. If I do, I'll be arrested for fraternizing with Jews."

Father was imprisoned in Vienna for two months.

31

Our group in the Zionist movement had received "certificates," papers permitting them to immigrate to Palestine. Everybody was ecstatic with the exception of me. I could not make up my mind whether to join my friends or stay with my family and wait for that necessary but elusive affidavit. I had grown close to the boys and girls and knew I would miss them once they were gone. It was also clear that to relinquish a certificate at this stage and give up the chance to escape Nazi Germany was a fool's choice. My friends did their best to overcome my indecision, but in the end the seductive vision of America won out and I gave up the certificate assigned to me.

But it was not only the dream of America or the insecurity of a 15-year-old that helped me decide which way to take. More than anything it was my desire to be with my family, and had they migrated to the South Pole, I gladly would have gone with them. As things turned out, I was not with my loved ones throughout the time of their tribulations. When eventually I was on my own, I always missed growing up in their fold. My parents died a vicious death that almost ended the life of my only sister as well. Millions of our people suffered the same fate as they were hunted and murdered for reasons that may have made sense to a superior being, but not to mere mortals like us.

Mother and I had gone to a small Jewish bath in the second district. There were only showers, but the hot water flowed freely, and that was something to be thankful for. The cleaning woman that serviced the place got into a conversation with mother about emigration. She said she was a widow and would soon journey to the United States. Her only son, living in New York for years, had sent her an affidavit, and she described how excited she was to join him. I don't know the reason behind their long separation and why it had to be something as drastic as the Nazi takeover to unite them again, but I felt sorry for the woman who had been without her child for such a long time. I felt so happy and grateful to be with my mother that impulsively I grabbed her hand and held it in a tight grip.

Parents of youngsters who were to go to Palestine often spent needed money to buy what was believed to be important for the journey and the new home of their children. Erich and other boys, proud as peacocks, strutted about in their black riding boots that were similar to those worn by the SS. At home, my friend showed me a hunting knife and a variety of other items he was taking with him. Moved by childish emotions, I envied him his outfit.

A girl named Susi and her friend Gretl were to travel with Erich. Until their departure we spent much time together. During the day or in the evenings we roamed as a foursome the little streets and alleys in the center of Vienna and discovered places not even I had seen before. We explored the city I still loved, ignoring the hate I felt for the people who were trying to deprive me of it. I wanted to go to America. But, I also wanted to be able to come back to the city of my birth and my youth whenever I chose without fear of my life.

Though the girls were also from Vienna, they did not know the Inner City the way I did. I guided them to legendary landmarks and places undisturbed by time and development. The entrances of certain houses led to sleepy courtyards where huge, old trees threw shadows over ancient wells. Some thoroughfares, created hundreds of years ago for horse-drawn wagons and carriages, are still thoroughfares for modern-day traffic. Along them, very narrow sidewalks, added at a much later date, run along buildings 200 years old and more. St. Ruprecht's church was started in the eighth century.

Frequently I accompanied Erich to the offices of the Zionist club and met the fellows who were to travel with him. Their cheerfulness, excitement and enthusiasm always aroused doubt about my decision to refuse the certificate. This indecision remained with me as long as Erich was in Vienna.

Meanwhile, the four of us met as often as possible for we wondered if we'd ever meet again after they departed. It was a long way from Palestine to the United States, where I wanted to go, and chances were remote we would ever meet again. The strained situation in Europe and the effect it began to have on the rest of the world made the likelihood of a reunion remote.

Parting with Erich was not easy. Where were the dreams we used to pursue together; the pleasures of Sundays; outings to the soccer stadium; the marvelous Prater; the movies in the evening; Brüder Seidler; and the juvenile interest we took in some apprentice girls? Our insecure approach to the opposite sex was common in most teenagers of my time. Youthful silliness, but how we enjoyed what life had offered! Just two teenage musketeers in a world full of wonders.

One Sunday morning, I dropped in on my family. Mother decided that all of us should visit grandma. After lunch we set out.

With the approaching winter, the weather had turned frigid and a fierce wind blew as we crossed the Danube canal over the Friedens-brücke. Despite the miserable cold, men shaking collection cans for the *Winterhilfe* (help for the needy in winter) had stationed themselves on the sidewalk in the middle of the bridge. They challenged passers-by to contribute to the cause. The reward for a deposited coin was a round piece of tin embossed with the profile of Hitler's face.

Most people already wore that emblem in their lapel and, as we did not, one of the men shook the can at us. "We are Jews," father said. For an instant the man hesitated, and after giving us a dirty look, he turned toward other people while we continued unmolested. We needed every penny now ourselves. Besides, we would not have wanted to wear that detestable image on our jacket as proof of our contribution. It would also have looked too much as if we were trying to pass as "Aryans", a charade that could have had dire consequences if we were caught.

I stayed with grandma until her daughters, my aunts in New York, sent for her. She received the affidavit and left Vienna in December of 1938. A refugee past the age of 70. We soothed her fears with the promise to follow very soon, but again, our predictions were inaccurate.

After grandma's departure, I moved back in with my parents and sister.

In late 1938 and until the beginning of the war in September 1939, families in England and Holland opened up their homes to Jewish children. I assume they were to have become foster children. In early 1939, my sister and I were to go on a comparable program to England but our transfer never materialized. A little later, Berta was slated to travel to Holland but here too nothing came of the plan.

At the time, the Nazis still wanted to get rid of the Jews through emigration. They later turned to mass murder when exit avenues became closed by war. While the way out of this mire of persecution, danger and degradation was still open, that road was studded with obstacles. Requests for passports and exit visas as well as letters imploring relatives outside Germany to send papers to help us escape Hitler's "Third Reich" were daunting tasks. To apply for a passport, people stood in endless lines outside the fence of the confiscated and plundered palace of the Viennese Rothschilds. The building had been converted to a passport office. In spite of the palace's many rooms and clerks, weeks passed before the necessary document was issued.

Once in possession of this travel paper, more days and weeks were spent at the doors and in the waiting rooms of consulates. The conditions imposed on immigrants varied from country to country. All imposed severe restrictions. A great number of Jews wrote to famous people, to many organizations or to the oddest of places asking for help to flee Germany. Their chance of success was usually as remote as an offer of help from Hitler would have been.

Many ran risks by crossing borders illegally. Contrary to the belief of many today, a successful crossing of this kind was no guarantee of safety. The threat of being returned to Nazi Germany if caught at the border or even inside the chosen country was real and was often carried out.

Central and South American governments demanded of prospective immigrants that they carry *Landungsgeld* (landing money). The minimum sum asked was five thousand dollars. Only well-to-do people or those who had not sent their money to a "safe" place could afford this amount. Some states required newcomers to have trades or professions beneficial to the host country.

A variety of provisions regulated the entry of immigrants into the United States, not the least of which was the dreaded quota system. The country of birth determined quotas. The size of those quotas varied according to country. Unfortunately, people from countries where they were not in danger of their lives enjoyed the largest quotas. To receive a number on the waiting list, one had to fill out a form with questions like: Do you have medical problems? A history of mental problems? Were you ever a Communist? (At the time, a Nazi had no trouble immigrating to the United States.) They also asked if one had been arrested, been a criminal, a beggar, and, if female, had been a prostitute – a rather degrading and insulting question. Candidates whose immediate family members were citizens of the United States bypassed the quota system.

A sponsor of immigrants did not necessarily have to be related to the aspirants. It was acceptable to the American government if he had (so it was said) a bank account of at least $10,000.00 and would be able to support newcomers should this become necessary.

Once these requirements had been satisfied and one was in possession of the necessary papers, misfortune could still be one's fate, as in the case of my family. After months of waiting, a distant relative in the United States provided us with an affidavit. At the time of our parents' births their birthplaces were in the Austro-Hungarian Empire. It made them Austrians. As those places belonged now to Poland, the American government placed them in the Polish quota. The difference was that the Austrian quota was open for immigrants while the Polish was filled for the time being.

It took another year before we were notified to appear before the American physician at the consulate. He diagnosed my father and me with a noncontagious, mild inflammation of the eyes. Notwithstanding this harmless condition, the doctor decided we had to cure it before being permitted to immigrate to the United States.

This postponement had its consequences.

After the departure of Erich and the group to Palestine in the fall of 1938, I joined another unit of our Zionist organization. I attended meetings with even greater fervor, but the chemistry that had bound me to the previous boys and girls was missing.

The more involved I became with the Zionist club's representations, the more I was torn between my conflicting desires. There was the land of my dreams, America, and there was Palestine, the country where my friends had gone. My feeling for the latter became stronger for it looked so much more attainable than far-away America. Both continued to tempt me, though for vastly different reasons.

America, as seen on pictures and in movies, appeared the land of abundance. It was a place of tall buildings, Broadway, endless rows of glistening cars crawling through deep concrete canyons and the continent to which huge ocean liners steamed. There were aunts, uncles, cousins, and diverse relatives I had never seen and I wondered what they were like. That was America. But, of course, it was also the country where my parents and sister were going to be.

In comparison, Palestine presented a mixed picture of unrest, attacks by Arabs, bombs, Kibbutz life, orange groves in sunlight, and the often-mentioned malaria-carrying mosquitoes. I had heard of Tel Aviv, a Jewish city run exclusively by Jews, something difficult to visualize. Could, or even would, Jews do every job and service necessary to run a city, I wondered! From street sweeper to bus driver, to letter carrier, police officer, to even judge or mayor. The setting and situation seemed unreal. Jewish attorneys, doctors, and businessmen I could understand, but all those other vocations and trades appeared out of character for Jews. I am certain that this misconception was shared by most of the world, Jews and non-Jews alike. If the latter were even aware of Tel Aviv's existence.

An exciting aspect of Palestine was that Jews defended themselves. One thing was certain, life would be neither dull nor prosaic. Perhaps this too could be considered adventure, though it had little in common with what I believed adventures ought to be like.

How naive was my comparison of the United States and Palestine! Both had facets I imagined them to have, but they were a small part of what life really was like in those two countries. Eventually I experienced the riches and vitality of both.

A school for Youth Alliyah was opened by Zionist organizations. Alliyah, ascend, meant: "to ascend to the Promised Land." It prepared young people for life in a kibbutz. Theoretical instruction filled the morning hours, and after a free lunch, trades were taught in the workshop of the school. I shared the activities with my new group and attended a locksmith and general fitter class in the afternoon.

Another place of instruction was in Moosbrunn, a village just outside Vienna. Boys and girls lived there for a few weeks, and were taught farming. Still hoping to go to America, I did not join them.

Always trying to keep the interest of us youth alive, the leaders of our club staged an evening of entertainment for parents and youngsters. The actors, boys and girls of different groups, performed funny and solemn sketches. One of the serious ones is indelibly imprinted in my mind.

On an improvised stage, a young fellow, his body in chains, writhed in agony. The scene, illuminated by flashlights whose lenses were covered by transparent dark-red paper deepened the gloom of the set. When the flashlights were moved back and forth, their reddish glow suggested licking flames. A small chorus of boys and girls, singing the haunting melody of the Yiddish song: "*Dos Stäterle brennt*" (the little town is aflame), may have supported a fear of things to come. The song lamented the burning of Jewish houses and people by crazed peasants in Poland and Russia during pogroms.

We did not know it then but not too far in the future those excesses would be repeated. The same kind of people were the victims, though instead of illiterate Russian peasants, a progressive and educated people perpetrated the crimes, namely the Germans.

The hushed audience was visibly shaken, moved by the predictive character of the performance and its hard-hitting quality.

This group also received certificates. Once more I declined to join them. Why I had been ready to walk with Erich to Palestine, but refused to make Alliyah with official entry papers may be because I thought that the initial undertaking belonged to adventurers.

Searching for ways out of Nazi Germany, father wrote to the U.S. State Department, begging them to find the address of the American consul who had saved his life during World War I in Krasnoyarsk, Siberia. He received an answer. The man was deceased.

In June of 1939 father was arrested again and detained in a district prison. After two months he was released on his promise to leave Germany with his family in the shortest possible time.

In a desperate attempt to flee the country, many Jews left Vienna and tried to cross illegally into Poland. Many succeeded. I wonder if the Nazis did not turn a blind eye to this exodus knowing they would soon overtake the escapees.

Hitler's tirades contained catchwords and slogans that nobody took seriously. He informed the world of his intentions and the world took it for bluster. Germany needed *Lebensraum* (living space), and *Drang nach Osten* (expansion to the east) was the solution, he screamed. He was judged a megalomaniac and his warnings were taken for mere ranting until it was too late.

Up to a time, the Germans found reasons for their aggression, however artificial. Later they did not try to pretend anymore but attacked when it suited them. Before the invasion of Poland, Hitler accused the Poles of murdering the staff of a small German radio station. After the war it was proven that Germans were the killers. The scheme was carried out to represent the Poles as provocateurs who had to be put in their place. This was the start of World War II.

Father decided we should try to cross into Poland. But life is like a country road. One travels it with a certain goal in mind and then, suddenly an invisible power places a detour sign across the way, thus forcing one to move in another direction. Sometimes there are two arrows, one is pointing to the left and another to the right and then it is up to the individual which arrow to follow. The decision, especially of the time I'm speaking of, was a matter of life or death.

A few days after father's return from prison, our fate and future were decided for us in a rather twisted way. It determined, in the long run, who was to survive and who was to die.

A Search for Adventure

When the urge struck I jotted notes on any piece of paper I could lay my hands on. Advertisements whose blank backside I might have used for my purpose were non-existent in those days in Vienna and paper to write on not readily available in our home. If a letter had to be written, the paper was bought in single sheets. (For people in the United States, where most everything is available and used wastefully, this may be difficult to understand.) Occasionally, I requested a blank sheet of paper that had not yet been turned into an imploring letter to help us escape Nazi Germany, and used it for my own purpose.

In a moment of weakness I even became a spendthrift, using part of the little money I had saved to buy a small diary. Conditions in Germany, however, made me cautious about what I entrusted to its pages. Later, and out of Hitler's clutches, I began to record memories that, like a prelude to the happenings 1938 and after, became the foundation of the current narrative.

Actually, I wanted to continue the above paragraph with: *On a later date and in the safety of the world beyond the Third Reich...* But this other part of the world I went to was no safe haven for me either. Not for a long time. Not for a very long time.

Young folks will dream of adventure. Some abandon those dreams early in life; I didn't. Not for an extended part of my life. I am certain that today's adults, who read mystery novels, adventure or science fiction stories, or watch movies of that kind, do not give up on their dreams either. They may not always be mindful of the fact or admit to it, but hidden in a corner of their hearts is still that, by now, remote youthful wish to participate in the adventures of a Mickey Spillane, James Bond, Indiana Jones, or a Star Trek character.

The heroes of my time had different names, but at the age of 16, I was as fascinated by their fictional prowess and their ability to survive as when I had first read about them. Hitler had forced emigration on the Jews, and this meant adventure. I dreamed of journeys to India, Australia, Africa, and America. I wanted to see the world and experience the excitement it had to offer. Living in Nazi Germany, I did not know that anti-Nazi movies in the free world found intriguing excitement right where I was. I never saw it that way. And how could I? Happenings in Germany were not my kind of adventures. They were not adventures where, in far away places, bloodthirsty members of a sect wanted to sacrifice a human being to some obscure idol. Or tangling with gangsters in the fashion of Edgar Wallace and writers like him. I did not recognize the times we lived in as they really were, and perhaps this was just as well. I did not foresee the murder of millions of people under a law written by the greatest mass murderers in history. A law that no gangster code could compete with and where the rapacity of a beast was tame in comparison with the savagery of our fellow creatures.

I knew of Dachau and Buchenwald and thought I could imagine the terrors the prisoners there were exposed to. But those were not the titillating perils of adventure I had in mind. Not until I experienced life in a concentration camp did I find out what fear meant and what hell is. The danger to life there was not an occasional occurrence, it was a permanent fixture in one's daily existence. It was a place where even the greatest hero would succumb to the dread of the vanquished. Fear that twisted the stomach, which spread over one's skin like burning acid, that made one's body shake as with fever. I experienced those emotions, was terrified by the way men, who looked like humans, dispensed cruelties and enjoyed them. How they coldly and unemotionally dispensed death and did not seem bothered by it. I observed and marked it down in my mind, never really certain I'd survive to tell about it. My desire to put my experiences on paper was, without doubt, one of two things that helped me get through the worst time in my life. The other one was the dream of seeing the world and finding the excitement I yearned for. I was to find excitement, but not in the way I anticipated.

For some weeks Viennese men had been appearing on the streets as soldiers. Some seemed uncomfortable in their ungainly uniforms and heavy boots, others, with a defiant grin on their face demonstrated their unconcealed pride in the field-gray of the German outfit. It was unclear, however, why so many fighting men were needed when Berlin, contrary to Hitler's slogans, consistently declared its non-aggressive intentions.

39

"Hitler does not want war. Hitler will never start a war. But one can't let the Poles get away with murder. One can take only so much." People in the streets repeated those characteristic statements that came from above and were printed in newspapers and believed them. And so, on September 1, 1939, Germany attacked Poland and World War II started.

The feelings of the Jews needed no interpretation. A feverish excitement took hold of every one of us. Events would hardly pass us quietly by. We were fearful of reprisals in case of German setbacks at the front. As no reversals occurred we sighed in selfish relief and hoped we had escaped trouble, at least for the time being. We were mistaken. The Germans needed no special incentives to persecute Jews; it came naturally to them.

But not only did the Germans advance victoriously, they also signed a pact with the Soviet Union. Poland was to be divided between the two former foes.

Among the Jews discussions about the war became more intense by the day. "Strategists" and war veterans of the First World War met at the offices of the Jewish Community Federation to discuss communiqués from the front. The strategy of the majority of Jews, however, was to crowd consular offices of countries not at war with Germany with increased frenzy. Chances of leaving, though, were drastically reduced when France and the United Kingdom declared war on the Nazi State two days later. American and Italian shipping lines – shipping lines of countries still neutral – were barely able to accommodate the travel-anxious Jews who had valid travel papers and enough money to pay for the trip. *Rette sich wer kann* (save yourself) was the motto.

Days passed and the German advance continued. The Jews waited. Something was going to happen, one could feel it; and something did.

Arrested by the Gestapo
Sleepily I sat up in bed. During the short interval between sleep and the first signs of awareness, I wondered why I had to get up so early. I had the uneasy feeling of having been aroused by something threatening. Judging by the darkness surrounding me, it had to be night. My eyes barely penetrated the gloom of the place where we slept and only slowly did they get used to the twilight in the room.

Against the white wall, which now seemed gray, I saw the silhouettes of my parents and sister also sitting upright in their beds, listening.

Ever since a Nazi had taken over our apartment without compensation, we lived in our former store. The place consisted of two rooms. The former sales room, our living and sleeping area, was secured toward the street at night by a thin corrugated metal shutter. The other room in the back was our kitchen from which a door, reinforced by thick iron bands, led to the hallway of the apartment building.

At the moment everything was quiet, yet the silence felt more menacing than any noise. Anxiety seized me. I suppressed the impulse to ask what had happened. I dared not move a muscle for fear it would expose us to something terrible. Still, I did not know what had awakened me.

I sat rooted to the bed while invisible fingers of fear tightened their grip around my throat, terrorized my mind, and made my skin crawl. I was afraid, horribly afraid.

Suddenly, fists and boots smashed against the kitchen door, and someone barked, "*Aufmachen, Staatspolizei*" (open up, state police), through the shaky barrier.

"Don't move," father whispered. We held our breath. Swallowing hard to suppress the sudden feeling of nausea, I continued to stare intently into the dusk of the room.

"They" had stopped beating on the door. Paradoxically, the ensuing stillness seemed filled with noises of which I had never been aware before. As if to spite and taunt us, sounds came from every corner of the room. The wooden floor creaked loudly, the wardrobe seemed to move creating a rasping grind and an invisible hand rustled noisily through hanging dresses. Everything in the room conspired against us, cried out to those men outside our door: they are here, they are hiding.

"Please," I prayed in my mind, "please be still."

How much time had elapsed since they first banged on the entrance I could not guess. No noise came in from the outside. Had they given up? Gone away? Seconds became minutes. Nothing broke the silence but the imaginary sounds of all those inert objects coming to life and our suppressed intake of air through open mouths, a more silent way of breathing. My emotions alternated between hope that the men had left and the fear that we still had to face them. The only constant in that turmoil of feelings was fear burning like acid in my stomach.

Suddenly the metal shutter to the street was kicked in and the room became bathed in the pale light of early morning. The cat-and-mouse game was over.

If the wait in the dark dragged on endlessly, what followed proceeded swiftly. Or so it seemed. The visit lasted more than an hour, but so powerful was the shock of the men's presence that time could not be measured by normal means.

Shortly after the first kicks against the street shutter, my father jumped out of bed and, grabbing a coat on the way, rushed to the door. He barely had time to pull the lock lever aside when three black uniformed SS men followed by a leather-coated individual, the leader of the group, and obviously the representative of the Gestapo, burst into the

41

kitchen. My father found no time to apologize for the delayed opening because the enraged agent, without any introduction, demanded money, gold, radios, and "Communist materials."

I was not concerned with valuables, but remembered something dangerous when father denied having any of those items.

In our possession was a voluminous book whose bound in red cover carried the popular declaration: "*Der Jud ist schuld*" (It is the Jews' fault). Nothing was more in line with the philosophy of the Third Reich than this often-used phrase. Unfortunately, however, the contents of this book contradicted its title and were written by communist and socialist authors of European countries. They disproved the trite clichés about Jews and demonstrated how they were unfairly made scapegoats for many adversities and misfortunes. To own this book in Nazi Germany was very dangerous for Jew or Gentile.

Always an avid reader, and not exclusively of the dime novels, I loved all sorts of books. Since we had little money now to buy them, I had built up an extensive library with books from persons planning to emigrate. Emigrants were permitted to take only a few of their belongings with them. Books, if not of special value or consequence, were not priority items.

That dangerous volume, among other books, had been given to me a few days earlier by a lady about to leave the country. I did not know what was in store for us, but I feared that the contents of that particular volume placed us in serious jeopardy.

Despite the small size of our living quarters, the SS men divided the task of searching, while the leather-coated agent stood in the middle of the room just looking on. My heartbeat doubled when one of the SS men turned his attention to the long rows of books on the shelves. Volumes wide and narrow, short and tall, a multitude of colors, but the one I furtively glanced at from the distance seemed to explode in its fiery red. The unlikely happened. The SS man, who picked up nearly everyone of the almost two hundred books ignored this "treasonable" publication.

The other SS men emptied the wardrobe, threw freshly washed laundry on the floor, looked under beds, in every corner, and found nothing. Then the two who had searched the room went to the kitchen. We heard them rummaging through things and suddenly they reappeared.

One held up an 8x5-inch lady's handbag that was made of flexible silver wire. I knew it to be soft to the touch and heavy in weight. The shiny fabric made from the silver strands seemed to have been crochet.

The other SS man had in his hand a few pieces of gold jewelry.

The unsatisfactory outcome of their search moved the Gestapo agent to a grotesque performance. He suddenly brandished an automatic pistol and pressed it against my father's forehead. "How long have you got to live?" he asked. He used the intimate German "du", whose usage either expresses a close relationship between adults, is customary when addressing children, or as in this case, was meant as an insult. Nazis always employed it when addressing Jews.

Mother, who had sat quietly on the bed next to father during the search, exploded into a frightening scream. Her cry reverberated through the room as she threw herself on the hand holding the weapon. Her fingernails drew blood. Red spots formed on the skin between the thumb and the forefinger of the hand that held the gun.

"Do you know what we can do to you?" the agent hissed at my father, as if he had been the cause of attack. The man seemed ready to pull the trigger, and my father screeched in terror, raising his arm defensively over his head.

I was too shocked to move. The three SS men had stopped what they were doing and became part of a frozen scene.

My mother was the first to stir. Frightened by her outburst, she pulled back. The silence lasted only a moment, and suddenly, as if nothing out of the ordinary had occurred, the agent replaced the gun in his coat pocket, and the SS men grinned. He had played with us. It was merely a sadistic game he found amusing.

"Get dressed," he commanded my father, and then pointing a finger at me, he inquired: "Who is this?" – "My son." – "How old?" – "Sixteen." – "Get dressed," he ordered me.

His questions proved that I was not on the list of those to be arrested yet was detained because of the man's whim. As it turned out, this freakish quirk of providence saved my life in the long run.

In the kitchen, the Gestapo agent filled out some forms (bureaucracy to the last) which he pushed toward my father. "Sign." My father did and returned the papers. When the man bent down to countersign, he ordered my father: "Turn around. You don't have to know my name." They did not seem as assured of their future as we thought they were.

As we were led away, mother and sister followed us to the house gate and, without touching, we said good-by. In the distance the bells of the St. Brigitta church tolled the seventh hour. The street was almost deserted. Only a couple of houses down the road some women waited for the butcher shop to open. Filled with curiosity they looked our way, having gotten over my initial shock and blissfully unaware of what awaited us, I almost enjoyed their stare and their furtively moving lips. I wondered if I knew any of them, but our guards gave us little time to study the scene. In a few steps we crossed the sidewalk and took our seats in a small black car parked at the curb. Obviously unafraid that the

43

cowed might attempt something desperate, my father had to take his seat in front beside the SS driver while I shared the back seat with a second SS man. The vehicle made a U-turn on our street and we sped toward an unknown destination and destiny.

We wondered why we had been arrested or where we would be taken but dared not ask. It was enough to be a Jew or a Christian anti-Nazi. As Jews, we were automatically guilty.

To our right the greenery of the narrow park that had hidden me once from the Hitler Youth ran between us and the Danube Canal. When we crossed the Augarten Bridge the sun rose in a fiery red ball over the housetops. Troubled thoughts occupied me. A foreboding, a fear of things to come came over me. Gazing at the beautiful sight outside the car, I wondered when and if I was going to see this again.

It was Saturday morning, September 9, 1939, and the war was nine days old. It was to drag on for six years.

After the bridge, we turned right toward the Rossauer prison or Lisl, as it was called with ironic affection by the Viennese. In front of that huge building most of Vienna's motor vehicles appeared to have gathered. Cars were delivering Jews from every part of the capital.

Growling angrily, our driver snaked his way through the maze of vehicles and found an open spot across the street from the prison. I was disappointed that he had managed this feat without damaging another car.

"Raus," one of them barked, and father and I hastily jumped out into the street. Flanked on both sides by our black uniformed guards, we were led to a small entrance. At the door another SS escort brought in Jacki Rumstein, a fellow I knew from our Zionist club. Furtively our eyes met and imperceptibly I lifted my head in silent salutation.

The room we entered seemed filled with SS men but most of them were pushing past us, on their way out. I had no doubt that their assignment was to pick up more Jews and this proved to be true as the day progressed. Because of the tumult we walked one behind the other, one SS man ahead of me, the other following my father. A narrow corridor led eventually into a big hall filled with Jews. Muffled murmuring filled the air which was stale and acrid with the odor of so many people roused from bed without having a chance to wash. On the left side, near the entrance behind a long table, uniformed SS men and civilians, doubtless members of the Gestapo, sorted valuables confiscated from the arrested Jews. We were pushed into the mass of people and for the time being, left to ourselves.

On one occasion our loosely congregated group was ordered to the rear of the hall. Everybody moved except one individual who, oblivious to his surroundings, rocked back and forth in prayer. The lonely figure in black caftan and wide-brimmed black hat faced the wall to the east, the direction of Jerusalem. Deeply absorbed in his devotions, he occasionally twisted to the left and right, revealing a fox-colored red beard. His preoccupation exposed him to great danger, and he was lucky the SS had not yet paid attention to his failure to execute their order. Some of our men called his name imploringly, but either he refused to interrupt his prayer or he was unaware of their urgent appeal to join us. Finally a few courageous fellows ran over to him and pull the resisting rabbi to the relative safety of our crowd.

Red-bearded Rabbi Luser was still a relatively young man. In the beginning of our confinement he shared his bread ration with individuals who said they were hungry. The only condition he placed on the recipient was that he should recite the blessing over the bread before consuming it.

The delivery of Jews continued and the hall finally seemed filled to capacity. Surrounded by people we could not see the table where confiscated valuables were still being collected by the Nazis. Their mocking laughter sounded across the room in a variety of accusations like: "Ah, a hoarder of silver." The sound of coins on the wooden surface could be heard, followed by the terrified stammer of the victim. "What's that? A *Persianer* (Persian lamb skin fur coat)? It'll never again keep your Jewish whore warm," called another voice sardonically.

The morning passed, noon came and went, and finally men were taken out of the hall in groups picked at random. Our turn came and we experienced our first physical encounter with those fiends in black uniforms. Two SS men began to chase our group up and down stairs and through corridors, calling out directions while we rushed forward. Running next to my father up front, I had not noticed that they carried rubber clubs, which they used indiscriminately to speed us on.

"Into the room," one screamed and for a moment there was confusion. Several open doors were on one side and in panic we crowded through the one closest to us. Inside sat SS men behind several small tables, and in front of each table stood a hapless person still terrorized by the unaccustomed viciousness of the chase. The prisoners looked pathetic standing at attention in response to their captors' orders.

The pursuit had been no problem for me, but the older men in my group panted and gasped for air, their chests heaving convulsively. The two SS men who had chased us and whom I now watched fearfully out of the corner of my eyes, showed no sign of exertion. Their bodies well trained and their minds brainwashed by the Nazi philosophy of Aryan superiority made them act the way they did. But all could not be blamed on indoctrination. Their vicious behavior had to be, in part, inborn.

They wrote down our names and other vital information. Those finished were ordered to face a wall, exposed and defenselessness. In confronting danger, I thought, one could tense his muscles and at least try to avert the worst by raising one's arms or crouching. How little I knew then of SS methods, and how naïve of me to believe that those physically abused could ward off punishing blows.

We became anxious when we were separated into two groups, one on each side of the room, after that. This did not necessarily have to be bad, I speculated. Perhaps there was even hope that for some of us the frightful experience of the last few hours was over and we would be set free. And if so, who would be the lucky ones? Those on the left or those on the right?

Some of us were lucky indeed – only we did not know it. Others were not. My father and I belonged to the fortunate ones. We were not let go but had to hasten in small groups to another section on the same floor. After a body search, including shoes, the SS gave us no time to get fully dressed, and another chase was on. The setting was terrifying, but it must have looked funny to the SS, for they laughed so hard they forgot to use their clubs on those running away. We ran down a corridor holding on to jackets, pants unfastened, flies open, and shirts fluttering. A hat got lost, someone lost a shoe, retrieving it, but had to limp along holding it in one hand. Chaotic disorder, but likely to be funny if you were on the side of the observers.

Our flight ended in a room where we were to remain for a while. The furniture of the place consisted of long wooden tables and benches arranged along three walls and straw mattresses stacked high in a corner.

Some of the men who had been sent to the other wall after questioning joined us. In time we became a band of about 40 inmates. As long as the SS was busy interrogating and sorting out prisoners nobody bothered us. During that calm spell, those who had been the unlucky ones and on the "wrong" side in the interrogation room began to tell their stories.

"They made me crawl on all fours and lick the floor with my tongue," one man told us. "But if things change..." He left the sentence unfinished, but took off his jacket to flex the unusually large biceps that had bulged his shirtsleeves. He was a piano mover.

"I was put opposite a man," another fellow related, "and ordered by an SS man: "Hit him." When I barely touched the other guy the SS man smashed his fist into my face, and screamed: 'That's the way to do it.'" And the poor fellow's countenance showed the marks from that blow.

They talked about the physical pain and degradation they had undergone in the last few hours – hair-raising reports. We wished we could strike back at our tormentors, but years passed before this became possible. And yet, even when the time came, many of the most vicious murderers got away with the help of an incredible assortment of helpers[10].

We heard more horror stories. Men had to face a wall once more and were made to stand on their toes, hands stretched high above their heads. When they fell back they were kicked in the rear with those high boots until they stood up again or collapsed to the floor. The frightening words: "Take him to the room" meant one was to be led to an empty room where SS men formed a circle around the victim to work him over. After kicking and beating from all sides, only an unrecognizable heap remained on the ground. We became familiar with sights of that sort when more victims were returned to us during the next few weeks.

In the late afternoon, bands of four or five SS men began to show up in our place. They appeared repeatedly but at different time intervals. During their first visit, they ordered us to pick a *Zimmerkommandant,* room commander, and then left. The choice was easy. A short, chubby fellow in his fifties had told us of his recent release from the concentration camp at Dachau. With his experience he seemed the best choice, and to his discomfort, he was elected.

Ten minutes later the SS men were back. "Zimmerkommandant," one roared. – "Jawohl, Herr Hauptscharführer," our new room commander shouted. – "How many present?" – "Forty-two men present. Herr Hauptscharführer," our fellow said smartly, standing at attention. – "And where is the Zimmerkommandant?" the SS man asked in a voice much too quiet for comfort. Many times a subdued tone was a prelude to a vicious action.

We could see our man stiffen even more. "Forty-one men and one Zimmerkommandant, Herr Hauptscharführer," he barked.

While this went on, the other SS men strolled around the room staring at people, all of whom avoided eye contact. It was as if an SS man, by forcing a person to look down, subjugated him mentally and physically. This "I dare you to look at me" was a sadistic game. It challenged a "lesser" creature to risk rebellion by looking back. And to challenge this power by just a look certainly would have produced the next victim. They left, only to reappear a while later.

"Zimmerkommandant. Count?" – "Forty-one men, and one Zim-

---

[10] They escaped justice because of bureaucratic confusion or absence of evidence. *Die Spinne,* the spider, a Nazi underground organization arranged passages to places in South America (mostly Peron's Argentina) and the Middle East (Syria). The Allies used their services after the war for their own purposes and most extraordinary of all the benefactors were members of the Jesuit Order.

merkommandant present, Herr Hauptscharführer" – "Forty-one prisoners and one Zimmerkommandant you have to report," shouted enraged the same SS man who had accepted the term "men" before.

More frightening visits by the SS followed, and again we heard: "Zimmerkommandant. Count?" – "Forty-one prisoners, and one Zimmerkommandant present. Herr Hauptscharführer" – "You brainless ass," bellowed the tormentor. "Forty-one Jews and one Zimmerkommandant, you say."

"Jawohl, Herr Hauptscharführer," yelled our man. It was obvious, he could never deliver a report to their satisfaction if they did not want him to.

In the evening we received our first meal. Beans boiled to a paste and spiced with lots of black pepper. A slice of stale bread.

During the three days in the Rossauer prison the composition and wretchedness of the food never changed. Breakfast was black water substituting for coffee and a piece of dried-out bread. Lunch, watery soup with a few lonely noodles in it. Bread. Dinner, beans or split peas cooked to a pulp. Bread.

Our stomachs rebelled against the unaccustomed food but this was suppose to be the diet fed to all prisoners here. A few weeks later we would have been very happy had we received as much as they served us here. At least there was a surplus of bread. Unconsumed slices were molded into chess figures. Almost everybody played chess. It helped to pass the time.

The SS continued to harass and torment us. They came to our room throughout the day. Once one of them asked for the youngest person. There was another fellow about my age and we looked at each other across the room, a few seconds went by with neither of us stirring. Father had grabbed my left hand under the table and, holding it down, tried to convey to me not to move. The silence in the room grew threatening, for it was obvious the SS would react violently to the none compliance of their order.

I raised my right hand.

"Come with me," the SS man ordered. When we passed the door I heard my father address the remaining SS. It was an act of desperation and his daring could have had serious consequences for him. Nobody spoke to an SS man without being addressed. As father later told me, he begged for my safety, saying he was a war invalid and I was his only son. Luckily he got away with his audacity. In my eyes he was a hero. Meanwhile, always half a stride behind the quick-stepping SS man, we walked down a long corridor, turned a corner, and stopped at a small table.

"Pick up the cigarette butts," he ordered me and obediently I squatted down to a floor littered with half-smoked cigarettes.

My heart beat like drumfire, and my fingers trembled when the other SS men showed up. For a while they talked among themselves and though I seemed focused on my task, I cast furtive glances at the group. Looking at their highly polished, knee-high black boots that could so easily become brutal weapons, I became uncomfortably aware of their glances toward me and expected the worst.

Suddenly they came over, positioning themselves around me. My muscles tensed to reduce the expected impact of a blow, and I was startled when, instead of a kick, a question came at me. "Why do Jews wear that thing with the tassels under their shirts?" (A ritual undergarment.)

As a child I had asked that same question. The answer at the time had been that it shielded one from harm. In our situation, I thought, it certainly had not helped any of the people that wore them. Without raising my eyes I said, "I don't know."

More questions about religion followed, and though I knew most of the answers, my reply was always the same: "I don't know. I'm not certain."

I was lucky. They took no offense, as they usually did in situations where one professed no knowledge of issues that one should have known at least something about. I must have sounded convincing, for one of the SS men suddenly said: "Let him go, he is not a Jew like the others." His classification of me might have been odd, but relieved, I raced back to our room.

Everyone wanted to know what had happened, and I gave a condensed version of my experience.

The SS reappeared. "Who can play the piano?" – No answer. – "Who knows how to type?" the SS continued. – The silence was tense.

"What? Nobody knows how to use a typewriter?" It sounded threatening. — "I know a little," one fellow admitted timidly.

He was handed scissors and told to cut off half the beards of the several religious Jews in our room. To make it more insulting, he had to shear off only the right side of the beard, from its lowest central point to the chin and up to the ear. It left a grotesquely pointed growth on half their faces.

With us was a friendly little fellow. He wore a small skullcap. The SS declared him to be a rabbi who knew how to read the torah. They made him a toilet cleaner, a job he had to do with one pail of water. After he finished one large facility, the foul-smelling liquid was poured over his head and body. Penetrating and sticking to his clothes, the poor man filled our room with his stench when he returned to us.

We had no doctor in the room. As we later found out, the Nazis singled them out for an extra thrashing. Jewish doctors, they said, raped Christian women and performed abortions.

After three days we were told to get ready to move. Rumors circulated yet nobody knew anything for certain.

We were apprehensive about the transfer, but when regular policemen moved us downstairs and into police vans we felt relieved. Father had on him a few Polish coins that had escaped the inspection by the SS. They were only worth a few German marks, but to keep them would have been foolish. During the trip he slipped them into a crack in the bench we sat on.

Inside the crowded van the air was hot and stuffy. Although the vehicle rolled through sun-flooded streets, only a little light entered our prison through the small window in the back door. The dimness surrounding us mirrored our feelings. We did not know our destination and this brought home, once more, the uncertainty of our future. Misery and hopelessness engulfed everyone.

Being near the door, I watched the scenery outside. People were going about their business, scarcely looking at the infamous "*grüne Minna*" or "*grüner Heinrich,*" as the green-colored prison vans were called. Had they known about us, I wondered, how many would have cared?

Still shaken by the horrors of the last three days, everyone worried about our destination. We were pleasantly surprised.

The Hermanngasse district prison was an old building in the seventh district of Vienna. I remembered the place for we had visited father there during his last imprisonment not that long ago. Now he was back and I was in his company.

Having left the van, we waited in the prison yard for things to come. It was late afternoon before a police inspector appeared to address us. He spoke for 15 minutes, and we listened to a human being for a change. He promised humane treatment if our conduct warranted it, as if any of these frightened men had any thought of misconduct or rebellion. His assurance of no violence by police was followed by an approving murmur of our people. This genuine expression of relief would hardly have been dared at the Rossauer prison – even had there been a reason for it.

One police officer read names off a list while other officers led small groups of our men into the jail. The end of the day found father, five more inmates, and me sharing one room. Prisoners still, but happy ones. A rather inadequate evening meal left us hungry but no one complained. The radical difference between the jailers of yesterday and those of today and the fundamental contrast between the places of detention were so overwhelming that nothing could spoil our contentment.

50

Before lights-out, straw mattresses were placed on the floor. Physically and mentally exhausted, we stretched out on them.

After the terrors of the Rossauer prison, the next four days at Hermanngasse felt like vacation time. Food portions continued to be small, yet, had it been up to us, we gladly would have chosen to stay here for the duration of our imprisonment.

The building had housed political prisoners in the past. Their penciled graffiti and party-oriented carvings on the wooden window frames of our room were still there. The three parallel arrows of the Social Democrats, the hammer and sickle of the Communists, and the swastika of the Nazis, appeared in harmonious company. Any free space was filled with faded initials and dates, some barely legible.

One day we were taken to bathe. The time allocated for undressing, taking the shower and dressing again was three minutes. Since we were told this ahead of time, we began to remove our clothes on the way in order to spend more time under the shower. It seemed funny and everybody was laughing. If this had been the rule for an extended stay at Hermanngasse it might have become less amusing.

Despite our preparations, we barely succeeded in getting thoroughly wet before the officers screamed: "Get dressed, get dressed." We had no towels, and in the short time allotted to us they would have been useless. Wet as we were, we jumped back into our clothing and speedily returned to our room.

On our second day at Hermanngasse, Mother and Berta came to visit. They were not permitted to see us. But for a moment, while we crossed the yard on our way to lunch, I glimpsed them near the gate to the street. They brought clean underwear, which we urgently needed, five marks (the German currency in use now instead of the Austrian schilling), and something that made me very happy, a little bag of hard candies. It seemed an eternity since I had last seen my mother and sister, though it had only been a few days.

For people who smoked, it was a trying time, but I found a way to alleviate their cravings. I had been given the job of sweeping and dusting the two rooms of the duty officers. Every morning, while emptying the ashtrays and garbage cans, I collected cigarette butts and hid them in my pocket. In our room everybody except father and me smoked, and my return was eagerly awaited. The tobacco extracted from the butts was rolled into any kind of paper the men could lay their hands on, mostly old newspapers. Then, like an Indian peace pipe, the cigarette thus produced, went from hand to hand, and mouth to mouth. Persons who never would have put anything to their mouth that somebody else's lips had touched smoked in brotherly union. I never saw such enraptured faces as when they inhaled the smoke of that primitive tobacco roll.

At one time, I decided to check the little stove in our room. Not having been cleaned out for months, I found a gold mine of butts among discards and rubbish. The tobacco, dry as fallen leaves in autumn, disintegrated to the touch. Yet despite its condition it was looked upon as a gift from heaven. The men puffed on that withered weed as if it were the finest of smokes.

Four days we spent here, four wonderful days, they were remembered like a peaceful island in a stormy sea of terror. We then put our meager belongings together to move on to a new and unknown fate. Closer to the hell that awaited us after our exposure to those two different kinds of law enforcers in the "genial city of waltzes," Vienna.

Strangely enough, our next abode was a large section of the Viennese soccer stadium. Our mode of transportation was again prison vans and the guards were once more policemen. But how different their behavior from the ones of Hermanngasse! They wore the uniform of the regular police force, yet behaved almost as barbarously as Stormtroopers. Screamed orders and pushing preceded every move we had to make.

It was our third transfer in one week, and it all began to look as if they did not know what to do with us. We had been arrested in the twentieth district of Vienna, taken to the Rossauer prison in the ninth, transferred to Hermanngasse in the seventh, and finally ended up in the stadium, which was in the second district. We were riding a merry-go-round in brutality land.

Once more, our names were checked off a list after which we were divided into five groups of about 200 each and placed in huge hallways under the bleachers. Each assembly was separated from its neighbor by a squad of rifle carrying police guards. Inside those big concrete and steel caverns, straw mattresses for the night were piled high, the stacks leaning precariously against walls and pillars. During the daytime we were permitted to sit outside on the concrete steps of the stadium, which in the nice weather we had was very pleasant.

We met people seemingly for the first time. In the big hall of the Rossauer prison still we had been dazed by the arrest, and the mass of captured had been just a blur to most. In the Hermanngasse, a relationship of sorts developed between my father, me, and our roommates. We also recognized the faces of Jewish prisoners we passed on our way to the shower and meals. At the stadium, we acknowledged more of those taken into custody on that unforgettable Saturday. But what we saw was even more appalling than what we had seen until then.

Bandaged heads with broken noses held in place by strips of gauze crossed over the face and then tied into a knot at the back of the victim's head. Some prisoners looked as if they had come back from a one-sided kickboxing bout. But the shocks wore off and an almost normal daily

52

routine developed.

People talked a lot, argued, played chess with bread figures, and took walks from one end of the restricted area to the other. The little bag of sweets mother had brought me lasted for a while. I kept to my resolve and consumed only one candy per day.

For a few days, our daily routine was interrupted. High ranking SS officers in the company of "scientists," as the rumor had it, appeared. They walked through our quarters, looked us over as if we were some extraordinary specimens, and then names of individuals were registered, mine included. The purpose of the registration became known a little while later.

The first few men on the list were called and then taken away. When they returned, we found the answer; "racial research."

The Nazis were obsessed with studies of race and breeding. In our case, presumably, they wanted to find out how close we came, or how remote we were, from what they believed a Jew should look like. It was an insane project they relentlessly pursued. For "scientific" studies of this kind, a great variety of subjects were essential, and Jews offered the best assortment. Although the more than 1,000 prisoners concentrated in one place provided a splendid supply of different types, I doubt the researchers found the stereotypical Jew the Nazi press displayed in their perverse cartoons. Many faces with "characteristic" features certainly were among us. Countenances varied from "Nordic" to "Semitic", from straight, blonde hair to curly black hair. Out of this mixture of men individuals were selected and I was among them.

Then my turn came.

I was taken to a room whose furniture consisted of a chair and two tables. Tools covered one tabletop; the other one had just one small pillow. A camera mounted on a tripod stood in front of a wall that was partly covered by a large, white sheet. Had I not known what to expect, the instruments would have given me the creeps.

A man in a white coat, the only person in the room, received me in a friendly manner, and throughout the performing of his work tried to set my mind at ease.

Against the white sheet as a background, my face was photographed from the front and side; then my name, age, and additional background information was recorded. Subsequently the man entered the color of my hair, eyebrows, and eyes as well as the complexion of my skin. While he picked the tools to measure the length and width of my nose, ears, lips and eyebrows, I glanced at the cluttered table. Among the calipers, rulers, and unfamiliar things were a metal bowl, spatulas of different sizes, narrow flat sticks, a jar of water, and towels. A bag of plaster of paris, its top torn open, leaned against the leg of the table.

Then, as far as I was concerned, came the main feature, the highlight of my contribution to the research. It seemed only fitting to me that I was able to contradict the stereotypes the anti-Semitic newspaper *Der Stürmer* tried to convey to the Germans: the Jew with the big, fleshy hooked nose and the thick, protruding lips.

My head on the pillow, I stretched out on the table and closed my eyes. The man advised me to relax, while he coated my face with a greasy substance. He applied it from the top of my forehead down to the throat and from ear to ear. The lubricant, he explained, was to prevent the hardened plaster of paris from sticking to my skin. He instructed me to breathe naturally through my nose and not move once he started to apply the mixture. I heard scraping sounds as he stirred powder and water to the right consistency in the bowl, and then felt the creamy paste being spread over my face. From time to time he used the narrow, flat stick to keep the passage to my nostrils open.

Eerie emotions and thoughts passed through my head as I waited for the plaster to harden. Perhaps I imagined it, but the soft mixture seemed to get heavier as it turned into a mask. After quite a while the man loosened the hardened cast by wiggling it from side to side. When he lifted it carefully off my face it did not hurt. The only sensation was a suction-cup effect. I would have loved to find out how I fit into their statistics. For all I know, my mask and personal details may still exist in some crates in a storage room somewhere in Germany.

Before I left, he smilingly handed me a cigarette. A precious gift for a smoker, but hardly one for me. At least I made one fellow prisoner happy.

Women came to visit, but no physical contact was permitted. They pushed against a fence some distance away, trying desperately to locate their men among the many hundreds of faces pressing against the huge windows two or three stories up.

One day Mother and Berta came, and we, like so many others before us, frantically attempted to get their attention. When we finally succeeded, joyful waving on both sides followed. The happiness of the reunion, though it had been only visual and from a distance, remained with us long after our family had left.

A package containing shirts, socks, and underwear, another little bag of candies, and five marks (money, useless to us, and surely needed more by mother), rounded out an almost perfect day.

The Way to Buchenwald

Three weeks after our arrest, Father was released, possibly because of his war record. I was kept. When he said good-bye he tried to comfort me: "*Sei nicht traurig, Gustl, ich hol' dich schon 'raus.*" (Don't be sad, Gustl, I'll get you out.)

I was happy about his freedom but suddenly felt terribly lonely. Sixteen years of age, the youngest person on his own among the 1,000 men, I felt small and insignificant. Father also advised me, "Gustl, wherever you are, and whatever happens, you are not alone. And, what others can overcome, you can too."

I wanted to be strong, yet felt miserable during the first few days.

Father requested my release on medical grounds. But the doctor who examined me found nothing wrong with my health; a correct assessment. When I was about to leave his office he dropped a rather ambiguous remark: "In any case, you (he used the German plural 'Ihr') won't remain here for long."

What did that mean? Were we to be released? I had not dared to ask for a clarification of his statement and after I left my regret came too late. Were we again to be moved to another prison in Vienna?

When I told others what the doctor had said, some of the fellows' eyes lit up with hope, others froze into a dead stare. For a while a word, or rather two initials of horror, haunted everybody's mind: KZ, concentration camp. If, on rare occasions, the unspeakable was touched on, the tone of voice was subdued. People had become superstitious, afraid a loud utterance of the two letters might conjure up or bring us closer to the unmentionable.

Perhaps it *was* better not to know the future.

Saturday, September 30, 1939. We were ordered to tie all our belongings into bundles, which were tagged and taken away. Only the clothes on our backs were to be retained.

Though the days had been sunny and warm, I decided to keep two shirts, another set of underwear, all of which I wore, as well as a small towel wound around my neck. We did not know where we would be moved to, and those extra items, I thought, might be useful. The advanced time of year also made me keep the heavy overcoat and peaked cap, though I perspired profusely in them.

What next?

The two letters, KZ, still haunted our thoughts. Now more than ever we lived in fear and apprehension. Yet, the idea that a *Konzentrationslager* (concentration camp) might be our destination was too terrifying a thought to dwell on. Confronted by that eventuality, however, some tried to reason that it would not be in the government's best interest to ship us to a concentration camp. Nazi Germany, embroiled in a war it had initiated, would only have an increased number of "unproductive" mouths to feed, and more guards might be needed as well. That reasoning, of course, was faulty because we were just as unproductive in Vienna, and the number of guards at a concentration camp would not have to be increased just because we added to the prison population. Nonetheless, to think along those lines made life more tolerable and eased some of the anxieties that plagued us.

Every speculation had to be countered by another, and if one group said 'A', another insisted that everything pointed to 'B.' We would walk that road to hell, some said, and speculated about what the Nazis would do to extricate themselves from this dead-weight – meaning us. These frightening prospects seemed real enough. Who would or could hold the Nazis accountable? Who would or could come to our rescue in time of war? The situation in Europe was against us. The rest of the world, alas, was too busy to worry about camp inmates in Germany. But war or no war and come to think of it, even during peacetime nobody in the world had cared or worried about the people in concentration camps. Had there been concern, it certainly never manifested itself or helped the captives. As for the present situation, the war had cocooned the Third Reich even more than before against the outside world. And although the Nazis never concealed the atrocities committed in the streets and camps, the prevailing circumstances gave their henchmen an even freer hand to commit acts of terror and murder.

Cautious inquiries among the friendlier police guards produced no answers. If they knew anything, they kept it to themselves.

On the evening of our departure each of us received a quarter loaf of bread and two small meatballs, made up mostly of bread. A tin can of jam was to be divided among five people. I became the caretaker of the jam for my quintet. Unwinding the towel from my neck I knotted the food into it and carried the bundle in my hand.

And while we waited in long lines in one of those huge rooms of the stadium to be move to our new destination, we had to listen to loudspeakers blast military marches. It was sheer torment, and we felt like being prepared for our execution.

In time we were led outside and loaded in groups of 20 into parked police vans.

Our trip began. Had we turned right after crossing the Danube canal we might have ended up at the Rossauer prison. That place of detention, so abhorred by us just a short while ago, seemed an alluring substitute for the unknown destination in our near future. At least it would have assured us of remaining in Vienna. But when the van continued straight ahead, I felt as if a noose had been placed around my neck that drew tighter with every turn of the wheels beneath us. And the straw we had clung to snapped as our last hope to stay in the city vanished. Little doubt remained about what awaited us. We headed for the *Westbahnhof*, the railroad station to the west, to Germany and its concentration camps.

I felt so frustrated I wanted to cry, but then my frustration turned to hate. I hated the Nazis as never before and that violent feeling, powerless though it was, made me feel good. "You are not alone," my father had said, "and whatever others can overcome, you can too." I looked at the others. None showed any strength, all trembled, their pallid faces projecting fear. It was a feeling I shared with them, but my hate was just as strong. I thought about my parents, my sister, my friends. When would I see them again? We were still in the same city, so close and yet so far away.

Our van stopped at the side entrance to the railroad station, and the vehicles that had preceded us waited in line to be emptied of their load of misery. Our turn came. A general sigh of relief went through our group when police officers, not SS men, awaited us on the sidewalk. But why were screams coming from inside the station? There was no time to speculate. We were ordered to fall in, two abreast, and march through the entrance door.

The shock was instantaneous. The inside teemed with SS men who took over the groups as they arrived, and here we got the first taste of what awaited us. The reception committee funneled us into a gauntlet of black-uniformed SS men and howled: "Run, you Jew dogs, you pigs. Run you sons of whores, you bastards. Two at a time. Run, run, run." So we ran between those black uniformed devils two at a time.

Fists flew, boots kicked, insults and sadistic mockery ridiculed the tortured. Pushed, pulled, and shoved, tripped up by an extended foot, hit with riding whips, we ran. The two abreast became one, the second man being lost in the mayhem or fallen to the ground. It was a long way from the outside door to the railroad tracks. I jumped over bodies, whipped around slow movers, and saw the wide-open gate of a cattle car at the end of the double line of SS men. This was the goal I had to reach, this was the door that led into the dark interior of the boxcar and away from this hell out here. Men jumped up to the rather high opening, most made it, many given strength by fear. Those who didn't were pummeled mercilessly by the SS.

I sprinted as so many times in school when getting ready for a high jump in gym class. I shot toward the black opening and kept to the left of it. The right side was blocked by one of our men who could not make it, and others who, in racing forward, had not swerved in time to avoid collision with the cluster of bodies. While still in a forward motion, I crouched slightly preparing for the leap. I felt a flash of pity for the people at the other end of the entrance who tried to ward off blows of the SS while attempting to board the train. I felt very confident that I had made it.

So I thought.

I was moving so fast that even had I seen the fist come toward my face I could not have avoided it. It was as if the last SS man on the left had been waiting for me and the only thing he had to do was to stretch out his clenched hand. It was like running into a train stop at the end of the line, and the impact was terrific. I actually flew through the air and toward another SS man who extended his hands to catch what came his way. He caught me, yet before he had a chance to recover from this surprise encounter, and react more in his "normal" way, I tore loose from his grasp and vaulted into the wagon.

I felt no pain, only numbness. It was as if my whole face had gone to sleep as a leg sometimes does. Luckily, the man had worn gloves that had softened the blow, leaving no mark.

In the dim light I saw rows of benches set up across the wagon, but the ones farthest away from the entrance, on both sides of the interior, were already occupied by others. Everybody tried to get as far away from the opening as possible. The most distant spot from the door I could find was two rows to the left, and I took my seat on a bench. More and more people stumbled in, panting spasmodically through their open mouths; on others, deep in shock, the white of their bulging eyeballs could be seen despite the poor light.

When the wagon was filled to capacity, and we sat shoulder to shoulder, the heavy door rolled shut. Sounds from the outside became muffled and a pall of gloom settled over our group. At least we were glad to be left to ourselves.

Everyone remembered stories of terror told by people who had come back from camps. They had told them to friends and families in strictest confidence, but the reports nonetheless made their rounds among the Jews. Terrible reports.

When Jews first were taken to concentration camps, transportation was by regular trains. SS guards would move up and down the aisle, and have their sport with the men. Their entertainment consisted in meting out physical and mental pain. Transgressions were invented and penalties executed. These ranged from being whipped across the face to being punched to a pulp. The SS took pleasure in forcing people to stare into the electric light without blinking. At times the horror ended with a murder. Persons were shot in the back "while trying to escape," when they wanted to go to the toilet. Yes, we were lucky to travel in cattle wagons.

I was unaware how long it had taken for things to grow quiet outside but suddenly I was conscious of the sounds in our wagon. Groans and sighs were signs of life and once in a while somebody sobbed. Time passed. For the next few hours I was in a daze. Not asleep, yet not fully awake. Perhaps I even slept for a while. Then suddenly I was wide-awake.

Our freight car jerked forward and backward. The rippling effect ran through the length of the train, and after a few seconds the staccato impact of bumper striking bumper gave way to the swish and click of wheels rolling over railroad tracks.

I guessed it to be about 4 or 5 AM when we first moved. Then people began to stir too. The foolish hope we might remain in Vienna faded with every revolution of the wheels and despair came over us like a poisonous vapor.

As the day progressed the sun shone brightly outside while inside our wagon gloomy twilight prevailed. People's faces, tinged a pasty gray, seemed to twitch as if on the verge of crying whenever flickering jets of light shot through cracks where the sliding door of the car failed to seal the opening.

Squeezed in between the shoulders of my neighbors, I could barely breathe, but all suffered from the same lack of space. I took off my heavy overcoat and laid it across my knees. It weighed a ton, yet shedding it did not gain me the space I craved. My neighbors expanded the moment there was room and our shoulders touched again.

Somewhere in the car people started to eat the food supplied to us and I also tried it. I couldn't. Every bite felt like a lump of lead and was just as dry. Nothing went down my throat. Our car prison resembled a steam bath. The stifling hot air grew worse in the burning sun.

Water. If only we had a little water. My throat was parched, and my mouth produced so little saliva that there was nothing to swallow.

An open pail in a corner substituted for our latrine and persons sitting next to it were really to be pitied. The stench was hard to bear. Even sitting at a distance of more than half the length of the wagon I was tempted to inhale the air through my handkerchief. I didn't. It was much too hot to do so. My lips cracked, and my head felt as if encircled by a ring of steel. Each jerk or bump of our freight car sent a pain through my brain. How long was this hell going to last? Knees of people sitting across from each other stuck together, and our clothing stuck to us. Socks and shoes, underwear and outer garments became fused to our bodies like a second skin that could never be shed. We sat and waited, waited for insanity to be the next stage in our drama.

The man across from me suddenly started to shake. I could not see him clearly, yet felt his knees twitch violently against mine. Then he began to groan. I asked: "What is the matter?" He did not answer, but he groaned louder and louder, and suddenly he was on his feet, howling: "Air, air, I am suffocating." The men around him forced him back onto his seat, and spoke soothingly to him. Finally he quieted down.

The incident shocked me profoundly. Never before had I been so close to a person who had lost his reason. It was frightening. But time and experience would teach me to get used to worse things – at close quarters.

If it had been fairly quiet up to now, this incident stimulated conversation.

Around five in the afternoon it slowly cooled off. Almost 24 hours had passed since we entered this accursed wagon, and still we saw no end to the trip. At times a breath of fresh air came through the cracks and whoever caught a whiff of it, drank it like water.

Suddenly the train reduced speed and then came to a halt. Agitated, the men began to whisper. We had no doubt that we were in Germany. But where? Outside somebody began to manipulate the sliding door and people sitting close to it moved away. Everybody tried to avoid unpleasant surprises for as long as possible. Slowly the heavy door slid open and clean air entered. After the stench it felt intoxicating.

I looked outside. The peaceful scenery bewildered me. It was a glorious autumn afternoon. Green meadows seemed to roll away from us and in the distance a lark trilled its song. Not too far from the train stood a small farmhouse. Out of its chimney blue smoke curled toward the sky. So friendly and pastoral was the scenery, so soothing that I suddenly felt a lump in my throat. People, crammed together in anguish and horror, the shock of the last 24 hours still etched in their faces, viewed a landscape more beautiful than any painter could have put on canvas.

It was a pleasant surprise to see two policemen, not SS as we had expected, outside the door. When our people implored them to give us water, one officer went with two of our fellows to fetch the precious liquid. The same was done for the neighboring cars. With the return of our men came the first bad news. In one wagon a man had gone berserk and had to be watched constantly; in another car a man had died. Though he may not have been our first fatality, the landscape suddenly lost its tranquillity and fate, staring us in the face, was again cold and menacing.

But for now we drank water, poured from a big pail into hats and caps saturated by perspiration. A jug, the policeman had handed to us, was snatched from hand to hand. I, too, succeeded in getting hold of it. I let the cool liquid run down my parched throat almost without swallowing until the vessel was torn from my hands. The pleasure was of short duration. The door rolled shut and the train continued its journey.

As at the Vienna stadium some men had tried to find out our destination, but here too the officers revealed nothing. The suspense continued and nerves were taut.

In spite of our bad situation, the fresh air and the little bit of water had worked miracles. People were vivacious, alive again. I squeezed past some benches to reach Herr Neumann, the father of my sister's girlfriend Edith. He sat a few rows away from me and when I reached him, I felt more relaxed. Though I had never been close to him in Vienna, at this moment he represented my neighborhood and, perhaps because of his age, my father. We talked about home and our families, whether they would be told where we were sent, and whether they would be able to help us. I talked of my hopes and what I wanted to do when I returned home, and he listened. When darkness fell I returned to my seat. Voices died away. The repetitious chatter of the wheels induced a sleep more relaxing than yesterday's, when we still were under the stress of recent happenings.

I awoke to twilight in our car. A man standing at one of the cracks near the door reported fog and rain. Eventually the train slowed, and came to a halt. Questions like: "What happened?" "Where are we?" "What do you see?" remained unanswered. The man by the door appeared stunned. People became impatient. "SS," he finally whispered loudly enough to be heard. It sounded like the hiss of a snake, and everybody fell silent. The knees of the man opposite me started to tremble again and I felt as if the hairs on my neck were standing up. Although all indications had pointed toward this for some time now, we still had hoped for a miracle. Hoped to avoid the terror of "KZ" and "SS." Now, however, when the dreaded calamity had caught up with us, and no escape from reality was possible it was evident that "SS" meant "KZ," and "KZ" would be the last place on earth for many of us.

Orders bellowed by the SS, followed by screams of pain from frightened men could be heard outside. My heart pounded so hard I thought it was going to explode. My neighbors' faces, distorted by panic and the twilight, became horrible grimaces. The scene was a nightmare, like a film of passionate fury, unreal, confused, indistinct, and hazy. But reality was just a few moments away. The door rolled to the side, and the "*rrraus*" (get out), we heard froze our blood. Like abandoning a sinking ship we tumbled and jumped through the opening, and out of the rail-road car that had been our security. On the station's platform we were pushed into rows of twos by the waiting SS.

The station's clock read nine, and a sign announced, Weimar. Now we also knew the name of the concentration camp. One of the most infamous at the time: Buchenwald.

Because of the rain and fog nothing could be seen of the city. I wore my overcoat and cap, and in my hand I still clutched the little bundle with the food. No time was granted to contemplate our situation.

61

Screams and punches continued as we were marched down the stairs to the street. Outside, a long column of Jews stood eight abreast in front of the station, and we joined the tail end of it. The very old among our people, some over eighty, stood to the side, facing a wall. They were taken to the camp in trucks. Except for a few idle onlookers who stared at us as if we were performing for their entertainment, the place swarmed with SS carrying rifles. They shouted commands, and although they were in German, they sounded foreign and strange to our ears.

As our car had been one of the last to be emptied, we remained close to the end of that big body of people, which was bad. In situations like ours, the head or the tail end of the group had to contend with problems. As it turned out, however, people at the beginning of our formation had relatively few difficulties during the march. We, at the end, bore the brunt of SS excesses.

Except for the few trucks, I saw no convoy of vehicles. Most likely we were to walk to the camp, and I wondered how far Buchenwald was from Weimar.

There was one person who, ever since I first had seen him, stood out from the rest of us like an inflated balloon. He couldn't have been more than thirty years old, and his body was of enormous size. He easily outweighed any two of us, and did not walk but rather waddled. Being the unfortunate oddity, he was like a lightning rod whenever the SS was near. He aroused their basest and most sadistic instincts and suffered more than most of us. I was told he was a devout orthodox Jew, but when I saw him he wore no sidecurls or beard. The SS had cut them off at the Rossauer prison.

This man was not far from me when our march began.

The SS surrounding us wore olive drab uniforms and not the familiar black ones. They strutted on both sides of the long column, one just a few steps ahead of the other, and carried their rifles at the ready.

While we were still in Weimar, things ran smoothly. We walked, and the SS was relatively restrained. As we left the city, the road climbed and we entered a forest. The rain had stopped, but mist kept the air saturated with moisture. The road was slick and covered in places by stationary rivers of black dirt, washed onto its surface from the rich soil of the forest.

Now the SS began to poke the men with their rifle barrels, while the SS bringing up the rear used the butt end of their weapon to urge stragglers on. To escape those painful attacks, our men crowded toward the middle, while the ones trailing now pressed forward.

The end section of our human serpent dissolved into chaos. People screamed, pushed, and fought to get away from their tormentors. I saw fellows rush by, blood running down their mud-caked faces. Presumably they had been knocked to the ground by a blow to the head but had recovered sufficiently to continue their flight. Pain and terror distorted their faces, and eyes bulged in crazed stares. The SS men's sadism became wilder the greater the distance from the city. They howled and laughed, prodded people in the back or ribs or wherever the point of their rifle found a target. Holding the rifle the other way, they wielded them like clubs. They hooted and screeched, imitated the wails and cries of the battered and continued with their brutal amusement as the march went on.

Among the thousand Jews were men of all ages. Some frail, some sickly, and most just not up to the pace set by the well conditioned, young SS. Although fear and panic drove them forward, delays were unavoidable. Some fell back, became obstacles to others, and the SS flailed mercilessly at them.

More and more people slowed down, and I tried desperately to get past them. When I succeeded, I ran as if the devil was behind me.

Just ahead a man had dropped to the ground and gave no indication that he intended to get up again. I wanted to pass by him but an SS man screamed: "Pick him up." To carry out his order was beyond my strength, but another young fellow who may have thought the order had been directed at him, also bent down and together we tried to lift the fallen man. Each of us grabbed an arm and tried to get him up and move him forward. The man had gone crazy or did not care anymore what happened to him. He fought and cursed us and refused to move. "Leave me alone," he screamed, "leave me alone."

In desperation I screamed now myself: "Are you insane? The SS are right behind us." We struggled in vain as he fought against our grip. Though thoroughly exhausted and with little strength left, I did not let go of the man's arm. My effort, however, was pure self-protection. Letting go of him would have been disobeying an order and would have brought the SS man's wrath down on us.

Held back by the struggling man, the three of us had lost ground. The tag end of our human column had almost reached us as the orderly rows had disintegrated into just clusters of terrified humanity. I could not drag this man any further without collapsing myself. Every muscle hurt from overexertion and soaked in perspiration I was at the end of my strength.

It came as a relief to hear another SS man shouting to us to let go of the man. We both dropped him to the ground where he just curled up and lay still. We took off as fast as our legs would carry us.

Just before I got away from the scene, I saw the heavy, awkward "balloon guy" fight off several SS men while he desperately waddled along. I was so close by then that in spite of the prevailing frenzy and noise I could hear him groan and moan, as he pulled himself along as best he could. He had the hunted look and bulging eyes of a deathly-frightened moose trying helplessly to defend itself against a pack of wolves attacking from all sides. He cried out in pain when hurt, and those penetrating wails followed me as I distanced myself from the rear and that sickening spectacle.

It is amazing how in a threatening situation many things are observed and registered by one's brain in the shortest of times. In those fleeting moments, when I was close to the end of our column, I caught sight of bodies lying on the road, left behind by the last cordon of SS. Further to the rear a truck and a group of SS men followed. They picked up and hurled the victims like so many logs of wood onto the vehicle. I did not know whether they were dead or alive. Probably both.

It was like having descended into hell in the middle of the day. Nothing resembling humans had been left in this small section of God's creation. I lack words to describe adequately this bedlam. The howling and screeching, the satanic laughter, the violence and the screams of fear all mingled together in a cacophony of unholy sounds and impious acts. Words are not strong or persuasive enough to convey what it was like. No one can feel the terror we felt or fully project himself into this situation without having gone through it. But it happened, and I was there, and I wonder how many are still alive who can tell about it?

Beside me hastened a man who apparently had been here previously for he hissed to no one in particular: *Die Todesgrenze*[11] (the perimeter of death). I did not know what he was talking about, but the words sent shivers down my spine.

We were ordered to run, and ran we did. We ran for our lives because whoever fell behind, and was met by the final unit of the SS, was either dead or might just as well have been dead.

I successfully kept to the middle of that stream of people and ran as fast I could in my heavy overcoat. Way ahead of me I saw a breach in the solid body of runners that grew bigger as I advanced.
Somebody must have fallen for when I neared the site I met a mountain of wriggling bodies over which more and more people tumbled. I tried to escape to the side, to bypass that twisting pile of humans, but everybody pushed to the middle. That barrier of hands and feet, gaping mouths and jerking limbs came closer. I tried to break my run, fight the people pushing me, yet, before I could think clearly I reached the spot. I strained every muscle in my body to vault over that barrier, but made it

---

[11] The Todesgrenze was not the electric fence surrounding the camp, but an undefined boundary created by a chain of SS guards that snaked through the woods. It was a line nobody crossed and lived to tell about.

only over the crest, and found myself lying on others. More men fell on top of me, and I struggled furiously to escape the heavy weights holding me down. I freed the upper part of my body but my legs were caught as in a vice.

Watching the SS advance from the rear and using their rifles in an atrocious way gave me superhuman strength. Fear, despair, and rage over my helplessness added fire to this frustration. I tore, pulled, and twisted my lower body, and slowly broke free. Covered with mud, I jumped up and ran until my breath gave out. All the while and completely unaware that I still clutched the knotted towel containing the food.

We reached a narrow three-storied building blanked by one-storied extensions on either side. Through a wide, grated gate in the center of the structure we entered the feared Buchenwald.

Konzentrationslager Buchenwald

The camp was 5 miles from Weimar, but it could have been five thousand miles away or on some cruel planet in another galaxy. Civilized behavior of those in power toward other humans was unheard of.

I had been lucky. Since that one blow to my face at the railroad station in Vienna I had not been struck or injured again; physically that is. Mentally I never have been able to overcome the traumatic ordeals I experienced in the Third Reich. Today, more than half a century later, I occasionally have nightmares in which Nazis play a role.

What a terrible sight we were. Some had torn clothes, many had bloodied and mud-smeared faces, all of us looked frightened like hunted animals. This was the way we moved into the camp, the place to be our "home" for no one knew how long – or forever.

We stood just beyond the gate on a big empty square that turned out to be the *Appellplatz*, where the roll was called each morning. Prisoners assembled here in the morning before being marched to work, it was the scene of punishments and the arena for many other displays of sadistic cruelties.

We were facing the double-winged building from inside the camp, and only now did I become aware of the short clock tower at its center. The barbed-wire fence around the camp carried high voltage and was interrupted ever so often by tall concrete watchtowers. Atop each structure sat two SS men behind a machine gun and a searchlight. At night SS guards in pairs patrolled around this circle of hell and, as we were told, more SS and attack dogs roamed the forest.

Behind us the camp sloped downhill and at the lower end of the assembly square a few rows of barracks were visible. A cloud of fog hid the remaining buildings and trees of the surrounding forest.

Apprehensively we waited to see what would happen. When it came, we were overwhelmed with terror and horror. A sickening spectacle, staged solely for our benefit, was in the making. Had it not been so terribly real, one might have thought one was attending an open-air theatrical production.

A group of SS men appeared followed by two guarded prisoners dressed in the dark and light striped gray-blue garb concentration camp inmates wore in winter. Two more prisoners, acting like roustabouts in a circus, planted a strange contraption made of boards near the assembled performers. It looked like a small table with a concave top, similar to a trough whose sides had been removed so that only the curved surface remained. The four legs were connected to each other, slightly above ground, by a strip of wood. This feared instrument called the "*Bock*," or sawhorse, was the central part of the flogging process we were to witness. The tool by which the punishment was delivered was a braided leather whip, perhaps five feet in length. Thick, where the hand gripped it, it tapered to a narrow point toward the other end.

The prisoner to be punished stepped with both feet behind the wooden strip of the Bock and then, bending forward, placed his upper body into the concave top. This position stretched his pants over his bottom. Yet, to insure a still closer contact of his posterior with the whip, two SS men, one on each side, pulled his trousers up some more, and then they held him down. A third SS man took up his post slightly to the side of the Bock and faced the victim. Raising and lowering the whip he playfully measured the distance between himself, and the buttocks of the victim. He took his time and I was shaken by what I imagined must have gone through the prisoner's mind while he waited for that first lash.

Suddenly the SS man raised himself up on his toes. His upper body and the right hand holding the braided weapon leaned back as far as possible. A moment later, and putting all his strength into the flashing whip, he flung himself forward. The impact of the whip on the prisoner was followed by a howl of pain. The tormented man begged for mercy, but the torture continued and his screams became a piercing screech.

After ten lashes, another SS man stepped forward, taking over the whip. To dispense ten lashes in this fashion was exhausting. One just wasn't up to full strength after ten swings. They changed places and the next SS man applied ten more to the defenseless body in the Bock. Yes, flogging in Buchenwald was not just flogging. It was a fiendish art honed to perfection.

We stood close enough to see the chalky countenance of the next victim. Fear had drained the blood from his face as he was led to the Bock. While this second exhibition of sadism took place, I felt a horror like never before.

66

I don't know if this inhuman punishment of the two prisoners had been a routine action or, as I had feared in the beginning, had been staged just for our benefit. Once the performance was over, the victims left on their own or had to be helped off the stage while we continued our thoroughly unnerving wait.

Individual prisoners, apparently engaged in different tasks, walked by us from time to time. Some glanced at us surreptitiously, most kept their eyes straight ahead as if we did not exist.

The elderly man who had been our room commander at the Rossauer jail recognized a passing inmate. Both had been prisoners in the concentration camp of Dachau before. In a subdued voice he called his name and for a moment the prisoner looked startled our way, but continued to walk. An SS man standing to the side had seen the encounter. He came over to our man who, in memory of his recent apprenticeship in Dachau, immediately came to attention.

"You know him?" The SS guard was polite. – "Jawohl, *Herr Hauptscharführer.*" – The SS man hit the face of our man. – "You know him?" he asked again smiling friendly. – "Nein, Herr Hauptscharführer," snapped our man, and the SS man turned away apparently satisfied.

At the time I couldn't understand why the 'no' had pleased him but eventually found that Buchenwald was the last place where one could look for logic. The SS needed no reason or logic when lashing out at prisoners. To behave sadistically toward the helpless needed no occasion. Many of those guards smiled when meting out pain. Their faces smiled, their eyes didn't.

We had a lot to learn about Buchenwald. Keeping a low profile, if at all possible, was the safest way to behave. We learned to be careful about topics when talking to inmates who were strangers and never in the presence of an SS man. Veteran prisoners we later met instructed us not to trust new acquaintances made in the camp. The SS had spies among the inmates, and no one knew who they were. It took a long time to make a friend in Buchenwald.

Names were called over the loudspeaker, and when sixty men were assembled, two SS led them deeper into the camp. Eventually, I also marched downhill. Out of the fog emerged more wooden huts, called Blocks. At some point we moved to the right, passed by the kitchen, and reached a building that turned out to be the bathhouse.

The "roads" did not warrant that name yet. They consisted of the original forest soil that in the rain and dampness had become a quagmire. But roads were being built, and two-storied concrete buildings were being erected to replace the wooden huts. Buchenwald, we learned, was eventually to become a holiday camp for Germany's youth. Recreational facilities were created with the blood, sweat, and suffering of those who perished here. Children would play on fields where fathers and sons had been tortured and died.

A short path branched off the so-called road and sloped toward the bathhouse. We descended that slippery route. The SS men disappeared through a door and while we waited outside a few veteran prisoners passing by whispered: "Do you have money? Give it to me, I'll give it back to you in camp. They'll take it from you. Do you have anything to eat?"

We gave all our food to those people. We never thought we would not be fed for a long time. I cannot forget the craving in their eyes when we handed them our bread and other edibles. Had we been caught, we would have been in deep trouble. The SS had threatened anyone handing watches, money, or other items to prisoners of the camp with severe punishment.

Eventually we entered a large, vault-like room where men who had preceded us were still assembled. It was crowded; yet more of our people were expected. The floor of the room consisted of the same mud as the ground outside. The whole camp was under construction. Kitchen and bathhouse exteriors were unfinished, and the walls of the place where we waited lacked plaster or whitewash. The floor was about five feet below ground level, and looking through square holes in the wall that eventually would be windows we saw legs of prisoners walking by.

While we waited, an SS man sauntered back and forth alongside our group. He seemed quite amiable, for though he knocked his riding whip playfully against his high boots, he made no aggressive move toward any of us. After a while he either got bored or wanted to familiarize us with more routines customary in Buchenwald: punishment for punishment's sake. An inmate passed a window opening and the SS man called him in. "You're out for a walk?" he asked the poor fellow maliciously, using the disparaging 'du'. "Nein, Herr Hauptscharführer," replied the man, standing at attention. "But I saw you." The SS man smiled. "Nein, Herr Hauptscharführer. *Kapo* (group leader), number so-and-so sent me for a spade." "So you shirk your duty by loafing." The SS man was still smiling. The prisoner wanted to say something, but the camp guard suddenly barked: "Shut up. What's your number?"

Inmates had their prison number conspicuously sewn onto the front of their jackets, yet it was obvious that the SS man was just playing a cruel game and was enjoying the fellow's panic. The man had every reason to dread a report by a camp guard. When an SS man noted an inmate's number, the prisoner became automatically a candidate for punishment, even flogging.

The prisoner uttered his number and dared to add that he never shirked work. His stammered excuses availed him nothing. He was ordered to exercise. The term was *Strafturnen* (penal exercise).

The man was ordered to squat and then get up by numbers. The SS man counted out the numbers agonizingly slow. At the command of 'one,' the prisoner raised himself slightly. At two, he got up a little more. At three his knees were only slightly bent, and at four he had to stand straight. Was the SS man really sadistic, he took his time between numbers and the pain in the victim's knees became unbearable. Besides squatting, the prisoner was ordered to jump sideways. Sometimes to the right and sometimes to the left. He had to run up and down in the narrow space between the wall and us, and all the while the SS man treated him with biting remarks and occasional kicks. The friendly expression never leaving the guard countenance. When the prisoner barely had any strength left, he sent him away. (In time we too participated in this sadistic game of *Kniebeuge* [kneeing].)

Resuming his walk he grinned at us as if to say: "Well, how did you like it?" It was again this insidious friendliness that camouflaged the inhuman coldness, the complete lack of feeling toward other humans which was so terrifying. The heartless robot with the smiling face and claws for hands that tore to pieces the body and spirit of victims. This exhibition of inhumanity demoralized us even more.

Not all of the SS smiled when committing atrocious acts. The smile only made things so much harder to take. I naively believed, at first, that a smiling person had to have a heart and feel compassion. With all that terror around us it was a natural wish to trust somebody friendly. I quickly learned, however, not to trust façades. Some SS men displayed no emotions while perpetrating atrocities; their faces were cold and expressionless. Then, of course, there were those who enjoyed the power they wielded and showed it.

We were finally moved to a room filled with naked and partly dressed men. There were no SS in sight. I was steered toward a table, handed an empty bag and a tin number (I believe it was 167) on a string, and pushed on. In an empty spot I took off my clothes and placed them into the bag as the others did. The string with the tin number I slipped over my head. In an adjacent room the bag with our clothes was taken away, and with it the last symbols of our lost freedom.

In the middle of this new room stood an enormous tub, a vessel made of wooden staves. Several veteran prisoners were scrubbing naked bodies of men with coarse scrubbing-brushes, normally used on wooden floors and with laundry. Mercilessly they pushed people under water and worked the brush indiscriminately over all parts of the body. Two SS men, standing on a nearby bench, laughed uproariously as the victims in desperation fought to reach the surface to get air.

Before entering the bath, veteran prisoners used mechanical hair

69

clippers to remove hair from all parts of our bodies and then propelled us toward the vat.

I tried carefully to step into the dirty, brown water but was grabbed and pushed under. I had barely had time to inhale and struggled furiously with the hand that held me down. Finally I got to the surface and inhaled deeply before being pushed down again. The stiff bristles of the brush went torturously over my back, hairless head, and chest. Then I was released.

While fighting for air and being exposed to the rough treatment in the water, I had not been conscious of the burning sensation that had spread over all of my scratched body. It felt as if the skin had been split open in a thousand places and acid rubbed into it. The pain was especially intense in the eyes and at the openings of the penis and nostrils. As we later learned, the brownish liquid in the vat was a water and Lysol solution used for delousing. We needed no delousing. We had no lice.

The next room to which we came had pipes with showerheads running the whole length of the ceiling. We had reached the actual bath.

While waiting for the place to fill up with people, our wet bodies shook with cold and our teeth chattered so much they hurt. But worse than anything else was the terrible burning of the caustic Lysol.

Fifteen minutes must have gone by when suddenly a deluge of icy water poured down on us. I wanted to die. I did not think life was worth living anymore. My dark thoughts faded, however, when the shower slowly became warmer. Contentedly we stretched our limbs, and even the burning eased as the Lysol solution was diluted and then washed away by streaming water. The good feeling was of short duration. The heat of the water increased steadily until it seemed to come down in a scalding torrent. There was no escaping; the room was filled to capacity with our bodies. People began to moan loudly and twisted as if it were possible to get away from the downpour. It was not, and the torture only stopped when the heat lessened. The temperature of the shower continued to change until icy jets hit us again. Finally it was over.

I don't know if this was a demonic game, a part of our initiation, for at a later date when we again went through the shower routine, the contrast between cold and warm seemed less drastic than the first time.

In single file we were led back to the first room and noticed with relief that the SS men were gone. We were handed our prison garb without any concern for fit. We received:

A shirt without a collar. If one was lucky it had buttons.

A pair of underpants.

Gray and blue striped trousers. A jacket and a round cap all of the same coarse fabric and colors.

70

A pair of socks, patched so often they contained practically none of the original material.

An old pair of leather boots, so heavy I had a problem walking in them.

My cap fitted me fine, but others looked like clowns. It was the first time since the Vienna stadium that I saw our people smile. It was indeed comical to see a man with a small head put on a cap that came down to his nose, while another with a large cranium had received a size good for a five-year-old. The caps were easily exchanged; more difficult were pants. The guy who had handed me mine never even looked at me. When I put them on, I found them to be enormous. They were Field Marshal Göring's size and certainly would have been rightfully due him. I found nobody willing to exchange his pants for mine and had to hold them up by hand while moving about.

Again in groups we were taken to a hut (an office as it turned out) and left waiting outside. By that time it was late afternoon, the rain had stopped, but we were hungry. After a 36-hour ride in cattle cars, a day in which we found out what hell was all about, and the kind of cleansing we had gone through, our hunger was fierce. We had barely tasted anything since our last meal at the stadium, and I missed what I had given away so foolishly to the veteran prisoners.

Finally my turn came and I entered the Block. To my relief we faced prisoners. They registered our names, the temporary identity number, home address, and more.

Still holding up my pants, I asked one of the prisoners for a string. I said "Spagat" the way it is called in Vienna. He looked at me a bit perplexed: "Spagat?" I pointed to my pants, and he laughed: "Bindfaden, you mean." (The German expression for string, never used by Austrians.) "Go to the next room," he advised me, "and ask for the string. But listen, among the prisoners we only use 'Du'. I had addressed him with the respectful 'Sie'. There is no difference here between rich and poor, or young and old. Everybody is equal. Don't forget it." I nodded my head, but it seemed strange to say 'Du' to people I had always addressed with 'Sie.' For instance to say to Herr Neumann: "Du, Neumann, what's new?" It came easy to say 'Du' to the veteran prisoners, but to our people I continued with 'Sie.'

I was reluctant to enter the other room, and the nice fellow saw my hesitation. "What's the matter?" I confided to him my worries about the SS. He assured me there were none in there.

Next door I received the string and the well-meant advice: "Don't hang yourself." I thanked the fellow for the string and the advice and assured him that nothing was further from my mind than to commit suicide.

Back at the assembly square and facing the main building we waited for all our people to assemble. I had paid no attention to an enclosure on our left that was surrounded by a double barbed-wire fence. It was to become our miniature camp, or, as we later named it, *Todeslager* (death camp). The reason for our being placed in that small compound remained a mystery forever. As we entered our section through a gate there was a small hut was to the right, in front of us lay our small assembly area and slightly further down to the left, was a wooden barracks. This part of the camp, being part of the main square, sloped downwards. Beyond our assembly ground stood three huge tents, our sleeping quarters.

Inside the enclosure we were supplied with a round battered mess tin and a tin spoon, and were told to stand in line for food. On a wooden table set up next to the barbed-wire fence that separated us from the big roll-call area, large pots had been placed. As we passed them, veteran inmates ladled a barley mush, mixed with some small bits of meat, into our bowls and handed us pieces of bread. Our ravenous hunger made it taste delicious, and we felt good. There were second helpings for anybody who wanted them, which made us believe that food was plentiful. Now if the SS left us alone, life might even be tolerable.

Night had fallen and each of us received two blankets. Inside the tents long rows of wooden platforms, four tiers high, had been erected, and I climbed to the very top. I was happy to find Herr Neumann and other acquaintances of the Vienna stadium on this upper deck and, being so very young, I wanted to know how the older people were feeling. None wanted to talk, everybody was exhausted, and they just nodded to each other and left it at that.

To make my sleeping place on the wooden surface softer, I folded one of the blankets and placed it on the boards. Jacket and pants rolled into a bundle became my pillow and the second blanket my cover. I had hardly cradled my head in the crook of my arm when I fell asleep. My last feeling was one of loneliness.

Loud shouting awakened me next morning. "Get up, get out. Up, up, up," somebody screamed down below. Startled, everyone jumped into his clothing and after quickly folding the blankets, we climbed from our lofty perches and out through the tent flaps. None of our people had watches anymore, but it had to be very early morning for the sky was still dark.

Veteran prisoners ordered us to our assembly area. Like the inmates of the main camp we assembled in groups of 100 to participate in the rigid camp ceremony. Strong lights from the clock building illuminated the congregation of prisoners, and from time to time, and coming from different sections of that huge assembly on the main square next to us, barked orders could be heard. Suddenly a voice sounded over the loudspeaker system above the main gate.

Achtung. Blockkommandanten zum Tor. (Attention. Block commanders to the gate.) Each camp barracks (Block) had an SS commander in charge. The first word had barely traveled over the square when every prisoner froze into immobility, and an absolute silence settled over the place. Our people, men torn from civilian life and unaccustomed to the strict discipline of the military or, as in this case, to that of the concentration camp, were so awed by the hush none dared to move or make a sound.

From the front of every formation of prisoners on the grounds an SS man quick-marched up to the main building. From our little camp one also rushed toward the main gate, and I had not even been aware that an SS man had been present in our compound.

Facing his subordinates and the assembly of prisoners, the camp commander received reports by the block commanders. After a while another order came over the loudspeaker: "*Arbeitskolonnen antreten*" (Work details take up stations).

A large band of musicians near the gate, hidden by the mass of prisoners between the building and us, began to play marches. The orchestra, inmates as well, played in their daily routine also the Buchenwaldlied, the theme song of the concentration camp Buchenwald. The words of the song I came to know later.

The groups on the main square began to move. One column after another marched in formation to its respective place of work inside and outside the camp. With the last work detail the orchestra disappeared and only we, the newcomers from Vienna, remained standing in our compound until told to disband.

The first few days passed peacefully. We were left to ourselves and nobody bothered us. The SS man in charge of our camp, Hauptscharführer Hinkelmann, appeared to be busy elsewhere. We rarely saw him, and when we did, he ignored us.

The daily food allotment may have been adequate for some, though most of us were continually hungry, including me.

Coffee delivered to our compound in the morning arrived lukewarm and did not taste even remotely like what we knew by that name. When, after drinking it, small chips of saturated wood were found at the bottom of our mess tins, it was judged to be made of tree bark. This declaration should not be taken as a complaint, for the dark liquid filled an empty stomach at the start of the day and helped us to bridge the hours between the distributions of food. During the day we also received one quarter of a *Kommissbrot* (army bread), a scoop of *Eintopfgericht* (stew), a

73

small section of sausage, a tiny cube of margarine, a spoonful of sugar-beet syrup, and occasionally an apple or cucumber.

The edibles supplied may warrant mentioning. They were not a starvation diet and the moderate quantities received made them always taste delicious.

The Kommissbrot, a heavy, small, rectangular army bread, was said to contain a large amount of sawdust in lieu of flour. The Eintopfgericht consisted of a variety of ingredients boiled to a one-course meal. The ingredients of the dish were variously dried beans, dried peas, or barley cooked with some vegetables and some little shreds of meat. Prisoners called the meat whale meat, though this remained unconfirmed; if found in the soup, it always tasted delicious. If enough items were used, the dish became a stew; at other times it was a watery soup. The undefinable contents of the sausage were made tasty by a liberal amount of salt, and the little cube of margarine supplied some fat. The occasional apple or cucumber was a popular dessert, and having a weakness for anything sweet, I loved the black, fairly thick syrup that tasted like burned sugar.

When on rare occasions food was left over, one of the three main camp prisoners, called elders, in charge of our little camp, gave some of it first to the young of our group.

Except for Hinkelmann, we saw no other SS on our side of the barbed wire. After the disastrous march to Buchenwald and the shock of being in the concentration camp itself, the absence of the feared SS guards lulled our anxieties, and life was quite placid for about a week. Beside our SS commander, the aforementioned camp elders acted as our supervisors. The title 'elder' had nothing to do with age, but with their task. They in turn answered to Hauptscharführer Hinkelmann.

One of them, Wolf, a tall, full-bodied man of about 40, for some reason outranked the other two. Walter, the second of the trio, was skinny and tall, and around 30. And Leo, about Walter's age, was a fellow of short stature. The Star of David on their jackets identified them as Jews, a definite handicap in a concentration camp. Wolf and Walter, however, were Jews by definition of the Nuremberg racial laws only. These discriminatory laws, concocted by twisted minds in the German Reichstag in 1935, labeled anyone racially impure if even one grand-parent was a Jew. As was the case of Wolf and Walter.

Though our first few days were spent in idleness, we were not permitted to be in our tents. The older men congregated in the center of our parade ground, the young clustered in groups. Being just 16 years of age, I often felt like a child among the older youth.

After a few days in camp we received our permanent prison number

74

and the red and yellow identification triangles. Tailors among our men stitched number and symbol to our jackets. When slipping into my jacket after the job was done I felt proud. It was as if I had put on a uniform to which signs of distinction had been attached.

My emotion, childish perhaps, may have been a spirit of resistance to a perverse system trying to humiliate us. The Star of David on our jackets was not only intended to categorize and identify us, it had always been used by the Nazis as a degrading symbol when characterizing and caricaturing anything Jewish. To me it was a mark of pride and dignity, a sign proudly displayed in synagogues throughout the world and honored at many Jewish functions. Even the black numerals 7439 on my jacket I recount with pride.

With our prison attire we had been issued a towel. It was of thin fabric and the size of a hand towel. Despite its poor quality it came in handy, though not only for the purpose for which it was intended. A camp elder had instructed us how to fold the two blankets and towel so that they would have sharp creases. This arrangement, placed on the spot where one slept on the wooden boards, had to be ready in case of an SS inspection.

The days were still sunny and warm, yet the early mornings had the nip of late fall. During the morning inspections our thin clothing, though called winter wear, afforded little protection against the cold wind sweeping over the exposed assembly grounds. Though our jackets had to be buttoned militarily to the top, the collar was loose enough to let cold air get to our bodies. Because we had to stand at attention for a long time and could not close the collar with one hand, the towel wound around our necks worked like a seal against the frigid air. Luckily it was not noticeable. It was a fine arrangement that could have had bad consequences had we been found out. An uncomfortable feeling never left me when I wore that "scarf," but the pleasant warmth this un-pretentious piece of cloth created outweighed other considerations.

During our second week in Buchenwald this peaceful life ended. Walter brought the bad news that we were to go to work. What kind of work? We'd find out.

It was not so much the work that worried us but the thought of having to leave the relative safety of our enclosure and enter the world beyond our area. Though we were able to observe the main assembly square and the first row of Blocks in the main camp on the other side of our barbed wire fence, it had seemed as remote as the Gobi desert until then.

Work

The first work day had dawned. Outside it was dark and the air felt icy when we left the tent. The sun rose late over the mountains to the east, indicating the nearness of winter. From the tower strong lights flooded the assembly square and forced us to squint. The Thuringian forest where the Buchenwald concentration camp was situated, was in normal times doubtless a beautiful place to hike and camp. It was fairly high mountainous terrain, and at the morning roll calls we shivered in our thin clothing as if with fever. The beauty of God's creation was lost on us.

On the main assembly grounds things proceeded in their usual way, and work details marched to their jobs to the sounds of the orchestra. On our side of the fence the forming of work details took longer.

"Everybody up to the age of forty step forward," Hauptscharführer Hinkelmann commanded, and about 400 men advanced. We young ones, a band of about 30, automatically kept together and were incorporated into a larger work detail. In groups of 100, lead by a Kapo, we left the compound and trotted in step through our gate. We crossed the adjacent big assembly area, passed through the main gate and on to the outside of the camp. It had only been a short while since we had entered Buchenwald troubled and frightened, but it seemed ages ago. I wondered what our job was going to be. Nobody had asked us about professions or trades.

Behind the gate our Kapo ordered: "Turn to the right. Quick march." We sprinted along the high barbed-wire fence that encompassed the camp, and I hoped that the barrier carried no high voltage during the day as it did at night. An accidental fall might have brought one in contact with the wire which may have been fatal.

A short while later we turned left and, leaving the fence, entered a wooded area. Now the Kapo permitted us to walk. He explained: "Shortly we'll reach the quarry. When you get to the pit, each of you grab a rock and put it on your shoulder. It better not be too small, for we may meet SS, and they'll inspect what you're carrying. Reassemble in the same order as you are now. You'll find out later where to take the rocks."

The forest thinned out, trees stood further apart, and we reached a clearing. To our left two-storied buildings were in different stages of construction; the future living quarters of SS who were to undergo their training in Buchenwald. Everywhere prisoners were at work. Kapos supervised and gave instructions. We had not met any SS men yet.

We traversed another short stretch of wooded area and not too far beyond the last trees a broad, bumpy dirt road led in a wide curve into a big quarry pit below. The Kapo ordered us to run, for SS could be close by. He added: "Move it fast down there. Don't dally."

In the quarry we searched for what we considered right-sized boulders. Nobody wanted to carry too big a rock, but everyone was afraid to be caught with one too small. It took a while, and the Kapo became agitated. "Move it, move it. Get a move on," he urged.

After a few trips to the pit, I found that rocks, not too thick but large in circumference, always looked good. They gave the impression of being heavy, yet were portable to carry. Ultimately, however, everybody came to the same conclusion and the search for the right rock became a problem. As time always was a pressing factor, and the SS frequently was present near the pit or stopped us for inspection when we were under way, our searches became shorter, and the rocks then hurriedly chosen did that much more damage to our shoulders.

The boulders were delivered to a place quite a distance away where a road was being paved. Along with other groups of prisoners we supplied the steady flow of material needed by the road builders, also inmates.

At one time I almost got into trouble. Once again we had run up the road leading out of the quarry and waited, the rock on our shoulder, for the order to march. Suddenly out of nowhere a bunch of SS men appeared.

"*Achtung,*" the Kapo howled, and everyone froze to attention.

The SS sauntered over, talking and laughing among themselves as if not aware of our group or the shout that had alerted us to their presence. How I hated their smirking faces, their sadistic games, and how deathly afraid I was of them. We stood erect, and yet seemed to shrink into ourselves.

They had halted, and while we waited, time seemed suspended. Suddenly some detached themselves from the group, and walked toward us; the rest just stood watching.

In the absolute silence only the grating sound of the advancing SS men's boots on the coarse ground could be heard.

I stood in the first row, clutching the rock I had chosen to my shoulder. I knew its size would attract attention and was dismayed I had not picked a bigger one. But those rocks hurt so much. And the skin of my shoulder under the thin material of the shirt and jacket had become raw and bloodied in places.

Out of the corner of my eyes I watched one of the SS man approach and, as I had feared, stop in front of me. I dared not look up to his face, but knew he had not smiled.

"How old are you?" He sounded cold. I shrunk some more into myself, and stared at his belt buckle. "Sixteen," I said.

At any moment I expected to be smashed to the ground or, worse, to be called out of formation. All kinds of thoughts flashed through my brain, tumbling over each other like bowling pins. Yet the one foremost on my mind was, how long, how long did it take to feel pain? Perhaps, I reasoned, I had been hit already and hadn't felt anything as at the railroad station in Vienna. Some say that if a bullet strikes, one does not necessarily feel pain right away. Crazy comparison. How much time had elapsed since I had said sixteen? An eternity? More likely just a few seconds. Suddenly I heard him say: "*Hast noch 'mal Glück gehabt.*" (You were lucky this time.) And he moved on.

I was so relieved, my knees felt like water. I wanted to shout with joy, and hug the man who had spared me. He was a nice man, like Hauptscharführer Hinkelmann. I listened to his footsteps as he continued his inspection, listened to the crunching of the dirt under his high boots, and again heard his voice not far behind me. "How old are you?"

Furtively I glanced back and saw him confront a friend I knew from the Zionist club. He was one year my senior, but bigger and heavier than I. "Seventeen," my friend answered. "*Raus,*" the SS man barked.

The frightful order exploded in the air and my stomach felt as if hit by searing shrapnel. Something dreadful was going to happen, and the agent was the "nice" SS man who had spared me. He had spared me all right, and I didn't know why. I had just been lucky as so often before and so often later in my life. I did not have to look back. It was common knowledge that if one was not attacked on the spot for an infraction but removed from a work detail or separated from a group, one was in line for more drastic punishment.

With horror I remembered the descriptions of beatings by the men who had been to concentration camps before. They told of the futility raising one's arms and try to shield one's body against the fists and boots of the SS. When the beating ended, all that was left in the center of the circle was a heap of misery and destruction. Today I wonder how many did not survive those punishments, and how many survived those beatings, did not tell about them, and are dead now? But, then, how many people would care about those statistics of more than half a century ago?

The shout of the Kapo: "*Laufschritt, marsch,*" (on the double) interrupted my thoughts. As we distanced ourselves from the quarry's rim, my friend's pleading cries followed us for a while and then faded away. – How close had I come to be in my friend's place?

Heini Pollak, a friend of my friend Erich, incurred the wrath of a guard on another occasion. He had run up from the quarry with the load on his shoulder when an older man collapsed next to him. An SS man who happened to be near ordered Heini to get the man off the ground and help him on his way. It was difficult to hold on to the rock with one hand and prop up the fellow with the other, but in Buchenwald no one argues a point. Heini did as commanded. A short time later another SS man called out to my friend, "*Schmeiss ihn hin*," (throw him down). Heini laid the man down. The SS had him pick up the man again, and screamed: "Throw, I said." As Heini once more lowered the hapless fellow to the ground, he was lashed with the whip for not complying with an order.

Fear, always a companion of Jews everywhere in Nazi Germany, was so much more palpable in Buchenwald. And yet despite its distinct influence on our conduct, others and I tempted fate at times.

A few days into our work assignment some of us found a way to evade the last and most hateful part of our route: the descent into the quarry to pick up a rock. I don't know who started this dangerous game, in which I participated, but invariably the young fellows played it. Whatever our gain, it hardly warranted the risk we took if caught by the SS, and only a survivor of a concentration camp can fully comprehend the pure lunacy of our daring. The SS asked no questions and we could have been shot *while trying to escape*.

When we entered the last wooded area before the quarry, a few men told the Kapo they had to step out to urinate. It was a request he could not refuse. As each group had to make a certain number of trips each day between the pick-up and the delivery spot, the Kapo had no time to wait for the men who followed their supposed urge. The work detail moved on, the Kapo expecting the men to rejoin the group on the way back.

There was no danger of anyone trying to escape. We were still within the perimeter of death surrounding Buchenwald. Though we were uncertain what this border consisted of, to pass it did not guarantee freedom for the fugitive. We were almost in the center of the country, Germany at war, wore striped prison garb, and had a shaven head. Nobody outside would have lifted a finger to help an escaped prisoner from a concentration camp. I never heard of a successful escape from Buchenwald in my time.

Staying behind while the others descended into the quarry presented us with two problems. First we had to avoid detection by SS who, for one reason or another, wandered about outside the camp and through the woods, and to hide was not easy. The underbrush grew sparsely on this tract of land. The other difficulty consisted of finding a rock that would satisfy the scrutiny of an SS inspection, and not too many large stones were on hand in the soft soil of the wooded area.

While waiting for the work detail to return, we scouted for rocks. We kept low and moved forward in a crouch, trying to use the low bushes for cover. While we were as quiet as possible, our eyes roved furtively about, looking for the olive drab uniform of the SS among the trees farthest from us. It was like a game of cowboys and Indians, only this contest was potentially deadly. If caught, a bullet might have easily ended our life.

After a few days most of us were convinced that the odds were against us, and we quit the perilous gamble. Eventually, all did.

From early morning till evening we carried rocks from the pit to the road under construction, interrupting our day's work only for lunch. It never was much of a rest, though. We had to get back to camp for our rations and left immediately after we finished eating.

As the day wore on, I switched my load more and more often from one shoulder to the other. In the beginning the change alleviated the soreness of my bony shoulders somewhat, but as the hours dragged on, the shifting did little good, and the pain intensified. I trotted along, trying to think of more pleasant things, but the attempt was hopeless. At times I played a game. I decided to do a certain number of steps before switching the rock. I started with three hundred steps, went to two hundred, then one hundred, forced myself to increase the number of steps between the intervals again, and so on. The number of steps taken between changes became smaller and smaller as the day progressed. Nothing helped. The insides of our hands were rough and the skin on our shoulders raw and bloody.

On the way to lunch we always passed on the outside of the camp fence two prisoners carrying between them a big container, covered by a lid. It was the midday meal for the SS guards in the watchtowers. The cover failed to hide the tantalizing aroma of the food when we passed. I don't believe the menu was the same every day; to me it always smelled like goulash, the meat-and-potato stew mother used to make. The aroma of the dish was so strong I could almost taste it. But it remained just another mirage.

Life took on a certain routine for us, yet uniformity did not make it easier. The weather changed for the worse as days turned into weeks. It was cold in the morning, and gusts of wind seemed like tiny darts on our faces. Sometimes it rained, which made the air feel warmer. The constant strain under which we lived affected people in different ways. Age was one factor. The young took camp life relatively well. Most of the old and very old seemed resigned with their fate and appeared unmoved by the rising death rate among them. For now, more and more people were dying. The middle-aged men were most affected by the strain.

The assembly of our people on the parade ground each morning was taking more time than usually allotted. To correct the situation, we were awakened one hour before the other prisoners in the main camp. After the groups were formed, we spent the remaining time waiting on the square for the daily ceremony to start. I don't think the lack of organization could be blamed entirely on the old and frail among us. In any large body of people there will always be those who move at their own tempo and do not care if the greater community is adversely affected by their behavior.

It got harder and harder to get up each morning, and the call of our camp elders "up, up, get up," lost its efficacy. Until the SS took over.

The first indication of trouble one morning was the blood-curdling scream: "*Rrrraus!*" It came from the floor level, and was followed by cries of pain. Young SS men now routinely enforced the wake-up call. Sometimes inside the tent or outside the tent flaps they clobbered anybody with wooden clubs who passed them.

After the first day people tried to leave through the rear exit of the tent, but more SS awaited them there. It was something new to adapt to, and everybody tried to rush by the guards without being struck. Through all those experiences I received only one blow but felt nothing. My agitation was so intense and my muscles so taut that I was not aware of any pain.

I had a special problem. One of the heavy boots I wore was too large and chafed the skin of my foot when I ran. When walking I adjusted to a certain limp that helped alleviate the rubbing against the sore spot. Still I hurt, and the sock was no insulation. I told Walter, our camp elder, about my trouble, and he kept me away from work for one day. But that was it. He could not get me another pair of shoes. Finally I stuffed newspaper squares – our toilet paper – into the boot, and eventually the affected area healed.

One day a young looking, middle-aged man approached me and smilingly extended a greeting. I looked at him, but he was a complete stranger. He laughed. "Don't you recognize me?" – I shook my head. – "I am Karp." – Herr Karp? The Karp I knew was an old man. He had worn a full black beard with some silvery hairs mixed in and sidelocks. His head had been covered by a big black hat religious people wore. This man before me was young; perhaps he was Karp's son. – No, it was Karp who looked 20 or 30 years younger after losing his hair and beard. It was an amazing metamorphosis.

For the umpteenth time I tried to move the uneven rock on my shoulder to a different, less painful position. But wherever it came to rest, the skin was sore and the shoulder bone hurt. Shifting brought no relief. Listlessly we trotted along the bumpy dirt road in the direction of the camp. We were just leaving the forest when a gunshot went off close by. As if pulled by a puppeteer's string, everybody's head shot up.

81

One automatically assumed the worst, for the only ones discharging firearms in Buchenwald were the SS and their game were not animals of the forest. Something dreadful must have occurred and everyone's face expressed alarm. Then I saw a scene I had not wanted to encounter.

I recognized the man as one belonging to our people from Vienna. He was a rather young person, perhaps in his early thirties, and a few minutes ago he had been alive and running, just like the other fellows in his group. Now he lay about 20 feet from where we trudged by and only a short distance from the first trees of the forest. His body was bent in semicircle, and his cap had fallen off his head. As if resisting the pull of gravity the small trickle of blood from his temple ran slowly down his cheek and disappeared into his shirt collar. He had been shot at close range and I was surprised how little blood he was losing.

I had viewed many corpses by then, but this was the first person I had seen shot. In spite of the nerve-calming bromide[12] in our food the sight made us tremble with apprehension.

The man had crossed the fatal line of the "Perimeter of Death", and the saying: "You cross it, and you are dead," had proved accurate. Our Kapo ordered us to run, and while we began our trot, I furtively looked at the two SS sentries who stood not too far apart from each other. Both had the rifles slung over their shoulders, but one of them had cold-bloodedly killed our man. They stared impassively at us while we passed.

Later we learned that the prisoner had told his Kapo of being thirsty and asked for a drink of water. The Kapo, not expecting the fellow to take his ironic advice, pointed toward the woods. Everyone knew the outcome of a walk between SS guards. They called out no warning to a transgressor but fired point blank. We assumed our man had lost his reason or had had enough of this kind of life and wanted to end it.

Of our three camp elders Wolf was the most remote. Nobody would approach him for anything minor. He was not unfriendly and would not have ignored an inquiry, but some persons have an air about them that keeps people at a distance. Even Hinkelmann seemed to talk differently to Wolf than to the other two elders.

Leo, the little camp elder I suspected of being really Jewish, had been replaced by Peter who in the eyes of the Nazis was without doubt pure "Aryan," but nonetheless politically "unsound." He wore only a red triangle on his tunic, labeling him merely a political prisoner. Peter was as friendly as Walter and despite the harsh life in the concentration camp both liked to laugh.

---

[12] Salpeter (KNO_3 or $NaNo_3$) is the suppressant supposedly used for this purpose.

82

Of the many things I missed in Buchenwald, was reading material. When food allotments were still adequate, I gladly would have parted with some of my rations in exchange for a book. I missed reading the way I later missed bread. Reading to me was more than a pleasure; it was something I thirsted after as an alcoholic craves a drink. I would not have been discriminating in my literary choices for I even read the square little pieces of paper that came from of an agricultural bulletin of a neighboring small town and were supplied to us as toilet paper.

Coming back for lunch one day, all the men from Vienna had to assemble on our assembly grounds. The young, the old, the well, and the sick.

What was that all about? A faint spark of hope jumped from person to person. Perhaps were we to be released. We stood on the parade ground just as on the day we had arrived. All were present. All present? Not quite. Our number had shrunk since our arrival in Buchenwald. Many were missing, and not because they had been freed. And yet, in spite of what we had gone through in our relatively short time in camp, we still clung to the hope that perhaps something nice might happen to us. We embraced this hope until twenty SS men and the commanding officer of Buchenwald arrived on the high ground of the square. Far too many of our tormentors merely for just a send-off. What was going on?

Deep concern supplanted the fragile hope, and a foreboding of approaching evil was in the air. The terrifying Bock was carried in and placed near the SS. A whisper suddenly went through our rows: somebody had stolen bread in our compound, and it had been found out. Following Buchenwald's policy of "one for all, and all for one," everybody in our little camp was to share in the punishment. The prisoners in the main camp did not suffer when we were collectively punished, though in the reverse cases, we were included in punishments meted out to them.

We were told of the "crime" and the penalty to follow. Bread had been stolen and, guilty or not, every fiftieth person was to receive twenty lashes. The speech was lengthy and seasoned with slurs about Jews.

While the prison numbers were read, the rest of us were terror-stricken by the mere thought that we might be called. As all Viennese prisoners had four-digit numbers, our hearts just about stopped when the first two numbers called were from our own group. It seemed an eternity until the remaining two sounded over the square, and the relief was great when they were someone else's.

The men to be flogged stood in a row on the high ground, among them the heavy, young rabbi. It was obvious that his number had not been pulled by chance. I tried to avoid looking at their faces, but had no control over my eyes. They were riveted on that abominable scene, and though I was relieved not to be among the victims, I felt pity for all of the men.

When the first man was led to the Bock, he begged for mercy just like the one who had been flogged when we first arrived in Buchenwald. But mercy has no place in a concentration camp. The man resisted half-heartedly, deadly afraid of the two SS men forcing him into the Bock. Then the initial lash came down. The dull impact of leather on body was heard clearly over the grounds. The man howled, twisted his body trying to tear himself free from the hands holding him down. After a few more lashes he screamed: "Please... please... no more." The sound hung in the air. It made us tremble like never before. Naked terror clawed at our insides, but the whipping was like clockwork now, slow and precise. With each stroke the lament of the wretch became quieter. Finally the SS man called out twenty, and it was over. The man was taken off the Bock, but he did not move. He was dragged away and dumped to the ground like a bag of garbage.

The next victim chosen was the young rabbi. He had lost much weight but was still heavy. When he was pulled toward the Bock, he put up a terrific, though futile, struggle. Several SS men had to move him, and nearly as many were needed to hold him down. He screamed and fought, and in the middle of the flogging tore loose. The whipping stopped for the time it took to restrain him, and when it resumed, the count started again at number one.

One after the other the selected victims suffered the punishment, and when it was all over, we were to receive our lunch. But who could eat? The food we usually craved stuck in our throat, and eventually we returned to work. I did not watch what happened to the flogged men after it was over, but those who survived, for certain, ended up in the Hendlstall.

Between the tents and our parade ground was a little compound called grotesquely *der Hendlstall* (the chicken coop). It was a small area surrounded by barbed wire where our sick languished during daylight hours. It accommodated invalid old men, infirm men, and foremost fellow Viennese who had had the misfortune to be beaten to a pulp. To some it happened at work, for others a chance encounter with SS men sufficed. They were a horrible sight. Several kept their upper bodies exposed, for it seemed the rough material of their clothing intensified the terrible pain they still suffered. Black and blue welts covered the naked part of their bodies, and the faces of some were smashed and disfigured beyond recognition. A few, getting over their initial pain, moved about more freely. The movement of others was zombie-like, or they sat on the ground and stared at nothing.

At one time I recognized a person in that enclosure. I had seen him in a Hebrew school where he had been director. I called out to him: "Herr Sonntag." And he came to the fence. "I know you," I said and he smiled sadly. "Look at me," he said. I was sorry I had called him. Discolored lesions from a beating covered his skinny upper body.

There was no system in our group determining who went out with the work force. It was enough to have the right number of people leaving our camp each morning. When the needed number was too small, Hinkelmann, with the help of the camp elders stood up front, looking over the remaining men by the floodlights over the clock gate. When they saw a young face, they would dive into the ranks and pull him out. Except for having to go to work, no further penalty was imposed. With no other SS man would our people have dared to behave in this fashion. Hinkelmann, for some reason, never touched any of us Jews from Vienna, though I saw him behave in a vicious way toward a Pole some weeks later.

This lack of control was exploited by some among us for quite another purpose. Despondent over our situation, they attached themselves to the work groups with a specific intention in mind. In their despair they had decided to end it all. Some succeeded.

Committing suicide in Buchenwald was easy. One needed no string, like the one holding up my pants, to hang oneself; no knife to cut one's wrist; no high building to jump off. One just had to join the work force in the morning and at the first opportune moment cross between the sentries. It was fast, easy, and perhaps the least painful way to leave this world of never-ending horror. It happened so often that one day, during the morning ceremonies, the voice over the loudspeaker screamed: *"Diese Saujuden sollen nicht über die Todesgrenze laufen. Eine Kugel ist zu schade für sie."* (Those Jewish pigs must stop crossing the border of death. A bullet is wasted on them.)

In time, carrying the rock on my shoulder became less painful. Skin and collarbone adjusted to the abuse more readily with each day. Meeting SS in the woods meant being hunted, chased, thrashed, and mistreated. These excesses could happen anywhere, but in Buchenwald it was a way of life. Families in Vienna received urns with ashes, and couldn't even be certain they were the remains of their loved ones. They rarely found out the cause of death, and that was just as well. But any death in Buchenwald was murder, even if the victim was as old as Methuselah. And if existing conditions were not severe enough, I developed a problem that complicated my life. Our latrine, situated on a little rise and some distance away from our tents, was in a clearing. It consisted of a big hole in the ground and two long boards on each side for seats. Men sat side by side like birds on a branch. The users of the latrine were exposed to the weather and with winter approaching it was certain to become a distressing process. For me difficulties started earlier.

Weather conditions had turned unpleasant. The wind blew hard at times, and intermittent rain increased our misery. I awoke one night and had to pass water. I climbed down from our high platform, and went out to the latrine. I was wet and shook with cold before I could get back to my sleeping place and was able to roll myself into the blanket again. The urge to relieve myself returned the following night and the one after, and before long, I had to get up several times before morning. Eventually the trips to and from the toilet just seemed a waste of energy. I lost precious minutes of rest each time. I no longer walked to the toilet but just went out the rear of the tent to relieve myself. The rain diluted and washed away the human water. Even so, urinating in the cold wind worsened my condition.

After the many interruptions of my nightly rest, the mornings found me dead tired. As the problem continued to bother me during the day, work became even more hellish than it had been until now.

We had no sick calls and at the time I was unaware of physicians among our people. Although they had no medicines to dispense they might have helped me with advice. Being on my own, I figured I had chilled my bladder and to remedy the situation I had to keep this part of my body warm. Lacking suitable implements for the job, I used my towel. I was at a loss for a while how to keep it in place but then used it as a loin cloth. One side of it was held up inside my pants by the string keeping my trousers in place, while the other side hung down in front of me, dangling between my legs.

Bloody Dysentery

I don't know how much benefit I derived from this device. I suppose it did some good. But shortly afterward another bad thing happened to us, which indirectly helped alleviate my problem.

One day we received cucumbers with our meal, and since anything edible was consumed regardless of its condition, we ate them though many were rotten. The bloody dysentery that followed we blamed on the cucumbers.

We stopped work because the danger of infecting the men in the main camp seemed too great a risk to the camp command.

The only wooden barracks in our compound was turned into a hospital where men with severe cases of dysentery were placed. There was no help to ease their condition, and they died. In a short time ten deaths a day became the rule, and the words "death camp" for our area started to pop up among us. Then it got worse.

Because we no longer worked, our daily food allotment was trimmed to a starvation diet. Even the black liquid called coffee was discontinued. At midday we received one fifth of a loaf of bread. As it was cut by hand, the slices varied in thickness between 1 1/2 and 2 inches. One felt lucky on receiving the thicker slice. To this was added a ladle of watery soup, and there was nothing else for the next twenty-four hours.

After receiving these rations we searched eagerly through the thin liquid in our mess tins, hoping to find some identifiable vegetable. A piece of potato larger than a die or a chunk of white beet was proudly displayed to the people around, and to discover a morsel of meat was hitting the jackpot.

A few days of this diet, and I was so hungry I thought I would never again be able to satisfy my craving for food. When I found a cube of dry bread the size of a die on the dirty boards we slept on, I hungrily put it in my mouth and sucked on it to make it last longer. It tasted of urine. I swallowed it anyway.

The month of November brought us more cruelties and more hunger as the SS command of Buchenwald found new ways to torture and decimate our group from Vienna. When the main camp was penalized and deprived of food for a day, the men in our enclosure became partners in their misfortune.

Accusing us of supposed infractions, the camp command, punished us with days of fasting. But a day of fasting deprived us of food for 48 hours. We received the slice of bread and soup at midday and lacked the willpower to save even a tiny chunk because we were so famished. The next day we waited in vain for our food, and another twenty-four hours went by before we could expect our rations again.

I say "could expect" because in November it happened several times that the penalty was extended to a two-day fast, making it 72 hours of hunger. During that month we must have had more days of fasting than days when food was provided.

The phrase "good times and bad times" hardly applied to life in a concentration camp. A more accurate expression would have been "bad times and worse times." It was bad for anybody to be a prisoner in Buchenwald, yet how much more so for a Jewish inmate who dreaded November 10, the anniversary of the infamous *Kristallnacht* (the night of the broken glass). One year had passed since those shocking events had taken place across the land of the swastika, and we dreaded its consequences now. The *Kristallnacht* was still vividly in our minds, and the flames that had consumed the synagogues in Germany still burned in our hearts. We feared the Jewish population faced new atrocities and the memory of last year haunted us as the date drew near. Our ordeal actually started on the ninth of that month.

On Wednesday, November 8, we received our slice of bread and ladle of soup at noon, and as usual devoured it. Thursday: no soup pots or bread showed up. Rumor had it that an attempt had been made on Hitler's life. On Friday, the feared anniversary, no food came. Saturday went by without any deliveries, and finally, at noon on Sunday, after a 96 hour fast, food was brought to our compound again. It was, however, only half the meager ration we had received before. A thin slice of bread and half a ladle of watery soup.

The two days of fasts that went before, and the four consecutive days of no food that followed produced a strange phenomenon. On the third day of this deprivation the desire to eat disappeared, and in its stead an apathetic feeling took over. Food seemed something remote and unimportant. Whatever section of our brain produced the pangs of hunger seemed to have died or no longer functioned. We were not hungry anymore, and the half ration on the fifth day was an anticlimax to the punishment. To be able to spend this time in our camp doing nothing helped us, and the days passed in half-sleep.

On the second day of the long fast I sensed the onset of a cold and the feeling of a slight temperature. I knew this without the use of a thermometer because my thighs hurt, a symptom I was familiar with. Our men congregated as usual in the center of our assembly square, and I sat some distance away on the ground, my back against the wall of the sick-barracks. I felt tired and sleepy, and it was pleasant to absorb the weak rays of a sun that promised more warmth than it provided. I did not expect anything pleasant to happen in the world around me and to escape the uncomfortable thought of getting sick and the vicious reality of camp life, my mind entered a dream world without being asleep. It was rather easy. My body was weak, and relaxing required no effort. I became detached from the adversities of my surroundings as a kind of self-hypnosis took over.

My eyelids were almost closed when through the slits I suddenly observed movement among our men. Quickly I was brought back to reality. I felt calmer when I recognizing the activity was not a response to the arrival of SS men. I was not especially curious to find the reason behind the activity and remained where I was. I watched as a group of prisoners put up tables on the high ground of the square and arrange things on top of them. Then our camp elders showed up and began talking to our people.

After a while our men started to take off their blouses and shirts and formed a line in front of the tables. Strangely, the prisoners seemed to be doing something to our fellows' chests, whereupon they moved on and began to dress again.

One of the camp elders walked toward the sick-barracks. He stopped next to me and told me get up there to get inoculated. Inoculated? It seemed bizarre to inject serum into the chest instead of the upper arm.

I had difficulties getting up and worse yet, starting to walk. I was weak, and for the moment my whole body refused to move. Haltingly I placed one foot before the other, stumbling giddily forward. Then slowly, as if driven by a force over which I had no control, I began to move faster. It seemed as if my upper body wanted to get ahead of my feet, for I leaned forward so that my legs had trouble keeping me upright. I lurched and reeled along, trying in vain to slow down. It surprised me as well as the other people who called out for me to stop, that I did not fall down full-length. It was unsettling to be able to think clearly and yet have no control over my limbs. I staggered past most of the men waiting in line, and for once nobody complained. It was obvious that something was wrong with me.

At the table the fellow with the syringe injected one man after another as long as the cylinder held liquid. He did this without changing the needle. I too had taken off my upper clothing, and exposed my chest to him. He jabbed me, and when he pulled back the syringe, the needle remained in my chest. He must have thought it funny, for he laughed. When he jerked out the needle he said:" Wait a minute. You didn't get the full amount." Once again he injected me, pushing the serum through the needle, and then waved me on before turning to the next in line.

I had felt no pain throughout the procedure, and was not angry at the seemingly uncaring attitude of the fellow. I was more alert now than before I had staggered up the incline to get my shot. I was still tired but had awakened from my dreamland, I went to look for the other young fellows.

I never found out why the inoculations were given in the chest instead of the upper arm. At the time it appeared to me merely another expression of Buchenwald's malevolence toward its inhabitants. If this had been their goal, the camp command could have taken pride in its accomplishment. Even without physical punishment, the resulting effect on our group was devastating. Morale and health had been undermined by the trying experiences of past weeks, the mortality rate of our people rose to new heights especially among the older prisoners.

One day several hundred men from Czechoslovakia were brought to Buchenwald and, after being put up in our small camp for a few days, were moved to the main camp.

Though we did not work, we had to attend the morning ceremonies on the parade grounds.

Hauptscharführer Hinkelmann had received reinforcements. Two subordinate SS men, acting on his behalf while he was absent, became the scourges of our enclave. Hinkelmann remained our camp commander; yet he appeared less often than before. But we saw too much of the other two, and worse, we *felt* them. They were devils incarnate and present everywhere. In the morning they sent the camp elders into the tents to get us up and waited at the exits to thrash us. Usually one at each end, switching from tent to tent, sometimes both waiting at the tent front, at other times both in the back. When we got through the tent flaps without being clobbered and thought ourselves safe, they suddenly appeared on the way to the parade ground and, wielding their wooden clubs, parted the stream of men like a jutting rock dividing the flow of water in a river.

We still rose an hour before the prisoners of the main camp and stood freezing in the icy wind waiting for the proceedings to get under way. Before the order "attention" sounded over the loudspeaker, we could move a little, and used the time to rub each other's backs with our fists to get warm. During one of those morning assemblies I had a sad experience.

On that day a little old man standing next to me moaned about the cold wind penetrating his prison suit. He was in a bad way, and I tried my best to comfort him. I rubbed his back and spoke of Vienna where he would surely return soon. My words had little effect. He just shook his head and the tears running down his pale cheeks glistened in the shine of the floodlights. He mumbled about his children and family but was talking more to himself than to me. Hoping that closeness would relief some of his pain, I put my right arm around his shoulders. "*Weinen Sie nicht*" (Don't cry), I said.

Then came the order to stand at attention. Acting against regulations I stood straight, but kept my arm about the man. He seemed to find comfort in my hug, for he leaned against me. Deadly silence lay over the parade ground, and my man also made no sound. He was about my height but quite frail. After a while my arm became fatigued for he seemed to depend more and more on my support. As I dared not move, I whispered out of the corner my mouth to him not to make himself so heavy because I had no strength left to hold him up. There was no answer and I ventured a quick side-glance to repeat my request.

I don't know how long he had been resting dead on my arm. His glassy eyes stared into a world he no longer saw, and his mouth hung open. I did not try to change his Hippocratic face, but while still standing at attention I slowly let his body slide to the ground. The morning

90

assembly continued, the count of prisoners on the square remained the same, though life had fled one of them.

The camp elders took care of the young people. To keep us from attending the morning roll calls, the occasional floggings and and other averse things in our compound, they placed us in the sick barracks. But there is no doubt that this could only be done with Hauptscharführer Hinkelman's understanding. Hut dwellers were excused from activities. People infected with bloody dysentery, other sicknesses or too weak to move, were regularly admitted. Still, the number of occupants in the hut remained almost constant. The death rate of its inhabitants kept the balance.

Bunks in the sick bay were similar to those of the tents; yet the space between the wooden layers was smaller, and the 4x2s holding them up were closer together. There were three tiers, the lowest being close to the floor. Anybody, who moved into the sick bay, picked the first open spot he found and settled into it. It was usually a place recently vacated by a dead body, yet nobody cared. The newcomer was glad to be inside the wooden building, and the ghost of the recently departed did not frighten him. The two blankets of the deceased had been taken away and the new lodger spread his own two blankets onto the planks and made himself at home.

I found a place in the second tier, actually the preferred level.

Because of the confined space we lay mostly on our sides, body crowding body, and when one tried to turn over he disturbed the others.

The toilet facility inside the hut and near the exit door was a wooden crate with three holes and large buckets underneath. Still not completely over my bladder problem I had to visit the toilet occasionally during the night. Once climbing down from my place I was startled when I stepped on something soft. The body of a dead man, pushed from his place by his neighbors had been my unexpected steppingstone. There was nothing vicious or callous about their action and the memory of a nature class in school came to my mind. Bees pushed their dead from the hive, the teacher had explained. Returning to my spot I pulled myself up to my sleeping place. My heart never would have permitted me to step on that body again.

More than once on my nocturnal trips through the dim passageways between the tiers of plank beds and the wall I stepped over human corpses. It was not an extraordinary occurrence to wake up in the morning and find one's neighbor, to whom one had talked the evening before, dead. Death had lost its dread for me.

The luxury of a warm stove inside the sick bay had a healing effect on my bladder.

More men in the barracks lay in the throes of death, but I felt no horror when my eyes traveled over the dying. Some died peacefully, others in torment. Their bodies twitched convulsively, their bulging eyes stared into the air or at people without recognizing them. Only the foam at their mouths when they moved their skull-like heads repelled me. My sensibilities had been dulled, and an indifference foreign to my character had taken over.

As long as it was daylight, the dead were placed outside the door. One body next to the other in a row on the right side of the path leading away from the entrance. The lifeless forms lay straight or contorted, frozen into the pose they had held when overcome by death. They created a hideous honor guard for people leaving or entering the sick bay. When I went to the toilet I always counted the dead bodies outside through a nearby window. I wanted to remember.

At daybreak, veteran prisoners came with wheelbarrows, loaded the corpses onto them, and wheeled them away.

Later the young people requested the camp elders to group them together, and eventually we came to lie side by side. After all, we had more in common than with the older people.

On occasion it appeared as if the camp command actually expected a number of our people to die every day. This theory gained credence when one morning when there were only five corpses in front of the barracks, all our men were ordered to assemble on the parade ground. For the first time this included the people from the sick bay.

Rarely was a reason given for penalties meted out to us by the SS command, but as a rule a rumor brought the explanation. In this case even the grapevine was mute. No cause for the punishment could be found, unless the SS wanted to rectify an unacceptably short count of the dead in our midst by killing us, especially the sick, through exposure to the elements. Outside it was raining. For a while it was just a few drops, then it came down in buckets. Dark clouds chased each other across a torn sky, and the wind, with the viciousness of late autumn, buffeted trees in the distance and the men on the square. Heaven had it in for us. Light rain or heavy downpour, the descending moisture was unceasing and relentless. Men too sick to stand collapsed to the ground. All of us stood there from early morning until late at night exposed to the weather without food or cover.

The following morning 30 bodies were placed in front of our barracks; 15 on either side of the walk. This time, however, not all corpses had come from the sick bay. People still living in tents contributed to the record-breaking number of deaths, and the name 'Todeslager' was again justified.

To remind us of the war in Poland, 100 Poles were brought to Buchenwald. They were not POWs, but "*Heckenschützen*" (snipers), as the Germans called them; civilians who, supposedly, had fired on Germans. But a different tale came to light when some of our people, who spoke Polish, talked to them. It turned out that most of the newcomers had been inmates of prisons when the Germans overran their city while others had been caught in the street after curfew.

The Poles lived in one of the big tents, now empty because of the mortality rate among our people. The Poles received their food separately, and with a few exceptions, kept mostly to themselves.

One exception was a man in his early thirties, a Jew who, after he found out that our people were Jews, moved into one of our tents. The other two were teenagers, one Jewish, the other a non-Jew. The camp elders placed those two young men with our group in the sick barracks. The assignments were easily carried out, since Hinkelmann did not seem to care who slept where inside our little camp.

One evening darkness had settled, and the lights were on inside our building when a commotion near the door got our attention. We could not see what created the ruckus, for the entrance to the sick bay was on the other side of the sleeping section behind us. We weren't really worried because the command "attention," indicating SS on the premises, had not sounded. Nonetheless, Hinkelmann, in the company of Peter, the camp elder, appeared around the far corner of the row of plank beds. Though we were not especially afraid of this particular SS man, we were shocked by his appearance.

They dragged between them a Pole, almost carrying the man, moved past us, and stopped at the wall were the sickbay ended. The prisoner screamed in his language, apparently defending himself against an accusation, and Hinkelmann was trying to outshout him. I had never seen our camp commander that furious.

The scene played itself out not more than ten steps from where I lay in my bunk. The Pole was propped against the wall and the SS man howled at him in rage: "*Du verfluchter Leichenschänder!*" (You damned defiler of corpses.)

"Who speaks Polish," Peter, the camp elder called in our direction, and the high falsetto voice of the Jewish teenager from Poland responded. He had a high pitched voice, and we called him *Quietschediger*, a word closer to Yiddish than German meaning the screecher.

The boy climbed out of his sleeping place and shyly moved closer to the three men near the wall. "Ask that bastard why he broke out the gold teeth of the corpses outside!" Peter told the boy. At the question the Pole started another tirade, which the SS man interrupted with a fist to the man's face. "He said he did not do anything," our boy translated in Yiddish, which is close enough to German to be understood. "We caught him using his spoon prying out teeth, and we found more gold teeth in his pocket," exploded Peter. "He probably thought it was too dark to be seen."

Then, as if by command, Hinkelmann and the elder, ignoring the frightened kid who retreated to his sleeping place, began to work over the Pole. Both men accompanied their blows with explicit expressions, the SS man repeatedly calling out the word *'Leichenschänder.'* When it was all over, the beaten man had to be carried out.

As far as I know, of the 100 Poles delivered to Buchenwald, only the three I mentioned remained alive. In a relatively short time the others, apparently healthy on arrival, died mysterious deaths. Perhaps it was the separate food they received; rumor had it, that it was poisoned. Even the bodies of their deceased were not mixed with ours, but placed in front of their tent from where they were picked up.

November came to a close, and toward the end of that month the additional SS men disappeared from our camp. Their departure was probably not their choice though they may have been happy about it. The thought of getting infected by a contagious disease or being exposed to the new plague that had spread to all of us inside the hut may have been the reason.

Lice

After the initial bath at the beginning of October, the second shower came a month later. It appeared that a bath a month was considered cleanliness enough for us. Washing facilities inside the hut consisted of one cold-water faucet, but by that time it made little difference to most. Many had become too apathetic, too despondent to care. The omnipotence death in our midst had reduced our chances of survival to almost nil anyway.

Since lice are not created by dirt but merely thrive in it, they first had to be imported into our hut. Our people did little to combat them, at least in the beginning. We had no experience with lice, and when they had multiplied to epidemic proportions, our rather feeble attempt to fight them by killing them one by one, did not alleviate the situation. In no time lice were everywhere. They thronged in our shirts, pants, and socks, abounding especially in the seams of our clothing. The blankets were full of them. On our body lice were particularly plentiful between our thighs, the length of our legs, our chest, and in the armpits. They clung to any part of the body with the slightest bit of hair. They could not be killed between two fingers; our skin was either too pliable, or their body too tough. We squashed them between our fingernails, and they made a popping sound like a tiny air balloon being burst. We were less repelled by the disgusting way we eliminated those pests than by the faintly odious smell that emanated from their crushed bodies. It was a futile fight and the continued slaughter of the parasites did little to reduce their number. There were too many, and they multiplied faster than we could destroy them.

A hand hair-clipper used at more or less regular intervals to keep us bald, still left enough stubby hair on our head that should have tempted the bloodsuckers. And yet we never had a problem with that part of our body. The lice just kept to parts below the neck.

The occasional change of clothing did not relieve our suffering. For suffering it was. The lice ate us alive. Their bites created a terrible itch and we fought the desire to tear the skin off our body. We scratched until we drew blood. Big sores and scabs developed everywhere. It was painful when inflamed places became infected with pus. Though we could restrain, to some extent, the urge to scratch during waking hours, we had no control over our hands while asleep. Many scabs were torn loose at night, frustrating the healing process.

There was almost no purpose in the change of our underwear and the bi-weekly change of our blankets. Our bodies were re-infested with the parasites in the shortest of times. I was unaware and glad about it that lice could be carriers of typhoid fever. An outbreak of the disease might have finished off the rest of us.

December turned out to be a quiet month, and we became rather indifferent to the daily routine. It was not that we had given up on life, but thoughts and events under normal circumstances affecting the behavior of people left us unmoved. Human emotions such as fear, horror, joy, or sexual desires were suppressed or reduced by what we believed was fed to us in the watery soup at lunch, bromide. This potassium suppressant may have been added to the food of all prisoners in camp.

The only subject to awaken response in our otherwise depressed state of mind was food. This theme was endlessly rehashed. We were continuously hungry, a feeling difficult to suppress. The thought of eating sausages made of horsemeat would have revolted me in regular times. In our conversations it was considered a heavenly dish. To talk about it made our mouths water and created aches in our neglected and withered stomachs. Otherwise the days dragged on in sluggish uniformity, interrupted only by the handout of bread and soup at midday.

Not surprisingly, people went less and less frequently to the toilet, and a week or more without stool became routine. Some worried about the unusual long periods between bowel movements, others saw the doctor, a fellow prisoner in the hut, only to bring a little variety to their monotonous lives. The physician had no office or special location where he met with his patients, and when he was not conducting business in his professional capacity, he lay in his bunk or walked around like other inhabitants of the barracks who had nothing else to do.

As he had no medications to relieve the suffering of the sick or help the dying, he may even have welcomed visits of men with simple problems or those who thought they had them.

I was not worried about my infrequent bowel movements but most men in the barracks had approached the physician with one thing or another and had received advice, I thought that I too could have a talk with the doctor.

Having no particular problem, I relied on the general complaint of no bowel movement. As I did not have the courage to lie about how long I had been constipated I counted the days, and when they reached seven, I felt entitled to consult him.

The predictably brief dialogue between doctor and patient ensued. "Doctor, I have had no bowel movement for at least a week." "Do you have gas?" "Yes, doctor." "Then don't worry," was his prognosis as expected. "Once we eat again, things will return to normal."

There came a time when I wondered if we young fellows who had been relatively well, had not made a mistake to succumb so eagerly to the temptation of the sick bay.

Helped along by the sedating effect of the bromide, we lay on our plank beds whiling away the hours in half-sleep. Sometimes we conversed with each other, mostly we did nothing. Everything seemed useless. The lack of movement caused our muscles to deteriorate and generally weaken us. I knew it was wrong to let myself go but thought that as long as I kept my mind active it would be all right. Eventually it required great exertion to just walk to the toilet. I staggered drunkenly as my shaking fingers clawed at the wooden boards of the plank beds along the way to steady myself. The people in the barracks lacked the strength and the will to do anything physical. Taking a walk for the sake of exercise was out of the question.

The wisdom of my decision, at the time, to enter the sick bay became questionable when, as was my habit, I looked through the window and saw the people outside moving about. Many resembled walking skeletons, yet at least they were active. I decided in time to do something about my lethargy but, like an addict, postponed any action on that decision from day to day.

I had lost considerable weight, and not having seen a mirror in a long time, I wondered what my face looked like. If it resembled my body, it had to be pretty emaciated. My ribs protruded and the skin over my hipbones, lacking the natural padding of flesh, had become leathery from sleeping on the side on the hard surface. We were covered with lice and crusty sores, starving to death, and looked like breathing skeletons. We were taken to the showers once a month, and changed our underpants and shirt every two weeks. Yet in no time lice covered us again.

Again and again I reminisced about home, about my parents and sister, and about my life in Vienna. How far removed it all seemed. Like a past on another planet, in another lifetime. Brüder Seidler, its people, and my friends, how long ago had that been? I loved to reminisce. It eased the feeling of despair that sometimes came over me. I fought any submission to black thoughts of doom and to the hopelessness of our situation. I believed that there had to be something after Buchenwald, beyond the Nazis and their cruelties, a world in which one lived without fear and hunger, and I had to get there. For the moment, at least, my thoughts conjured up that dream.

And a song I had learned in school came to my mind. Not in its entirety at first, but in bits and pieces. And when I forced myself to think of its words, more came to me. I did not know who had composed the song or written the lyrics. But what we as kids had sung in class with such indifference emerged suddenly in its true meaning, conveying its message. I racked my brain to remember more of the verses, and when I eventually believed I had the whole song, perhaps I was mistaken. I may also have changed some words, but the meaning was there.

Die Gedanken sind frei, wer kann sie erraten?
Sie fliegen vorbei, wie nächtliche Schatten.
Mein Wunsch und Begehren, kann niemand verwehren.
Ich bleibe dabei, die Gedanken sind frei.

Und sperrt man mich ein, im finsteren Kerker,
Das alles sind rein vergebliche Werke,
Denn meine Gedanken zerreissen die Schranken
Und Mauern entzwei, die Gedanken sind frei.

Thoughts are free, who can guess them?
They fly by like shadows of the night.
My wish and desires, no one can restrain them.
I insist on this point, thoughts are free.

And if I'm imprisoned in the darkest of dungeons
It would clearly be a wasted effort
For my thoughts break barriers
And walls into pieces. Thoughts are free.

The neighbor to one side of me was a few years older than I and we both liked to talk of our life in Vienna. He told me of his home and younger sister. Sometimes his father, who lay next to him, spoke of his own past life. Like my father he had been a soldier in the First World War and a POW. The lives and experiences of both our families paralleled each other to the extent that persons and events could easily have been interchanged. Except, of course, that his father was here in Buchenwald and mine was at home.

A fellow in our group whom I knew from school had another story to tell. His home life was harsher than usual though it resembled tragedies many Jewish families had to cope with. His widowed mother had five sons, four of whom had fled Vienna. When the Gestapo had come to arrest one of them, they found only his mother and him. So they took him. Now his family was scattered. His mother was in Vienna, one brother in New York, another in Argentina and one in England. The one the Gestapo had been looking for had escaped to Switzerland while he, the youngest, was in Buchenwald.

I liked to talk to people, but often I just wanted to daydream. Then, despite the lice, I pulled the blanket over my head, and my thoughts took me to lands I had only read about. My imagination conjured up pictures that provided me with a kind of energy. Like recharging a battery. It made me forget for a while the evil times I had come to.

I saw a dark-blue ocean, bright sky, white yachts, and elegantly dressed people with golden buttons on their suits. There was a big bay surrounded by hills, which, I felt, had to be the Italy of the song "Santa Lucia." My dreams took me to America, India, to a foreign and tempting life, to China, to jungles, and to rain forests. It was just as the song said: "Thoughts are free." Yet it was also an effort to overcome the apathy, the indifference that held us prisoner. It was so much easier to drowse and let time flow by than to force one's mind to think.

Thus one day followed another. Many nights we lay awake, for there was little difference between what happened during the day and the night. Outside it snowed. The glistening white was hiding the ugly earth and the lifeless bodies outside our barracks. In the morning when the red globe of the sun rose over the mountaintops, the snow that covered the corpses glowed pink. Everything was peaceful, quiet, not at all like a concentration camp. Yet before the first light, the thousands of prisoners of the main camp had trotted to work to the snappy tunes of marching songs. Then quiet settled again over the campground. The sun climbed higher and prisoners came to collect our dead. They pulled the cadavers from the white mounds that now looked like desecrated graves. A new day had started. The question reoccurred: who will be next? Who won't live to see the evening, and who won't be alive tomorrow? But it was always the other men I was thinking off, never myself.

Each day a few more people lay in their last agony. Their bodies twitched slightly, as if touched by low voltage wires. The two doctors in our group, who had no medications to dispense, were powerless, and for those in the throes of death help would have come too late anyway.

Outdoors it was deep winter, and many of our people were brought to the hut with frozen fingers, feet, noses, and ears. The only remedy for them, and this just for their hands and feet, were *Wechselbäder.* Dipping the frozen limbs alternately in hot and cold water. We were lucky to have the stove in our barracks; it made it possible to heat water in a bucket.

It was another of the many nights when sleep evaded me. I lay awake in my bunk hoping that Morpheus would defeat my troubled thoughts and take me beyond the barbed wires of the camp and the world of Nazism and into the abyss of an unconscious dreamless sleep. Dreams inevitably turned into nightmares. Not only the world we lived in was troubled but also our dream world.

Time moved in slow motion. Minutes stretched into painful hours while I attempted to escape the thoughts that kept me awake. I began to count: one, two, three. The sands of time trickled through the neck of the hourglass, yet weariness failed to produce the desired result.

I was awake, but my left arm had fallen asleep and pinched me painfully. When I tried to shift position, my neighbor to the left moved too. He sighed and raised his head. He is still awake, I thought happily.

"What's up?" he asked. "I can't sleep." "Me neither," declared the neighbor to the right of me.

Before long about twelve of us were involved in conversation. Not for long. From the other side of our plank beds angry words demanded quiet. Yet even our lowered voices traveled far and this gave me an idea. Every evening, I suggested, one of us would narrate a story he had read or a movie he had seen, and I would start. One voice certainly would not disturb our neighbors on the other side of the barracks. The fellows agreed, and I got ready.

My two neighbors made room for me and I turned on my back. I stared at the naked wood above me, and while the darkened lamps in our barracks spread their gloomy shine, I narrated the movie "Babes in Toyland."

In time the steady stream of my words turned monotonous, and their soothing sound, drifting through the semi-darkness, took effect. Fantasy liberated us from reality.

I'm not in Buchenwald. I never heard of a concentration camp, and I don't know what it means. As so often before, I am sitting on the curb of a sidewalk with a group of friends recounting a movie. I have seen so many. My audience listens attentively. They stare at my mouth so as not to miss a word, and yet they don't react as expected. They don't laugh at the antics of Laurel and Hardy I know how to mimic so well. I am puzzled and almost apprehensive by the unusual silence around me. I see the streetcar moving on its tracks, but I can't hear it. Cars and horse-drawn wagons rumble soundlessly over cobblestones, and it is like watching a silent movie. The eyes of the listeners still gape at me while I tell a story now void of substance. Meaningless words flutter into emptiness and disappear without trace.

Suddenly I remember not having done my homework yet. I shouldn't be sitting here, jabbering away. My first class tomorrow is physics. Or is it chemistry? I have to know chemical formulas by heart. Herr Scharmer is a tough teacher and feared by the whole class. He confronts me, and in his hand is the infamous little red book that somehow is gray now. We are familiar with this little book; he records the grades in it. I don't feel well. What in hell is the chemical formula for Lysol? I know it isn't HO. Is it H SO ? Why Lysol? Letters and numbers begin to dance in front of my eyes, and Scharmer grins at me. We were not taught the chemical formula for Lysol, I said without sound and stare defiantly at my teacher's face. Yet in spite of my denial, there is this nagging thought in the back of my mind that tells me I am lying. I know that smelly stuff which proves that we have had it in our studies.

"Why are you staring at me," my teacher says, and I feel hurt. He says it without moving his lips, but I understand. He is right. I shouldn't look straight into anyone's eyes. It's dangerous. How do I know that, and why am I afraid? I try to reason this thing out, bring order into my thoughts, but I can't. I look into two eyes that gleam sneeringly at me now. This isn't my teacher. This thing confronting me has the lifeless face of a death mask, but the eyes are alive. It wears a uniform, and I know this kind of clothing, and yet I have completely forgotten how I came to know it.

Why do I ask so many questions and then answer myself?

Wo zum Teufel? (Devils). It must be the devil, and that's why I'm so frightened. No, it can't be Satan. He would not cover his horns. The figure I look at wears a beautiful, very dark, peaked hat. Its front is adorned with a skull. I am rather surprised; everything I see is in different shades of gray, but the badge on the cap has a silvery shine. I almost think I know the meaning of the skull. Or do I? I am so mixed up and try so hard to keep my thoughts straight.

Somewhere in my madly whirling mind lies the solution, often tantalizingly close, at other times way out of reach. Almost physically painful is the search for the answers to my many questions. To escape that nagging pain in my brain I hold on to a thought that has popped up like a jack-in-the-box. I always wanted to own a silver ring decorated with a shiny skull. It is so eerie to look at and all my friends would envy me. A grinning skull and two crossbones. Perhaps I own such a ring? Suddenly I feel proud. Proud? Proud of what? The men I have met recently are very haughty, very arrogant. Is this the same as being proud?

My thoughts flicker from subject to subject, and I wonder where it all had started. What's wrong with me? My head spins like a top, and I am now unable to concentrate. The more I try, the more jumbled my thoughts become. Blinking stars dance around me, and unexpectedly they turn into objects: the devil, numbers, letters, and chemical formulas, individual boys, my school building and more. All whirl around me and I rotate furiously in the opposite direction. I feel extremely dizzy and chilled to the bone but keep myself straight and stiff. A warning like a red light looms up: If I fall, I'll be dead. I don't want to die. I decide to move and fight against that rapid spin through a void from which there is no return. I lose my sense of up and down and break into a cold sweat. Suddenly I whirl toward something that seems downy and soft. "Relax," a voice whispers "you won't die if you fall into cotton candy." Something tells me not to trust the voice. I see the skull hidden in the soft feathery blackness, and it is as solid as a rock. I don't want to smash against it. My hands and feet try to resist the fall, but I push air ...

"Hey," says a voice beside me, "stop flailing around." He laughs a bit when he sees my bewildered face "You fell asleep in the middle of your tale, but so did we. That makes us even."

I say nothing. The dream, still real and vivid, weighs heavily on my mind. I lie awake until the first light breaks outside, and the wooden rafters regain their clear contours. Then I fell asleep again. I sleep dreamlessly this time, and awake only after the sun is high in the sky, and life, such as it is, has resumed in our building.

I had suffered through nightmares before, but none had affected me as deeply and stayed as long with me as this one. I read serious meaning into it. Besides mirroring our distorted life, the dream, especially the last part, seemed like a warning. A caution against surrender to the pleasant numbness prevailing in our hut. To let go and submit to lethargy was so easy, so pleasant, but like dope, it eventually destroyed the will to live.

I write in great detail about this nightmare because for a long time the thought of it haunted me. The first notes about my experiences in

Nazi Germany I jotted down right after I crossed the German border into freedom. In the ensuing years I had to record it several more times. In later years I was always on the move, and in those turbulent times, I lost my writings more than once.

Life *was* bad, and our chances of survival diminished with every passing day. And yet I dared not give up hope. When I expressed this belief to an older person, he said: "Hope? That's a beautiful word. But it's not for us anymore." It was so easy to lose faith.

Still under the spell of the dream I decided to get myself moving and went visiting. In the beginning it was a laborious undertaking. I walked down a few bunks to the left or the right of my place, eventually making longer excursions. It made me feel good to be doing this merely for the exercise and not out of necessity like going to the toilet.

Just before Christmas, to everybody's surprise, our rations were returned to their original level. Again we received a quarter of a loaf of bread, a spoonful of syrup, a slice of pasty sausage, and a little cube of margarine. The soup had not improved, yet we were happy with this turn of affairs.

After the first euphoria people began to wonder about the reason for the change and suspected ulterior motives. Fewer people were dying now, and the SS command did nothing to increase our mortality rate. Actually we had fewer corpses because the old, the infirm, and many of those who had given up hope had already perished. The survivors clung desperately to life. It was said we had been 1,056 men at our arrival in Buchenwald; only a few more than 400 were alive now. The expression "extermination camp" did not even exist as yet. It came into use later when, with German efficiency, millions of humans were being murdered.

A few people still tried to commit suicide, sometimes in the craziest ways. A man who had thrown himself on the barbed wire surrounding our enclave was brought into the barracks. He had wanted to electrocute himself though everybody knew there was no electricity in our fence. The man's arms were torn to shreds by the barbs, and he suffered terribly. No doubt the man's mind had snapped.

At Christmas everyone received a whole loaf of bread, and at New Year's an additional half loaf. This was a supplement to our daily ration.

When we received this extra food, one of our young fellows went crazy and ate the whole thing at once. Luckily he vomited before it killed him. His shrunken stomach could never have digested that amount of coarse bread.

I had eaten a portion of my supply and then rolled the rest into my towel, which I kept firmly against my stomach when going to sleep. Many people finished the extra ration in a few days and could be expected to steal any carelessly unattended bread they saw. Although the toasting of bread atop the stove may not have been permitted, the heavenly smell nonetheless filled the barracks.

A man I knew casually passed by my bunk late one evening. He stopped to chat with me and, as if by the way, mentioned his intention to toast some of his bread. He indicated willingness to do the same for me, and naively I entrusted him with a few pieces. On his return he told me that the bread had been stolen. He had left it for a moment unattended on the stove and, when he came back, it was gone. – Of course. – Bread was more precious than gold in Buchenwald, and I should have kept that fact in mind before trusting the man.

Then a miracle happened. A few days into the new year of 1940 an event initiated by a most unlikely person radically changed our hopeless existence.

On that mid-afternoon our dreary life was interrupted by the feared shout of "Achtung" Attention! It was Wolf, our camp elder, who alerted us to a visit by the dreaded SS.

A huge SS man, whose size alone was intimidating, came into view followed by Wolf. The symbols on the SS man's overcoat collar denoted him as a ranking officer. The gold-rimmed monocle in his right eye added to our nervousness.

To our dismay he stopped in front of us young folks.

"At ease," he said, and we hesitantly relaxed. As we later admitted to one another, none of us had dared to look straight at the man's face but cast furtive glances to be prepared for the unexpected. Eyes, always more eloquent than speech, revealed true intentions, and his seemed quite amiable. It was nonetheless difficult to trust a man in that feared uniform.

Unexpectedly the SS officer turned and walked away. Trailed by our camp elder, he disappeared around the end of the bunk beds, and we were left wondering about the visit. A short while later Wolf returned. "Everybody under the age of 20 get dressed and follow me," he ordered.

The air inside the hut was horrid. We had not showered or cleaned ourselves for a long time, and the open toilet added to the stink of the interior. So to exit the hut became an experience. The fresh, clean air outside made me to feel almost tipsy, and we trembled in the unaccustomed cold as we faced the SS officer. He smilingly looked us over and then asked no one in particular how we were. He did not wait for an answer, talked to Wolf, and then left.

We returned to the sick bay wondering about this visit. The seniors in our hut expected our discharge from Buchenwald. (I was 16 when arrested, and no youths of this age had ever been sent to a concentration camp before.) Still, none of the young inmates dared to believe in the miracle of a mass release. It seemed too compassionate an ending to the nightmare we had lived.

People said tomorrow was the day. But what?

In spite of my great anticipation, I slept better than I had in a long time, and early next morning we eagerly assembled again in front of the barracks. We still did not know what was to come. Yet things could not be worse than what we had here.

Wolf marched our little group across our parade ground and through the little gate leading from our "death camp." On the big square beyond our fence we turned right, walking downhill toward the blocks of the main camp. Mixed feelings of dread and hope filled us. We were not sent home but incorporated into the main camp!

The days of darkness and despair grew brighter, and though the terror of the concentration camp continued to be with us, there now seemed to be a chance of survival. The prisoners in the main camp were not purposely threatened with extinction the way we had been, and I hoped that from now on we would be treated just like the rest of Buchenwald's inmates. It was said that of the 12,000 prisoners in camp 2,000 were Jews.

In the shower building, and before submitting to the infamous "*Lysolbad*" to get rid of our lice, we encountered the huge SS officer again. In his company was another SS man who sat at a primitive table with a ledger-like book in front of him. We had to call out our prison number before stepping on a scale, and a veteran inmate announced the weight of each individual. I was recorded in the ledger of the SS man as weighing 38 kilograms (82 pounds). There was one fellow who weighed only 33 kilograms (73 pounds).

The cold-hot-cold shower seemed less of an ordeal this time, and after being issued clean clothing we felt reborn.

While getting dressed, I was talking to Jacki Rumstein. He sat on a bench pulling a sock over his foot when suddenly he stopped in mid-sentence. Surprised, I turned toward him and was shocked to see his upper body and head lean against the wall, while his eyes stared into nothingness, and his mouth hung wide open.

It was the face of death I had seen countless times but never on somebody so close to me. In terror I screamed his name and shook him violently, not believing he had suddenly died. Then he moved again. "What happened?" he asked.

"You fainted," I said, relieved at his resurrection.

Our new living quarters, Block number 8, was declared a sick bay for one month by our benefactor. He appeared to be Buchenwald's medical doctor. We slept in three-tiered metal beds that had mattresses, and it felt as if we had ascended from hell to heaven.

During one visit by that giant man he inquired again how we were, and in answer we were able to look into his eyes and smile. It is still a mystery to me why this man had saved us from our little enclosure, the place we had called a death camp. He was a human being in that inferno. At the time we did not speculate about why, but were excited by the turn of events and our new fate.

Other benefits denied us in our former living quarters were standard here. The hygienic and living conditions were luxurious in comparison to our previous situation. To fill my cup of happiness, a letter from home arrived for each of us. For unexplainable reasons we could not keep them and they were just read aloud to us. After three months of uncertainty this sign from my parents and sister was soothing ointment on my festering worries. It stilled the emotional hunger that had tormented me ever since I had been taken by force from home.

In spite of the comradeship among the young people, each of us, I assumed, had fantasies, desires, and a private universe he shared with no one. Only between Erich and myself had there been complete openness, a condition I did not experience with any other fellow. Even when fantasizing about life Buchenwald, I kept my reveries to myself. It was, however, not merely to hide my innermost wishes but because despite my skepticism concerning superstition, a nagging little fear in the back of my mind warned me that a daydream recognized as such will not come true. On the other hand, I convinced myself that a positive night dream had a chance of becoming reality. Such notions, confused and unconventional, may be the imaginary straw people cling to in times of stress and danger.

I truly felt more confident of our chance to survive Buchenwald than I had in a long time. My optimism may have stemmed from several factors, not the smallest of which was the cleanliness around us. We were rid of the lice, the sores were nearly gone, and my bladder problem was almost nonexistent.

Weather conditions became important again. Clearly, sooner or later we would have to join the work force again, and because we were weak and lacked warm clothing, the exposure to wintry conditions outside would surely decimate our number.

Our food ration had not been changed, but occasionally we received extra provisions. That supplement of our daily diet came from the camp hospital and was ordered, according to our block elder, by the SS doctor.

For now we followed the proceedings on the parade ground each morning by way of a loudspeaker system installed in every barracks. We listened to orders and announcements by the SS command, generally warnings to the inmates about their behavior and actions, and enjoyed the music played by the orchestra. Less entertaining was the vision of the individual prison groups marching to work to those tunes.

At other occasions we were forced to listen to punishment being inflicted, which was distressing, but the broadcasts over the loudspeakers in our barracks could neither be muffled nor turned off.

One freezing winter morning a group of prisoners on the parade ground apparently kept moving to keep warm. Suddenly a voice over the sound system shouted: "*Diese Tschechen Hunde sollen stramm stehen.*" (Those Czech dogs must stand at attention.)

For a while it was quiet and then again the voice came over the loudspeaker: "If those Czech bastards don't stand still, they'll see what's going to happen to them."

We heard no more about the men from Czechoslovakia, but a few days later, some delicacies arrived in our barracks as a direct result of their misfortune. As it turned out, to penalize this group for their disobedience, the SS command confiscated the Christmas parcels they had received from home. The SS doctor took part of that loot and gave the gifts to us young fellows. Each of us received half a bar of chocolate and could choose between a piece of salami or bacon, a chunk of cake, and other goodies.

Again one had to wonder why this SS man behaved in the way he did toward us. I never found out.

In the middle of January we were visited by about 20 veteran Jewish inmates who brought two guitars with them to entertain us. They must have been around 30 years old. They played their instruments, sang songs, and then talked to us about all kinds of subjects, but mainly they answered our questions about life in the main camp. They stressed the importance of keeping up one's spirit, and we felt enchanted by their presence. We also learned the story of the Buchenwald song.

Every concentration camp in Germany had a camp song and Buchenwald, being rather new, needed one. The camp commander arranged a competition among the prisoners, and Beda, a Jewish author of popular hit songs, wrote the lyrics, to which a professor, also an inmate, composed the music. When being punished, prisoners were forced to sing the song on the parade ground. A surprising demand, considering its lyrics. The words sing of revolt against tyranny.

It became my ambition to learn the song, and though I had no pencil or paper to write down the lines, I eventually memorized words and tune. Much later, when not under the Nazi yoke anymore, I tried to write down the verses, but remembered only two of the three.

Wenn der Tag erwacht, eh' die Sonne lacht,
Die Kolonnen ziehn, zu den Tagesmüh'n
Hinein in den grauenden Morgen,
Und der Wald ist schwarz, und der Himmel rot
Und wir tragen im Brotsack ein Stückchen Brot
Und im Herzen, im Herzen die Sorgen.

(Refrain) O Buchenwald, ich kann dich nicht vergessen,
Weil du mein Schicksal bist.
Wer dich verliess der kann es erst ermessen,
Wie wundervoll die Freiheit ist.
O Buchenwald, wir jammern nicht und klagen,
Und was auch unsere Zukunft sei,
Wir wollen trotzdem Ja zum Leben sagen,
Denn einmal kommt der Tag, dann sind wir frei.
(The second is the one I forgot.)

Und die Nacht ist kurz, und der Tag so lang,
Und ein Lied erklingt, das die Heimat sang.
Wir lassen den Mut uns nicht rauben.
Halte Schritt, Kamerad, und verlier nicht den Mut,
Denn wir tragen den Willen zum Leben im Blut,
Und im Herzen, im Herzen die Liebe.
(Refrain) O Buchenwald etc.

My English translation:
When the day awakes, 'fore the sun starts to smile,
And the columns move to their daily toil
Into the graying morning,
And the forest is black, and the sky flaming red,
And we carry in our bag a small piece of bread,
In our heart, in our heart we tote worry.

(Refrain) Oh Buchenwald, I can not forget you,
For you are my fate
How lucky is the man who has left you,
For only he values freedom's state.
Oh Buchenwald, we don't complain or lament
And whatever our future 's going to be,
We'll say yes to life in spite of all,
For there'll come a day when we'll be free.

107

And the night is short and the day so long
And a song rings out that our homeland sang
We won't be robbed of our spirit.
Keep in step, comrade, and don't lose your gut
For we carry the will to live in our blood.
In our heart, in our heart our love.

(Refrain) Oh Buchenwald... etc.

It was not yet a month since the SS doctor had declared our block a sick barracks, when the older men from our little "death camp" began to arrive. After a few days of rest in our barracks, the men were moved to a permanent block in camp. Subsequently we younger people also changed our quarters and were transferred to block 3, which bordered the parade ground.

By order of the SS physician we were afforded an additional month of "*Blockschonung*," (grace) which excused us from morning assemblies and work. It gave us more time to prepare for the hard life out there.

The barracks windows overlooked the parade ground, so we now not only listened to the proceedings on the square, but also had the dubious thrill of observing what happened there. Mostly we avoided watching, and if we did, then only furtively. We feared chance eye contact with an SS man passing our window; there was no telling his reaction. Yet mesmerized, as birds are by snakes' eyes, we watched some of the horrible events on the square. Especially one "*Strafturnen*" (exercise punishment), I shall never forget, and I had witnessed some bad ones before.

Contrary to the camp policy of one for all and all for one, about sixty prisoners were harassed by several big SS men in a way I had never seen before. I don't know what their transgression had been, but they were chased, beaten, and subjected to all the harassment this kind of punishment entailed. One huge tormentor played his own game with the prisoners. When they lay flat on their bellies, he grabbed one by the back of his jacket, and the seat of his pants and, raising him above his head, he threw the hapless prisoner through the air as if he were a bundle of rags. Punishment rarely inflicted on animals, much less on human beings.

Our *Blockältester*, (barrack elder) Stephan, seemed in his early forties. He was tall and slightly stooped; a condition perhaps brought on by years of prison existence. He had been a newspaper reporter, and when the Nazis ascended to power, he was arrested and sent to a concentration camp.

Stephan chose two others and me to be table elders of the three tables taken up by the young inmates. Selected adults headed the other tables in the room. He instructed us how to behave in camp and in certain situations and satisfied our curiosity about the different colored triangles the prisoner wore on their tunics:

Red triangle: *Politischer Gefangener*, (political prisoner).

Green triangle: - *Gewohnheitsverbrecher*, (habitual criminal). Often those classifications were incorrect.

Purple triangle: *Bibelforscher* (Jehova's Witness) It was rumored that if a member of this religion renounced his association with the group, he could be released.

Purple triangle bordered by a black stripe: *Rassenschänder*. (Defiler of the race.) Generally, a Jewish person who had intercourse with a Christian woman.

Black triangle: *Arbeitsscheu* (malingerer).

Brown triangle: *Zigeuner*, (gypsy).

The badge of a Jewish inmate was two triangles, one superimposed on the other to create a Star of David. The colored triangle on top revealed his alleged transgression. The yellow one below it marked him a Jew. Eighty percent of Buchenwald's inmates wore the political color red and so did every one in our transport from Vienna. A narrow red stripe above the red triangle meant once released but because of "continued hostile activity against the state," returned to the concentration camp.

As a last item I want to mention a display only very few inmates exhibited. It was a large red dot in a white circle, sown to the front, the back, and the right sleeve of their jackets. They had attempted escape but failed. I felt deep respect, even awe for their daring, and was very sorry their effort had been unsuccessful. At the time of their capture they must have undergone severe punishment.

In block 8, the sick barracks, we had no SS visits. In block 3, we did. It seemed so long ago since we were willfully subjected to the persecution of the SS that it came as a shock when two of them suddenly appeared in our barracks. At Stephan's call to attention we jumped up and froze.

"Report," one of the SS barked at our block elder, who called out the number of people present. It was frightening to see that phony smile on their faces again. We stood stiff as ramrods, staring straight ahead. We wanted no excuse for punishment; yet of course, they needed no special incentives to act in their villainous ways.

We thoroughly cleaned and dusted the block every day and diligently made our beds to specification so that the top blanket had not the slightest crease and lay perfectly flat atop the mattress. A wrinkle would have raised the ire of an SS inspector. To accomplish his feat, the blanket was smoothed over and over with a wooden board. It was a frustrating enterprise because not enough boards were available and arguments ensued about the length of time boards could be used by each of us. Where the blanket met the rather flat pillow, it turned upward in a 90-degree angle and became another sharp corner at the top, to cover the pillow in flat, horizontal fashion.

On this one visit the SS men did not inspect our sleeping quarters but walked around the room looking for dust. Their fingers went over furniture and any protrusion that could accumulate particles of dust. Finding none, one SS man ran his hand along a rim near the ceiling. When he brought it down and looked at it, he made a hateful grimace. "This place is filthy," he roared.

There was really nothing wrong with the cleanliness of the room, and even the place he had touched had been wiped. But every survivor of a concentration camp is familiar with those inhuman creatures that derive pleasure in torturing their fellow men for no reason at all.

We were lucky. Except for the difficulty in carrying out the SS's orders to hit the floor several times at full speed — we were wedged in between tables and benches that stood close to each other — we escaped injury.

Permission to write home a postcard was a happy event. We were shown a printed text that we had to copy.

Despite my faith in the future how could I ever hope to escape this hell? Yet hope was the emotion that kept us going. During the last few nights my dreams were the extension of thought that haunted me during the day: home. And while sitting at the table in the morning, I threw superstition to the winds and recounted to my fellow prisoners the repetitive fantasies of the night before. They smiled tolerantly.

Dawn February 7, 1940.

On that Wednesday morning I once more awakened from a dream of home. The impression was so lifelike that I had to talk about it. While distributing the food, which was one of the duties of a table elder, I said to Jacki who sat next to me: "You can laugh as much as you want. But I dreamt again of home."

The dream was a short scene. I was walking along the street where our store had been. I knew I had been away for a long time and was curious whom I would see first. It was Edith Neumann, my sister's friend, and my grandmother standing in front of our store. Edith recognized me first, and I felt deep pleasure when she called into the store: "Frau Ziegler, Gustl is home."

And Jacki laughed. I could not even be angry with him for thinking me funny. By that time only about 10 men out of our whole transport from Vienna had returned home while almost 60 per cent had perished. Our chances of release were poor. The war was in its sixth month, and we knew little of the general situation outside. Germans had more important things to think about than the few Jews who were prisoners and could die in Buchenwald. But I would not give up hope.

Over the loudspeaker came the voice of the SS man in charge of the morning assembly and, following procedure, he read out orders and directions to the inmates of the camp. Then the murmur that had filled our room fell silent. The voice at the gate began to read names, date of birth and places of origin of persons to be discharged. We were afraid to breathe. "Gustav Pimselstein, geboren am 30. April 1923, aus Wien." I had scarcely heard my name when I jumped out from behind the bench I was sitting on, and stared in disbelief at the loudspeaker. Was it possible? I was to be released? It seemed too good to be true.

The people in the room mobbed me. They shouted names, addresses, and greetings for their families at me, while I stood dazed in the middle of the crowd and stammered: "Perhaps I am being called for something else and not my release."

Release

A few minutes later Stephan, our block elder, appeared and, pulling me away from the people and through the barracks door, called out: "*Schnell, Du bist entlassen,*" (Quick, you are being released.) Outside he impulsively hugged me and I looked into his face. Perhaps his eyes behind the glasses only glinted because of the electric light nearby or perhaps he felt like crying, as I did. He was an exceptionally fine fellow and in the short time we knew him, he had become a friend to all of us.

Overwhelmed with happiness, I also threw my arms around him, but suddenly he tore free, grabbed my arm, and pulled me in quick step toward the big square. Prisoners to be released had to be on the parade ground, and I joined a small group that had assembled for that purpose.

From then on things moved fast. Labor details marched to work to the sounds of the "Buchenwaldlied," and many an envious glance was cast our way. For the first time in a long while I hummed along with the orchestra as it played its repertoire, and finally they too disappeared.

We were a motley group of about 20 prisoners. We stood on the square until we were marched to a barracks for medical examination. Our band consisted of five Jews from Vienna, one Jew from Berlin, and the rest non-Jews with different kinds of colored triangles on their chests.

111

For the last time I met the tall SS doctor and his assistant with the ledger. One inmate after the other stepped onto a scale, the weight was announced, and the prisoner rejoined us.

The procedure seemed routine until something happened to one of our men from Vienna. When the man's weight was announced, the doctor told him to step to a place in the room where nobody else stood. "*Nicht transportfähig*" (unfit for discharge), he added, rejecting the man because he was underweight. He burst into tears and pleaded with the doctor to let him go. His promise to gain weight at home in Vienna availed him nothing, and the SS man's decision remained.

I was deathly afraid of being rejected with freedom almost within my grasp. I had not realized that I might be returned to camp. Considering the way I still looked, I certainly was the perfect candidate for this underweight category. Though my ribs still protruded, my face had filled out somewhat as I saw in the mirror we had in the block. When I stepped on the scale my stomach felt queasy, and that sensation worsened when my weight was called out. 42 kilos (about 91 pounds). I was certain to be pronounced "Nicht transportfähig," but instead the doctor seemed pleased. "He has gained 4 kilos (9 lbs)," he announced with a grin to the other SS man who, without changing his stony expression, entered my weight in the ledger. I had gained the pounds since our transfer from death camp but was happy that my weight had not been registered at our arrival in Buchenwald. I might have been rejected in that case.

Back in our civilian clothes — and what a wonderful feeling it was to get into them! — we were taken through the main gate. In the left wing of the building were offices staffed by SS. In one of the rooms a three-star officer, *Untersturmführer* Rehrick (I never forgot his name), gave us "educational" indoctrination. His harangue was full of threats. "Don't ever tell anybody about life in camp," he warned. "And should someone insist on knowing, tell him to come here, and we'll gladly show him. Behave properly in the future (This was directed at non-Jews, who were to act according to Nazi principles) for we'll make it quite unpleasant for those who return. Get out of Weimar as fast as you can. People in that city are always on the lookout for shaven heads."

And then he asked: "Are there any Jews?"

A bit fearful we raised our hands. "You Jews," he said, his voice becoming more ominous, "better watch out. And those of you, who go to a foreign country and think you can safely spread lies about the German Reich, you especially watch out. We'll get you, and attend to you wherever you are."

During the half-hour tirade one of our fellows from Vienna grew sick. His face was white, and he finally raised his hand to get the SS man's attention. He begged permission to go to the bathroom, but the officer was in no mood to be bothered and gruffly told him to shut up and not interrupt again. A few moments later the poor fellow vomited all over the carpet on the floor.

The SS man was almost apoplectic. "You. Get me a bucket of water," he howled at me, and I shot out of the room. I was in the corridor of the building, but where could I find a pail in these SS offices? I was afraid to knock or just open a door and look for one. An SS officer confronting a little person in a wrinkled civilian coat might react violently.

Suddenly the door to Rehrick's office was thrown open, and his enraged face appeared: "Why in hell are you taking so long? Shall I shove a rocket up your ass to make you move?" he screamed at me and vanished again.

I had not known that women worked in those offices, but one appeared in the corridor and to my relief she wore no uniform. Evidently they came from Weimar. Inside or outside the camp, I had never seen a female since my arrival. I asked her for a pail, and she showed me a little storage-room. I picked up a bucket and filled it with water. Because of the weather outside, the water was freezing cold. I ran back with my load to Rehrick's room. The SS man grabbed our fellow by the arm and, pulling him from the office, he ordered me to follow. "Open the window and lean out," he screamed at the man. Taking the bucket from me he poured the icy water over the sick man's head, and then announced: 'Nicht transportfähig.'

At this verdict the fellow broke down. Here too his pleading had no effect. In his case, the ruling was even harsher. He already was out of his prison garb and dressed in civilian clothes. As it happened, I met the man later in Vienna and was happy to learn of his eventual release from Buchenwald.

None of us three from Vienna had money for the fare home. In an adjacent office another SS man chose me, and I signed for 100 marks to buy the train tickets to Vienna. It was a loan to be repaid to the Gestapo, or if we had no funds, by the Jewish community of our city.

No words can describe my feelings when I presented my release order to the SS guard at a barrier a little distance from camp. In the shortest of times I went through a range of emotions that were not always of a positive nature. Even the air outside the camp seemed different and hunched backs grew straight. Then suddenly my happy mood changed. For an endless moment I was agonized by the fear that this was one more of my vivid dreams. This fear chilled me for a moment. My dreams were always so real – until I woke up. But this was no dream, and with the awareness of reality my excitement returned.

Tomorrow I would see my family. And life *was* beautiful.

As we walked away from the barrier, an empty delivery truck was also on its way out. Overcoming my shyness I asked the driver's permission to let us go with him, and when he agreed, all of us climbed onto the rear platform of the vehicle.

At the time of our discharge, each of us had received two sandwiches, and I had hungrily eaten mine while walking away from the last SS office. Now, on the truck, one of my older partners, one was over 40, the other one over 50, asked me if I wanted one of his sandwiches. He seemed so happy about his discharge that he felt no hunger. I accepted.

The truck rolled into a factory yard at the outskirts of Weimar, and I suggested to my two fellows from Vienna a gift of five marks for the driver. Kindness has no monetary value, but I wanted to show our appreciation to this stranger.

My companions agreed, but the driver refused to accept the money. "No, no," he said, "you need it more than I do." What a wonderful experience to meet a friendly person just outside the camp. I thanked him and he smilingly waved to me as he walked toward the building.

Marching on to the railroad station, I spied a small grocery store. In my insatiable hunger I asked my partners' permission to spend one mark of our money on rolls or bread, and they consented. Inside the store I aroused the curiosity of the few women customers, for without much thought, but in accordance with camp law, I snappily removed my peaked cap, exposing the short hair beneath it. My behavior and hairstyle revealed who I was, though to no ill effect. Unfortunately there was nothing to buy except a few candies; everything else was rationed.

In spite of the disappointing shopping trip I was comforted by the belief that representatives of the Weimar Jewish community would meet us at the railroad station. According to Jewish prisoners who had been discharged from Buchenwald before and then rearrested at a later time, people of the Jewish community were to welcome us at the station with food and, if needed, a little cash. It seemed a wonderful event to look forward to.

Nobody was waiting for us at the station. Most probably after seven years of Nazis rule, Weimar was "*Judenrein,*" (free of Jews).

Another disappointment awaited me when I tried to purchase rail tickets to Vienna. I was short the one mark I had spent on candies. The oldest man of our trio wanted to cable his children for money, but the other two of us insisted it was wiser to get out of Weimar as soon as possible. I had no intention of waiting around and perhaps spending a night there, especially without accommodations. We could easily be picked up and, if the worst happened, be returned to Buchenwald.

Besides, I was anxious to get home.

The train station was a busy place as I went looking for the Jewish fellow from Berlin. When I found him and asked for a mark he refused at first. He had not been home for a long time and did not know what to expect. He finally gave me the money.

At the ticket window, I was handed a single ticket for three people, and the ticket agent, obviously aware of where we came from, provided friendly instructions on how to get to Vienna. We were to take the train from Weimar to Jena and then from the Saale station in Jena continue on to Munich. There we were to change trains again for the last leg of the journey to Vienna.

We left Weimar at noon, and it brought back memories of our arrival. Was it really only a little over four months since that frightful day or had it been years? It might well have been years. So many things had happened during that time, and so many of our people had lost their lives. Buchenwald, in spite of our horrible experiences and the many killings, was at the time like all other concentration camps in Germany only a place of detention. The full horror and force of destruction was not unleashed until the decision to exterminate the Jews was taken in January 1942. In my time the policy of the Nazis was to get the Jews out of Germany, not to destroy them. Auschwitz came later. Almost two years after my release, "the final solution," the murder of every Jewish man, woman, and child in Europe was planned and set in motion by people who thought themselves to be human beings.

Being young, less than three months away from my seventeenth birthday, I wanted to put the emotional tribulations of camp life behind me and look only toward a brighter future. And everything seemed to point that way. The train rolled through the snow-covered countryside of Thuringia and my eyes and heart became entranced by the beauty outside the window. It was exciting to watch the white rolling hills, the leafless trees, and the soundlessly flying black birds with the blue sky in the background. Freedom was reflected in every creation of nature that flitted by, and I was amazed at the people in our car who did not see what I saw, shared nothing of my enthusiasm, but just sat there indifferent, talking or sleeping. What a pity to miss all the wonderful things life offered. But then, the sense of freedom and the thought of going home intoxicated me.

At first I had felt as if everybody was staring at us. This unpleasant feeling disappeared, however, when we arrived in Jena and had to look for the Saale railroad station. Having spent the last penny on our tickets in Weimar, I wanted to have at least a small amount of spending money.

I informed my two partners of my intention to earn some money, and they consented.

The platform of the station was packed with people. Everybody seemed to be traveling. Men, women, and children dressed in city clothes and farmers' attire. But outnumbering all were soldiers who carried rifles and other gear. Even though there was no fighting going on, the country was still in a state of war.

I saw a woman dragging a big suitcase and carrying several small packages, all of which seemed to make her life miserable. I offered my help and she gladly accepted. "You know," she said, "I was looking for a porter, but couldn't find one. They must all be in the army."

I carried the suitcase to the outside of the station, across the road, to what seemed the end of a streetcar line. When I sat down my burden the lady held out a paper mark. "Do you have change," she asked. I had none, and she handed me the bill telling me to keep it.

It was the first time I had seen a paper mark instead of the familiar coin. Apparently metal was needed for the war effort.

About to return to my partners, I saw the streetcar arrive, and the conductor change the nameplate to "Saale Station." Luckily my two companions had become restless in my absence and had come looking for me. Climbing aboard the streetcar, I again helped the lady with the suitcase. We stood beside each other in the crowded car. "Are you KDF travelers," she asked me. *Kraft durch Freude*, (Strength through Joy) was a Nazi organization that rewarded industrious workers with holidays at vacation spots. "No," I said, smiling slightly. "Where do you come from?" she inquired. "Weimar," I said evasively and was not even lying.

From a distance I saw the conductor push through the crowd. He sold tickets on the way. My partners, unaware of my earnings, fidgeted uncomfortably. They may have seen us already ejected from the streetcar or worse. They looked at me and I winked at them reassuringly. It was fun to see them breathe a sigh of relief when I paid for our tickets.

The lady's destination was also the Saale station. I carried my benefactor's suitcase to the luggage clerk since she was to travel on a different train. When I said good-bye, I raised my cap and then she may have guessed where we came from. By that time, however, I didn't think it mattered to the people we met. They seemed indifferent.

I had spent 45 pfennigs for the three streetcar tickets and decided to use the remaining money for something to eat. At the station restaurant 55 pfennigs couldn't buy anything. On my return from the restaurant my partners told me the lady had been looking for me. I found her and she offered me a couple of wrapped sandwiches. In regular times I would have modestly refused. Here, still craving food, I overcame my shyness and accepted.

On the station platform and waiting for our train I was puzzled when the conductor near the door who had punched our ticket, beckoned to me. "A woman in there wants to talk to you," he said pointing to the waiting room.

It was the same lady. This time she invited me to have breakfast with her. I would have loved to accept, but expecting our train at any moment, I regretfully declined her offer. She insisted: "Please, come with me," she said. "Surely you must be hungry. We'll have coffee and rolls, and then you can continue your journey." She must have intended to use her ration cards for the purchase of the rolls. I thanked her once more, pointing to the train that was just pulling into the station. "Ours," I said. She bid me good-bye again and wished me a pleasant trip. Another wonderful experience to meet a person like her.

The train was packed. Every seat in every compartment seemed occupied. Only after a long search did we find two places for my partners. I did not want to sit but preferred standing in the corridor and admire the swiftly passing panorama through the window.

Late in the afternoon a uniformed pageboy came through the passageway, beating lightly on a gong. People were called to the dining car, and I wondered whether they also needed ration cards or could simply pay for food.

A man standing at the window next to mine stopped the young fellow with some questions. The boy's reply got my curiosity. He said: "We ride along the Rhine river and can clearly see the French soldiers on the other side. Nobody is hiding. They see us, and we see them, and when we're outside the car, we can hear them play loud music." That was an interesting kind of arrangement of coexistence. Over five months at war, and the enemies just watched or even entertained each other.

A little earlier I had noticed the younger of my partners in animated conversation with a stranger. A little later the pageboy tried to serve me a cup of coffee. I refused it. Even the man's reassuring wave of his hand through the glass partition failed to impress me. I thought he had merely ordered the brew, and with no money to pay for it, we would have gotten into trouble. Any food or drink on that train had to be very expensive, and coffee most certainly was no exception. I put my head through the compartment door. "We can't pay for this," I said. I then learned of the stranger's kind gift, a cup of coffee for each of us.

This traveler, my partner told me, was Jewish. He had also been a prisoner in Buchenwald at one time. Now he was on his way to Shanghai. He had missed the Italian steamer in Hamburg, and he hoped to catch the ship at the Italian port of Genoa. Italy was not in the war yet, and Italian ships still plied the waterways of the world.

117

Every Jew's life in that time and in that nation was a story in itself.

The trip from Weimar to Jena is relatively short; from Jena to Munich takes a long time. Our express train reached Munich at 9 p.m. Throngs of passengers, more than we had encountered anywhere until then, crowded the railroad station. Military personnel were as numerous as civilians. We had just a few minutes to change trains and were glad of that. The sooner we left the better.

Not that it particularly bothered me, but the railroad car to Vienna was not very comfortable. It had no cushioned seats or individual compartments like the previous train but rather wooden benches that were filled to capacity with travelers. Floor space was limited too. Boxes and baskets, parcels and packages cluttered the place, so that even standing was a problem. My two companions found seats, and I, being tired by now, squeezed in between a soldier and a fat lady, who agreeably pushed her neighbor to make room for me. I was too excited to sleep, and occasionally would have liked to get off my seat and run up and down the aisle. There was just no room.

At dawn the train rolled through the Tullner Basin and each wheel revolution bringing me closer to Vienna made me more excited. A worry, long in the back of my mind, took shape. At six o'clock in the morning we arrived at the *Westbahnhof*, (West Rail Station) and I really began to fret about my mother. How was I to face her? I was afraid the sudden excitement of seeing me might harm her. I thought of asking the caretaker of the building we lived in to prepare my parents before I showed up. Then I changed my mind, hoping things would turn out all right.

I said good bye to my companions but was so agitated that I did not think of how they would get home without carfare. They took a taxi for which they intended to pay at home. I took she subway. From the Friedensbrücke station I continued on foot. My feelings were in turmoil, and I needed the extra time of to steady my nerves. How I had waited for this moment to happen, longed for it in my dreams, and how difficult it now seemed to face my mother! Equally strong feelings of happiness and fear were battling inside me.

Wallensteinstrasse, Klosterneuburgerstrasse, Traunfelsgasse, Jäger-strasse. Carefully I hastened along the streets, keeping close to house fronts, always afraid of being seen and stopped by acquaintances. Nothing happened. The metal shutter the SS had kicked in was repaired and still lowered. I entered the building through the gate. Silently I walked the short corridor to our door and knocked. My heart beat furiously, and I knocked again.

"Who is there?" I heard my mother call out.

"It's me, Gustl."

There was a cry, the door flew open, and we were in each other's arms.

Now I learned why I had been released from Buchenwald. Behind my discharge was the persistent effort of my father who had repeatedly mailed letters to the Gestapo begging them to let me go. He reiterated his story of being a war invalid from the First War and the many years he had spent as a POW in Siberia. He wrote that if I, being his only son, was released, we all would leave Germany – not very likely this late in the game. His persistence had paid off, and I was freed.

Thus ended 152 days of hell, one part of my life. A new one was just beginning.

Back in Vienna

How wonderfully good it felt to be home again, to know that my life as prisoner number 7439 had ended. The only sadness in this otherwise happy scenario came from the deeply lined face of my mother. She looked terribly worn out and had suffered physically and mentally much more than I. I thought that my return from the concentration camp and being together would help her overcome the pain of the past, but was only partly right. All too soon I left Vienna, never to see my parents again.

On that first morning home I devoured at great speed eight Kaiser rolls, drank two mugs of hot cocoa, and only stopped so as not to alarm my mother even more. I could have easily continued eating and thought that nothing would ever satisfy my hunger. I suppressed the desire for more food and without thinking reverted to the Buchenwald habit of picking up even the smallest of bread-crumbs with two fingers and placing them in my mouth. I was not aware that my behavior was odd and felt uncomfortable under the shocked glances of my parents and sister as they watched me eat.

As weird as my conduct may have seemed, behavior of this kind can only be understood by someone who has suffered the agony of starvation. Someone who did not even have the luxury of a garbage can to rummage through, and was deprived intentionally of sustenance so he would waste away and die a slow death.

Just before we left his office in Buchenwald, SS 'Untersturmführer Rehrick had instructed our group to report immediately to the Gestapo Head Quarters in our respective hometowns. It was to be done upon arrival and before visiting home. Anyone in a small community with no

Gestapo was to report to the nearest police station. "Do not go home first," he had warned, "and don't lose your discharge papers. They won't be replaced."

For a long time I had deliberated in my mind this order not to go home first before I decided to disregard it. It was not an easy choice. I distrusted the Gestapo, the feared Secret State Police, and besides I was dying to see my family. I hoped that defying the order would have no serious consequences.

Then I had to go. My parents insisted on accompanying me, at least until we reached that Gestapo building, the place many entered, only to leave on a stretcher for a hospital or the morgue.

To soothe my mother's growing anxiety about my visit there, I pretended to be indifferent, but my heart beat furiously when I entered the huge complex of the former Hotel Metropol on Morzin Platz, the Gestapo H.Q.

On the left side of the big reception hall, in a glass-encased compartment, sat an SS guard who had to know my name and the purpose of my visit. I had taken off my cap in military fashion when I entered, and my shorn head brought a mocking smile to the man's face. Having survived hell, I felt more like a hero than ashamed of my baldness. It was not easy to enter here, but the exit at times was even more difficult. Thanks to the camp's discharge paper, permission for my reluctant visit to the domain of Herr Eichmann, who had not achieved his subsequent notoriety yet, was promptly granted. My name and exact time of arrival were entered into a ledger whereupon I was told the room number I had to report to.

With a sneer the Gestapo official on the third floor inquired: "How was it?" "Good," I answered humbly. My discharge paper was taken from me and never returned. I was left without proof of incarceration, though at the time I did not care. The Germans were thorough in their bookkeeping, however, and my name was in surviving files. After the war I was compensated with 100 dollars for the 152 day imprisonment, 66 cents for each day spent in hell.

The SS man's parting instructions were familiar. Camp prisoners who had gone through this procedure before, but had the misfortune to be re-arrested and returned to Buchenwald had described them to us. The order was to report twice a week to the nearest district police station, and once a week to Gestapo HQ. My discharge paper gone, I was just glad to be able to leave that place unmolested.

As time went by, and I reported week after week to the Gestapo, their verbal approach to me became more aggressive, but they never touched me. "You're still here?" the SS man would say, "we're going to send you back to Buchenwald." I hoped he was only trying to frighten me, but never felt certain about his intentions. SS men were unpredictable and vicious and, as I knew too well, no particular inducement was needed to make them act in their atrocious way. How many times had I witnessed that! They felt superior to everyone who did not fit the pattern of the master race or who, though Christian by birth, did not share their political views. The Nazis' mildest form of abuse was to taunt, scorn, and insult. In their more violent expressions they displayed a lack of human emotion that seemed incomprehensible. How else could they stand in a circle around another human being, smash their fists into him, laugh at the victim's futile attempts to shield his body against their pitiless blows, and ignore his cries of pain and pleas for mercy? When the victim finally succumbed to the inhuman punishment sinking to the ground, the SS men kicked him with their shiny black boots until he showed no sign of life.

Thus the master race ruled in its Teutonic splendor, proudly displaying many of their "Aryan" characteristics, some of which were their appearances. Blond, tall, slim and well built. How little those characteristics fitted the race, and especially the "masters" I found illustrated in an unexpected way two years later in another part of the world. Walking down a street in Alexandria, Egypt, I came upon a shop displaying a variety of funny cartoon postcards. One especially amused me. It showed the three leading figures of the Nazi movement, and captions above each of them stressing their main characteristics in relation to the "Aryan race." They read: "As blond as Hitler." (The "Führer" had dark hair.) "As tall and even-bodied as Goebbels." (The Minister of Propaganda was short, and suffered from a clubfoot.) And "as slim as Göring" (who looked like an inflated balloon).

I am still sorry I did not buy that card.

The following days were like the dreams I used to have in camp but, as if to remind me that Buchenwald existed, the postcard I had written home arrived. It seemed incredible that I was able to be with my parents and sister, to step out into the street whenever I felt like it, except during the curfew for Jews between sundown and sun-up, and talk to people who were not wearing the striped garments of the camp. Another great satisfaction was to eat. Just eat. In the shortest time I grew plump, an unusual condition for me, and my face looked like a full moon.

Father took me to see Dr. Murmelstein, formerly rabbi of the Klucky synagogue, who was a big shot now in the *Kultusgemeinde* (Jewish Community Federation) in Vienna. We sat opposite the man behind the big desk and, acceding to my father's insistence I tell all, I told as much as I could in the short time allotted to us. Dr. Murmelstein sat there and shuddered at my experiences.

Four years later, the man was in charge of the Austrian Jews in the ghetto of Theresianstadt. Ordered by the Nazis to list Jews for deportation, he sent my parents and sister, who by that time had been deported from Vienna to Theresianstadt, to the death camp of Auschwitz.

One thing that depressed me during those first few days at home was speaking with visitors. They came from all over Vienna. They were women whose husbands or fathers had been in Buchenwald with me and who wanted to find out about their loved ones. I knew only a few intimately, the others were faces I had seen but probably never talked to. Some women had received urns with ashes and had been informed by the Gestapo of the death of their men. They came to me in hope that it all was a mistake and that I had seen this person alive. When I was able to confirm the death, I never told how the person had died. I was happy when I could tell a wife or mother about a loved one being alive and well. It was, however, a half-truth, for nobody was well in Buchenwald.

My parents tried to ease the strain I began to show and begged visitors to stay just a few minutes. They promised to observe the time limit yet never did. Minutes passed, half an hour or even an hour. In often-repetitious questions the visitors wanted to know all I knew down to the smallest detail. Other people arrived and waited patiently in the kitchen till it was their turn. Then everything started anew. I really did not mind their coming. I felt a deep pity for their woes, but all too soon, and not of my choice, I was relieved of the job of dispensing information.

I developed a fever, and a stabbing pain in my chest accompanied every breath I took. Primitive home remedies like tea, keeping warm or staying in bed for a few days had no effect. I finally gave in to my parents' wishes and went to see a doctor at the Rothschildspital, the only Jewish hospital in Vienna. I insisted, however, on going by myself.

Though the hospital was about a mile and a quarter away, I went on foot. During the trip I thought about the winter weather. Had it been summer, I believed, the warm sun would have relieved the pain in my chest and cured my ills. But the weather was as frosty as the times and our surroundings and the sun brought no warmth.

At the hospital my sickness was diagnosed as pleurisy. A moisture built up in the space between my lungs and the thin skin covering them had to be removed. The doctor contradicted my belief that sunrays would have improved my condition, maintaining that exposure to the sun might have worsened my case. He advised me to remain in the hospital, but I had to inform my parents. Since we had no phone, I walked home to tell them.

On the way back to the hospital my father accompanied me. When I tried to register at the reception desk, I was informed that the hospital was filled to capacity. This did not deter my father. After a less than friendly exchange of words with the hospital management, I was accepted, if only because I had recently been released from Buchenwald.

I stayed in the hospital for two weeks. Because of my refusal to let them tap[13] the fluid built up in my pleural cavity, I was told to leave. The doctor at the station urged my father to persuade me to undergo the treatment. When I stubbornly refused, I was given the choice of submitting or being dismissed. I left voluntarily and had to sign a paper that I left of my own accord and at my own risk. Two weeks at the hospital and hot compresses had done me good. I had no pain, and the fever had disappeared as well.

On the surface life on the streets of Vienna had not changed much. Newspaper kiosks and newspaper hawkers did a thriving business. The headlines and reports coming from the "*Oberkommando der Wehrmacht*," (the German High Command) were intoxicating for the Austrians. The victory over Poland had been won at lightning speed, and what could be sweeter than being part of a powerful Germany. But black-rimmed announcements stating, "He gave his life for Führer and Fatherland" appeared on house walls posted by families who had lost someone close. Those declarations of grief did not dampen the proud feelings of those who had not lost a loved one. If a loyal Nazi lost a close relative, he or she might even feel inspired by the sacrifice.

Feelings about such losses had to be guardedly expressed. When getting a haircut or shopping in a neighborhood grocery store an overzealous patriot might misconstrue what he had heard, and if he reported it to police or Gestapo, a ticket to a concentration camp might be the outcome. Parents had to be wary of what they said in front of their own children. The influence and indoctrination of the Nazi Party on the young was powerful. They were encouraged to denounce "enemies of the state," meaning anybody including parents. To inform on dissenters was their duty to the fatherland.

Food was rationed and Jews still received almost the same amount of provisions as non-Jews did. The individual pages, good for different items, were divided into coupons that were clipped off by the stores where purchases were made. To distinguish our ration cards from that of non-Jews, a big red J, for *Jude* (Jew), was emblazoned on them. Some of our coupons went to the Jewish community kitchens that dispensed free dinners – the main meal at noon in Vienna – to Jews without means, my

---

[13] A painful procedure. A thick needle siphons out the liquid that has collected between the thin skin that covers the lungs and the lung itself.

family among them. Our community kitchen was in a small empty store, and at noon one or two members of our family went there with some pots, stood in line, and received warm food to be taken home. It was a plain diet. Mother, using the same food ingredients as the kitchen, created delectable dishes at home. The high cost of fuel, however, made these feasts a rarity. As kosher meat was unobtainable, no meat was cooked in our home. Yet when mother made a fake Hungarian goulash, consisting only of potatoes and homemade gravy, the dish tasted so one could almost believe it was made with beef.

Depending on our finances, meat coupons assigned to us bought sausage or cooked meat; yet because they were not kosher, father, my sister, and I ate them off the paper in which they had been wrapped. All ration coupons were dated. If the allotted provisions were not bought in time or were out of stock, the ration was lost.

When I asked why we could not use the money that was in a "safe" place, I was told it was not in Germany, and we could not get to it.

Father, in the worst of times always the businessman, made some money selling small furniture items and eiderdown quilts. Emigrants donated home furnishings to Jewish organizations that, in turn, supplied them to people in need. Donations were so plentiful they gathered dust in storage places. Occasionally father requested such articles and at intervals received them. Once he borrowed a small wooden cart, which we took to such a distribution place in the second district. We received pieces of furniture and pulled our cart through the streets toward home. I felt embarrassed when people stared at us.

Father listed the items for sale on a piece of paper that he tacked to the wooden fence of the closed factory across from where we used to live. This wall, a popular spot for people to advertise second-hand merchandise for sale was next to the Hannover market and a place with heavy pedestrian traffic. The items we had received sold quickly, providing us with some money. When lack of money forced our parents to sell our record player and records, it was like losing a family member. I remember how carefully I used to crank the handle so as not to break the spring inside.

The war situation was depressing for us Jews. In April of 1940 the Germans invaded and conquered Norway and Denmark. In May, Belgium and the Netherlands fell and in June France surrender. Italy, not blind to the ease with which Germany incorporated country after country, declared war on the Allies on June 10. Loudspeakers installed in strategic places all over the city blared forth Mussolini's declaration of war in Italian, a language hardly anybody understood.

Later that month and of course breaking Nazi laws applying to Jews,

I watched an elated Hitler do his chicken step in a newsreel as he gloated about the defeat of France. The people in the theater went wild in their excitement.

By then the only West European enemy country not occupied by the Nazis was England. Hitler ranted against Churchill, the Jews, and England, which he promised to conquer at any moment. To honor this anticipated achievement a song was written: *Wir fahren gegen Engelland (England)* (we advance toward England). The song was a smash hit and was sung with great enthusiasm by all.

When time went by and nothing happened, a joke started to make the round among the Jews. Question: Which country in the world is the farthest away from Germany? Answer: England. The Germans advance and advance but never get there. Necessity produced a new shoe fashion. The streets rang out with the clicking and tapping of wooden soled shoes, replacing the vanishing leather requisitioned for army boots. There was also talk of clothing being made of paper, and butter from coal. I can't say whether either was true.

Spring had come and gone, and in this summer of 1940 life was still bearable for us in Vienna. Jews did not have to wear a yellow star on their clothing – yet. One could almost have forgotten the Nazis were in charge had not that invisible pall of danger constantly hung over us. With no choice, Jews lived with the restrictions placed on them, accepting them for one of the lesser evils that could befall them. We got used to the curfew between sunset and sunrise that prevented visits to friends in the evening or strolls after dark we used to take; Jews got accustomed to being excluded from entertainment establishments, I am an exception here. We were not allowed to enter recreational facilities such as public swimming pools or even walk across a park to shorten the distance between two points. In one place nobody checked for Jews: The *Überschwemmungsgebiet* (flood plain) an uncultivated, potholed strip of land running along the left side of the Danube, whose purpose it was to save Vienna from high water in case the river overflowed.

We took Sunday outings on foot, a two mile walk from our home to this wide stretch of land, enjoying the unspoiled nature of the region. On sunny weekends this area was frequented by hundreds of Viennese families who picnicked, played ball, or just enjoyed the outdoors. I don't know how many more Jewish families took advantage of the place, but there was no guarantee against possible mistreatment by other groups had they found out we were not Christians. To avoid this risk we kept away from crowds.

My friends, Kurtl and Otto, a different Otto from the one of school days, always joined us. Usually some of my sister's girl friends also came along. Kurtl was a funny guy who entertained us with his antics and his imitation of speaking English, French, or other languages he did not know.

Otto introduced his cousin Jenny, a girl of about 16, into our group and she became a frequent guest in our home. I thought her pretty. She had a nice laugh, a good figure, and especially enticing to me were the breasts concealed by her dress. I never mentioned this to anyone and would have felt embarrassed had my fascination been found out. Her attire was not meant to accentuate her bosom. It had been acquired when she was younger. As most Jewish families had little money, her parents presumably wanted her to wear this dress for as long as she could fit into it. As it was, her dress spread tautly over two perfectly shaped spheres, protruding like two tennis balls hidden behind the material.

To save money we gave up electricity and used a kerosene lamp. The back room had to be lit even during the day and perhaps because of that the room appealed to me. It gave me a feeling of privacy because parents, sister, and friends were mostly in the front. I liked to work in that back room on my stamp collection. Jews wanted to emigrate. Consequently they carried on an intense correspondence with far-away countries. I begged and often received foreign stamps from friends and acquaintances. By the soft light of the oil lamp I carefully washed the stamps off envelopes, dried them on newspapers, and placed them between the pages of a book to flatten them.

Everything went well until my sister's girl friends decided to disrupt my peaceful pursuit. With mischievous intent they sneaked up behind me and with a quick puff of air blew stamps off the table. It was upsetting, but my rage when I chased after them, was just pretense, and they knew it. When I caught one of them and ostensibly tried to wrestle her to the ground, she squeaked and squirmed in my hug, pretending to be in fear of me. They enjoyed the game as much as I did.

In the evenings my sister and I read or played cards, sometimes with friends who defied the curfew. During daylight hours I continued my long strolls through the city. On these hikes I never encountered problems perhaps because I did not look typically Jewish or appeared cautious. I felt safe and so continued with my daring visits to movie theaters.

Foreign nationals in Vienna wore little metal flags in the lapels of their jackets. It reduced the risk of being molested by Nazi thugs. If ever challenged, they were better able to prove their nationalities. Otto brazenly wore the American flag, insisting he was entitled to do so as he was going to emigrate to the U.S.A. I thought rather that the emblem could cause trouble for him and anybody in his company.

After my return from Buchenwald I had been to movies six times already and foolishly decided on another visit to a theater. A film with my beloved comedy team of Stan Laurel and Oliver Hardy was playing. When Otto found out he wanted to join me. I disliked the idea for several reasons. It doubled the danger of exposure, I was afraid he "looked Jewish", and third, the little emblem in his lapel bothered me. It attracted attention, something to be avoided at any cost. Having no heart to refuse my friend I insisted on the removal of the flag from his jacket if he wanted to accompany me.

The sidewalk in front of the Kreuz Kino on Wollzeile, a busy street in the Inner City, was crowded with young people. At least half of them wore the uniform of the Hitler Youth. Summer vacation was on, and the afternoon performance promised to be mobbed. Vienna's kids were as crazy about Laurel and Hardy as I was. To safeguard my anonymity at least to some extent I took certain precautions in this dangerous game. The movie theater had to be some distance from home. The ticket was purchased at the very last moment, and I entered the cinema as a latecomer after the lights were out. And finally, I left the theater just before the words "The End" appeared on the screen, feigning the wish to beat the slow exit of the crowd. Those steps reduced the chance of an unexpected encounter with someone familiar, though the possibility of being recognized by a person who knew me always existed.

On Wollzeile Otto and I strolled the sidewalk across from the theater, pretending to be interested in window displays. I was waiting for the right moment to cross the street quickly, like two fellows late for a movie. I had noticed the three foot high sign next to the ticket window from afar, but it looked even more menacing now that I stood next to it and asked for two tickets. No other theater I had seen displayed the proclamation this large and in capital letters: JUDEN IST DER EINTRITT VERBOTEN (Jews are forbidden to enter). It almost tempted me to abandon the visit. But then, it was Laurel and Hardy, a picture I'd hate to miss, and I purchased the tickets.

The place seemed sold out and it took a while to find two empty seats in the darkened theater. The problem was that a teenager in the uniform of the Hitler Youth sat between the two places.

"Never mind," I whispered to Otto. "Sit on the other side of him."

The fellow must have understood that we were together, for after we had taken our seats, he asked me in Viennese vernacular if I wanted to sit next to my friend. I said yes, and we changed places.

In Vienna's movie houses a ticket was good for one show and once the lights were off, they only came on again after the performance was over or if something was wrong. We had sat through the newsreel when, to my alarm, the lights came on. I looked about and saw a policeman enter the hall from the rear of the theater. While he walked down the aisle to the first row, I promised myself that if I got out of here unscathed I would never, *ever* again tempt fate by going to the movies. I had no idea what the policeman wanted, for after reaching the first row and looking over the sea of faces, he turned and marched back the way he had come. As he disappeared through the exit, the lights went out, and the movie came on.

I don't know if I would have stuck to my resolve had I stayed on in Vienna, but not too long after that event things began to happen.

We still hoped that one day the mail would deliver that anxiously awaited letter from the American consulate, authorizing our immigration to the United States. Every day we watched for the mailman, and when he failed to stop at our door, we said perhaps tomorrow our dream would be realized.

Then the letter arrived. It again ordered my father and me to appear before the American physician. My father passed the test, but I was told to return in six months. The doctor said there was no change in the condition of my eyes. Asked if a diagnosis by a Viennese eye specialist would have any influence on the consular doctor's decision, we were told it would not. No recourse was open to us.

The Rotgasse Transport

The immigration of Jews to Palestine had been going on for decades. It was a trickle while the Turks were still masters of the Ottoman Empire, of which Palestine was part, but increased after the country became a British mandate at the end of World War I. To placate the Arabs, however, London restricted the influx of Jews into the country in later years, and the Jews resorted to illegal entries.

The Rotgasse Transport was the last of its kind to leave Nazi Germany during the war years. Organized, so it was said, by a right-leaning Zionist party, the transport was to sneak past the British blockade and land on some deserted beach in Palestine. A group of men in charge and a body of young men trained by that organization were to keep order among the refugees while in transit.

Doubtless there were Jews in Germany (and former Austria) who even at this late date thought they could weather the Nazi menace by remaining where they were. The majority did not subscribe to this myth and were looking for a way, *any way* out of there. But by the summer of 1940 the chances of leaving the Third Reich had shrunk to almost nil. Though no one could predict the future, an ex-inmate of a concentration camp appeared to be in greater danger than others. The threat repeated at my weekly reports to the Gestapo, "You are still here? We are going to return you to camp," I did not take lightly.

The Jewish Community Office added my name to the "Rotgasse Transport," a group of prospective émigrés. The number of participants eventually swelled to over 4,000. To join this undertaking was expensive, but exceptions were made and travel charges waived in special cases. My imprisonment in Buchenwald, my trouble with the Gestapo and my parents' inability to pay for the trip made me a special case. Not all participants were Austrians; many came from other parts of greater Germany.

Although our official destinations were South American countries, the Gestapo was well aware of the transport's real objective. The tour I was to join resembled in part what I had envisioned and had suggested to my friend Erich.

This mammoth group of ours would have to endure a perilous 2,800-mile journey. An itinerary fraught with obstacles and trouble spots not marked on any map. We would have to traverse East European territories that, with the exception of the Soviet Union and Greece, were controlled by Fascist governments. Travel the Danube River to the Black Sea, through the Bosporus, the Sea of Marmara, the Dardanelles, and the Aegean Sea. On this last leg to Palestine we'd be at the mercy of Great Britain's naval forces and axis' warships and submarines as they faced each other in the mine infested Mediterranean Sea.

The unexplainable benevolence of the Germans toward our escape can be seen in a different light when one considers that they believed our trip to benefit them. If we came to harm, no nation would shed a tear, least of all the Nazis. If we successfully broke through the blockade and landed in Palestine, the Arabs would accuse England of having closed its eyes to a mass influx of Jews. The Moslems' hate of the British and their flirting with the Nazis was well known. With a little goading by German agents or even without their encouragement, the Arab world might stage uprisings in the Near East, creating a potentially disastrous situation for London in this time of war. It was the last thing Great Britain needed in its already precarious situation. But even were conditions to remain calm in the country after our arrival, the government in London had on its hands 4,000 refuges, men, women, and children who had no place to go. The Nazis, it seemed, just could not lose. What we were unprepared for, however, was Britain's ingenuity in its effort to solve the settlement problem when the time came.

Our departure was repeatedly postponed. Not because of the Germans' reluctance to let us go, but there were complications with authorities of the many countries we were to traverse. Permissions for transit required lengthy negotiation, not the least of which had to do with money. The delays did not bother me as much as they should have. Remaining in Vienna, intentionally or not, was playing with fire. Still, I was not eager to leave, for it meant separation from my family for an indefinite time. But since I had no say in the matter, I consoled myself with the awareness that this daring enterprise came as close to an adventure as I ever would get.

I had a return bout with pleurisy and ended up once more in the Rothschildspital. Being hospitalized, fate seemed to play into my hands. My trip with the Rotgasse transport, unavoidable until then, could be canceled because of my renewed illness. Not even the Gestapo, I reasoned, could blame me for not leaving Vienna in my condition. I would stay until the American consulate allowed me to leave with my family for America. I requested my father to withdraw my name from the transport, and he did.

The overcrowded Rothschildspital was the only Jewish hospital in the city. I was placed in a small room on the lower floor with a thirteen-year-old boy who had a heart problem. Two days later he died.

To spare me the sight the nurses wanted to place a divider between our two beds until he could be removed from the room. I assured them that I was not squeamish about dead bodies. Where I had been, I had seen many people die and often been closer to their corpses than here.

I was moved to a big sunlit room on the second floor with a door leading to a large roofless veranda. It would have been beautiful here had I not been contending with two problems: the stabbing pain in my chest when breathing and the continuous pestering of doctors to agree to the tapping procedure. If a stay in a hospital could be called enchanting, it was for me. A group of teenage girls studying to become nurses steadily flowed through my room. One looked especially attractive. When Stella, one year my senior, had the night-shift and was not occupied otherwise, we would sit on those warm summer evenings on the veranda and talk till lights out at 10 P.M. My parents and sister, her girlfriends and my friends came every day during visiting hours. If alone, I read or did crossword puzzles, which I loved. About to be expelled again from the hospital, I agreed to the medical procedure. After this painful process I felt better, but sooner than expected my holiday was over.

One morning Stella came to say good-bye. I was stunned. The girl was to leave with the *Rotgasse Transport*. "Me too," I blurted out elated when I suddenly recalled that I had withdrawn from the trip. Impatiently I awaited visiting hours and a talk with my father. My parents smiled when they heard the reason for my unexpected travel excitement and father promised to do his best to sign me up again. He succeeded, and a few days later I left the hospital.

After weeks of postponed departures the 'Rotgasse Transport' finally was to leave Vienna. A postcard arrived in the afternoon mail on September 2. "You are requested to come with your luggage to Grosse Mohrengasse at 10 A.M. on September 3, 1940."

The many postponements had made the trip seem doubtful and now, confronted with the departure, they gave me sixteen hours to prepare for a journey from which there might be no return. One good thing though was that the time of painful parting was shortened. It became evening and curfew time as my father and I hastened along darkened streets to bid friends farewell. In our home it was Edith, my sister's best friend, who was our last guest.

My relationship with her was built on years of a mutual fondness that was expressed by continuous teasing. Edith was a smallish girl of 14, and though the signs of womanhood had barely begun to appear, I nonetheless felt greatly attracted to her. I nicknamed her *Floh* (flea) and explained to her that she was as small and as pesky as this insect. But she just laughed and took no offense. She liked me as much as I liked her, and our continued teasing gave promise of a more intimate friendship later. But this was not to be; fate had other things in store for us. On this last evening, however, and unaware of the future, our good-natured bantering continued till it was time for her to go home. We exchanged pictures, and the inscription on the back of hers read: "Recall the naughty flea, always teasing. Remember me whenever you feel like it. Mischievous Edith. Vienna, the 2nd of September 1940."

The city was blacked out, and I wanted to walk her home, only one short block away, but she declined. "Stay, I'll walk alone."

Though Jews were not allowed out after dark she was in no danger of being recognized as Jewish unless somebody knew her. She bore little resemblance to what Nazis expected a Jew to look like. Her features were fine and small. A little nose popped out between blue eyes, and a smiling mouth with permanent dimples at each corner created the small pixy face I found so attractive. Her face was encircled by blondish hair combed flat on top with braids on both sides.

I would have preferred to take that walk but gave in and stood in silence beside her in the doorway of the apartment building. Minutes passed and we did not speak. I was having confusing thoughts and unfamiliar feelings. The strange emotions pulsing through my body made me feel uneasy, and where I assumed my heart to be, something wanted to explode. I did not think of Stella and the unexpected infatuation with her that had placed me in the present situation. My feelings for Edith were different; they were of a closeness that was based on years of friendship.

We just stood there staring into the night. Nobody walked by, and only an occasional car with headlights painted black, leaving just small slits for the light to shine through, drove along the deserted street. Yet the silence between us was not meaningless. It expressed what my heart refused to recognize and my lips shied away from saying. Feelings that were incomprehensible to me.

"What are you thinking about, Gustl?" she asked, breaking the silence.

"About you and a lot more."

"Tell me about that 'lot more'."

She avoided the first part of my answer, and I felt relieved. "I think about what lies ahead. And how long it will be till I see you and my family again?"

I felt dejected and gloomy, and she sensed it. "It'll turn out all right," she consoled me.

Though her face was only a faint shadow, I knew she was smiling and the dimples on both sides of her mouth had deepened. We were very young, she 14 and I 17, yet we both were affected by the impending forced separation.

"I have to leave," she said, turning toward me.

I nodded and, though reluctant to do so, timidly tried to touch her breast.

"No, Gustl," she said, pulling back ever so slightly. "It's no good."

Somewhat hurt, I extended my hand to shake hers. But when she murmured, "*Servus*, Gustl," I experienced a feeling I had never really felt before. It was warmth, sadness, and perhaps love. "*Servus*, Edith," I replied, and she walked away from me. I could see her cross the road, then she faded into the dim canyon of the side street where she lived. For a while I gazed into the blackness that had swallowed her, and for a moment I felt how much I really cared, and how I would miss her for a long time. We had not even kissed, I thought in disappointment. Tomorrow I would see her again, but this had been our good-bye. Edith did not survive. She was murdered like so many others.

Escape on the Blue Danube

The big day had arrived. I woke up for the last time in the place I called home, the place that held memories for me I would never forget. We did our best to behave as if it was just another day, not the day of a separation whose length none of us knew or dared to guess. Everybody acted out a performance that lacked the sincerity of our customary relationship but in doing so avoided displaying the feelings that pained us.

I evaded my mother's glances, knowing that each encounter aroused sad feelings. She went through the sorrow of every Jewish mother whose child was leaving the family fold. Happy to see her young one get out of Nazi Germany and yet heartbroken at losing a child she might never see again. When it became inevitable, and we had to say something to each other, I looked past her face as if I had no time to chat but was in a hurry to get something done. She was the hardest person to deceive. My emotions went from a giddy high to a despairing low and quickly back up again. When I was mindful of our final separation, my throat muscles contracted and swallowing became difficult. The strong ties that bound me to my family made me feel as if I was deserting them. My conviction that they were safer remaining behind helped little to ease my troubled feelings. Tormenting thoughts made it difficult to keep up the façade of normality.

Then, without any reason my mood changed, and I grew excited at the prospect of adventure but was too ashamed to admit it. Mother would never have been able to participate in this thrill, and as much as she wanted to see me happy, she certainly could not join in my enthusiasm. The thought of the impending trip sent shivers down my spine. It was like getting ready for a journey to the other side of the moon, for that's how a trip to the world beyond the confines of Nazi Germany seemed in September of 1940.

Years later I often wondered what really had made me pass up earlier opportunities to leave this place of oppression. For to leave promised adventure regardless of the destination. The primary reason no doubt was my desire to stay with my family and emigrate with them to America.

I never saw Stella again. She traveled with the "Rotgasse Transport," but on another ship. My incarceration in Buchenwald may have made me eligible for this trip, but Stella had moved me to undertake it.

This time I *was* leaving. It was not up to me any more whether to stay or leave the country of Gestapo and police. And whatever the motives behind this decision, it probably was the wisest I ever made in my life.

The suitcase intended for my journey was battered from long use and on this morning of departure appeared to me in poor shape to withstand the rigors of a trip. To buy a new one confronted us with a problem. It was 8 A.M., only two hours before the scheduled meeting at the place of assembly, and Jews were not permitted to purchase anything in stores before 9 o'clock in the morning. Furthermore, to demonstrate their adherence to Nazi policies most stores displayed signs saying "Jews unwelcome" or "Forbidden for Jews." Hoping to find the right store and not be recognized for who we were we went to a neighboring district.

133

But living under the Nazis for two years had its effect on Jews. They acted more like oppressed creatures than free man. I was preoccupied with what lay ahead of me, and inattentive to my father's sudden disclosure as we strode along in search of a luggage store.

"I have to tell you something I don't want you to forget and thought that the best time is shortly before you leave. (How wrong he was.) Remember I told you a long time ago that we had money in a safe place?" I nodded to please him, and he handed me a slip of paper with the name of a bank in Lucerne, a code number, and a name. "Tell them that you are our son and you need money from the account."

There was a war on, Switzerland was surrounded by the Germans, and I was too busy escaping dangers for a long time to think of that last conversation with father. Also, with all the tribulations I endured in the years that followed, it was easy enough to forget. Decades went by before I thought of it. But the issue was academic. I had no paper, remembered no particulars, and without them who would believe me? It was one of the less important things the Nazis had robbed me of.

The luggage shop we decided on was not big. The owner, nice enough, said right out: "I can't sell you a suitcase before nine." And he hadn't even mentioned the word Jew. My father begged him to make an exception, as I was to leave the country in two hours. We could not wait for the curfew to end. He showed the man my notification and passport, that contained a visa to Uruguay[14], and the man finally consented to the sale. In the course of their talk, the two men found that both had been POWs in Siberia in the First World War.

At the gathering place in the *Grosse Mohrengasse* confusion reigned. The noise inside the building made conversation nearly impossible. People hugged, kissed, cried and said silent and effusive good-byes. Some laughed, others seemed depressed. The entire range of human emotions was on display. It looked as if all the Jews of Vienna had met here and it was impossible to discern who among those present was departing and who was staying. Groups formed and broke up releasing people to form new groups. Throughout the building there was a constant coming and going, a never-ending flow of men, women, and children. For this reason, two couples and I missed the special busses that had taken the

---

[14] The visas in our passports were for different South American countries. They were authentic and had been issued by proper consulates. It was said that big pay-offs had been made to the right persons in those states who had ordered their issue. Everyone was aware, however, that though the permits were official, entry into the involved countries would have been denied. It was a pro forma arrangement, a charade to satisfy the German bureaucracy, which, needless to say, was aware of the scam and our real destination.

travelers to the railroad station.

The five of us ordered a taxi. *Servus* Mama, Papa, I said, and kissed my parents. *Servus* Berta, and I kissed my sister. That was it, I thought. But after saying the little word *Servus* and looking at the face of my mother, feelings repressed until this moment came to the fore. I looked into her eyes and saw love and hurt in them. The love was like a soft, warm breeze of spring air caressing me, while the hurt pressed painfully against my heart. I felt homesick for the home I had barely left and a longing for the people still before me.

But *Servus* meant farewell and nothing could change that. For better or worse I was on my own the moment the taxi pulled away. The long suppressed tears of my mother flowed freely, and her promise not to weep dissolved in the misery she must have felt. I turned my head. I did not want to see the retreating figures of my family or the profound suffering of my mother. It didn't befit a young man who was about to enter the seductive world of adventure to surrender to tears.

In my adolescent naiveté I did not consider Buchenwald and the dangers a Jew was exposed to in Vienna to qualify as adventure. The excitement for me seemed to lie in the future and in an exotic world beyond the Nazi Reich. Of course my experiences until then should have satisfied any sane person's wish for adventure and should have lasted me a lifetime.

I did not know then that Hollywood had created heroes, who in thrilling escapades always overcame the bad guys in Nazi Germany at the end of the film. Having lived under the Nazi rule for two and one half years, it would have been difficult for me to visualize this happening. It may have been that going to the movies before and after Buchenwald and hiding in thin underbrush from the SS when avoiding a trip into the quarry of the concentration camp was stupid to be sure, but also an attempt to experience some kind of adventure. It had certainly raised my adrenaline level.

As our taxi rolled toward the railroad station I considered the people in the car. A white-haired man, his elderly wife, and a one-armed invalid with his spouse. How dared "old" people join an undertaking like ours, I wondered? As the future was to prove, my estimate of their chances of survival was wrong. It was not necessarily the young who survived the perils of our trip.

For the time being none of them could imagine what awaited us, and their conversation flowed unconstrained. They laughed and joked, immensely happy to leave Nazi Germany. For most of the time I sat lost in thought, uncertain now about my feelings. Despite my wish for adventure I felt vulnerable. Having reached the point of no return and being on my own, I was aware that once the journey ended all of life's decisions would be up to me.

The law permitted each emigrant to take just 10 German marks out of the country; yet more important than the money may have been the advice of my father on parting. "Wherever you'll be," he said, "if you're hungry look for a *mezuzah*[15] on a door post. Knock and when somebody opens it, say you are Jewish and you are hungry. The people will always feed you." This was good advice I was fortunate enough never to need.

September 3, 1940. Our special train left the *Ostbahnhof* (East Train Station) at 12:30 P.M. The inside of our railroad car resembled a warehouse struck by an earthquake. Boxes, suitcases, packages lay helter-skelter in such numbers in the aisles that it seemed impossible for anyone to ever find his luggage or bring order into this chaos. It reminded me of my train ride from Munich to Vienna. How different the circumstances, however!

We crossed the Danube over the Stadlauer Bridge and Vienna, the city of my birth and youth, disappeared behind the trees of the Lobau. Leaning out the window I tried to catch a last glimpse of the city behind the retreating trees, but to no avail. Disappointed I turned my gaze toward the passing fields. As the train gathered speed, the fleeing countryside had an hypnotic influence on me. My mind wandered and my thoughts entered a domain where reality and dreams mix. It was pleasant to let my mind roam while under this spell. After a while I reluctantly tore my gaze from the scenery outside to return to the present.

In my compartment was a young fellow who during the journey became a good friend. Bunjo (pronounced Bunyo), one year my senior, also had left his parents behind and hoped eventually to meet up with them in the United States. Our upbringing though was different. He came from a very religious family, while I grew up in a more relaxed atmosphere. Notwithstanding our different ways of life until then, we stuck together and got along well.

With little else to do I began to listen to the other people in the compartment, curious about their thoughts. None of my fellow travelers, including Bunjo, perceived our trip the way I did. Adventure was not on their mind. They recalled letters of earlier travelers who had written home about their journey, the troubles, and dangers they had faced. But their reports had always ended on a positive note, emphasizing the happiness of being in the new home. The prospect of belonging one day

---

[15] A small parchment scroll encased in metal, and inscribed with lines from the fifth book of Moses and the name of God. Jewish families place it on their doorpost as a sign of their faith or tradition.

to these fortunate ones must have helped many aboard the train to view our uncertain future with confidence. No doubt, in the minds of many, my father's advice to me when he was released from prison in Vienna and I stayed behind, ...what others can overcome you can too, played an important role here. They were happy to be on the way to freedom and agreed that their successful escape from Nazi terror at this late date was close to a miracle.

While still on the train I wrote a postcard to my family in Vienna, which I mailed in Marchegg at the Hungarian border. For the first time in my life I saw border police, but my compatriots did not share the thrill I experienced at their sight. They also failed to see the small, nondescript railroad station we had reached as anything out of the ordinary while I found it to be my gateway to adventure.

We arrived there at 2:30 P.M., and our patience was put to the test. The day was hot, and so were the railroad cars. We were not allowed to leave the car until called to a nearby shed for baggage inspection. When after three hours of idle waiting my turn came, I had lost all romantic feelings for that border crossing.

Time continued to drag as we waited in long lines inside that wooden building for our baggage to be examined. The inspector who checked the contents of my travel-gear found everything in order. He even ignored the expired date on the document permitting me to take my extensive stamp collection out of the country.

On the way toward the exit, a German border policeman stopped me. "Have you been inspected," he snapped at me. − "Yes." − "Show me who it was."

I did not see my man, nor was I certain I would recognize him if I saw him again. Frightening thoughts assailed me when I was ordered to stand with my luggage against a wall. The situation was resolved when the inspector showed up and I was able to identify him. He confirmed the inspection, and I was permitted to exit the shed.

Everybody was eager to leave this last stop in Germany, but our impatience had to be contained, for our train did not steam out of Marchegg until 9:30 that evening. Ninety minutes later we arrived in Pressburg (Bratislava), the capital of Slovakia, the country recently created by the Nazis. What pleasure to see a city in lights after one year of blackouts in Germany. It was a different world. Our train moved closer to the banks of the Danube that flows past Bratislava, and it was after midnight on September 4, 1940, when I stepped aboard the steamship Uranus.

The Uranus belonged to a group of steamers, all similar in build and design. They were pleasure craft that plied the waters of the river and had their home base in Vienna. The ships' owner was the *Donaudampfschiffahrtsgesellschaft* (Danube Steamship Company) a name, that because of its inordinate length, aroused amusement even in Germany. Now the vessels were flying the German flag, the swastika.

We were unaware at the time that three more ships of that company carried émigrés from Vienna. They also belonged with our transport, and the four craft were to rendezvous later in a distant river port.

The people on the Uranus, 1,000 in number, were to be my travel companions for the entire journey. Not built to house or even carry that many passengers, the ship was overloaded. She lacked sleeping accommodations and also storage space for our baggage. To ease that problem we were told to select a few personal items from our suitcases and then deposit the luggage in a designated area on deck for the remainder of our trip. I placed toilet articles, a change of underwear, socks, and shirt in a little backpack. I also added reading material and the diary I had started to write the moment we crossed into Slovakia. It must have been an unusual sight for people on land to see the high stacks of suitcases and packages on the deck of a ship known to be a pleasure boat.

Extremely tired, I looked for a spot to lie down. My roving took me through much of the ship, but passengers, many of them asleep by then, had occupied every bench, chair and bit of floor area I passed. In my search I stepped over people, and on short stairways where they sat next to each other like birds on a branch I negotiated the climb or descent only with difficulty. In a room, whose floor was also covered by sleepers I spotted an unoccupied corner. Mindful not to disturb those at rest I reached the spot and settled down. Actually it was a miserable place. I just had enough space to sit but not enough to stretch my legs.

As the confusion and noise aboard the Uranus abated, weariness crept up inside me like rising water. My eyelids dropped and my chin came to rest on my knees. I looked forward to a bit of sleep, but my uncomfortable position kept me awake. By 4:30 A.M., and having been without sleep for over 20 hours, I had had enough. I left my corner, snaked my way around and over sleeping people to the deck to await our departure. Here too people were rolled up in blankets and filled every vacant space. They were oblivious of the cold wind that shredded the dense morning fog as it blew over ship and water. I felt cold but stuck to my post at the ship's rail. I did not want to miss another first in my life: the vessel's release from her moorings and her glide to midstream.

At 5:30 A.M. the ropes tying the Uranus to the quay fell away. Her idling motors sped up and facing the strong current of the Danube she held her own as she slowly moved away from the landing. After performing a big half-circle, she pointed her bow downstream and with her increased speed she moved faster than the rushing waters of the river.

Awakened by the ship's rumbling turbines more and more people appeared on deck and activities spread throughout the boat. A crowd surrounded a group of young men who, singing Hebrew songs, were harmoniously accompanied by an accordion. Only now did the sense of deliverance from Nazi repression and the dawn of new life come over me. The invisible pall of terror that hovered over ever Jew in Germany had dissipated, and a lighthearted smile illuminated every face. The world might be at war, and our people did not know what fate had in store for them, but for now the refugees aboard the Uranus had tasted real freedom and they loved it.

The land on both sides of the river was flat and monotonous as we passed pastures, little islands of trees and cattle in the distance. To me, however, nothing was boring. A stork circling overhead and then disappearing behind trees was a beautiful picture. I was just as excited when seagulls, birds I saw for the first time in my life, trailed our ship while we steamed through northern Hungary. Toward noon the Uranus navigated the bend where the Danube, in a 90-degree angle, turns south, and by 2:30 P.M. we had entered Budapest.

I had never been to this city yet recognized the parliament building on the left side of the river. This imposing structure was familiar to me from old Hungarian stamps in my stamp collection. From embankments and bridges onlookers waved, a salutation that was enthusiastically returned by our people. Shortly after leaving the residential sector of the city, the Uranus tied up at a dock to take on water and provisions. Two hours later we were moving again. The passing scenery on both sides of the Danube where the level tracts of land stretched into the distance continued to be monotonous. At dusk the far reaches to the east and the darkening sky fused while the sinking sun to the west painted the horizon a flaming red. Not far in that direction lived my parents and sister but with every turn of the ship's propeller the distance between us increased as we steamed south toward Yugoslavia. How long had it been since I had left my family? Was it really only yesterday or, as it seemed, a lifetime ago?

I made precise notations about our journey and recorded at the time: Thursday, September 5, 1940, our second day on our journey. Passed Mohacs and Bezan, both cities in Yugoslavia. I am still up and it is late at night when we anchor at Semlin, a suburb of Belgrade. I watch the loading of water and bread onto our boat and can also see the blinking lights of the Yugoslavian capital ahead of us. At midnight we pass illuminated Belgrade and dip into inky blackness. As my eyes adjust to the dark, I gaze at a night sky that is dotted with twinkling stars. Like a glowworm the light of a lonely house appears occasionally on the riverbank only to be swallowed up after we pass.

Under a portrait of Hitler, adorning the wall of a passageway, I found a premium spot on the floor, and after 40 hours without sleep sank into a dreamless void.

On September 6, the third day aboard ship, we passed a small boat with refugees. Anchored in the middle of the river because they were not permitted to land, they were unable to continue on their way. We saw only young men and women aboard. Some girls were hanging washing from clotheslines; men were busy with other things. We waved and they waved back, without enthusiasm. Had they reached Palestine, I would have known. They must have shared the fate of the rest of the Jews in Yugoslavia when the Germans overran it shortly thereafter.

The Danube, from its origin in the Black Forest of Germany, winds its way almost clear across Europe. Yet, nowhere on the part we traveled had the river's course been forced to detour more from its path than when its left bank became Rumania, and the region mountainous. To me it meant that a geographical point of interest was just around the corner: The Iron Gate. This narrow spot between Orsova and Kladover, two small towns, is where the Danube river breaks through the Banat mountains. Until Austrian engineers in 1890 cut a channel through this gorge, the narrow stretch was almost impassable for riverboats.

Back in school we had been told that the Danube flowed so rapidly through the Iron Gate that a railway line had been built along the riverbank, and a locomotive pulled ships upstream through the rapids.

I don't know what I had expected to see. I was unimpressed, however, by our voyage through the passage and the fast-flowing stream around us. Soon afterward the region flattened out and another change, unrecognizable to the eye, occurred. The shore on our right had become Bulgarian territory.

Until then the cruise had progressed smoothly. Despite the close quarters, people were generally patient with one another. Nobody minded the long lines at mealtime or the extended wait in the morning to wash up. And although the toilet facilities on the ship were too few to satisfy the needs of a thousand passengers, people were considerate of each other and gave way if necessary.

The first involuntary interruption of our journey occurred in Giurgiu. It was September 7, a Saturday, and our fourth day under way when the Uranus stopped at this Rumanian port. We did not know the reason, but the grapevine supplied two answers. One explained that because of a Bulgarian threat to the province of Dobruja, the Rumanian government was in an uproar and therefore had canceled our transit

140

through Rumanian territory. The other rumored that the palms of certain persons in the local hierarchy had to be greased to permit our journey to continue.

Our ship described a circle and then headed slightly upstream toward the opposite side of the Danube. Our goal, Ruse (Russe), a Bulgarian river port. Two days passed before the Rumanian authorities let us continue on our way. After another short stop at Giurgiu on September 9 we proceeded down the river and deeper into Rumania. The next day we reached Braila and the day after that, September 11, our eighth day aboard the Uranus, we saw Tulcea, a city at the beginning of the river delta.

I had often wondered how we would complete the journey. Obviously not on the ship that had brought us here. Flying the German flag on her stern and being a river boat, she could hardly take us to Palestine. Soon we had the answer. The Danube is very wide in Tulcea and we anchored in the middle of the river. The three other boats carrying our people from Vienna arrived the next day and positioned themselves not too far from us. Loud communications sounded across the watery divide between the vessels when friend recognized friend, but I searched unsuccessfully for Stella, the nurse from Rothschildspital.

Life on the SS Pacific

On the afternoon of September 14, three ships detached themselves from the right bank of the Danube and maneuvered into position alongside our riverboats. But, heavens, what kind of ships were they? They looked as if they had been taken from a mooring where retired ships were placed to disintegrate peacefully. The Atlantic, the Pacific, and the Canisbei, later renamed Milos, had been Greek steamers that now, except for their bombastic names, had nothing to be proud of. They were old and rusty, and the only place the paint was not peeling was huge Panamanian flags freshly painted on their sides. The symbol of that Central American country was to display the registry and prove our neutrality later in the dangerous waters of the Mediterranean. We were to be transferred to these ships.

The mountains of baggage on the deck of the Uranus had been spread out so that people could look for their belongings. As dusk settled the chaotic transfer to our new ship, the Pacific, got under way. Suitcase in hand and knapsack on my back I boarded the vessel over a narrow plank and, like everybody else, had orientation problems. People who had reached the deck of the Pacific hesitated for a while, then moved on through one of the several small doors into the unlit interior of the steamer. Illumination on board was unpredictable. It was unclear if it was

141

the fuel or, as in many instances later, because the generator failed.

Joining one of the lines I entered a pitch-dark opening. In the narrow confines of a stairwell the steady flow of people thickened to a solid mass from which there was no escape. All were borne along without being able to resist the current or control the direction of the flow. Once in a while the wavering beam of a flashlight pierced the darkness, but as the illumination was no help, it was turned off almost immediately to save the battery. I carried my flashlight in my free hand but did not use it.

The stairs ended and I was on a flat surface. Many flashlights now illu-minated a corridor made narrow by wooden bunk beds on the left and a planked wall on the right. The sleeping facilities, three tiers high, were deep enough for two people to lie parallel to the wall. The fingers of light flitting probingly over the wooden platforms searched for empty bunks. All places were occupied, and the human serpent moved on.

Progress in that narrow thoroughfare was difficult. There was barely enough room for two people to pass shoulder to shoulder. In regular times this part of the ship had been the outside passageway along the railing. Now the section had become an artificial corridor, a tunnel created to protect the sleeping quarters against bad weather.

Without letup the forward push continued. Once more stairs were underfoot and complete darkness around us. But there was no danger of falling; the moving mass of bodies carried me along. Had there been light, we might all have looked like an oversized caterpillar in a science-fiction movie slowly descending the inside of a shaft. The air was stuffy and hot, and wearing my winter coat did not improve my comfort. There was no chance to take it off and after a while I was soaked in perspiration.

We encountered another flat surface and more bunk beds and finally, though we were still quite a throng, the steady stream of my compatriots thinned out. More and more people crawled into makeshift beds before I could get to one, and finally I reached a room that, after a hasty examination by my flashlight, looked like the inside of a tomb. I found an unoccupied space in the middle of a three tiered bunk and, tired, settled into it. The suitcase by my side, the rucksack for a pillow, I closed my eyes and, in spite of the commotion still going on in the room, fell asleep. This was the welcome to our new home. People on the other two vessels fared no better. It is hard to imagine what would have happened had an emergency arisen.

Loud talk awakened me. My first impression was a pale light that came from above and it exposed bunks and people. For a fearful moment I was back among the bunks in Buchenwald. It turned out to be the ship's hold. It was not a big room, yet, in every available space, except

142

under the opening, racks for sleeping had been constructed. In a short while the grayish sky took on the first red of the rising sun, the room became brighter, and our first day aboard our ocean liner had started.

The statistics of our ships were as follows: Our flagship, the Atlantic, the biggest vessel in our fleet, was 700 tons and had taken in nearly 2,000 people. The Pacific, the ship I was on, 400 tons, carried 1,000 passengers. And on the Milos, approximately 300 tons, were about 900 refugees.

Bunjo had been close behind me when I had searched in the dark for a place to settle, and he found a spot in the same hold. Though we had some common interests, he shared none of my curiosity about the ship or my prickly feeling of adventure in sailing aboard her. His aim, like that of the other passengers, was to reach Palestine and its relative safety in the shortest possible time while I was in no rush to get there. I wanted to enjoy the extraordinary features of the enterprise and the thrills of the unexpected that our voyage might serve up. And in all my enthusiasm about the intriguing prospect, I was unaware that this unrealistic attitude of mine actually made the hardships of our journey much easier to endure. If realities occasionally got the upper hand in my life in adventure-land, homesickness may have been the reason. Though the longing for my family was always present, I was uneasy and in low spirits at rare moments and only for a short time.

The Pacific appeared to have been a cargo vessel in her prime with just a few cabins on the main deck. Judged by her size, she probably did not roam the oceans but confined her travel to the more immediate region around her homeland, Greece. Everything on board pointed to the fact that she was Greek. Painted instructions on walls were in Greek and so were doorplates. The captain and the few sailors were Greek. They were rarely seen and never fraternized with our people. Rumor had it that our captain was an alcoholic, but he nonetheless proved himself to be the perfect navigator.

The ship was not outfitted to handle emergencies. Only three life-boats hung from rusty winches, and no life vests were available. We never had a safety drill, which in our situation would have been pointless. Nothing and nobody could have handled a mob of people on the small decks of our ship in a crisis. Though our journey in the Mediterranean Sea was to be as inconspicuous as possible, I wondered later if there even was a radio transmitter aboard to send out SOS signals. I doubt it. But even had we possessed the luxury of such equipment, Eastern Europe was insecure and in ferment, and I don't believe the governments of the Balkan countries would have been overly worried if our ship was in trouble. The organizers of trips like ours had to be happy to find a craft that still floated on water and somebody willing to steer her to where they wanted her to go. If such a man was found and did not mind the danger of landing in a British prison for running the blockade of Palestine with 1,000 refugees from Nazi Germany, that was good enough. He was paid a lot of money for the chance he took but certainly needed good nerves for this engagement or a 'bottle' to strengthen his nerves.

I don't want to pass judgment, but rather emphasize the difficulty of making the necessary arrangements for an undertaking like ours, a task that required money, guts, and cunning.

Life on board was tortuous at first, but people adjusted to the hardship with the passing of time. Drinking water, brought aboard at various points during our journey, was not available in Tulcea. Perhaps the city wanted too much money for it. We were forced to drink river water. Not straight from the river, but the liquid from the ship's water tanks was ultimately river water. To pacify us we were assured that it had been filtered. It tasted abominable. When one considered all the sewers emptying into the Danube for 1700 miles upstream, it took a real thirst to overcome the nausea when drinking this water. Once in a while dead animals, mainly cats and dogs, floated by, which did not enhance the taste of the coffee or soup our cook, a German Jew who had owned a restaurant in the days before the Nazis, prepared for us. The only comforting thought was that the water the coffee and soup were made from had to be boiled.

The bread delivered from the city was uneatable. It smelled musty and was covered at times with mold. Its quality improved after a general uproar and the ominous threat that something drastic would happen, such as throwing the leaders of our transport overboard.

Considering the circumstances, our food was fairly good. I even started to help in the kitchen to overcome the tedium of our idle existence. It also meant more food. As cigarettes were used in place of money on board, I bought cigarettes for a couple of marks, and they served me well. The scarcer they became the higher their value in barter. I exchanged them for jam, sausage rations, and even ink that I needed for my Waterman fountain pen.

People with items of greater value supplemented the ship's diet by bartering with men that came in little boats from shore. Those rowboat entrepreneurs offered sticks of salami, cheese, pickled and smoked fish, fruits, vegetables that could be eaten raw, and other foodstuffs in exchange for wristwatches, gold rings, gold chains and anything of value. Some customers paid with the ten marks they had been permitted to take out of Germany. Those business transactions were theatrical performances, and with not much else to do, the ship's railing was always crowded with spectators.

The deck of the Pacific was not very high above the waterline, but still the exchange of goods had to be made with the help of a string.

Valuables were lowered into the rowboat, and then the food was pulled up in the same way.

Food in Rumania was very cheap yet the exchange of valuables for edibles did not reflect this. The buyers were helpless, and the hawkers just seized the opportunity to make easy money. Some of those boat traders were real scoundrels. They grabbed the valuables offered to them but failed to send up the food. Followed by the frustrated screams of everybody watching, they quickly rowed away from our ship.

On one occasion a man rowed a Rumanian army officer to the side of our vessel. When the barter with one of our people began, he was offered, of all things, a two-foot-high pendulum clock. They agreed on an exchange, and the clock was carefully lowered over board. When the officer held the clock in his hand, the man who rowed the boat took off in haste. The howl that followed was probably audible for a mile. But that army man was honest. He apparently was as surprised at the rower's behavior as we were, for he ordered the man to return to the dangling string to which he fastened the purchased item.

The reason for the forced layover in Tulcea may have been the occupation of the Rumanian province of Dobruja by Bulgaria. Unfortunately this episode took place just while we were anchored in Rumanian waters. Though we traveled under the Panamanian flag, Panama apparently had no intention of intervening on our behalf. Panama had been paid for the permission to hoist their flag, but that was all the responsibility they extended to us. The longer our boat was stuck in Tulcea, the more it felt like being on an island prison. People became irritable. Faced by an uncertain future, they reacted angrily to the slightest provocation. Small quarrels were viewed as a kind of diversion in the daily humdrum. Contestants were separated when the battles became physical.

During the heat of the day, the lower part of the ship exuded the odors of all the cargoes she had carried in her holds. On deck one tried mostly in vain to find shelter from the stinging rays of the sun. Only sun freaks, who in the year 1940 were apparently unaware of the dangers of skin cancer, roasted their bodies slowly to a deep red in the heat. Seekers of shade devised makeshift sunroofs by attaching blankets, shirts, or cardboard to stationary objects. Creators of those sunscreens shared their contrivances with others as the cover usually covered more space than one person's body area. And space was scarce.

A few days after our transfers to the "ocean-going vessels," the Milos began to leak. Luckily she was the closest of our ships to the shore, and the passengers were permitted to take refuge on land until she was repaired.

At night tempers mellowed and people became more sociable. I recorded in my diary:

"Only here in Tulcea have I become aware of the magnificence of a star-studded sky whose enormous canopy is not reduced to a narrow channel by walls of tall buildings and where their brilliance is untarnished by the fumes and vapors of a city's emanations. During the day life aboard ship has lost some of its romanticism, but night brings back to me the world of pleasant unrealities seen only in movies or read about in books. When the heat of day yields to the cool of the evening the travelers flee the humidity of the ship's interior and stream on deck. They relax on planks still radiating the warmth of the sun and are seemingly unworried about the impasse we are in.

My favorite spot is on the railing where I sit and listen to the bubbling sound of the flowing water as it splashes softly against the ship's side. My thoughts escape the confines of our surroundings and travel back to Vienna, my family, and friends, or into the veiled future that is just as far out of reach.

On one side of the deck a group of boys and girls assembles, and soon songs sound over the dark waters of the Danube. Sad melodies that express sadness over personal loss or patriotic songs that look to the future in a Jewish land.

At times homesickness becomes overpowering, and I almost feel like crying. I am filled with longing that makes me vulnerable to dejected moods. And yet it is a sentiment I rarely succumb to. Songs sound through the night, and I remember Vienna. Trips with my parents and sister to the Kahlenberg and Prater. Streets, narrow and wide, games, roving through the Inner City, Brüder Seidler, my cousins Leo and Hugo, their friends and girl friends. And Erich and Susi, whom I hope to meet at the end of the journey. I have been well off but not aware of it. One has to be lonely to discover the true meaning of closeness and home. I do not blame myself; most people take good things for granted. I find that writing about my innermost feelings eases the blues and softens the pain. I stay up late into the night, contemplate life, and then go to bed. On the morrow the bad images, if there have been any, have dissipated. What remains, however, are the thoughts that occupy me most: When are we going to leave? When are we going to arrive at our destination? Will we reach our goal? And how many of us? The future will tell. And with no choice, we continue the tedious wait."

Finally it was over. The long delay came to an end. After we had been stranded in Tulcea for 27 days, the Rumanian government permitted our departure. It was 10:30 A.M., October 7, 1940, my thirty-fourth day aboard ship, when the neighboring Atlantic weighed anchor and began to glide downstream.

She had hardly moved a few hundred yards when she stopped. Not knowing that she had suffered a broken steering mechanism, we passed her like winners of a race with howls of triumph followed by the Milos.

Though the landscape we traveled through was flat and offered little of interest, we were enchanted. *We were moving again!* Willow trees, little groups of shrubs, dilapidated houses, small herds of cattle, and now and again a few horses made up the scenery. The familiar seagulls circled overhead, accompanied us for a while, and when finding no food in the ship's wake, flew off with angry cries. The scenery rolled by, distanced itself behind us, and disappeared.

We traveled a straight waterway, an arm of the Danube delta. It appeared to stretch endlessly to the rear and ahead of our ship. An obelisk on shore caught my eye, but what it stood for in this lonely spot I could not guess, and so it just became part of the moving scenery.

At 4:30 P.M. we began to pass ships anchored at piers along the left bank of the river. With a happy howl we greeted sailors of an oil tanker on whose stern the Union Jack fluttered; the paradoxical sign of our approaching freedom. A short distance ahead we saw Sulina, the city near the end of the Danube delta. When we came closer, everybody was ordered below deck. No reasons given.

Behind Sulina our people crowded the ship's deck again, searching eagerly for the Black Sea ahead. Fifteen minutes later we departed the secure delta of the Danube and entered an immense body of water, slightly bigger in size than the state of California. The Black Sea was calm enough yet the gentle up and down motion under our feet made a few people seasick. Outside the river's mouth the Pacific stopped and dropped anchor. People did not take kindly to another delay. Once again the grapevine provided a reason: we had to wait for the other two ships. We remained on that spot over night, but on the following morning the Rumanian government, apparently wanting to be rid of us, sent a motor boat that escorted us out of their territorial waters. We had lost sight of the Milos between Tulcea and Sulina, but as she failed to show up, we proceeded south. To the left of us the Black Sea met the eastern horizon, on our right a thin line, as if drawn by a pencil, indicated land.

A ship coming toward us aroused our interest. It eased that feeling of being alone on that wide expanse of water whose depth in places reaches 7,000 feet. Cheerfully we awaited the encounter and pressed against the railing to get a better view of her and her passengers. It was a freighter. Then our joyful welcome died in our throats when we recognized the hateful swastika flag fluttering in the wind. She was German.

147

Our ships passed in silence. No sound, no waving. I suppressed the hate that welled up inside me and wanted to express itself. I was still afraid of them and their symbol. Onward went our thoughts and our ship. No more would we be stopped and restrained by forces that wanted to be rid of us in the first place.

Toward evening of that first day at sea I too fought a slight dizziness that affected my stomach. Following an instinct, I went to the forward section of our ship and let the wind blow against my face. It was not easy to make my way across the deck. As on the Uranus, people were rolled up in their blankets to sleep in the open rather than below deck. Stepping between the bundled-up bodies, I reached the forward section where I stood with closed eyes facing forward. It made me feel better. After a while I descended to our bunker to lie down for the night.

Next morning I felt fine. I decided to try out a special soap bought in Vienna. Regular soap produced no suds in salt water and was therefore useless for cleaning. This particular soap was supposed to overcome that problem. I waited in line for the pail on a rope used to fetch water from the sea. After people had their wash in the container, they poured the used water back into the ocean and handed the bucket to the next person in line. When my turn came I threw the pail overboard and, hoping the salt water would rinse it, pulled the container along our ship. I then pulled up the load, and tried to get foam out of my soap. Nothing happened.

On the second day at sea I already felt like a seasoned mariner. The queasiness in my stomach of the day before was gone, and I decided that to overcome that feeling I just had to stand exposed to the wind sweeping over the ship and fill my lungs with fresh sea air.

The uninterrupted progress of our voyage and the assumption that Constantinople (Istanbul) was just ahead promoted a cheerful mood aboard. We did not make it to Constantinople's minaret skyline but anchored closer to a coastline of steep rocks with a lighthouse on top of them. It reminded me of a picture postcard I had seen of Helgoland. The place, still in Bulgaria and called Noss Kaliakra (Noss in Bulgarian means nose) actually looked like a rocky nose sticking out into the sea.

By the next afternoon, October 10, a small Bulgarian warship appeared. Our captain was taken on board their vessel. When he returned he was accompanied by a group of Bulgarian sailors. We must have been taken for a dangerous lot, for those sailors strutted around our boat with fixed bayonets attached to rifles over their shoulders. In the company of the warship we traveled south, reaching Varna at 8 P.M. Night had descended and only the blinking lights of that harbor city were visible.

Curiosity got me up early next morning. I wanted to see the place that had been concealed by darkness the night before. Expectantly I climbed to the deck and found our ship surrounded by an impenetrable fog. The opaqueness of the heavy mist concealed the city more effectively than the darkness of the previous night. When the fog gave way to the sun, I gazed at a distant city set on a hill. From the shore a mole stretched into the sea, and at its end stood a lighthouse. Bulgarian, Italian, and Russian ships lay moored side by side while little boats rushed back and forth all over the harbor. I was tremendously impressed. It was, after all, my first saltwater port.

The day passed quickly as I watched the bustling harbor life. Other people, less enthusiastic about our presence here, demanded to know the time of our departure. By evening I shared their feeling, though for a different reason. Varna was interesting, but to the south a world of new places I wanted to see awaited us.

Next morning the fog again hovered around our boat. As I leaned against the cracked wood of the railing and stared into the wafting dampness, my thoughts began to wander. The cool air seemed familiar and appeared to have little to do with the weather conditions or the fog. Something physically intimate was present that also manifested itself in an emotional sense. And then I understood. It was the spirit of Yom Kippur in Vienna.

Yesterday people had talked about this holiest of holy days, and the devout among our travelers had prepared themselves for the occasion. I had paid no attention being busy looking at Varna. Since my bar mitzvah I had fasted on Yom Kippur, but now I actually found it unfair to be expected to go without food and water for the next 26 hours after my many days of fasting in Buchenwald. Yet I was still influenced by the traditions of home, and I was going to fast like most people aboard. Tradition was not easy to break. My daydreams of past Yom Kippur days in Vienna were interrupted when I became aware that the fog had lifted. It brought me back to the present, the Pacific, and Varna harbor. Yom Kippur, October 12, 1940, my thirty-ninth day aboard ship.

Our patience began to grow thin. The city was beautiful to look at, but six days of Varna was too much for anybody. Each day another reason for the delay was given, and some had merit. The generator needed repairs, the compass was out of whack, food had to be brought aboard, water tanks refilled, coal loaded, and finally, emigrants had to be taken aboard.

On the fourth day of our stay eight Bulgarian Sephardic Jews were accepted onto our vessel. The fifth day saw a wedding performed by a rabbi among us. On the sixth and final day, though few believed it to be the final day, our boat was moved to the quay to accept 20 more emigrants. At least twice as many stormed the gangplank and boarded our ship. Once aboard, nobody had the heart to force them off. If those responsible for our transport refused to take in all the Jews who wanted to board us, it was not ill will. There was no more space, and more passengers endangered the lives of all of us.

When we finally left Varna at 2:15 P.M. on October 17, it was into heavy seas. Our vessel resembled a floating Tower of Babel. Most of the nations of Central and Eastern Europe were assembled in our small world: Austrians, Germans, Hungarians, Czechs, Slovaks, Poles, Rumanians, Russians, and Bulgarians. Later I found a woman in my bunker who was born in Safed, a city in the mountains of Galilee. She had lived in Vienna for a long time with her husband, a Jew from Poland. In every corner of our boat a different language or dialect was heard.

That night the heavy seas developed into a full-fledged storm, in late fall and winter a frequent occurrence in the Black Sea. It tore tarpaulins off the deck and crushed the wooden walls erected to shelter bunk beds in the gangway against high waves. The gangway was flooded. During that terrible night when the captain almost gave up the ship, as was reported by the grapevine the next day, a healthy baby was born. In that same night and despite the calamities threatening the SS Pacific, the captain steered us to safety. Unaware of the catastrophe that had almost struck us, I slept through the whole thing. The next morning, in the company of others, I stared in disbelief at the havoc the storm had wrought on our ship.

We spent the day anchored in a lonely bay, while everybody lent a hand to bring some order into the devastation. The Black Sea, still rough, could have endangered our craft had we sailed on. According to rumors we were in Turkish territorial waters.

The next day, October 18, at 4:30 A.M. we left the sheltered cove and entered a sea choppy with waves. Not too far from the coast, we traveled in a southeasterly direction. At 1 P.M. a lighthouse in the distance marked the entrance to the Bosporus, a waterway that separates Europe from Asia. At 2 P.M. we steamed past mountains, villages, beautiful mosques, and, as they looked from afar, palaces of the *1001 Nights*.

In a suburb of Constantinople we had a visit by police, their stay was short, and we soon continued on our journey.

I had been waiting anxiously to see Constantinople, and at 4:15 P.M. it came into view. With the setting sun in my eyes it was hard to judge whether it was fantasy or reality what I saw. The many minarets, the countless domes of mosques, the houses, all immersed in a golden light, were like pictures out of a beautiful fairy tale. The sight of the city and especially one of a big mosque in that ocean of buildings I remembered with clarity for a long time.

150

Without further delay we reached the Sea of Marmara, and in the afternoon of the following day, October 19, we traveled through the Dardanelles. This channel, four to five miles at its widest point and about half a mile at its narrowest, was of strategic importance. At certain points of the passage we were ordered below deck. I therefore missed Gallipoli, the place where allied forces suffered a disastrous defeat in the First World War.

At 6:30 that same evening we reached the Aegean Sea.

As if hexed, the moment we entered the new waters the generator gave out and we were again without electricity. The few kerosene lamps placed in strategic corners at night provided modest illumination. The poor light barely penetrated the dark interior of our boat. The consequences of an emergency would have been unthinkable. At night we were buffeted by another storm and the lamps in the corridors had to be extinguished because they were a fire hazard on the rolling ship. Though the weather was beautiful the next morning, the SS Pacific still bobbed up and down as she progressed on her southerly course.

Later we found out that the compass also had quit functioning. How our captain managed to find his course I don't know, but he steered our ship unerringly to her final destination.

Between two and six on the same afternoon we stopped at a small Greek island to clean tubes from accumulated soot. Islanders assembled on shore staring at us with the same interest as we observed them. A Sunday entertainment for all. Three policemen, rowing their boat toward the Pacific, engaged our crews in a lively conversation. We followed the verbal intercourse in Greek with interest but little understanding. It all seemed fun.

Life on the Pacific had settled into a routine. One could forget one was on a ship. Our boat and its people were a little world of their own. Like travelers in space searching for the Promised Land that was to give them shelter and home. The regions we touched and people we met were like stars in the void that, after contact, thrust us away as if we were two magnetic poles with the same charge. Despite the difficulties and complications we lived together peaceably a thousand souls, from the youngest baby born during that storm on the Black Sea to the orthodox old men who, in any weather, rocked back and forth in their prayer shawls to communicate with God every morning and evening. The people of the Pacific did not possess much, but whatever they owned was visible to everyone on the ship. The most secure place for anything of worth was a suitcase, and though it was always left unguarded on a bunk, I never heard anyone complain that something was missing.

Though we were confined in a small space for a long time, thanks to our progress there was comparatively little strife among the travelers.

Most people on board were like folks one met as neighbors in an apart-ment building, strangers encountered by chance on the street, or casual acquaintances at shopping places. Nondescript individuals who blended into the fabric of everyday life in any city. Some were more pleasant than others, and some stood out in obnoxious ways.

Among the people our small living quarters accommodated was Bunjo, the woman from Safed, and her husband, and just above my sleeping place, in a bunk a little wider than mine because of the curve of the ship's side, a couple from Germany. She was blond, slender, and good-looking, he was just as tall and slender, but bald and cross-eyed. Both spent their days tanning in the sun and their nights with endless sex.

Lustig, a dark, handsome, young man, whose brother had been in Buchenwald with me, appeared to me as if he could have made it in the movies. In my mind's eye I saw him dressed in top hat and tails, tap-dancing to a tune from a Ginger Rogers–Fred Astaire film. He laughed when I told him this and damped my imagination by saying that he did not know how to tap-dance.

The woman from Safed, Palestine, always sang the same Yiddish song whenever I saw her. I still remember it, for it fitted our situation.

Yach fuhr aheim,	I'm going home,
Yach fuhr aheim,	I'm going home,
And will net mer sein kein Ger[16]	and won't be a stranger anymore
Wie gevehn bis aher	As I used to be before,
Yach fuhr, yach fuhr aheim.	I'm going, I'm going home.

In a small cabin on deck lived an elderly couple. Both were short and their faces wrinkled like dried fruits. She reminded me of a Fury, one of that spiteful spirits of Greek mythology. Whenever I passed, she was yelling at her husband. I never heard him say a word.

The corpulent cook from Germany with his brush-like mustache always seemed agitated. During the serving of the meals he wielded the big ladle like a saber and shouted to the people in line: "Move on. Move on."

Shani, a young, tall, skinny fellow from Vienna, was well known because he belonged to the group of entertainers who on some evenings amused us with funny sketches. They were performed on the small forward deck, near the ship's bow. I met Shani later in 1941 at a highway crossing somewhere in Palestine while waiting for a bus. He did not remember me, I had been just one of the thousand people on our boat.

---

[16]Ger in Yiddish and Hebrew is a stranger.

He was down and out and very unhappy. In later years I met several more people like him who were unable to adjust to life in Palestine, could not forget Vienna, and were waiting for the first opportunity to return. I wonder what eventually happened to Shani.

Another fellow known to all males aboard ship was in charge of the men's toilet. His volunteering for the job earned him every user's gratitude. This important institution had been set up at the stern of our boat, just below deck. The toilet and washing facilities on board ship were inadequate, and a larger, improvised latrine alleviated the crunch. We sat on a bench made of long wooden boards, which followed the semi-circle of the ship's stern. Under it tin sheets, bent hollow and riveted together, served as a gutter. Here, with no privacy, men sat side by side, like pigeons on a roost and while answering nature's call, discussed politics, the war, and our chance of survival. No one felt embarrassed in the presence of others in this most private of functions. Still, there were some men who held their bowels in check all day and waited for nighttime when the facility was deserted or almost vacant.

The keeper of the place would throw a pail on a string through an opening in the ship's side, haul in seawater, and continually flush the waste through another opening into the sea. This section was called: WC or The Parliament. Women had their a similar latrine somewhere else on the ship.

Personal hygiene was a problem. There was neither the space, nor were there the necessary facilities to bathe or shower. One tried to keep clean the best one could. Despite the cramped quarters and the lack of sanitary accommodations, no vermin or illnesses related to them were found among the travelers.

A father and his retarded teenage daughter created a disgusting scandal. They slept together and he violated her. At the internment camp later in the year it was learned she had become pregnant.

One day I met a man on deck I had not seen for a while. He looked terrible. His face was a pale green, and he looked as if he suffered from acute jaundice. He told me that when we had crossed into warmer climate, an attack of malaria, which he had contracted as an Austrian soldier on the Isonzo front in Italy during World War I, had put him into our infirmary. It seemed malaria was a disease that could not be cured and which reoccurred under certain conditions.

Our infirmary was a small wooden hut built atop the wheelhouse.

We steamed past the innumerable islands of the Cyclades on October 21 and reached San Nikolas, Crete, in the afternoon of October 22. Another misfortune had occurred on our ship. The water tank had sprung a leak, and because we no longer had the luxury of the dirty

Danube waters at our disposal, the precious liquid still left in the tank was rationed. From the island we received provisions and water but no help with our light generator, the leaky tank, or the disabled compass.

We remained anchored at San Nikolas until October 28.

On the day we left, the islanders we saw from our ship were not their usual selves. Something had caused anxiety and stirred up the place. We learned that Italy had invaded Greece from occupied Albania. An Axis power was just one step behind us.

After we reached the open sea, an aircraft looking like a fighter plane approached our ship, circled us twice, then flew off again. We were unfamiliar with its markings, so the plane's nationality remained a mystery which left us with an uneasy feeling. For the first time since leaving Germany had we been exposed to a weapon of war.

To display our neutrality to the opposing military forces in the Mediterranean Sea a kerosene lamp on a string was lowered overboard on each side of the ship at night. They illuminated the Panamanian flags that I am certain were indistinguishable even from a short distance. If we safely plied these waters, it was either because we had not been discovered or did not seem worth a torpedo.

A ship with two kerosene lamps!

It was apparent by then that we were nearing our final destination, and the happiness aboard knew no bounds. People laughed, joked, sang, and played. On the forward deck a festival was in progress. It was October 29 and my fifty-sixth day aboard ship. It could have been the last day of my life.

I stood on the small roof of the wheelhouse with the infirmary to my right and watched the proceedings from my elevated position. On the small area not covered by the little hut of our miniature hospital people sunned themselves while others played chess on boards placed on suitcases. Suddenly our ship, while still moving forward, listed slightly. First to the left, then to the right, then stronger to the left, and even more to the right. While this was happening, the people on the deck below me, in their confused effort to keep the ship in balance, dashed always to the high side of the deck, thus increasing the pendular motion. The pieces on the chessboards toppled over, and as the back-and-forth running of the passengers below intensified the ship's roll, men began to howl, women screeched, and children wailed in terror.

The rocking of the SS Pacific became so severe that things began to slide. To me the motion of the ship was an alarming experience. I sometimes lay with my back on the wall of the infirmary gaping at the sky, and the next moment, when the boat's position reversed itself, I seemed to carry the hut on my back, while I stared straight down into the sea. Yet, in spite of the ship's swaying motion, she never lost her speed or direction.

It was obvious that another few extended swings would capsize the ship, and most of her passengers would have perished in the middle of the Mediterranean Sea. "Sit down," our security men bellowed, "sit down." They waved their arms and grabbed the bolting people, forcing them onto the deck. The few sailors around also screamed, and although nobody understood Greek, the frantic motions of their arms conveyed what their language failed to express. Luckily, the orders were obeyed in time. The ship slowly settled into her upright position, and when the vessel sailed on without interruption, the people calmed down.

It all had begun with the festivity on the forward deck. The narrow ship needed only a few extra people standing on one side to unbalance her. This started the action that could have ended in disaster.

My friend Bunjo, down in the bunker, was taking a footbath in a basin. As he later told me, the water in the container started to swap back and forth, and he almost lost his seat. That unexplainable motion frightened him, although the movement down below was not as pronounced as above.

Looking back at his mishap, we both had to laugh.

On October 30 our coal supply was used up, and the captain ordered the burning of all available wood aboard. This new kind of fuel sent a magnificent stream of sparks through the ship's smoke stack, a display that was far more noticeable in the distance at night than the feeble light of kerosene lamps swinging on strings.

On October 31 we broke up and chopped to pieces the rail surrounding the small deck of the wheelhouse, the infirmary above it, the walls little kitchen hut, two of the three life boats, leaving one life boat for 1,000 people, cabin doors, and all the bunk beds. Everyone slept on the floors that night. Any wooden item that could be done without was used as fuel. (I hope some Britisher took pictures of our stripped ship after our arrival.)

We sighted land November 1. It was still far in the distance and appeared as thin as the Bulgarian shoreline in the Black Sea. At that point, however, similarities ended. We now steamed not parallel to the coast, but toward it. This was to be the end of our journey.

But we were not alone. We had been expected. As we later learned, the plane circling us upon our leaving Crete had been a British Spitfire. The fighter aircraft had alerted the Mandate authorities in Palestine and as we approached, vessels of the British Navy began to follow us. Any plan to beach the Pacific on a deserted stretch of coast and disappear into the interior had been foiled.

At 7 A.M. on that beautiful morning a warship of His Majesty's Navy directed us into Haifa Bay. We were the first of our three ships to reach our goal. Our long and dangerous journey had found its conclusion, but we were at the mercy of the British blockade.

Nonetheless, in the general euphoria over our safe arrival I recorded in my diary:

This time our journey has really ended. Two months have passed since we set out into the unknown and all troubles and anxieties appear to have vanished with our entrance into Haifa Bay. Fifty-eight days of uncertainty, are behind us, and this fifty-ninth day has, at long last, seen our wishes and hopes realized.

I was never in a hurry to get here, but now that we have made it, I feel elated and happy and can't wait to leave the ship and see the new country. It is hard to believe that we have reached our goal! To leave this floating miniature prison that until recently I had not considered as such, is wonderful. It is difficult to believe in the beauty of things when despite the wish to forget hard times, one still is weighed down by events of the recent past.

The deck of our little freighter, that has carried us for thousands of kilometers, resembles an aroused ant colony. People rush back and forth across deck trying to find an opening behind the wall of gawkers pressed against the ship's rail. They want to have a glimpse of the city whose houses cover half a mountainside. Haifa and Mount Carmel. On top of this mountain is a building (Stella Maris, a Carmelite monastery and hospice) that looks like a fortress. It has a commanding view of the entrance to the bay and the Mediterranean.

Several miles inside the entrance of the bay and north of Haifa I see an oil refinery. It brings to my mind the front page of the *Kronen-Zeitung*, the Vienna newspaper that showed an aerial view of that refinery smoking after – so they had claimed – an aerial attack by Italian planes. Everything seemed peaceful and undamaged.

Near the north end of that gulf of blue water I see the skyline of another city.

It looks almost as unreal as a Hollywood movie set for an Arabian fairy tale. It is Akko (Acre). Its dark buildings, mosque domes, and minarets are in stark contrast to the light colored houses of Haifa. It seems beyond comprehension that I am on another continent, will mingle with people who have different customs and are dressed differently. It is Arabs that I am thinking of. From now on I will have to fend for myself. A somewhat disconcerting feeling.

At the time I had not even considered the fact that I knew none of the three languages (English, Hebrew, and Arabic) spoken here. Being aware of it certainly would have increased my discomfort. For the next few months, however, I didn't have to worry.

To our indignation the Pacific reduced speed and eventually came to a full stop. We had expected to be taken straight to the enticing warehouses and buildings lining the distant waterfront. Like parched wanderers in the desert, we saw in Haifa our long sought oasis.

The seasoned captain of our ship was more familiar with procedures. In a short time a motor boat flying a yellow flag at its bow raced toward us: health and quarantine inspectors. In its wake followed another boat with uniformed men; they were Palestine Police, men of British origin and some native policemen. The latter wore furry headgear similar to that of Russian Cossacks. Everything looked exotic, unreal, and dreamlike.

Just before the police appeared, our leaders collected everyone's passport. It was the last we saw of our documents. That foolish attempt to conceal our identity availed nothing. We had nothing to hide, and when interrogated, everyone volunteered his particulars without reserve.

In the wake of the police, food arrived. It was a welcome change from our monotonous diet. White bread tasting like cake, fresh meat, not seen for so long and, best of all, an abundance of drinking water, in short supply during most of our journey. *Chalva,* a mixture of honey and nuts, a delicacy from the stories of the Arabian Nights, was distributed twice daily, a spoonful each time. One could not be happier in heaven than we were on our flimsy boat. *Schlaraffenland* (Land of Cockaigne).

A period of quiet followed. The nearness of the coast gave us a sense of security and freedom. This self-deception was succeeded by a creeping anxiety about the state of affairs, as our situation remained unresolved. Rumors of liberty after quarantine seemed less plausible with each passing day. Yet the majority of us clutched at straws. What could the British government do with this ragged lot of homeless tramps but let us land? We couldn't very well be sent back to Germany. In one short year the war had become a disaster for the Allies. Western Europe and Scandinavia had been lost to the Nazis, the British Isles were at the mercy of the Luftwaffe, and the Italians were 70 miles into Egypt where they had captured Sidi Barani in September of 1940, the month we had left Vienna. For all we knew when we set out on our journey, the Italians could have reached Palestine before us. Axis submarines infested the all-important shipping lanes of the Atlantic Ocean and Mediterranean Sea. The government in London, we surmised, surely had more pressing affairs to attend to than the matter of immigrants who had reached their Promised Land.

Then came the order for women and children to pack their belongings and get ready to be moved. For a brief moment this seemed to promise freedom. It did not. Women and children were not taken to the nearest pier but rather transferred to a big, gray ship called, Patria. The vessel was moored near the end of the breakwater and was far from the port's facilities.

In subsequent days men in groups of 20 were ferried to the same craft. After two days of transfers our boat resembled a battlefield. Broken glasses, lumpy mattresses, discarded clothing, pieces of wood that had escaped the fires of the ship's boiler, lay helter-skelter beside empty sardine and diverse other cans, bread and zwieback leftovers, papers, cardboard boxes, and objects I had never imagined to have been on board. Yet, in spite of the chaotic surroundings we who had not transferred yet had no complaints. The fewer we were on the Pacific, the more food we had to eat. We lived a life of gluttony, and had only part of this abundance been available to us during our trip, it would have been like meals on an ocean liner, without the liner's extravagant services to be sure.

On November 6 we experienced our first air-raid alarm, to be followed by many more. Being on a ship with nowhere to hide, we felt very exposed. Luckily, no German or Italian planes reached Haifa at that time.

The Sabotage and Sinking of the SS Patria

On November 8, 1940, my sixty-sixth day at sea, I too was moved to the Patria.

The British had seized the Patria, a 12,000-ton French steamer, after France's surrender to the Germans. The ship appeared to have been a cargo vessel that had been partly converted to a troop carrier. She seemed massive, and everyone boarding her was impressed. Having been previously on a riverboat and the small and often unsteady SS Pacific, this new ship seemed as solid under my feet as good old *terra firma*. Walking fast I could have moved from bow to stern on the SS Pacific in about a minute; on the other hand the corridors of the Patria seemed without end. There were several decks, but our movements were restricted to only a few sections of the vessel.

We showered for the first time in almost three months, and our luggage was disinfected. After being vaccinated, inoculated, fingerprinted, and interrogated, we were assigned iron bunk beds in one of the ship's huge holds.

About that time the Milos, our smallest vessel, was led into the bay by a British Navy craft. Her passengers, too, were transferred to the Patria, and now only the Atlantic was missing.

When more days passed without official statements about our fate, an increased number of people voiced fears that the British government had no intention of putting us ashore. Others called them *Miesmacher,* (defeatists). Yet the transfer of people to the Patria made sense to the believers in British magnanimity, and the Patria's size certainly afforded us more humane accommodations until we could find a permanent place.

And yet the prevailing uncertainty was made for elation or depression depending on the latest grapevine story. After a while I gave up listening to rumors and depended more on my usual belief that things would turn out all right. The negative assessment of the others, however, had roots in reality. British policy in the Middle East adhered rigidly to the infamous "White Paper" restricting Jewish immigration to Palestine. London's uncompromising attitude precluded a favorable solution, as nobody at Whitehall seemed concerned in the least about our plight.

Rumors flew when on November 15 a large contingent of Arabs and black Africans came on board our ship to supplement the British crew. An uninterrupted chain of men loaded great quantities of sacks of coal and they looked like hunchbacks under their burden as they walked, in a stooped way, over the gangplank. They disappeared through an opening in the lower part of the ship's side. Provisions needed for a lengthy ocean voyage were brought aboard in boxes and crates. These unmistakable preparations for departure ended the wishful thinking of even our diehard optimists. The rumor described our future, and it sounded like the sentencing of a criminal in a medieval court of law. We were to be taken to the British colony of Mauritius, an island in the Indian Ocean, and interned there for the duration of the war, whose length and outcome nobody could predict.

By that time my priorities had shifted again. The possible extension of our journey sounded like a new adventure. Suez Canal, Red Sea, Indian Ocean! For a 17-year-old Viennese youngster those were places to get excited about. But I may have been the only one among our voyagers who felt that way. People on the Patria, and especially those with relatives in Palestine, became unruly. To prevent disturbances or quell uprisings an increased number of Palestine Police were brought aboard.

Trouble was really on the rise in Jewish parts of Palestine, and I noted in my diary:

November 20, 1940. In opposition to the British plan to deport us, hunger and work strikes are being organized throughout the Jewish community of Palestine. All Jewish men on our vessel follow suit and refuse food. Young men and women try to escape from our boat, but most are caught.

November 24, 1940. The Atlantic, the last of our sister ships, reaches Haifa. Though the Patria's boilers now under steam for two days confirm our impending departure, the arrival of the Atlantic changes the British plan. Our journey is temporarily postponed, and for now we remain in the safe waters of the harbor.

November 25. British authorities began to transfer people from the Atlantic to the Patria. The morning started no different than any other morning, it only appeared to have brought us closer to our departure. Immediately after breakfast I left the ship's hold, intending to catch up on my neglected diary entries. I usually did this in a room on the steerage deck. Its gray steel walls had several square portholes that let in enough sunlight to make the drab place quite pleasant. The room had several long tables and benches for people who wanted to read, write, play chess or cards. It was a haven of peace and quiet in otherwise noisy surroundings, respected even by those noted for their passionate debates and fervent outbursts. At this moment, however, the place was a noisy forum for angry arguments.

'What is our stand going to be?' – 'Nobody asks our opinion.' – 'We shall make ourselves heard.' – 'Who is going to listen?' – 'We shall show them.' – Impotent ravings fueled by frustration.

I listened for a while and then turned to my diary. I tried to concentrate, but the paper in front of me remained blank. I could not shut out the noise and diversions and eventually gave up the intention to write. Annoyed I returned to the ship's hold.

Here it was worse.

With the arrival of the first two hundred refugees from the Atlantic, the British moved people from the places to which they had been assigned earlier. Intending to settle the remaining 1,800 refugees of the Atlantic on the Patria as well, the sizable bunker near the bow of the Patria, spacious and comfortable until then, became crowded. The floor began to fill up with more baskets, bundles, and suitcases. In the midst of this bustle a lone British policeman, his rifle at port arms, unsuccessfully tried to bring order into this chaos. He shouted orders in English that nobody understood, and he looked like Don Quixote fighting the windmills. Rescuing my belongings from this pell-mell situation by moving them away from the stairs and deeper into the hold, I wondered where all this was going to lead to. It truly led to something.

The muffled sound of a distant explosion jarred the ship. It felt as if a short, but violent earthquake had shaken the Patria. The hold, resounding up to then with the growling, fighting and cursing, froze into silence. During the few seconds of calm, theories about what might have taken place shot through my head. A bomb from an enemy plane? A seaquake? A boiler explosion? Whatever it was it set in motion events that began to move rapidly toward a disastrous climax.

Though nobody knew what had happened, people around me exploded into pandemonium. They fled in haste storming the two staircases leading to the upper decks. I too was shaken, but also too naive

160

to grasp the seriousness of the disaster whose extent no one could even remotely imagine.

I retraced my steps from the depths of the hold until I stood directly under the cargo opening and looked up. Several stories above me I saw the thick, tall mast of the Patria standing straight and undamaged, and the square of blue sky gazing down at me was its old sunny self. About to turn away I became aware that I was not standing straight. My left leg was stretched slightly and the right one bent at the knee. The big ship had listed to one side.

This discovery changed the situation. I still saw no reason to panic like the others, but went to my belongings in the forward part of the bunker to pick up a few things. I slipped into the jacket that held my pride, the Waterman fountain pen, a gift from my parents. From the suitcase I took my stamp collection, an envelope holding snapshots from home, documents, travel notes, and the German ration cards I wanted as souvenirs. I placed these items next to the rubber bag of toiletries in the small valise. I also stashed one of my little adventure booklets into the back pocket of the shorts I wore just in case I found time to read. The title of the novelette I had so carelessly grabbed was *Die letzte Fahrt* (the last voyage), the story of a cutter that sank.

All this took only two or three minutes. As I carefully ascended the stairs, the roar of many voices above me grew louder. To judge by the clamor, most everybody had fled upstairs. The ship was listing some more, and I steadied myself by holding onto the railing.

Insanity dominated the scene. People were pushing madly, cursing, and shouting in frustration: "Fritzi, where are you?" "Ernstl..." High-pitched calls of mothers broke through the roaring sound of mass hysteria, but there were no replies. Appeals to people rushing by: "Please, have you seen...?" stopped the addressed person for less than a second before he stormed on with a blank stare on his face, unaware of what had been wanted of him.

Children, lost and terrorized, called in heartbreaking voices for their parents. But most of the people on the Patria had turned a deaf ear to requests, questions and pleas. They were too busy with their own fear and their effort to escape the approaching disaster.

The stairs I had climbed ended on the gangway. I had really no idea what direction to take though I understood by then that time was of the essence and not too much of it was left for reflection. Not fond of heights, I wanted to get to the part of the Patria closest to the water. But a loose cordon of two British policemen and some of our young security fellows were blocking off this section.

Their action at first seemed senseless but later I learned that scores of those who had taken this apparent short cut to salvation were struck

161

and killed by wooden and metal objects that slid off the large decks and struck swimmers in the water.

I saw a man with two clubfeet cling to a rail with his right hand, his left arm stretched out imploringly toward people rushing by. "Help me. Please, help me. Oh God, help," he shrieked. His shrill, piercing voice revealed his fear of death.

While these events were developing like a bad dream, I remembered a movie matinee I had gone to as a kid in Vienna. The film depicted the sinking of the Titanic. Toward the end of the show, when on the badly listing ship furniture began to slide and panic-stricken people filled the screen, I got so scared that I left the dark theater to seek security and reassurance in the sunshine outside.

Now, looking at that excited anthill of humanity, I felt detached as if I had nothing to do with that crawling, screaming, and fighting mass. Some women ran about with hair disheveled, eyes wide open with fear, and half clad. But I could not run away as I had from the film. I was forced to watch the disaster unfold. And yet, though the world around me had gone mad, I never feared for my life. That preposterous attitude had nothing to do with heroism. It was mostly my misjudgment of a serious situation. It just never entered my mind that I might die during the next few seconds or minutes. I did not even think that other people would lose their lives. If most people were overreacting, I underreacted. Their irate behavior, considering the circumstances, may have been more rational than mine was. *Rette sich wer kann* (save yourself) was the order of the moment.

I entered the room where a short while before, I had tried to update my travel notes. Here too all hell had broken loose. The room, about 12 feet wide and twice as long, swarmed with people. A few wore swim vests, most did not. All were struggling to reach the few relatively large, square portholes that led to the outside of the ship. Bunched together like grapes on a vine, writhing bodies overflowed from the windows a few feet into the room. This seemingly solid mass, however, changed swiftly into different patterns as people pushed, elbowed, and separated the clusters of bodies in front of them to reach the openings behind which they hoped to find salvation from the nightmare. Then I observed a strange thing. Not all that reached the desired spot moved on to the outside. Many froze at the window, refusing to budge one way or another. The pressure behind them built up to the point where they quickly had to choose between jumping or returning to the presumptive safety of the room. Forced to act, some disappeared to the outside, others, unable to keep their position at the porthole any longer, forced their way back into the room.

Standing a few feet away from that mob, I wondered what made the people hesitate at the exit. Clutching my little valise, I fought my way to the window. When I arrived, and looked down the ship's side to the water below, I understood my predecessors' reluctance to climb out. This was the elevated part of the Patria and it was a long drop to the water. I decided that I was neither experienced enough nor sufficiently crazy to make what seemed to me a break-neck leap.

Another reason for my hesitation was the big expanse of harbor on which there were no boats coming toward our ship to pick up swimmers. As I later heard, assistance came late (although only in terms of minutes) because would-be rescuers were afraid the big boilers of the Patria, under steam now for two days, might explode when hit by the cold water of the bay entering through her funnels.

I worked myself back into the room, and it was then that I became aware of a drawn-out shriek. Its high-pitched crescendo rose above the din created by the people milling around in confusion. Then I realized that the scream that had startled me came from my friend Bunjo. A nightmarish panic had taken hold of him. At his side of the room, a narrow pipe came through the ceiling and exited through the floor. Bunjo clutched that slender pole in desperation, his eyes bulged, and his throat was emitting that piercing sound. For a moment I stared at him in disbelief, for he seemed out of control. I placed my valise on the table next to me, and, keeping my body in a slant to adjust to the listing of the Patria, carefully walked over to my friend. "Bunjo," I called, shaking him by the shoulders. "Bunjo." For a moment his blank stare fixed on my face, but he failed to recognize me and continued to scream.

Suddenly I felt crazy myself and for a moment had to fight off the desire to laugh at this grotesquely distorted face. His eyes seemed to pop out of their sockets, and in the wide open mouth I saw the uvula in his throat vibrate in the stream of air escaping his lungs. Pointlessly I wondered how he could hold that scream for so long without inhaling. Suddenly he stopped, took a deep breath, and the penetrating sound returned. He was completely traumatized.

Not knowing what to do about him, I returned to the table and my valise. By that time it had become obvious to me that my little valise was a luxury I could not afford to take with me. I had never jumped off a swimming pool tower, nor was I a terrific swimmer. I could swim, but that was all. When tables and benches began to slide and were stopped only by the gray wall of the room, I decided the time had come for me to take the plunge. From then on I moved fast. Taking the rubber bag from the valise and emptying its contents on the table, I replaced the discarded items with documents, the envelope with the snapshots of home, and the ration cards. I ripped written pages from my diary and, losing part of them in my haste, added the rest to the papers in the little sack. Pulling the string of the bag tight, I stuffed it down the front of my shirt. With pain in my heart I left the valise containing my stamp collection on the table and started anew for the window.

Just as ungraciously as the others I threw myself into the melee of bodies and struggled toward the window. At the porthole again, I squeezed past persons hanging onto the frame, still undecided, but mostly in fear of jumping. I was in the center of the opening, and the people behind me who thought they had more resolve than I pushed forward. For one short moment I was permitted a glance at an incredible sight. Some people were dangling from ropes thrown over the rail above us; others, having crawled through other openings, clung to the ship's side like starfish. The water around the Patria was dotted with heads of swimmers and a few rafts floated about. I felt greatly relieved when I recognized a multitude of different-sized boats, British and non-British, racing from the wharf toward the crippled ship.

I clung to the porthole only for seconds. Then, facing the water, I released my grip expecting to fall. The Patria had listed to a degree that prevented a free drop, but her side was too steep to permit a slow slide down her hull. The moment I let go of the window my body rushed downward at ever-increasing speed. The trip over the ship's side normally above the water line was like riding a rasp file. I lost the seat of my shorts, parts of my underpants, and a bit of skin. The short section of the hull that had been below sea level, but was now exposed to air because of the tilt, was covered by a thick, slimy layer of sea vegetation. It afforded a smoother ride. While shooting down that last part of that steep incline, I noticed a multitude of small sea creatures clinging to the greenery, among them little crabs running about. The force of the descent took me deep below the water's surface and moments later my woolen jacket had absorbed many times its weight in water and created a deadly pull.

No doubt I made several mistakes during the entire episode. The most foolish one was the refusal to shed my jacket with the fountain pen. Today my behavior is difficult to understand. At the time, however, I was aware that I had lost everything of material value and because of this it made sense to me to hold onto my jacket and pen.

Struggling to rise to the top I vigorously treaded water and after a long while returned to the surface. I inhaled deeply and then looked for the nearest boat. I spied the small British water-tanker that had supplied the Patria with drinking water and swam toward it. The boat had come to help, yet for some reason, had stopped quite a distance from our ill-fated vessel. I passed a raft where people helped other swimmers aboard but stuck to my intended goal.

When my woolen knee socks and canvas shoes slowed me down, I stopped swimming and discarded them. While ridding myself of the footwear I looked back toward the Patria. By then she was listing to an alarming degree. People were still climbing out of openings; some ran irresolutely back and forth over the side of the ship's hull that had become an almost level surface, while others slid down to the water. Nobody knew where the giant steel body would come to rest.

On the heavy cables tying the ship to the breakwater rows of people tried to swing themselves hand over hand toward the rocky strip of the mole. From a distance they looked like herring on a string hung out to dry. Some of them, losing their strength, let go of the cable, and plunged into the water.

At the water-tanker a short section of rail had been removed and on a rope ladder thrown over its side, swimmers were climbing aboard. While awaiting my turn, I treaded water to keep afloat. I finally clutched the bottom rung of the ladder and tried to lift myself up, but I lacked the strength to do it. The water-soaked jacket weighed me down, a condition that could have been easily corrected by shedding the garment. Foolishly I refused to abandon it. After a few unsuccessful attempts to climb the ladder, and impatient calls from the bobbing heads around me, I felt so frustrated that with one last great effort I finally succeeded in grabbing hold of the next rung and a moment later climbed aboard. I felt no gratitude for having been saved and accepted it as a natural development in the succession of events. I was unaware, of course, that I had escaped circumstances in which more than 200 of the Patria's 2,000 people had perished in 15 minutes.

I had seen many shocking incidents in my life, but none had disturbed me as much as the one I saw here. Not far from the tanker a naked baby was floating on its back. It was less than a year old. The head, legs, and little arms were below the surface, and only the bloated belly stuck out above the water. Eyes and mouth were open, but the body was not moving. Help seemed too late, but when I wanted to turn away, I saw air bubbles escaping the child's mouth. A dark-skinned sailor aboard our tanker had seen it too and before a moment had passed, he was overboard. Reaching the baby he lifted it with one arm into the air and then swam to a nearby raft where he placed the infant. The incident is as vivid in my mind as the man dying in my arms on the parade ground in Buchenwald. I do not know what happened to the baby afterwards.

Many had found refuge on the tanker, and more were climbing aboard by the minute. The feelings of the survivors were easily discernible. Some were zombie-like, starring at nothing. Others, squatting down, their backs against the wheelhouse, kept their woes to themselves or uttered them in tearful laments. Many bent over the ship's railing, desperately searching for persons close to them among the heads in the

165

water. They yelled names into the bay at the top of their lungs.

The Patria capsized, but a small part of her remained above water. This saved people who could not swim and who were eventually picked off the hull. Swimmers lost their lives, and non-swimmers survived. Pure chance often determined survival or death. The crippled man with the clubfeet, my friend Bunjo and others remained in the part of the vessel that stayed dry as did the room where I had left my stamp collection. Nevertheless, I never saw my stamps again.

Years later I met the one-armed invalid who had shared our taxi in Vienna. I reminded him of our cab ride and asked about his wife. She had drowned on the Patria. A young woman from Vienna who used to compete in swim contests died in the water. A motorboat, streaking toward the Patria, ran over her, and its propeller cut open her abdomen.

With a load of survivors aboard, the crowded tanker finally steamed toward the pier. What an incredible feeling it was to step onto firm ground again after almost three months of seafaring! We were taken to a warehouse where in the shortest time bundles of used clothing and big boxes of second-hand shoes arrived. An emergency call for the needed items had gone out to the Jewish population of Haifa, and the response was immediate. The rescued people were in various stages of undress, and I too hunted for a pair of pants to exchange them with my torn shorts. To complete my wardrobe I picked a pair of shoes that fitted me tolerably well. When shoe pairs were held together by shoestrings, the picking was easy; had they been thrown into the boxes loose at the last minute, searching for a matching mate could prove frustrating.

Indifferent or unaware of their exposed bodies, some survivors still ran about half-naked. They were either in a daze or so absorbed in finding loved ones that nothing else mattered. Tears of joy flowed freely when family members found each other. Though it was too early to know the fate of those not present, searchers were weeping in anguish. The repeated question asked of newcomers was: "Have you seen... ?" More and more survivors came through the gate of the warehouse, which reverberated with the outcries of happiness of those who had found each other. Long lines formed to receive hot tea and sandwiches The sick and injured were taken in ambulances to hospitals; the survivors were counted. In the afternoon busses began to take people away; my turn came after nightfall. To prevent escapes or an attack on the busses to free the prisoners, British military vehicles escorted us.

I saw little of Haifa and after a few minutes the city was behind us. The road described a 90-degree turn, and now led south. To the left hovered the black hump of Mount Carmel, on our right the star-filled sky and the dark Mediterranean Sea merged into one. The highway led away from the water but continued its course parallel to the sea. After half an hour of travel we turned west on a narrow road lined by tall, slim palm trees. The trip ended after a short ride. We had arrived at our destination: Clearance camp. But why not call it by its real name: The Atlit Detention Camp.

Imprisoned in the Promised Land

The busses stopped near a gate. On both sides of it a low barbed wire fence disappeared into the darkness. Behind that barrier, and before one reached the tall fence surrounding the camp, lay offices and lodgings of the British camp commander and some of his underlings as well as the living quarters of the guards and storage facilities. We were issued three blankets, a small pillow, knife, fork, spoon, and plate, and then taken in small groups to one of the many wooden huts inside a high, wire stockade. Small steel watch towers and poles with electric lights overlooked the enclosure that was patrolled by native policemen, called gafirs. Those guards on patrol wore the Cossack-type headgear and shouldered rifles. It seemed an ironical twist of fate that all of the sentries were Jews. The camp consisted of two sections, separated from each other by a passageway. The left part was for men, the right for women. Small children stayed with their mothers.

Inside each hut two rows of beds, standing side by side, lined the long walls. I deposited my things on one of the beds and sat down to rest. I contemplated my situation. Except for the old pair of pants I wore, the shoes picked up at the warehouse, and the jacket and fountain pen I had saved from the Patria, I had nothing to my name.

Actually, that was not true. I had survived another calamity and saved my life. Surely an irreplaceable item. Aside from that, I had salvaged the unpretentious rubber bag that held most of what I deemed important. The river of my life continued its flow as if nothing of consequence had happened. And I just had to stay afloat to see where it would take me, a prisoner in Vienna, in Buchenwald, and even on the ships with their restricted space, my incarceration here was just more of the same. Somewhat relieved, though not without sarcasm, I consoled myself that at least I would be suffering no great hardship and would be fed as well. Although I wondered how long my confinement in Atlit was going last.

I spread my blankets on the bed, stripped down to my torn underwear and lay down with my eyes closed. I was concerned about Bunjo unaware that he had been saved. People around me chatted about the events of the day, but most were too tired for conversations. Before falling asleep I became aware of an eerie quiet in the room, nobody was

167

talking anymore. The silence, after the tumult of the day, was deafening. A short time later I too was asleep.

Leaders of the Hagana, the Jewish defense underground, had planned the sabotage of the Patria. The reason was, so it was said, that international law forbade the deportation of shipwrecked persons. Members of the underground, disguised as Arabs, were among the men carrying sacks of coal onto the ship, and hidden in a sack or sacks was TNT. The explosives placed against the ship's hull were to blow a hole in the Patria, a hole too big to plug, yet small enough to make her sink slowly. The scheme miscarried. The saboteurs were apparently not skilled enough to do the job right and misjudged the power of the explosives. Our ship capsized in a short time.

At the time the Patria was capsizing, my grandmother in New York was in a hospital. When I met my cousin Leo years later in New York, he told me a story fit for Rod Serling's Twilight Zone.

On that day after work he visited her in the hospital and she told him frightened: "Gustl is in great danger. He is on a ship that is sinking." Leo wanted to know who had told her a crazy story like that, but she insisted she had not heard it from anybody. She just knew. None of my family in Vienna or New York could have heard of a ship called Patria or could have known that I was aboard. No newspaper could have reported the sinking of our ship that soon or found it important enough to do so in the middle of the war. And anyway, grandma could not read, write or speak English. How *did* she know? Telepathy halfway around the world? It is puzzling, but to quote Shakespeare: "There are more things in heaven and earth, Horatio, than are dreamt of in your philosophy."

Services were held for the people who had died, but the Jewish population could do nothing more to help the survivors. For weeks personal belongings removed from the Patria arrived in camp. Sometimes dry, when the items where picked up from the part that stayed above the water line, but mostly wet and moldy when they were fished floating up from inside the ship. Articles were laid out on the sandy ground or hung onto the barbed wire fence inside the camp for people to inspect. I found none of my belongings. Of all the things lost I missed my stamp collection most. A lot of my devotion and time had gone into that book filled with thousands of stamps, and it hurt to think that somebody must have found and kept the album. The room in which I had left it had remained above water.

To supplement my wardrobe, I reluctantly picked clothing sent to us as donations. I never had worn second-hand clothes before.

I searched for Bunjo and was very happy to find him alive. In

168

accordance with his religious upbringing he had moved into the hut of the orthodox people. He persuaded me to move in with them. Reluctantly, and not at all certain how I would adjust to their way of life and conform to their practices and restrictions, I agreed to try. I joined them in morning and evening prayers, the Saturday services and, for the first time in my life, learned how to put on "tvillim."[17]

The barracks also served as synagogue and had a primitive holy arch for a Torah. Worshipers came from other huts to attend services and because there was so little room, they stood between our beds.

The rabbi and several men of our hut oversaw the ritual fitness (kosher) of the camp kitchen.

People from the Atlantic who had not transferred to the Patria before her sinking were also brought to Atlit. Their stay was short.

In the evening of December 7 the camp inmates were instructed that, by order of the British camp commander, everybody was confined to barracks until further notice.

At 5 A.M. the following morning, it was still dark, I was awakened by shouts and recalling Buchenwald I jumped off my bed in alarm and stared into the gloom. Reality quickly returned, and we knew that the people of the Atlantic were in trouble. Stealthily looking through a slightly opened door, we saw a number of soldiers moving about. When they went into the barracks of the Atlantic people, shouts and screams followed, and then the soldiers came out again. This went on for a two hours. For a while we thought things would be all right, and the soldiers would be ordered to leave once it became clear that they could not move the people. But we were wrong. Hoping to discourage the soldiers from moving them, the men from the Atlantic had stripped naked. It did not work. As daylight broke, the soldiers returned and began carrying the naked and struggling men away, four soldiers to a man. Some of these inmates were covered by blankets that in the melee often slipped off their bodies. But their desperate resistance was futile. The fight was unequal, and the end predictable. None of our people tried to interfere. We were still afraid of men in uniforms. Then it was over. The people of the Atlantic were no longer residents of Atlit, but seafarers again on their way to the island of Mauritius.

Atlit had already prisoners when we arrived. They were people from Bulgaria who had come to Palestine several months earlier and on a boat like ours. Once captured, they were interned here. Why no attempt was

---

[17] The pair of black leather phylacteries (small square leather boxes containing slips inscribed with scriptural passages), which are bound to forehead and left arm for morning prayers during weekdays.

made by the British to send them to some distant shore, I never found out. Perhaps the few hundred of them did not warrant the bother. Months later, released from camp, I saw their ramshackle ship "*Libertad*" (freedom), rotting in the southern corner of Haifa harbor.

At my first chance I sent a Red Cross letter dated, December 18, 194, to my parents and sister in Vienna. It was the only permissible way to communicate with people in enemy countries. Their answer had to be written on the backside of the same Red Cross stationary, which was then returned to the sender. One was permitted only a personal message of up to 25 words. I wrote in German: "*Liebste Eltern und Schwester! Bin glücklich und gesund hier angekommen. Hoffe, dass auch Ihr gesund seid. Herzliche Grüsse und Küsse. Euer Sohn Gustl.*" (Dearest parents and sister. Arrived well and happy. Hope that you are well too. Kindest regards and kisses, your son Gustl.)

Almost four months later, on March 6, 1941, their cable-style answer of 25 words reached me in Atlit. They were well and extremely happy with my letter. They advised me to write to grandma in New York who wanted to send me money. Money was later sent from New York, but it never reached me.

Of the few letters going back and forth between my family and me, two are still in my possession. The very first one, mentioned above, and the last one mailed by me on January 17, 1942 to Jägerstrasse in Vienna. Their answer was dated June 12, 1942.

Life in Atlit was like that of a small town. Although the camp was cut off from the outside world by barbed wire and guards, life inside was almost normal. A few inmates received financial help from relatives outside the compound, but for most, money was scarce. Business was transacted using services or personal item for payment. Professionals and tradespeople exercised their skills, and some entrepreneurs managed to obtain small stoves to bake cookies and cakes for sale. People somehow found ways to acquire the materials needed for their ventures, and a canteen catered to those who could afford to pay. A library lent books free of charge, the several hundred volumes, mostly in German, having been donated by the Jewish community of Palestine.

On one occasion I received a gift from an outside source. I remembered that my father had a second cousin living in Haifa. I don't recall how I got in touch with him, but one day I was informed that one of the *gafirs* (native policeman or guard), walking the beat along the camp's perimeter wanted to see me. My informant pointed out the man to me and left. Because it was forbidden for guards to talk to us and vice versa, I strolled along the fence on my side, in step with him. He asked me if I was Gustav Pimselstein, and when I said yes, he said he had regards from Mr. Pimsler and something else for me. With an inconspicuous flip of his hand he tossed a five-piaster coin my way.

That was the first and last time I heard from Mr. Pimsler while in Atlit. Later I visited the man perhaps three times, but when no special relationship developed, I stopped calling on him.

An empty lot inside the camp was turned into a soccer field but was later taken away because the British camp command wanted to build more prison huts. Conditions, were not bad as prisons go. Still, the question of our release was on everybody's mind. To protest our detention, a large group of men grew beards. The British showed little concern, so the men removed them.

In some way married couples suffered more than others. For only one or two hours around midday were men and women permitted to mingle. Frustrated by the lack of privacy, some husbands had sexual relations with their wives in huts while other people were present. People ignored the blanket-covered movements on beds.

Callers came and we could talk to them through the double barbed wire fences near the camp's entrance. I wrote a postcard to Erich, my friend from Vienna, and he came from his kibbutz to visit me. He had changed his first name to the Hebrew Eli (pronounced Ely), a common name at the time, meaning: my God. He suggested that I join his kibbutz after my release, but the opposite happened. Erich (I never got used to calling him Eli) eventually joined me in Haifa.

The fateful year 1940 came to an end, rains came, and people stayed inside the barracks. The hard baked earth turned to mud, and the abundance of water created rivers and rivulets in the muck between the buildings. We were restricted to quarters, not by order of the camp commander, but by the foul weather. To break the monotony of rainy days, people read, wrote letters, played cards or chess. In our hut, the only game played was chess.

On Friday nights after prayers the rabbi sat at the center of the table, discussing local and general affairs. He touched on controversies characteristic of Jewish life in Palestine. One problem the rabbi brought up I never forgot. Should there be Hebrew newspapers? The rabbi was against it. "Hebrew," he said, stroking his beard in familiar fashion, "Hebrew is the language of the Torah and our prayer books. This in itself may not make it wrong to use it in a newspaper, but the word adon[18] appears on those papers, and this is unacceptable. Outdated newspapers are used for

---

[18] The Hebrew word "adon" means mister, master and because a Jew is forbidden to say the word God, it is one of several words used in its place.

171

wrapping and worse things.[19]" His face showed disgust as he mimicked spitting out twice. His followers murmured agreement.

I had questions concerning our religion or rather its history. I dared not ask the rabbi or any other men in our hut, so I asked Bunjo. "If Adam and Eve had several sons, how did things continue when Eve was the only female in the world?" For a moment my friend was stunned, then he admonished me: "If you believe, you don't question."

Bunjo and I talked a lot about our dream of meeting our families in the U.S.A. once this nightmare was over. And yet, as fervent as our hopes may have been, we were aware that the chances of this happening soon were remote.

To pass the time and make a little money, I bought a needle and a spool of white thread at the canteen to sew and bind together prayer books that had come back from the Patria in pieces. The payment was three to five mills for each of the repaired volumes, depending on its size. As the Palestine pound equaled 1,000 mills or 100 piasters, I would have had to repair between 200 and 333 prayer books to earn one pound. I never even came close to the astronomical value of that bank note. The rabbi made the payments. Since I had no expenses and did not buy anything I hoped that the money earned would come in handy after my release.

The rabbi had come from Berlin. The corporal in charge of the camp guards was his son. At first it did seem odd to see this tall, soft-spoken man in uniform come to our hut and visit his father, with the permission of the camp commander, of course. We still felt uncomfortable with men in uniform, but after a while we regarded him with pride. This policeman was a Jew, and that made a world of difference.

Dr. Blan was a right-wing Zionist from Czechoslovakia. He had traveled extensively in the Middle East and other parts of the world before the Nazis took over his native country. He was fluent, it was said, in almost every European language and versed in several Arabic dialects as well. Dr. Blan gave talks about his travels and expanded on his political views. On those occasions the hut he lived in was filled to capacity with listeners, and I too enjoyed attending his lectures. He spoke in German. I remember Dr. Blan's pronouncement word for word: "The Jews have inalienable rights to Palestine because of historical facts and because they are conquering the land through work. Even Rousseau and Karl Marx said the land belongs to those who cultivate it. The Jews who came to Palestine found mostly deserts or swamps. The Jews bought arid

---

[19] At the time newspapers were still used for toilet paper.

172

land, cleared it of rocks and planted crops where only exhausted ground had been before. They bought swampland, dried it, and created fields. And that is a fact."

When the Italians retreated before the British in North Africa, the Germans sent the Afrika Korps under General Rommel to aid them. The German and Italian forces then advanced to Solum on the Egyptian border. German paratroops also captured Crete, which gave them air bases of relative safety. The eastern part of the Mediterranean Sea, Palestine, and Egypt were within easy reach of the Axis air forces.

On May 7, 1941 we were told to dig trenches. During the night of June 9 to 10 we or rather Haifa, fewer than ten miles to the north, experienced our first night attack. Again I took notes:

At half past midnight I was awakened by strong shaking. Distant thunder aroused me and it took only a moment to slip into my shorts, shoes and jacket and shoot out of the hut. Air raid. A full moon, intermittently obscured by scattered clouds, illuminated the countryside. Half the population of the camp was up, all staring toward Haifa. We could not see the city on the other side of Mount Carmel, but the sky above it was lit up by constant antiaircraft fire. Reddish-yellow blobs appeared, and the brilliant spots in the sky showed where the shells were bursting. Feeling chilly, and not just because of the cold night air, I pulled my jacket tighter around me. The dull hum of enemy planes sounded overhead, and I shuddered at the thought that Atlit, its barracks in perfect rows, might be mistaken for a military camp.

After one o'clock it became quiet. Relieved, I returned to bed but had hardly relaxed when the racket started anew. The dull explosions, the rolling thunder and the steady hum of the planes scared me. Again I jumped into my clothes and left the hut to watch the sky. This time the raid lasted one hour. I was almost asleep when the third group of aircraft arrived. After 4 o'clock in the morning we heard the planes for the last time. Still in doubt if it was over, I laid down at 4:45 with an uneasy feeling, but fell asleep.

On May 12 I saw the first enemy planes fly over Atlit in broad daylight. They flew toward Haifa, but at such a high altitude that I was unable to tell whether they were German or Italian. A short while later the antiaircraft batteries on Mount Carmel opened up. Planes and antiaircraft fire became less sensational as time progressed. Not because they were less frightening, but because they became more frequent.

In January 1941, British forces began their campaign against the Italians in East Africa. By May of that year Italy had lost Eritrea, Ethiopia and Italian Somali. In early June the British were victorious in

Iraq, which had been under German influence. Then with the help of their Allies (Free French, Australians, New Zealanders, and others, as well as Jewish scouts – Moshe Dayan lost his eye in the campaign) they invaded and captured Lebanon and Syria from the Vichy French. Lebanon's border is a scant 25 miles and Syria's 35 miles from Haifa. With all the bad tidings coming from Europe and North Africa, the victories in this part of the world so close to us were morale boosters.

Then came a wonderful surprise. The British started to release people of the Patria from Atlit. (The Libertad internees had been freed some months earlier.) My discharge from camp took place on June 18, 1941, after almost seven months of internment. Other Patria survivors remained prisoners for up to a year. I had just turned 18 and could look back to a full year of incarcerations. One month by the Gestapo in Vienna, more than four months in Buchenwald, and seven months in Atlit. Quite a record for a teenager whose only crime it was to have been born a Jew.

On My Own for the First Time

A bus took our group to a three-storied building in Bat Galim (how poetic a name: Daughter of the Waves), a suburb of Haifa. The building, called *Beit Olim* (House of Newcomers), was not much larger than a one-family house in the United States. Each room contained several beds, and I placed my little bundle of clothing on one of them. In a small building across the street we had lunch. For the limited time people were guests at the Beit Olim meals were served free of charge.

I had many wonderful moments in my life, moments when an extra shot of adrenaline rushed through my body, times when my stomach quivered with the anticipation of something thrilling to happen. In many of those instances I felt as if the outer shell of my being was torn apart by an explosion from within, exposing an inner self that strove to get out and participate in the expected excitement. Many times it was like that. But nothing reached the intensity of two occasions: passing the perimeter of death on my way out of Buchenwald, and stepping off the bus in Bat Galim after the long imprisonment in Atlit. Though they can not really be compared, the feeling of freedom was overwhelming in both cases. No more barriers of barbed wire or guards to restrict my movements, no door or fence to hold me back. The awareness that I could walk anywhere intensified freedom's sweetness. I now wanted to taste liberty, explore this new world, walk streets again, and Haifa was within reach.

Five teenagers, led by an adult, set out for the city. Though the main part of Bat Galim was behind us, there were still some houses on the left side of the road while to our right the area was uncultivated ground all the way to the highway. After half a mile the road turned 90 degrees, and we walked toward Mt. Carmel whose massive hump was about one third of a mile in front of us. We crossed the Haifa-Tel Aviv railroad tracks and came to Jaffa Road that also connects Haifa with Tel Aviv.

Meeting Arabs on the street here for the first time in my life was thrilling. Their presence in the adventure books I had read about North Africa and the Middle East had made them into exotic figures, an impression later contacts quickly dispelled.

For the moment they seemed strange men with somewhat different features and dusky skin. But what mostly made them appear strange to me was their dress. I recorded my impressions, albeit inexperienced, later on a sheet of papers that I added to those I had saved from the Patria.

Traditionally the Arab male wears a coat, called galabia, which reaches from his shoulders to his ankles. It is made of linen or, if he is wealthy, of silk. Most materials have dark, thin, vertical stripes.

An Arab in European clothes wears at least traditional headgear. The red fez with the black tassel is a left over from the Turkish Empire, the *kaffiye*, a vestige of their desert ancestry. The kaffiye, a big square of a usually white cotton fabric, is folded from one corner to the opposite one to create a triangle. It is placed on the head, so that the distant corners hang down on each side of the face and the third corner covers the neck. The kaffiye is held on the head by two rings of black cords.

The third kind of Arab dress, worn mostly by poor people, are baggy trousers of thin material that hang loosely around the lower body and are fastened tightly below the knees.

A short distance into Jaffa Road we were stopped by a man who said something to us in Hebrew. When we did not understand him and responded in German, he switched to Yiddish. Were we interested in making a little money? Of course we were. He pointed to a pick-up truck parked near the curb. The vehicle piled high with sacks of cement, had to be unloaded, and the bags taken to an empty room on the ground floor of the building next to us. We did not ask how much the pay was going to be because we had no idea what a fair wage would be. We trusted the man because he was Jewish. When the job was done, he thanked us and handed each of us a 50 mill (5-piaster) coin. Better than a fair wage for unskilled labor and for the time we had spent on the job. With the cement powder still on our faces and clothing we resumed our stroll.

After a while we decided to postpone our walk to the main Jewish section of Haifa, the Hadar Hacarmel. Not used to exertion, the job had tired us out, and ashamed of our dusty appearance, we returned elated and happy to Bat Galim. We had earned our first money in the new country.

On June 22, 1941 the Nazis invaded the U.S.S.R. which was, in a weird way, good news. We thought this would surely mean the end of Nazi Germany and the war. Russia, we believed, and we did not have to be Communists to think so, was the mightiest nation in the world.

What terrible disappointments were in store for the free world and us? During the next 16 months the scales of war continued to tip in favor of the Axis. Not until the fall of 1942 did the long awaited change in balance take place.

While still at the Beit Olim I spent my time roving through Bat Galim and the city of Haifa. I did not want to think of the moment when I would have to leave the House of Newcomers to make room for new arrivals. For now I wanted to enjoy life and not worry about the future; not even for the days just ahead. It may have been the wrong attitude, but having gone through such hard times, I became carefree when life turned easy.

When visiting the Hadar Hacarmel, or Hadar as it was called for short, I always walked. A bus ticket from Bat Galim to the German Colony at the foot of the mountain was half a piaster or 5 mills. A trip, all the way to the Hadar, cost one piaster. I walked because I liked walking and also to save money.

The Hadar, which is halfway up Mount Carmel, was thrilling. There were moments when life felt as unreal as a dream, and then there were times when the pulsating life of the streets overwhelmed and dizzied me. I had missed the hubbub of a city for so long, and Haifa certainly provided it. Though its buildings were modern, the city was altogether different from anything I had seen. Shouting newspaper boys on corners, cars, bicycles, buses, and a great variety of people. After my first few visits to the Hadar, however, I felt relieved when returning home to the peaceful Beit Olim. I had to get used to city life again.

In our neighborhood I walked a short boulevard from our street to the beach. At the end of that tree-lined avenue was a building, called Casino. It was not a site for gambling, but a café and nightclub. Having no money to spare, I never visited the place.

In the evening I strolled the boulevard to the beach road near the sea. To the right and diagonally across from the Casino was an outdoor café restaurant where music played over a loudspeaker system. I fell in love with one often-repeated tune, a hit at the time. Much later I found it to be "Over the Rainbow." But it was not the café I visit. My goal was a bench on an empty beach road where I would sit and stare over the dark waters of the Mediterranean. I looked in the direction of Vienna, and my thoughts traveled back to my family, so far away. I missed them terribly and almost wished I had never left them. Homesickness, a painful emotion, was always worst at night. Then the feeling passed and the hope that one day I would see my family again dispersed the gloom.

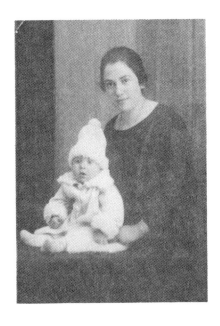

1923
With Mother

1930 Second Grade
Sitting 4th from left, 5th Otto, later Yakov

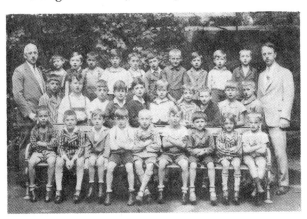

Mother, 1938

Father, 1938

My Sister Berta, later Betty
1942

Self, 1940

Grandma, 1938

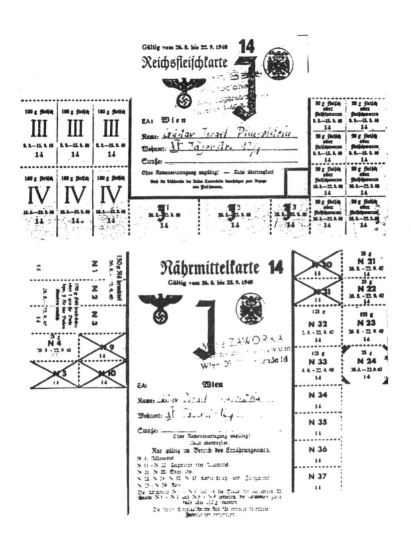

Ration Cards

179

SS Patria, 1940
The author thanks the National Maritime Museum, Greenwich,
London for permission to reproduce this picture.

With the British Army in
Alexandria, Egypt. 1942
Left to right: Schmulik,
Joshi, self and Fritz

Photo copy of the original British "WAR DAIRY"
The Author

MOST SECRET.

WAR DIARY.

28.11.40.
Thursday.

FOREIGN STATIONS.

Mediterranean. (Contd.)   **785**

Enemy Units. (Contd.)	3 Battleships. 5 Cruisers. Unknown number of destroyers. Unknown number of Merchant vessels Taranto. (Nore W/T 1205/28).

This was the last entry in a series of statement in the War Diary about the sabotage & sinking of the SS Patria, November 25, 1940.
The Author

	Following has been read. Addressed TRIUMPH from N.O.I.C. Malta. Air raid approaching +Malta. (Nore W/T 1329/28).
PATRIA **Sabotage.**	My 2130/25. Final muster indicated 254 refugees at present unaccounted for but believed that a certain number were smuggled from ambulances. Only 1 member of the crew missing and 1 British Police guard. (N.O.I.C. Haifa 1114/28).
Roumanian ships.	Suggestion again received Roumania State Line (S M R) anxious to sell Liners TRANSYLVANIA, BESSARABIA, and Motor Ships SULINA, BALCIC, CAVARNA all three new 3,600 Gross 14 knots. Possible to arrange for second transfer flag, or to work ships for British account under Panama Flag. If ships remain in Black Sea they will be certainly used by Germans. (N.A. Angora, 1225/28 to C.in C. Med.)
Potential A.M.C's.	Ref: telegram 1225 28/11 from naval Attache, alternatively it has been suggested that possible to induce S.M.R. sail the two which are suitable A.M.C. for Salonica on pretext of picking up refugees thus giving you an opportunity to seize them at sea. Should this line be pursued? (Wolffson 1226/28 to C.in C. Med.)
UPRIGHT.	Leave patrol as requisite arriving Malta dawn on 4/12. Route. (Capt: S., 1413/28 to UPRIGHT).

This is the last entry in a series of statements in the original British War Diary about the sinking of the SS Patria, November 25, 1940

Convoy, Spring 1949
3rd from left, standing

Regimental Training, Suez Canal
1944, 2nd from right

Israeli Army, 1949
Road to Red Sea, Arava, Southern
Negev: 2nd from right, standing

With the Israeli Army,
1949, Ma'ale Aqurabim
(Scorpion Hill) Negev

Israeli Army, 1949
Near Ras el Nageb, 1st left, standing

With IDECO rig rotary drilling in
Kibbutz Revivim, Negev, 1951/52

Engaged to Rina (Desi)
1952

Drilling in Ein Radian, Arava,
Southern Negev, 1950

Marriage, 1952

Tel Aviv, 1947

Rina, Clara, self and Shabtai in Colorado, 1964

In another of my early impressions I wrote:

Haifa is a modern city built at the foot and halfway up the slopes of Mount Carmel. In the lower part of the Haifa is the Arab section, the business district, created and managed mostly by Jews, and the German Colony that is now empty of Germans. They have been deported and interned. Half way up the mountain is the most modern part of the city, the Jewish section; Herzl Street is its main thoroughfare. On top of Mount Carmel other cities are beginning to take shape, Har Hacarmel and Achusa. A winding road climbs up to the peak where one can view a beautiful panorama. At the foot of the mountain is Haifa Bay, and beyond that the intensely blue Mediterranean Sea. The city of Acre can be seen at the northern end of the bay, and even Ras el Nakura, on the Palestine-Lebanese border is visible further north. Buses take care of most of the public transportation in the city as well as in the rest of the country, but there is also a train line all the way to Egypt. There are no streetcars to remind me of Vienna, but the innumerable coffeehouses, though different in appearance, are a fair substitute. Of the three movie theaters on the Hadar, the "Ora," the most modern one, burned down several months later. The movies shown are mostly American and English productions with French subtitles. But translations into Hebrew, Arabic, and German (German later discontinued), as well as several other languages, are projected onto spots on both sides of the screen. – – – –

Toward the end of June I was informed that my carefree life at the Beit Olim was to terminate July 1. It was a message I had been expecting all along, yet when it came, I felt anxious. I had been aware, of course, that my free ride was soon to end but had avoided thinking of the alternative. The country was still alien to me and I would have to face situations I had never confronted before. I had no skills, had learned no trade, spoke only German and some Yiddish, whereas the languages of the country where Hebrew, Arabic, and English. Worst of all, I felt lonelier than ever before. I seemed a solitary earthling who, after leaving the safety of his space ship, was to live among the beings of another planet. The thought that I could communicate with no one in an emergency was disquieting. I had never asked for a handout but had never been self-supporting either. Not while living with my parents or grandmother, in German prisons or on the trip to Palestine. Not as an internee in Atlit or the short stay in the House of Newcomers. I had always been fed (even if it had only been the starvation diet in the concentration camp) and been furnished a place to sleep, as on the hard planks in Buchenwald.

These apprehensions dissipated once I left the Beit Olim and found that life was not just black and white. The solutions came in the shape of a jovial man with a winning smile, a representative of the Jewish Agency. He appeared at the Beit Olim shortly after we were informed that we had to move. The man encouraged teenagers to join a kibbutz and talked to us in groups or, if prodding was necessary, individually. Even before the man had come and exerted his promotional skills, I had weighed the advantages of kibbutz life. I was to some extent still influenced by the meetings of the Zionist movement in Vienna. However, twice declining the offer in my hometown, I wondered if my attitude had changed that radically and I was now ready to take that road after all. It should be all right, I tried to convince myself. Half a day I would study or learn a trade, the other half I would work for the community. This program was the concept of Youth Aliyah.

Though I decided to join, I still felt reluctant to make my commitment to the man. In spite of all the positive aspects, I hesitated at the thought of spending my life in a kibbutz. Then, after more soul searching, I mastered my reluctance and told the smiling gentleman in German: "Ja, I'll join the Youth Aliyah."

His smile vanished. "Not Youth Aliyah. You are going to live and work in a kibbutz, and eventually become a member in good standing," he said in Yiddish. With all my good intentions, I had hardly been enthusiastic about my decision. His disclosure made the prospect even less attractive and I told him so. "You're 18 and therefore too old for Youth Aliyah," he explained.

We argued back and forth and finally, as if he had the power to force the issue, he stated: "We don't let young people like you go to the city." This clinched it for me. Instead of acquiescing to his "order," I rebelled, and exploded: "I am going to the city." And that is what I did.

Looking back after so many years and despite my reluctance at the time, I believe I would have become a good Kibbutznik had my wish to join the Youth Aliyah been granted. Whatever this man's reasons, his refusal to accept my request puzzles me to this day. Extraordinary situations overrule standard policies, and the survivors of the Patria certainly belonged in that exceptional category, I believed.

Three days before leaving the Beit Olim another representative of the Jewish Agency showed up. He handed each of those who were to leave the House of Newcomers one Palestinian pound, the equivalent of about three American dollars then, to help us over the initial transition from dependency to independence. It was a loan for which we signed. I felt rich. One pound could be divided into one hundred piasters or one thousand mills. I was ignorant of food prices, but having bought a glass of *gazoz* (a carbonated soft drink), for three mills, I felt that life in this country could not be too difficult.

The riches in my pocket improved my disposition and I set out confidently to search for a new place to live. I did not know where to look, but a small grocery store a few houses down the road seemed the right place to ask. I was lucky. The owners, a Russian couple, and the few customers present displayed a touching willingness to advise me when they learned that I had been on the Patria and had been released from Atlit just a few days earlier.

After a short palaver in Yiddish and other languages among the people in the store, I was led outside. Everybody came along. We walked to the corner of the building, where a small, cube-like house a little ways off the road was pointed out to me. It was called House Wollmann, and its residents were the Levin family. Somebody had heard they had a room for rent.

The house was only a short distance from the Beit Olim, and its location in a familiar neighborhood made it reassuring. I knocked at the door and a young, slim woman opened the door. An abundance of bushy, auburn hair framed a narrow, friendly face, and two inquisitive eyes looked at me as she addressed me in Hebrew. "I am sorry," I said in German, "but I don't understand." She smiled. "What can I do for you?" she asked in German. – "Do you have a place for rent?" – "Yes. It is 85 piasters a month." She looked at me, and something made her ask: Do you have blankets and linen?"

It was a harmless question, yet it made me wince. "No," I said, and felt as if I had admitted to something offensive, like being a drifter. My own blankets had never come back from the Patria. "I am from the Patria," I added as an explanation for having no bedding. Suddenly I felt ashamed at being almost destitute.

"All right," said the woman, "for 10 more piasters I'll supply the blankets, a pillow, and linen for the bed. The linen I will change weekly."

This was a bargain. I assume it was compassion on her part, but luckily I was too naïve to recognize it then. I might have been stupid enough to refuse her offer and spend part of my meager money supply on the purchase of bedding. Being independent now, the last thing I wanted was pity. I failed to recognize that all the clothing I owned, with the exception of the woolen jacket, were gifts sent to us by compassionate Jews.

I gave her the pound, and she returned five piasters. "I'll just get my things from the Beit Olim. I'll be right back," I called out to her and took off.

I arrived at House Wollmann with a small cardboard box containing my possessions. My wardrobe consisted of an extra pair of shoes, a second pair of pants, three more shirts, several pairs of socks, and a few undershorts.

The place I had rented sight unseen was a small, narrow room. The furniture consisted of a bed below the only window, a low chest of drawers opposite the bed and near the door, and a small table and chair on the narrow side of the room. My whole wardrobe fitted into one of the chest drawers. I was happy with my room. It was my own, and I could come and go whenever I liked.

With little choice, and as much as I hated it, I knew I had to approach the man from the Jewish Agency again. Of the one pound received, five piasters were left, and even with the 45 piasters I had saved in camp, the amount could never last me until the time I could expect to get paid for the work I hoped to find. I needed another pound and went to see the man who had previously advanced me the money.

I found that kind man the next day and explained my predicament. He came up with another pound, and I signed for it again. I also asked where to look for work and was told to go to the "Yard" on Carmel Avenue in the German Colony. He said to be there before eight in the morning. It sounded easy, though I was worried about finding a job I would be able to handle. What did I qualify for? Not much. Nevertheless, the prospect of work and making money elated me. I decided to live dangerously and spend a whole piaster of my replenished money reserve on a trip to the Hadar. It was not just pleasure that motivated this extravagance, but the wish to acquire a moderately priced alarm clock. I hoped to find a greater selection and cheaper models in Haifa. I wanted to make certain that once I had a job, I would never be late for work.

I walked the short distance from our house to the boulevard and the bus station and waited with a few other people for the bus to arrive. Everything was exciting. The people, the houses, a dog that understood Hebrew, and even the few cars that passed by. Besides the license plate, cars displayed a disc with the letter M for mandate. To me this still meant distant *Palästina*, not Palestine or Eretz Israel.

I still was a stranger in a strange land.

I bought the clock and returned to Bat Galim. I went shopping for food that I needed for my first day at work. I took it for granted I'd be working tomorrow, and just the thought made me feel light-hearted and tingling with anticipation. The world looked rosy.

Up until then I had experienced no language problems and began to believe that everybody spoke German or at least Yiddish. I had not as yet had any contact with Jews, who spoke neither of those two languages even though they came from Europe. That came later. For now I went to a bigger grocery store on the boulevard, spoke German, and had no problem. I bought a loaf of bread, a package of Blue Band margarine, and a few ounces of *Lakerda*, a smoked fish that smelled heavenly, tasted even better, and was inexpensive. I also purchased a small piece of halvah, that delicious sweet to which I had been introduced on our arrival in Haifa and which I thought I should not deny myself. Home again, I borrowed a knife from Mrs. Levin, and prepared my sandwiches.

I was so happy, I had to talk to someone. Mrs. Levin smiled as she listened to my preparations for tomorrow and my fear that my alarm clock might fail to perform next morning. No problem, she calmed me, she would make sure I got up on time because she also had to wake her husband. The safest bet, she added in jest, was their little daughter who, though not of school age yet, was an early riser.

The following morning I awoke before my clock had sounded its alarm and could just see the door to my room open slightly. A hand appeared and a glass of steaming tea was deposited on the chest of drawers.

"Ho," I said startled, and the smiling head of Mrs. Levin appeared.

"I thought you might like some tea in the morning," she said. I wanted to protest, but she withdrew.

It became routine to expect a cup of sugar-sweetened tea every morning on my dresser, and for the time I lived at House Wollmann it never failed to arrive. It was doubly nice of Mrs. Levin to do this because sugar was scarce during the war.

There are moments in a person's life when one steps over an invisible barrier and commits oneself to responsibilities one did not have before. One reaction to the imminent confrontation of that new reality may be the feeling of a vacuum in one's stomach. Two circumstances that may cause this feeling of trepidation is the decision to get married and raise a family; the other is being 18 years of age, with no experience in making a living, and with no possibility of returning to one's former state of dependency.

As I set out on that two-mile walk to the Yard that morning, I was certain that my face mirrored my thoughts. It made no difference, however, whether the few people I met were aware of it or not. Life and nature moved on like my alarm clock at home. The sun was shining, the sky was blue, and there was nothing in the air that pointed to the importance of my mission.

Moshava Hagermanit (German Colony) of Haifa had had a large German population before the war. Enterprises in the area still displayed their German signs: Restaurant Probst on the corner opposite the Yard, the small barbershop across from it, the butcher shop half-way down the road and almost invisible behind its shrubbery, and the small grocery. Almost two years into the war the original owners had been interned, and mostly Arabs now ran the businesses. It was, however, a pleasant surprise when the man at the butcher shop spoke fluent German.

189

The Yard on a corner lot on Carmel Avenue belonged to the British army. It consisted of an office building, several room-sized workshops and storage facilities, all surrounding an inner yard. In its center was an air-raid shelter. The short tunnel, covered by a mound of dirt, had two exits. Also inside the yard and near the entrance was a small wooden hut with a narrow window in the front. What I did not know was that the hiring was done through this window.

The inner yard was filled with people when I got there. Many sat or reclined on the hardened ground, apparently waiting for work to be assigned. Judging from their swarthy complexion and by their cloths, they were Arabs. They were dressed in tattered shirts, thin, baggy pants, and a headgear made of something like burlap. Their ragged attire was characteristic of the Arabs from Houran, Syria. Many of them were barefoot or dressed in old shoes, the backs of which, pressed down by their naked heels, made them into slippers. Others wore pieces of tire cut to the size of their soles and held in place by strings. The soles of their feet were hardened from lack of footwear and exposure and their hands were callous from hard work. Some were porters, carrying heavy loads on their backs, and I never saw one begging on the street as other Arabs did. They were motivated and always looked for work. Houranis lived under impoverished conditions; they may even have been homeless, but seemed fatalistically resigned to their way of life. I would later see Houranis wash their feet and faces at public spouts, but because of the heat and their primitive cleaning habits, they exuded odors that were hard to take at close proximity. They were primitive and illiterate and other Arabs showed little compassion for their brethren from across the border. They looked down on them.

When I asked one of them what to expect, my German failed to get a response. None of them understood, though my question seemed to amuse them. They laughed. I stood on the fringe of that crowd and idly looked about.

Suddenly the window at the little hut opened and all the men who had sat on the ground jumped up and pressed toward it. It was the Patria all over again. Survival depended on what lay behind the opening.

I did not make it to the window before it fell shut again. The quota of hired hands had been filled for the day and for the rest of the men there was nothing else to do but leave. Disappointed and resigned faces look the same the world over. We were out of luck, but somehow I was relieved. I had one more day when I did not have to worry whether I qualified for the jobs given out.

Next morning, though, I was very early at the window. I did not sit down but eagerly awaited the opening of Sesame. When the window was raised, a somewhat familiar face looked at me. It was not that I knew the man, but he looked Jewish.

"*Kann ich Arbeit haben?*" (May I have a job), I asked. He seemed surprised to see somebody like me. He gave me a slip of paper and told me in Yiddish to climb aboard an open military lorry that was waiting on the street. I did not understand the English word lorry, but would not have understood the word truck either. I followed the other men holding the same slip of paper in their hands.

I wondered about the task I had been assigned to without being questioned about my abilities. Apparently the man at the window believed me qualified. Why else would he so readily hand me the slip of paper that detailed me to a job? I was happy and felt a kind of rapport with those poorly dressed men who were slowly filling the truck to capacity. I grinned at them, and they grinned at me. Our sense of community prevailed over the language barrier. We all were happy to have found work.

The truck delivered us to the harbor area where each of us received a shovel. Under a merciless sun we shoveled sand and gravel all day long for buildings under construction. The job required no mental effort, but lots of stamina and muscle. I was a skinny little guy, not used to this exertion, and in that hot climate I perspired profusely. The salty liquid seeped through the pores of my skin, dried on my body, but refused to dry on my face. Fed by a sheer inexhaustible source, the rivulets of sweat ran down my forehead, stung my eyes, and collected in the corners of my mouth. I continued to shovel, having learned in Buchenwald not to give up. I worked at the same pace as the men in my group and rested when they did. To an observer my complexion and attire must have made me stand out among those broad-boned men like a half-sized, white asparagus stalk on a plate of artichokes.

At lunchtime everyone sought a shady place. While each of my Arab fellows undid the knot of a not too clean piece of cloth and removed from it a *pita* (pancake-like bread) and green onions, I leaned against a wall, too tired to eat. For the first few minutes I kept my eyes closed against the glaring sunlight, watching orange disks chase each other across the insides of my eyelids. It would have been easy to fall asleep, but the thought that I would be more exhausted when I woke up made me open my eyes to slits occasionally and watch the others. Despite the frugality of their meal they seemed to enjoy it. Afterward they drank water from a faucet, rolled and lit cigarettes, and relaxed on the ground.

I wasn't hungry. Even the thought of the lakerda sandwich in my paper bag failed to tempt me. I eventually ate the halvah and then went for a drink. I opened a faucet to catch the water in the hollow of my hand, and almost burned it. The sun on the exposed pipes had brought the water almost to a boil. Letting it flow for a while cooled it to a degree, and eventually I drank the tepid liquid to quench my thirst. The sweet halvah and water sustained me for the day.

Early on the following mornings I was again at the window. After a few days I was not bothered any more by the annoying procedure of being hired on a daily basis. I received 18 piasters for eight hours' work, wages for unskilled labor, and though I did not intend to make shoveling sand my career, I was not unhappy with the situation. Five days of work paid for almost a month's lodging, and since my only expense was food, I began to save a little money.

During the next few workdays I acquired blisters on my hands, but also an appetite for the food I brought with me. I learned my first few Arabic cuss words and spicy they were and days became routine once more.

In my second week of work, Herr Diamant, the man behind the window, told me one morning to stand to the side and wait for him.

I was curious and complied. When he had finished distributing jobs, he came out of the hut and told me that I would start working with one of the plumbers. – Plumbers? – *Installateur*, my benefactor translated.

I was hitting the jackpot.

Herr Diamant (I always called him "Herr"; "Mister" sounded strange to me) took me to one of the shacks, the inside of which smelled strongly of open fire, hot metal, and melted grease. An array of items made of galvanized tin and in various stages of completion, were on the floor, the workbench, and hanging from the wooden walls. Five people were present. Two were easily identified as Arabs; the other three were Jews. Herr Diamant said something that obviously was an introduction, for he pointed at me, and said: "Gustav." He then rattled off the names of the others, but for the moment only one stuck to my mind: Moshe. I was told in Yiddish that he was the plumber I would work with.

My new boss's parents had emigrated from Rumania to Palestine, where Moshe and his younger sister were born. He was seven years my senior, slightly taller than I, spoke Hebrew, Arabic, English, and to my relief, Yiddish. He was quite a ladies' man, and I have no doubt that his wavy, light hair, the blond mustache above his full lips, his ready smile, and the Sunbeam motorcycle he rode attracted girls. He enjoyed telling me about his sexual prowess and made me slightly envious. Moshe was bursting with vigor, except when he was tired from an evening out the night before, a not unusual occurrence. For all his antics he did his job well and knew what he was doing. He was a nice guy and I liked him.

In time I became acquainted with the other people at our work place.

Chaim, also a plumber, was in his early thirties, married, and father of a young child. He and Moshe were always competing to see who was the better plumber. Moshe loved to annoy Chaim with real or fictional work problems, and Chaim was the perfect patsy for my boss's tricks. The poor guy always got upset and tried to hide this behind arguments he never won.

The third Jewish man connected to that particular shack was Yitzhak. He was 60, yet looked 20 years older. Palestine's climate had been unkind to him. Yitzhak was originally from Poland and had come here as a young man. He spoke Hebrew, to a lesser extent Arabic, and almost no English. He seemed most fluent in Yiddish. The old man still had something of the "*Galut Jude*"[20] in him though he would have vehemently denied the accusation.

Still thinking Arabic to be a romantic language and wanting to talk with those people who spoke no Yiddish, I made an effort to learn some words of their language.

Yunis, one of the Arabs, was tall and dark skinned. His black hair was silver streaked and his bushy, deep black mustache made me suspect that he used dye to achieve this color. To an Arab the mustache is not only handsome, but is his pride and proof of manhood. The worst insults is to touch a spot above one's own lip with thumb and forefinger, make a twisting motion and, while looking at the opponent, emit a Bronx cheer. For this insult an Arab is (or at least used to be) ready to kill. Moshe often joked with Yunis, and they laughed a lot. During their verbal banter Yunis would act out that insulting motion, and Moshe would be the only one who dared to return that gesture.

The second Arab to work here was Yahub, a man in his forties. He rarely participated in conversations except when job-related. Months later, during our lunch, I saw Yahub do a curious thing to a cigarette. With the help of a thin wooden stick, he carefully extracted tobacco from his cigarette. When it was half empty, he rolled a dark paste into a small ball, inserted it into the hollowed out paper, and then refilled it again with the loose weed. I asked him in Arabic: "*Shoo hada?*" (What's that?) He grinned up at me. "*Chashish. Bedak? Chamsi girsh.*"

It was hashish, and he had asked me if I wanted some, the price being 5 piasters. I had no intention of trying the stuff. I distrust narcotics, and besides, one smoke would have set me back one fourth of my daily earnings, and that was more than I would have been willing to spend on a piece of Viennese chocolate cake, which I loved. "*Katacherak,*" I thanked him, adding: "*Mishlasem.*" (I don't need it.)

---

[20] Galut means Diaspora or Exile. Galut Jew alludes to Jews who, for two millennia in exile, lived in an atmosphere of intolerance, persecution and humiliation and who, for that reason, behave in a subservient and cowed way. It is the characteristic behavior of minorities in all times and places, even the USA.

A third Arab, who only occasionally came to the shack in the morning, was Yussef. He was about my boss's age and also worked as a plumber for the British Army. He spoke Hebrew with the Jews (Moshe said he spoke it fluently), Arabic with his own kind, and English with the British. He was stocky, and his biceps were as wide and muscular as those of a bodybuilder.

A Plumber's Apprentice

The British army had taken over houses in the German Colony in which they billeted soldiers who worked in military offices. The army had also commandeered the big Italian hospital three blocks to the west, and the German hospital one block to the east. The German hospital, a dark, low structure with a garden growing wild, was as inviting as a witch's hovel. The Italian hospital, on the other hand, was a modern, light-colored building of several stories where wounded soldiers of the Lebanese and Syrian campaigns were taken. For lack of beds and rooms wounded men were lying on stretchers in the corridors. Here I came face to face with graphic consequences of war.

Moshe, Chaim, and Yitzhak tended to plumbing needs in the many places in the city the army had occupied. Most houses had old plumbing that was in constant need of repair. Bigger appliances, such as boilers and water tanks, with serious breakdowns were disconnected and transferred to the Yard where Yunis and Yussef, both tinsmiths, repaired them.

People in other trades worked in the compound as well. A fellow immigrant from Germany painted signs. His letters and numerals, large and small, were as perfect as print. I liked to watch the man at work during my occasional breaks at the Yard. He chain-smoked and coughed a great deal. I suspect he suffered tuberculosis. I liked his company for he spoke the familiar German.

With my advancement to plumber's apprentice, my daily pay was raised from 18 to 20 piasters. The extra money paid for the plate of *Chumus* (humus) I liked to eat at a small Arab restaurant on Jaffa Road. Though my visits were infrequent, my menu was consistent. I proudly called out my order in Arabic: "*Uahat chumus, tnin pita uh uahat moye, minfadlak.*" (One humus, two pitas, and one water, please.) When I felt especially good, I ordered as an afterdish: *"Uahat au-ee,"* (one coffee).

A dish of humus and green onions cost two piasters, the flatbread pita half piaster. A reasonably priced meal in line with my budget. I loved that food and never tired of it. I enjoyed my visits to the restaurant except for one time when a new Arab waiter served me.

Humus is spread onto a plate with a wooden mallet that leaves the pasty food's edge uneven. To improve its appearance, this waiter held the rim of the plate between his thumb and forefinger and with his other hand rotated the dish. From time to time he licked the collected paste off his thumb and then continued with the beautification of the plate. When he had created a shiny white circle around the food he licked his thumb clean before bringing it to my table. My visits to the restaurant ceased until I made certain that this budding artist and beautifier of gastronomical delights had quit his job or was fired.

Every morning an Arab coffee vendor showed up at the Yard, selling strong, sweet Turkish coffee in small cups. The coffeepot the man carried in his right hand was of Middle Eastern design, concave at its waist and with a short spout. In his left he held two of the small coffee cups which he clicked with great dexterity against each other. It created sharp clear sounds and advertised his merchandise. From a rope encircling his waist dangled on a short string a tin can with a narrow S-shaped pipe for a spout. It contained water needed for the rinsing of used cups. When a customer had finished his coffee and returned the cup, the vendor poured water from the tin can into it. As the water flowed, and using only the fingers of his left hand, he deftly turned the cup around and around while his thumb freed the inside of the cup from grounds and the film the coffee had left. Now the cup was ready for the next customer. Often I was that next customer.

The coffee's price was half a piaster for two cups, which made it 2 1/2 mills per cup. Since half mills did not exist anymore, one had to drink both cups of coffee at the same time or come to an arrangement like mine with the coffee vendor. I paid him half a piaster, and we settled for one cup in the morning and a second cup at lunch if I was there. Otherwise I got another cup the next morning.

I still think fondly of my encounters with the absolutely delightful and delicious coffee in poorly cleaned cups and the tasty foods consumed in atrociously grimy restaurants in Palestine and Egypt, and I wonder if those delightful flavors have gone down the drain of time like the years?

My Jewish co-workers advised me to sign up with the *Histadruth* (the General Federation of Labor). Most Jews and also some Arabs belonged to it. The organization oversaw the working conditions of its members in the civilian sector of the country, as well as of those employed by the British army. For the first three months I was exempted from paying dues, but after that it made a dent in my finances. As a member I was covered by *Kupat Cholim* (the Workers' Health Plan), an important consideration in joining the federation. I delivered a photo of myself to their office on the Hadar and was issued my membership booklet with the picture in it.

A duplicate photo submitted to a government[21] office adorned my identity card, the one required of all residents of Palestine. The card had to be carried at all times and shown to persons of authority on request. I don't believe, though, that the British were foolish enough to believe in the infallibility of their control system. The identity cards were easily falsified. There was no guarantee that they were genuine or that the examiner of the document was adequately trained to recognize a counterfeit, and the underground[22] took advantage of this.

Most plumbing repairs Moshe and I made were within a few blocks of the Yard. Vehicular transportation was thus unnecessary. If on occasion help was needed in the more distant downtown area, we still walked to our assignment. When, in rare cases, Moshe used his motorcycle to get us to a job, I rode the pillion. I loved to ride behind him on his motorcycle, leaning into the curve when he took a corner or, if we got onto the highway, feel the pull of the strong wind on my face. In those days safety precautions were low on the list of riders' priorities. Moshe and I rode the motorcycle, like most everybody else, without goggles or leather cap.

Life with my boss was not just work. When assigned jobs were finished by early afternoon, Moshe occasionally would say, "Let's go to the movies, but let's not get caught". The theater we then visited was the Ain Dor movie house in the southern part of the Arab district. The matinee audience consisted mainly of male teenagers and the films reflecting their taste, were Hollywood B pictures about smug detectives, mechanical monsters, sinister doctors, and menacing inventors. Once in a while, as if by mistake, an Arabic movie was shown at matinee time. In the evening the priorities were reversed, and Arabic movies from Cairo took precedence over English and American films. We bought tickets and the inevitable bag of sunflower kernels, the popcorn of the Middle East. Rows under the balcony were avoided, for during the show shells of empty sunflower and pumpkinseeds were spit way out into the room below. The racket in the theater was as intense as that during youth matinees in Vienna. The language was different, the commotion the same.

---

[21] 'Government' here refers to an administration controlled and run by the British.

[22] The Hagana, the illegal self-defense organization, though it exercised self-restraint to the extent of frustration during the Arab riots and terror actions of the 1920s, 30s and even later, was nonetheless outlawed and hunted by the British, as were the members of the illegal military right wing.

At other times when Moshe had gone out the night before and was tired, we went to the attic of the Italian or the German hospital. My boss took a nap while I was instructed to hammer at some pipes should a military person show up. The noise woke my boss and also gave the impression we were busy. In spite of its uninviting appearance I preferred the German hospital to the Italian. In its attic I found several small, red-covered books in German published in the 1920s. They contained old-fashioned love stories and poems. It was not my kind of reading material, but it helped me pass the time when Moshe was asleep.

During the year I was with my boss, we twice sneaked off to Kayat Beach on his motorcycle during working hours. Kayat Beach, perfect for bathing, was a popular seaside spot on the Mediterranean Sea. About five miles south of Haifa, it was frequented mainly by Jews, but British civilian and military personnel also liked to spend their free time there. I mention this, because it took a lot of gall on Moshe's part – I was the reluctant fellow traveler – to court trouble that way. A military person or a staffer of the Yard who spent a free day at the beach could easily have recognized us. A report of our misconduct would have gotten us fired.

I enjoyed my hours at work, but not because of job-related activities. Our tasks lacked variety and required little mental or physical effort. Unclogging sinks and toilets or fixing and soldering leaky faucets and showers quickly became monotonous. What made working hours interesting was our being constantly on the move and meeting people. The occupants of the houses we visited as repairmen were British military personnel. Moshe was a sociable fellow and when occasionally residents were transferred, he quickly established a friendly relationship with newcomers. I envied my boss's fluency in their language and felt left out when they talked and laughed. I knew a few English words but was too shy to use them. I felt less restrained when trying out my limited Arabic vocabulary on Arabs. Being almost completely ignorant of Hebrew did not bother me. I had no problem conversing with Jews.

Hoping to overcome my ignorance, I mentioned my wish to learn English one morning at work. Itzhak, the old gentleman I always respectfully addressed as *Adon* (Mr.) Bermann, suggested the missionaries' office on Hechalutz Street where English was taught free of charge. I protested that I had no intention of converting just in order to be taught English. He assured me, however, that this would not be required of me. He was right. I did not have to convert, but it was strongly recommended that I show up at Bible meetings in the same building. I attended once and recorded the experience in my diary:

The access from the street led into a long room. Though rows of pews and a lectern at the far end made it look like a place of worship, the place lacked any spiritual aura. I received a hymnbook at the entrance and took a seat in the last row. The worship service began with a song quite unlike the ones I remembered from the village-church our maid Julie had taken me during my Vienna days. Instead, this particular service developed into an unrehearsed farce.

On the empty seat to my right lay the homburg of a man in the next seat. He was singing with great fervor. Suddenly a young fellow burst through the door and with a quick eye spotted me. We knew each other from work but were unable to converse much because he spoke only Arabic. With a friendly grin of recognition he entered my row and, facing the preacher, squeezed past me to take a seat. He dropped into the seemingly empty seat. Unperturbed and without any show of remorse, he drew the flattened headgear from under his posterior and nonchalantly handed it to the disconcerted owner. The following outburst interrupted the devotion of the 20 or so worshippers.

When things had settled down again, the proceedings continued.

In front of us a middle-aged lady, looking like the storybook old maid, followed attentively the words of the man at the lectern and joined passionately in the singing of every hymn. At the same time she seemed to have taken my young neighbor and me to her heart, for every so often she turned in her seat, smiled at us, and pointed to the hymn in progress.

At irregular intervals a hush settled over the congregation in observance of a silent prayer. My neighbor, who appeared to share my tedium, pulled from his pocket a soft-cover Arabic novel and, searching for the right page, made enough noise to make our spinster friend and others in the congregation turn around and shush him. It stopped the fellow's pursuit of diversion but also the silent worship of the man at the lectern. After an accusing look at the congregation the preacher, his head bowed again, continued his soundless prayer.

Two benches in front of me sat a bald man. He was bothered by a persistent fly that found the blank and perspiring surface of his head an attractive place to park. The reverent silence and the sermon were interrupted by the man's slaps to the top of his head. This failed to discourage the fly but was very disruptive.

During the closing hymn the preacher's voice broke in the middle of the song and ended far off key. Despite the distraction, the congregation finished the song with a fervent Amen. I felt sorry for the preacher who, no doubt, had seen better days. But for me it brought to an end a study of English that had not even started yet.

Despite the soft spot in my heart for Bat Galim I would have preferred to live in Haifa. But the price of a rented room on the Hadar was beyond my means. I missed the hustle and bustle of a city, the teeming streets of my youth. So on Saturday, the Sabbath, I went to

Haifa to visit the Jewish Hadar, the Arab section, or both. The leisurely walk to the city brought back memories of my Sunday strolls with Erich in Vienna. I would have liked my friend to share my experiences but in his last letter he had been still very much the enthusiastic kibbutznik.

With the exception of the Arab areas, the lower part of the city was deserted on Saturdays. Few people strolled on Kingsway; the business district was empty.

If I chose to spend my free time in the Orient, as Europeans referred to the Middle East, I lunched at the familiar Arab restaurant on Jaffa Road. On the way I took a side trip to the Ain Dor Movie Theater to find out if they were showing something I liked. When they did I remained in lower Haifa until it was time for the movie.

Chamra Square was alive with men in red fezzes, flowing headgear, long robes, or suits. Married Moslem women wore black dresses, a head shawl of the same color, and a veil that left only the eyes exposed. Unmarried girls wore no veil, and Christian Arab women often dressed Western style. Hawkers, loudly extolling their merchandise, peddled lemonade, fruits, vegetables, small houseware items and honey-dipped cakes on which pesky flies feasted. The cake sellers carried the pastry on big, round trays balanced on their heads. I liked those syrupy triangles of flaky dough despite the insects, and ate the pastry with no ill effect. The fruit and vegetable merchants sold their wares from the backs of overloaded donkeys and weighed the merchandise on a balance using different sized rocks for weights.

The discordant sound of Arabic music mingling with the hum of human voices, the noisy braying, bleating and guttural noises of animals constituted the symphony of the Middle Eastern market scene. A multitude of smells wafted through the air. The effluvium of animals, human sweat, and other odors failed, however, to spoil the intermittent aroma of roasting meat. The tempting fragrance of kabobs and shashlik roasting on spits over open fires on small stoves made me hungry. But I didn't have enough money to indulge myself.

I liked to crisscross the square, look into shops, have one or two little cups of sweet Turkish coffee while viewing the people, move about and write in my mind a report of my observations on invisible paper. The narrow streets of this neighborhood were mostly without sidewalks, but to one especially I would return time and again. This street led away from the square and had many little shops. The air smelled of spices, condiments, and other unidentifiable things. I liked to watch the men do business with each other, get excited when things did not go the way they expected, and use all those intriguing expressions and movements I had seen Yunis, the plumber, employ. Pulling down the skin just below the eye with one finger, and mockingly say, *alena ya sheich?* meant, you want to fool me? Or, you think I'm stupid? Lifting the head and click softly with the tongue meant "no."

I was shocked at first when Arabs at work belched loudly after their meal, until it was explained to me that it showed their satisfaction with the food they had consumed. If a guest expressed his pleasure after the meal in this way, it was a tribute to the host.

At seven I would go to the Ain Dor theater and at nine walk home to Bat Galim. On a moonless night, the way home was less pleasant. The blackout left everything in almost total darkness. Was the moon up, it was beautiful. But it was a bombers' moon and often the air-raid sirens would start wailing.. I used the bus only when exceptionally tired. It never entered my mind that walking home over that long, silent road by myself was dangerous. Nothing ever happened.

When my Saturday trip took me to the Jewish Hadar, it was an altogether different experience. The Hadar was westernized. The only thing that took time to get used to was the use of Hebrew and English on signs. The only Hebrew writing I had seen at home had been in prayer books. Though stores were closed on Saturdays, cafés and restaurants were open and did a thriving business.

On Herzl street, behind a row of stores and up the hill, stood a distinctive building: the *Technion*, the Jewish Institute of Technology. On the corner, across from the stores, was *Beit Hashaon* (the House of the Clock), the hub of social life. Here boys and girls, couples, and groups gathered and the phrase "Let's meet at Beit Hashaon" was widespread in Jewish Haifa. I did not participate in this part of city life, but Haifa was then my favorite city in Palestine. I drifted along with the crowd, looked at display windows, and had a cup of coffee, so different from the Turkish brew in the Arab section, in a café. It was served with a tiny can containing a syrupy liquid, which substituted for sugar.

In the evening I invariably visited the Armon Movie Theater, and with the German translation on the side screen I was able to follow the plot. The Armon had a roof that rolled back during the performance. It admitted fresh night air and exposed twinkling stars. When air-raid sirens sounded outside, a red light came on below the screen, and the roof returned to its original position. Few of the patrons, including myself, left the theater for an air-raid shelter. It was an altogether crazy situation, for when the anti-aircraft batteries around Haifa and atop Mount Carmel – a rather short distance away – thundered, it was difficult to concentrate on the show.

Haifa was plagued by frequent air raids. There was actually not much physical damage to the city, but nerves were frayed. The city lay on the slope of Mount Carmel, and incoming German or Italian bombers had a difficult target. Enemy planes arriving from the sea faced heavy anti-aircraft fire from the ridge of the mountain as they flew over the narrow target area. The industrial belt around the bay and north of Haifa had anti-aircraft batteries and floated barrage balloons in the evening to defend against planes.

Night air raids in Bat Galim were unpleasant for another reason. The only shelter in the neighborhood of House Wollmann was the cellar of a building near the road. The place was damp and home to millipedes the size of a man's hand or larger. People sitting on benches avoided leaning against a wall for fear one of those millipedes might slip into their shirt or dress. During one of the raids with the antiaircraft guns noisily booming, a man sang sarcastically in a low voice: "*Leise, ganz leise, klingt's durch den Raum...*" (Softly, so softly it sounds through the room) words of a song in a Viennese operetta.

Another repulsive insect that occasionally invaded my room at night was the large cockroach. After getting ready for bed and turning off the light, I opened the window to let in fresh night air. The move was an invitation to this repulsive intruder. Once when I heard the buzzing sound of its wings come through the window, I turned on my flashlight. The bug had settled on the floor, and I crushed it with a shoe. I planned to clean up the remains next day. Next morning the messy body had disappeared. A few nights after the mysterious disappearance of another squashed cockroach the mystery was solved. Using the flashlight one night, I saw a steady stream of ants busily taking the insect's big body apart and carrying it away piece by piece. The bugs thrived in the hot climate and old buildings and nothing could eradicate them.

Some weekends I remained in Bat Galim. On my strolls there I never met persons my age. Even the couples dancing in the evening at the beach café were older than I was. They seemed carefree, and I felt no kinship with them. During the day I walked to the beach, sat on my bench, and read a German book borrowed from Frau Levin. Often I stood at the water's edge and watched the waves hit the rocky shore. But when my eyes slowly rose above the expanse of the sea, I always thought of home. When I visited the shore of the Mediterranean in the evening, it offered me two different faces: glittering and friendly in the moonlight or forbidding and unapproachable, water and sky fused together.

The United States was not yet at war with Germany and this opened up an illegal way to correspond with my family in Vienna. The Red Cross would transmit a letter of 25 words to an enemy state, and then one had to wait for months for an answer. To circumvent that problem I wrote a long airmail letter to my parents and mailed it to one of my aunts in New York. She placed it in another envelope and forwarded it to Vienna. My family reversed the procedure. This correspondence of a homesick teenager with his parents worked twice. But then I received an official notice from the British censor to appear in his office. Still not having gotten entirely over the behavior of the Nazis toward enemies of the state, I feared the British might take me for a German spy. It was obvious to me that my letter had been intercepted and was in their hands.

The expected inquiry was conducted in a large room by a man behind a big desk. In front of him on the desk lay my letter, mailed a few days earlier.

To his questions in English I could only answer in German: "I am sorry, but I don't understand you." – He switched to my language. "To whom did you write this letter?" – "To my family." – "Where is your family?" – Always loath to lie I answered awkwardly: "They must be in America now. They were suppose to go there." – He did not buy this. "They are in Germany and that's where this letter would have gone had we not stopped it." – I did not try to contradict him and just stood there in silence. But Palestine was not Germany and an Englishman was not a German.

"Don't do it again," he warned me. "This time I'll let you go, but the letter stays here."

I was relieved, but it was painful to have wasted the postage. An airmail letter to America set me back a quarter of a day's pay.

Partly because of loneliness, and to some extent out of curiosity, I began to smoke cigarettes. I had observed the pleasure smokers seemed to derive when they inhaled and exhaled the smoke. To find out I spent a whole piaster for a box of ten "*Atid*," the brand name meaning "future."

In the evening I went to the dark and deserted waterfront where the sound of waves and the distant music of the café created a romantic atmosphere. Feeling like one of my dime novel detectives, I lit a cigarette and inhaled. Smoke filled my mouth and windpipe, and the frightening sensation of having swallowed a cork which had got stuck in my throat and prevented me from breathing turned out to be just imagination. Getting my wind back I bravely, but cautiously took some more puffs. Suddenly I broke out in a sweat. My stomach felt queasy and was on the verge of rejecting the meager meal I had consumed prior to my experiment.

What an experience! Still, I refused to give up, and decided to have another try a few days later. The second cigarette, too, tasted terrible. I had another one in a few days' time, and the more often I smoked, the better the cigarettes began to taste. I was hooked and became an avid smoker. For 35 years, despite many attempts to quit, I remained a slave to the pleasure of smoking.

202

I persuaded Erich to leave the kibbutz, and in August of 1941, he moved in with me. We had never lived together before, yet his coming to Bat Galim seemed an extension of our life as friends in Vienna. Even there we had shared more waking hours in each other's company than with our families. After all, we had worked side by side through most of the week and also spent the weekends together.

I talked to Frau Levin about my friend, and we agreed to raise the monthly rent to 1 1/2 pounds. Paying half of that amount saved me 20 piasters a month. It was a day's earnings and was not much, but it was not the money that mattered. The companionship of my friend, I hoped, would compensate me in part for the longing I felt for my family. I got Erich a job at the Yard and, as in my case, he worked first as a laborer, and then advanced to the rank of assistant to a craftsmen. Like two brothers, we bought and shared our food and took the same sandwiches to work. As in Vienna, we again talked about girls, went to the movies, and attended soccer games. We walked together to and from work. We shared activities. It was almost like Vienna, and yet so very different. I introduced Erich to my bench at the beach, the music that drifted into the night from the café, the Arab restaurant on Jaffa Road, the Ain Dor Movie Theater in the Arab quarter, and my visits to the Hadar. We were the best of friends, yet there was something about Erich that was strange. He was holding something back.

After a few weeks he started to go out evenings by himself. When I asked where he was going, he answered evasively. For a while I believed he had a girl in Haifa, but as we continued to talk about the opposite sex, I rejected the thought. Though we still shared worries about our families, were uneasy about the war situation in Russia, England, and North Africa, speculated on the length of time it might take for things to get better, the lighter side of life was missing.

When in November 1941 the British went on the offensive in North Africa, the war situation close to us improved. They advanced into Libya, relieving the besieged garrison of Tobruk, and continued to El Agheila on the Gulf of Sidra. On December 7 of the same year Japan attacked Pearl Harbor and brought the United States into the war. Our hopes were raised that this would hasten the defeat of the Axis powers.

In my life, Erich's secretiveness made me feel uncomfortable. He went out at night more and more often and several times failed to come home at all. It was then that I began to worry that he was involved in something unlawful, not criminally, but politically. What made me suspect was that in answer to my questions he finally admitted that he could not talk about his activity. A week or two later Erich informed me of his intention to leave House Wollmann. He had found a place in Haifa, which he was going to share with two other fellows from Vienna.

On December 21 my friend moved to the Jewish Hadar.

His refusal to talk about the reason for his move and the unwillingness to disclose his new address to me confirmed my suspicion. The thought that he belonged to one of the outlawed right-wing underground organizations made little sense. Erich had spent two years in kibbutzim of the *Shomer Hazair*, a left-wing Zionist party. The British did not hunt them unless they were members of the Hagana, the party's underground defense unit.

Once more I was alone and wanted to leave Bat Galim. Again Old Man Itzhak came to the rescue when I voiced my wish to move to Haifa. In a house on the street behind the Yard lived a Jewish family that rented out places, he told me. This was exciting news, and I only wondered if I could afford a place in the city. The building must have been a century old. It looked neglected and dirty and apparently had not seen fresh paint for decades. When my knock went unanswered, I entered unannounced. In a large anteroom I was met by the heavy smell of oil cooking over a fire, the sharp aroma of raw onions, and other indefinable odors. If I rented here, I would have to get used to the smells, I thought. I was about to leave, when a short, skinny woman appeared. She wore a light cotton dress of faded colors and an apron of like material. Her sparse, unkempt hair framed a lean face, and her small, squinting eyes made me think that she needed glasses. I had been pleasantly impressed when I first met Frau Levin, but this woman repelled me.

Surprisingly, she addressed me in Yiddish. My wish was to get out of there without being rude, but I felt too embarrassed to do so. I asked how much the rent was. Seventy piasters a month. That softened my resistance and made the place more appealing. It was a bargain. The dwelling was not on the Hadar, but at least it was in the city. I could sleep longer because the Yard was just around the corner and also save money. As in Bat Galim, I almost rented the place unseen, but something held me back. "Where is the room?" I asked.

The woman led me to the rear section of the house and a big room. Despite the two windows and the brilliant sunshine outside the place was only dimly illuminated. Beyond the windows a wild growing curtain of tall greenery was blocking the sunlight. But it was not the lack of light that disturbed me. It was five beds along the walls, the only furniture visible, that made me wonder.

"This is my room?" I asked incredulously.

She pointed to the bed in the right hand corner. "This is your bed," she said. Then she added: "*Es sennen noch vier Menschen mit dir im Zimmer.*" (Another four people are in the room with you.)

I was shocked. It was not a room I was about to rent, but a place to sleep. An accommodation with four strangers was not my idea of a home. After all that had happened to me in the past two years, I craved privacy. Undecided about what to do, I weighed the pluses and the minuses and finally convinced myself that a change from the German Colony to the Hadar was easier than one from Bat Galim. I decided to move.

Living in Haifa

Leaving House Wollmann was not easy. It was almost like leaving home for the second time. Frau Levin's friendliness had helped me over the awkward time of adjustment and my first tentative steps in the new life. It had been easy to relate to her and to the atmosphere of her home. When I had walked into House Wollmann, I had entered a familiar world.

But to what kind of a place had I moved this time! The house was dirty, and the woman of the house was given to hysterics. She was mother to several children (the husband I saw only fleetingly on a few occasions) and also had her old mother living with her. Nothing was handled in a civilized, calm manner. Frequently the house resounded with her screams, the whining of kids, and the moaning of the neglected and at times abused grandmother. The old woman came sometimes crying to me, but I could hardly do much in the defense of her. When I said something to her daughter, she jumped at me: "Es is nischt eier gescheft." It's none of your business. I had never expected anything of this kind to happen in a Jewish family and it disgusted me.

In my living quarters I was a stranger among strangers. With the exception of two young men in the room who appeared to be friends, the rest of us kept aloof from one another. The closest I ever came to my roommates was to say "shalom." The house had no electricity, and the feeble shine of the tiny oil lamp I had bought and used in the evening, supplied just enough light in my corner to get ready for bed. I began to regret having left Bat Galim.

Erich and I met less and less often. In April he mentioned his intention to join the British army and asked me if I would do likewise. I declined. Instead I hoped he would ask me to move into his place on the Hadar when he left. As the days passed without Erich ever mentioning about this, I asked him if I could have the room he was about to vacate. He declined my request, saying that he had no say in the matter. I refused to believe this and found his behavior callous and unfriendly.

When Erich became aware of my vexation, he tried to smooth things over by admitting he was a member in an illegal political organization. Since clandestine meetings were held in their living quarters, I, as an outsider, could hardly live there. He warned me not to mention this to anyone because it might mean trouble for him if the British found out. He still refused to divulge where he lived or his political affiliation. He only said that he shared the room with two other fellows from Vienna who belonged to the same political group.

I tried to be understanding, but was troubled and unhappy by what I had learned. The place on the Hadar had seemed within my grasp until my friend had introduced political complications. And yet I still had hope. Perhaps Erich could convince his partners to accept me as an outsider. I naively argued that even though I was not one of "them" (whoever they were) my Viennese origins should have calmed his partners' fears about me. I promised complete secrecy, and my friend could vouch for me. Erich finally agreed to look for an opportune moment to ask the fellows to consider me as their new roommate. He promised to do his best.

During the next few days I was jumpy. Whenever we met at work in the morning, and I looked at him expectantly, he would shake his head. It meant another day of uncertainty. One morning he said he had to talk to me. He wanted us to meet at a "safe" place where we could not be overheard. Because we spoke in German (still the only language I knew), I proposed the Arab restaurant on Jaffa Road. We were to meet there at 9 P.M., a time when the place most likely would be deserted.

Driven by impatience, I reached our rendezvous early. As expected, the restaurant had only two patrons, and they sat in the back of the room playing backgammon. They rolled their dice and paid no attention to their surroundings.

I settled at a table near the blacked-out window and ordered Turkish coffee. I nursed my coffee, and smoked two cigarettes before my friend showed up. His face was noncommittal, and the smile, I had hoped for was not there. "Wait," Erich said when I was about to say something, and I curbed my curiosity until his coffee arrived. Afterward I asked in German: "*Nun?*" (Well?)

"What I tell you now, you are not to mention or discuss with anyone," he said in a voice just a notch above a whisper. Then, without any further ado, he dropped a bombshell: "I belong to the Communist party."

In Palestine this was just as bad as belonging to the I.Z.L. (*Irgun Zvai Le'umi* or National Military Organization) the extreme right-wing group called terrorists by the British and even by some Jewish organizations. My friend's disclosure stunned and frightened me. "How could you?" I blurted it out louder than intended.

Erich shushed me angrily though there seemed hardly a chance that anyone understood German here. "Don't ask questions," he said. "I talked to the people in my cell, and they agreed to let you move in if you are willing to join our cause."

"What does this mean?" I asked bewildered.

He presented me with the clichés of Communist politics and propaganda. "We are against the capitalist system. We want the workers of the world to unite under the red banner. The Soviet Union is the motherland and engaged in a life or death struggle with fascist forces."

I could not believe it was my friend talking. My question had been purely rhetorical. I was aware of the Communists' goals and they were diametrically opposed to mine. My parents had owned a store, and if that meant that they were capitalists, I was all for capitalism. I wanted to go to America and perhaps, become a capitalist myself. The struggle in which the USSR was engaged was worthwhile, but my friend had forgotten that this same Communist regime had quite recently concluded a pact with the same fascists it now fought.

I liked my friend too much to argue with him about his political views[23] and for the moment, anyway, was more concerned with the question of the place on Hadar he was to vacate. I was given time to think things over before moving into their quarters. Under the circumstances an extraordinary concession. My friend must have spoken well of me and apparently had succeeded in dispelling their suspicions. What I did not consider was that if they should get into trouble with the law, it would mean for me: *mitgefangen, mitgehangen* (caught together, hanged together).

I had to agree further that once I moved in and was still not a member of their group, I would never talk to anybody about things I saw or heard. Leave the house half an hour before their political cell met (twice a week in the evening) so I would not to be able to identify members. I was to return three hours later. If I eventually joined the group, I would have to pick another first name by which the members would know me. The names of the others were all fictitious.

It was not a bad deal. I did not have to commit myself to anything serious, yet was allowed to take over Erich's bed, and would finally be living on the Hadar. If there was something worrisome in my future, it was not the Communist Party, which I had no intention of joining.

On April 10, 1942, Erich joined a Jewish company of the R.A.S.C. (Royal Army Service Corps), a branch of the British army. Soldiers of that military branch drove trucks that supplied army units with materials and provisions. The excellent performance of those Jewish truck driver

---

[23] Eventually it became clear that the attraction of young people from Vienna and Germany with the USSR had been a fad. It came about by their belief that the latter seemed to have become the most potent foe of Nazism.

companies greatly helped the war effort of the Allies during the African campaign and later in the European Theater.

Five days after Erich had left, I moved from the German Colony to 41 *Rechov Hashomer* (Street of the Guard).

I was now living in Haifa but learned that the seemingly desirable is not always up to expectations. Even exotic places are only mysterious and exciting as long as one is only visiting. Once one has settled in, life becomes routine and loses its intriguing aspects. I still liked Haifa for its beauty, but the romantic aura it had once radiated was gone. The romantic thrill of the Arab quarter and its people, the camels used for commercial purposes and not housed in zoos, the donkeys and sheep that I had only seen in pictures, all had become routine. Even the Hebrew lettering on signs in this land of the Bible failed to impress me as something out of the ordinary anymore. Hashomer Street rekindled for a while that vanished feeling of living in exotic surroundings. All too soon, however, life in the neighborhood became unexciting.

The three-storied building to which I had moved was still on the Hadar, but it was a Hadar I had not known existed. The Jews here were different from the Jews I had met. They spoke no German or Yiddish. Their often noisy dialogues were in Greek, Bulgarian, Turkish, *Ladino* (the Judeo-Spanish dialect), or *Farsi* (Persian). Jews from Arab countries spoke Arabic. Kids played clamorously in the street and washing hung from several rows of cords that stretched between brackets fastened to walls below windows. Women gossiped over a natural telephone: the air between balconies and windows.

Though 41 Rechov Hashomer was on the bottom edge of the Hadar, across from our apartment building, and still in the Jewish section, lived Arabs in a narrow three storied house that had two stores on the ground level. The street was a neglected stretch with a crumbling sidewalk on our side and none on the other. The rear of our building overlooked a large empty tract of land that dropped steeply toward the Arab sector of eastern Haifa.

The owners of the apartment, husband and wife, had immigrated to Palestine from Russia as a young couple. Now they were parents of several boys and a teenage girl named Zipora.

My roommates were Dov and another fellow whose name I forgot. They were not their real names anyway. Dov was the head of the group that met on certain evenings in our room for political studies. I had no idea how many groups of this kind existed in Haifa or how big they were, but had no wish to find out. I never met the other cell members, with the exception of Bathsheva (not her real name) an attractive young woman, also from Vienna. She was Dov's girlfriend and visited often. When, on occasion they wanted privacy, the other fellow and I went for a walk until around ten at night.

Living here had the advantage of a steady supply of German books I could borrow. I did not know the source of the books and did not ask where they came from. They satisfied my hunger for reading. These were not books of Communist indoctrination, but thrilling fictional stories by leftist writers. I was not worried about being converted to the cause by *Der stille Don,* (The Quiet Don) or *Die Republik der Strolche* (The Republic of Hooligans), a story that takes place in a Russian prison. Those and other novels were just entertaining works of fiction for me.

This apartment too had no electricity, and we used a kerosene lamp to light our room in the evening. As much as I had hated the lighting in the house in the German Colony, here the glow of light seemed warm and cozy. When my roommates were away on some evenings, and I was alone at home, the orange fan of the light inside the lamp chimney conjured up memories of our home on Jägerstrasse.

One day Dov told me that the German novelist and playwright Arnold Zweig was to speak at the Armon Movie Theater. Zweig, a Jew, had fled Nazi Germany and had found refuge in Palestine. The Nazis confiscated all his property before he left. I wanted to see the man, not because of his leftist leanings, but because he was a well-known personality whom I otherwise never would have had chance to meet. When I got to the Armon, it was filled to capacity, and I was not admitted. People milled about in front of the building, and they were excited and angry. Groups formed, arguments ensued between supporters of Zweig's political views and those opposed to them. Some vocal disagreements ended in shoving matches. Later I learned that inside the theater the situation was equally raucous. Naively I thought that Jews should never behave that way. I could not understand their conduct and was dismayed when I heard that a friend of Dov had been stabbed in a melee inside the theater.

After coming home from work, I sometimes stood on the little veranda behind our back door and watched the barrage balloons rising. I had a clear view of the *Mifratz* (the land around the Bay of Haifa), but was fascinated by those blimps that rose every evening into the sky. I hoped to see or at least hear of a case in which an enemy plane had hit the anchor cable of one of the huge balloons and crashed. It never happened in my time.

I did witness, however, a tragedy involving British Spitfires over Haifa. Walking toward Carmel Avenue on the side street next to the yard, the noise of airplane engines made me look up. It was a group of Spitfires flying in untidy formation. Suddenly the wings of two planes touched and a moment later both were spiraling toward the earth. As their corkscrew descent appeared to be away from Carmel Avenue, I sprinted in that direction. In the next few seconds the sound of the dropping plane grew louder, and when I looked up, one of the doomed Spitfires, like a huge monster, seemed right on top of me.

That's the end, I thought. I threw myself into the dirt behind a trash barrel, hiding my face in my hands. With an enormous crash the stricken plane hit the ground. An intense heat wave swept over me, and then rounds of the machine gun aboard the plane started to explode rapidly. For a few seconds I remained frozen in my position expecting at any moment to be buried under the second plane. When nothing happened, I jumped up and rushed into the inner yard of our compound.

Here everybody had taken shelter believing we were under attack by enemy planes. I hastily recounted my experience, and still shaky from the fright, a few of us crept warily across the yard toward Carmel Avenue to have a look at the calamity. The Spitfire had nose-dived into one of the short rock towers lining the avenue and was burning fiercely. The spot happened to be a bus station, but luckily no people were present when the disaster took place.

The other plane had crashed downtown. Its pilot, it was said, had jumped to safety. The pilot of the Spitfire on Carmel Avenue was killed when he abandoned his plane too late. His parachute had no time to open, and he crashed only a short distance from his aircraft into one of the big trees along the avenue.

A few days after the removal of the aircraft, I counted the distance between the trash barrel behind which I had hidden and the point of the plane's impact. They were just fifty steps apart.

The war situation in North Africa had turned more ugly than ever before. A few weeks after Erich joined the British army, the Afrika Korps under Rommel was on the offensive and before long crossed into Egypt. Somehow the Jews in Palestine showed no particular anxiety, and life continued as if the advancing army of Hitler was no danger to them. Their indifference may almost be excused since there really was little that could be done about it. Had all able-bodied Jewish men and women in Palestine joined the British army at the time, it would have helped little to improve the situation. Weapons for Jewish soldiers were scarce. And yet, unbeknown to most, Jewish underground troops, hunted by the British, were preparing for a last stand should the enemy reach Palestine.

I was very much afraid of again falling into German hands. The Nazi army's apparent effortless advances in Africa and the Soviet Union threatened not only my physical world, but also that of what was left of the world of my youth and my belief in a just higher being. My friend Bunjo had said, if you believe, you don't question. But my heart and brain told me I should question. Why was it right that a people which had not the slightest compassion for other human beings triumphed in all their undertakings? In my relatively short time in Buchenwald I had tasted hell and witnessed the annihilation of 60% of our men from Vienna. And though we did not know it then, the Nazis would kill about an equal percentage of the world Jewry by the time the war was over.

My experience was still too vivid in my mind, and I could not ignore what was going on or what might happen in our immediate future. To me the danger the Germans presented was real. It seemed clear enough, and not much imagination was needed to guess what would transpire if the Germans overran Egypt and reached Palestine. The Arabs of Egypt and most Arabs in Palestine waited to receive the Germans with open arms. Haj Amin el Husseini, the ex-Mufti of Jerusalem, was in Berlin and was a good friend of Hitler. He organized the Moslems of Bosnia to fight on the German side, and his anti-Western propagandizing was well known. Arabs would have worked hand in hand with Hitler's death squads to kill Jews just as the Croats, the Ukrainians, people of the Baltic states, and others did, some even surpassing their masters' cruelties.

For me the time had come to join the British army. Never again, I promised myself, were the Nazis going to get me without a rifle in my hand. I would not go into hell as sheepishly as before. I did not feel like a hero, and I felt both happiness and fear. Only recently I had turned 19, and it seemed exciting to become a British soldier. On the other hand, there was that fear of war's consequences. Perhaps it was not so much the dying I was afraid of, but the possibility of becoming an invalid. I remembered men I had seen in Vienna who had lost both legs in World War I. They sat on little wooden platforms with small ball-bearing wheels and propelled themselves forward by pushing the ground with small leather pillows they held in their hands. It was a frightening thought.

But my mind was made up. I would join the British army and this as soon as possible. My only hope by then was that I would reach Sarafand, the big army induction camp in the south, before the Germans did.

In the British Army

The British army recruiting office on Kingsway that sunny Sunday morning, July 12, 1942, was a busy place. Many young fellows like myself, and some older men milled around the big room, sat on benches along one wall and in front of the big windows, or stood in line facing several tables, behind which soldiers took down particulars of those ready to enlist. All of us apparently had wanted to spend one last Saturday as civilians before volunteering our services to King George VI.

Sitting on a bench near the wall, I listened in vain for the familiar sound of German in the chatter around me. I was worried that the language problem might be an obstacle to my enlistment. I was also bothered by something I had not thought of in a long time: the disastrous diagnosis of my eyes by the physician of the American consulate in Vienna. Would I be found physically unfit to join the army because of a slight inflammation of my eyes? Half a century later it seems an unreasonable worry, but for a lad of 19 who never again wanted to fall into the clutches of the Germans without a weapon to defend himself it was real enough.

I dreaded the thought of being rejected. I watched the men around me, trying to guess who spoke my language. I wanted to talk to somebody my age. Living on Hashomer Street had taught me that not all Jews spoke German or Yiddish, as I had believed until recently.

As I found out, Danny, who had been sitting beside me all the time, was my age, spoke German, and came from Berlin. He told me that I could choose the army group I wanted to join. I intended to join a fighting outfit to get back at the Germans, but Danny told me that the British took no Palestinian Jews into combat units. The closest one could get to be a foot soldier was to join the Buffs, an army group doing only guard duty. My new acquaintance advised me to join the R.A.O.C. (Royal Army Ordnance Corps). It was a technical group and one could use the skill one knew. But I had no skill. Don't worry, Danny said, tell the recruiting guy you are a "fitter general," and he'll accept it.

I considered the idea. At the trade school of the Zionist club in Vienna I had had some training as a locksmith, the equivalent of general fitter. But the truth was I knew only the absolute minimum of what a person in this vocation had to know. I asked Danny if he was a fitter general, and he said yes. He had learned the trade in a kibbutz.

I liked the guy. Soon we stood in the queue and signed up for the R.A.O.C. The British army could not have functioned without the word queue, its partner word, "bloody," and the standard expressions "stand in the bloody queue", "move back into the bloody queue", "get a bloody move on," and so on. After signing up we were not soldiers yet. Before being dismissed, we received bus tickets, and were told to report to the famous army camp Sarafand the next day.

Danny (I never learned his family name) wanted to visit his girlfriend in Jerusalem before going to Sarafand. I never saw him again.

I had another 24 hours in the city, and since I was near the Arab section, I strolled through the area, lunched in the Arab restaurant on Jaffa Road, and then walked up to the Hadar, as I had done so many times before. People were at work, but for me the day was a holiday. Sentimental, as always, I took my leave of places I knew, saying good-by in my own way. This part of my life had come to a close, and not knowing where my new life would take me, I wondered if I would ever see Haifa again. The British were spread out over half the world in their fight against the Axis powers and Japan, and who knew where I would end up?

Next day in Sarafand I passed the medical examination without trouble. Given leave until noon of July 17, when the swearing-in ceremony was to take place, I accepted the time off as a pleasant surprise. Because the free days, or rather nights spent in a hotel would take a big bite out of my savings, I returned to Hashomer Street where lodging was free. It felt silly to come back a civilian, but it had not been up to me.

By July 15 I was restless and decided to spend at least one day in Tel Aviv before returning to Sarafand. In the morning I took the bus to Tel Aviv.

I visited Susi who, with her girl friend and Erich, had accompanied me on my evening stroll through downtown Vienna before they left with the youth group for Na'an, a kibbutz in southern Palestine. She and her father lived in one room divided by a canvas partition. They were a most friendly couple and I enjoyed listening to the old man with his distinct Hungarian accent. I did not tell them that I might spend the night in the city, knowing they would invite me to stay. To me it seemed an imposition on their privacy. When Susi eventually found out that I had been in Tel Aviv that night, she scolded me for not staying with them. I could have slept in her father's part of the room, she said.

When I left their home on Bar Kochba Street to resume my wandering, I was still undecided whether to remain in the city or take a bus to Sarafand. As darkness fell, I ate in a restaurant on Dizengoff Circle and then sat down on one of the benches in the park-like ground of the square to enjoy the evening.

It was a beautiful night like so many in this part of the world. The heat of the day had yielded to the cooling breeze of the evening, but the summery warmth of the vanished sun still lingered in the air. I sat on the bench with my head resting against the back of the seat and looked up at the firmament. My eyes, mind, and thoughts, captivated by the glitter above, looked into the dark sky and its twinkling stars that looked like a swarm of glowworms caught in a spider's net. The luminous dial of my wristwatch displayed 9 o'clock, then 10, and as the hands on the dial moved forward I felt less and less inclined to leave my place. I stretched out on the bench, fingers entwined behind the back of my head. Why not sleep here, I thought, and then I slept.

Something nudged my shoulder. Sleepily I tried to open my eyes, and the blinding beam of a flashlight in my face made me blink. I sat up, and the light was turned off. My eyesight, still impaired by that sharp beam, made out the shapes of two men standing in front of me. One of them wore the headgear of a British Palestine policeman. The other one said something to me in Hebrew.

"*Ich verstehe Sie nicht.*" (I don't understand you) I said in German.

He changed to Yiddish and wanted to know why I was sleeping here. I told him that I had joined the British army and was on my way to Sarafand tomorrow. While he translated my response to the other policeman – I had not really answered his question – I wanted to get up and leave. He held me back. "Stay. We don't mind," he said, and they left.

Sunshine awoke me, but the air was cool. I wanted a cup of coffee, but shops were still closed in this part of the city. I crossed some streets walking to Allenby Road and continued up that main thoroughfare to the overland bus stations in the southern part of Tel Aviv. The place teemed with people, and coffee shops were doing a brisk business. I had coffee and a cigarette and then got in line to board the bus to Jerusalem with a stop at the gate to Sarafand.

Near the camp entrance many riders got off. Returning soldiers showed their passes to the MP and marched right through the gate. They knew where they were going. After an identity check we would-be soldiers were directed to an office inside the camp where we *queued* up for the final registration. A man behind a desk helped me fill out a form which I could neither read nor understand. I signed and officially ceased to be a civilian though I still wore no uniform. The paper read: PAL. NO. 6585. Name: Gustav Pimselstein. Corps R.A.O.C. The young fellow who at one time thought himself an Austrian now swore his allegiance to His Majesty King George the Sixth of the British Empire.

In a noisy and crowded mess hall I took my first army meal. Three men were sitting at a small round table. I said Shalom and asked in German if could join them. The man on my left, heavy set with Slavic features, answered shalom and in Yiddish: "Sit down." The other two, slim and dark skinned, with square, black moustaches just looked on.

I apparently had interrupted an argument, for the three of them, talking in Arabic, were speaking sharply to one another. I felt uncomfortable, yet decided to sit out the argument. After another heated exchange of words, the man on my left suddenly grabbed a knife, and with a violent stabbing motion brought it forcefully down onto the table top, where it stuck, quivering.

For a moment his frightful expression of rage left me dumbfounded. Then I voiced my shock: "*Was machst Du?*" (What are you doing?) Never taking his eyes off the two men across from him he shot back at me angrily in Yiddish: "Be quiet. Stay out of this. That's the only thing they understand."

214

I expected a reaction from the two men, but they never said another word. They left, and I didn't see them again.

That is how I met Getzl, who originally came from Poland. For the next four years we were together in the same army unit but remained no more than acquaintances. During the Arab unrest of 1947-48 he was murdered in a raid on a gas station near Petach Tikva. He was at the time only a customer.

Two days later we new recruits were taken to a workshop inside the camp for a skill test. I was handed a flat piece of iron and a blueprint of a *spanner* (British expression for a wrench) and told to make the tool. I felt like a student of music who had learned to read a score but was now asked to write a song. The English soldier who had handed me the job, and with whom I could barely communicate, was helpful. Whenever he passed my workbench he stopped, gave me verbal pointers accompanied by sign language that eventually resulted in a poor imitation of a spanner. My qualification as a fitter general was duly marked in my soldier's book on July 22, 1942, but with no classification.

While in the army, I passed tests that were recorded in my soldier's book: Reclassified to class III, November 15, 1942. Reclassified to class II, February 10, 1943, and finally after passing the trade test, I was upgraded to Group A class I General Fitter, December 8, 1943.

For almost six weeks, until August 25th, Sarafand was our home. Other soldiers had warned us that the barracks in Sarafand were infested with bed bugs. Well, that was not true. But another bloodsucker was plentiful: mosquitoes. When night fell, they came out in swarms. We slept under mosquito nets, which was stuffy and stifling, but was supposed to keep those miniature vampires away. Unfortunately, the nets were old, and the netting often had small holes, small enough to be missed by the eye but big enough for the mosquitoes to find their way to a meal. After a night of blood orgy, and not finding their way out again, the mosquitoes settled inside the net. Retribution followed when the bloodsuckers were picked off in the morning, and each of us proudly announced how many of them he had dispatched into the afterlife.

The size and fat content of the breakfast was hard to get used to. We were served sweet tea enriched with condensed milk, porridge, fried bacon or sausage (made of Soya beans), a fried egg, a slice of toast fried in oil, sweet fried beans, marmalade, and bread. Lunch and supper left something to be desired. Many of our fellows complained about the cooking and the small amounts served. Not being a big eater, I was only unhappy with the taste.

We were issued summer weight khaki uniforms, black boots, and a cloth cap that looked like the hull of a capsized ship. It was worn jauntily over the right side of the head. I liked that headgear much better than the beret we were issued two or three years later. Underwear, shaving kit (I still have and use the safety razor), two blankets, a kit bag, back pack, and haversack.

As members of a technical group we were never issued personal rifles. For the fortnight of regimental training we received every six months, rifles supplied to us had to be returned to the storeroom after the exercise. Much as I liked the rifle range and though I always did well in the practice, I hated the cleaning of the weapon afterward. Drill and rifle exercises, menial jobs, cussing and sweating under a hot sun, sore muscles, bayonet training. The order was translated for those who did not understand English: "Forward, run, run, run, scream at the top of your lungs, it intimidates and frightens the enemy. Push it in and twist before you pull out, it's deadlier". Kitchen duty, learning English orders, spit-polishing heavy army boots, keeping brass parts of belt and shoulder straps at high gleam, receiving a steel helmet and a personal gas mask – all this was required to become a soldier.

Foot and rifle drill were a frustrating part of our early training. Many recruits spoke no English, and orders given on the parade ground might just as well have been in Latin. Yet when necessary, we learned fast. Once I understood the orders, executing them was easy and fun for me. My training in the youth group of the *Judenstaatspartei*, the first Zionist group I had belonged to, helped.

Some of our fellows, and not necessarily the older one, had a harder time. Occasionally it was as if a spoof of army life was being acted out on the parade ground. To the instructor's vexation we could not help laughing when after an order of "left turn" (left face, American) some of the men turned right and stood face to face with the others. Some of the men just did not seem to be able to start out on their left foot. When "present arms" was called, some did port arms. Executing the right or left turn sounded like machine-gun fire instead of the singular sharp sound of teamwork. Yet at the final parade, orders were executed to perfection, which brought a proud smile to the drill instructor's face and raised the twisted ends of his waxed moustache toward heaven.

Full battle dress included a gas mask. The square fabric bag, strapped to the chest during training, held a rubber mask that was connected by a corrugated hose to a metal container filled with a chemical air filter. We were led in groups of 20 into a little hut to test the efficiency of the respirator. While pulling the mask over my face, I was surprised to see the instructor lock the door behind him. Standing in a circle around the man, I watched him bend down to a canister in the middle of the dirt floor. After he worked on it, vapors began to rise. The masked faces around me looked like goggle-eyed heads of insects. None signaled a leak in his mask. A few minutes passed in silence, then we heard the muffled voice of the instructor saying, "Take off your gas masks." Nobody moved. I thought I had misunderstood. "Take off your masks. We're not going to leave this room before they are off." I thought the man had gone crazy.

When his command was still ignored, the instructor turned to the man next to him. He grabbed the connecting hose of the fellow's respirator just below where it entered the mask, expertly pulled down, away, and up, and our man stood there eyes popping with shock, his face exposed to the vapors in the room. In a few seconds more masks came off that way and with little choice, the rest of us followed suit.

Just before I took off my respirator, I inhaled deeply, hoping to have enough air in my lungs to hold me until we got out of the hut. But I was mistaken. The instructor knew the trick and kept us in the biting vapor until everybody's eyes were running and all coughed. We had been unaware that the training required us to taste gas. It was not poisonous, yet it hurt eyes and lungs.

Then, with the grind of the training over, we hoped that the worst the army had to offer was behind us and a more pleasant time would follow. It did, but the military situation in Africa had not changed. That was something to keep in mind. Rommel and his Afrika Korps were only about 50 miles away from Alexandria. A very short distance when compared to the hundreds of miles his army had advanced.

On a string around my neck I wore two dog tags that identified me as PIMSELSTEIN G. JEW 6585, a man who would become a member of the 515 Workshop Company. Considering that our enemy was the German army, it felt less than reassuring to advertise my religion so openly. What if we fell into the enemy's hands? To ease our apprehension it was explained that should we get killed, we would be buried as Jews.

After boot camp, the army base Tira, just south of Haifa, felt like heaven. Food was plentiful and tastier than Sarafand's, and the army's regimentation less strict. We found that a six-hour pass, 6 P.M. to midnight, could be obtained every evening and a 30-hour pass every weekend. Yet before we had a chance to enjoy Tira, we were moved. After a four-day stay, Kurdani, inland from the Bay of Haifa, became our new camp.

Kurdani was in every respect a new camp. It was not even finished yet. The rolling sand dunes of the region reminded me of Foreign Legion movies I had seen, and I almost expected a bunch of wild Berbers on horses to race toward us when we arrived. But of course this was not Marrakesh, I was not in the French Foreign Legion, and the most that could have happened here was a local Arab galloping on his donkey while shouting *Marchabah* (welcome). The enormously large camp area, veined by new asphalt roads and dotted by a scattering of big camouflage-painted buildings, greeted us instead. A number of these were already in service as workshops, many others were still empty hulls.

A misconception of mine about the habitat of scorpions was set straight on my day of arrival. I was assigned to a small, round tent already occupied by two of our fellows. They had beds; my place was a straw mattress on the sandy floor across from the entrance. The trucks had dropped us off on a road inside the camp but a long way from our housing. The day was hot, and after carrying my gear over sand dunes I was bathed in perspiration when I entered the tent. I was grateful for its shade and had no quarrel with the mattress on the floor; sooner or later I would be issued a bed. My great disappointment, however, was the transfer to Kurdani. It seemed an out of the way place, though it could not have been much farther from Haifa then Tira was.

Dropping my equipment to the sandy ground, I plopped with a sigh of relief onto the mattress. Perspiration ran down my face, irritated my eyes and disposition, but there was little I could do to ease the discomfort of both. While I vented my annoyance about my transfer and smoked a cigarette to relax, a head peeked through the tent opening. It was a British soldier. He shook his head when he saw me sitting on the mattress and even my poor English was good enough to understand his warning: "Don't sleep on the floor. There are scorpions here."

I thanked him and his head disappeared. I laughed after he had left. Everyone knows, I told the fellows, scorpions live under rocks, not in sand.

Having rested, I began to store my equipment against the tent wall and tried to turn over my mattress. I raised it up on its side but immediately let it fall back to its former position. Under it two big, yellow-white scorpions, roused from their hiding place, flitted about, their tails with the venomous sting at the tip curved threateningly upward.

Overcoming my shock I quickly leaned the mattress against the wall and trampled on those long bodies, glad for my heavy army boots. The sand gave way under my stomping feet, and the scorpion disappeared into it. I had no way of knowing the result of my attack, but hoped to have gotten rid of them. There were no beds at the storeroom, and not until the next day was I issued one. I spent the night on the mattress without a further encounter with scorpions – this time. Years later, drilling for water in the mountains of Jerusalem, I changed shirts in our little hut and was stung twice by a scorpion that had settled in my garment.

Living conditions here were worse than at Sarafand. Our drinking water was drawn from a sheet-metal container without cover, which was capped eventually with a wooden board to keep insects out. A tanker truck filled the vessel once a day with our water ration for the next 24 hours. Since the kitchen building was still under construction, food, cooked in the open, often contained drift sand blown in by gusty winds. It was disgusting to bite into food and feel fine sand grit between teeth. Many lost their appetite, and so did I.

Detailed to a workshop, I worked at the repair of cannons. Requesting a transfer, I was moved to tanks and worked now with two British soldiers from whom I picked up a few more scraps of English. They were friendly fellows and we got along superbly. I should have been content with life but felt restless. I wished for an indefinable something, a change of some sort. Nothing seemed to satisfy this vague need, and nothing produced an answer or explained this unaccountable feeling until a change did occur.

At morning roll call on October 3rd, "Palestinians" were separated from the rest of the assembled soldiers. Rumors buzzed through our ranks: we will be sent to a place outside Palestine. My unrest changed to a prickly excitement not experienced since my departure from Vienna. An officer read the names of 28 soldiers and I felt devastated when mine was not among them. Some of the fellows selected were unhappy, and I gladly would have changed places with them. I felt cheated and angry. Work that morning was painful for me, and my British partners finally took notice. When they asked why I was so upset, I explained my "misfortune" in broken English. The two laughed. One said: "Don't look for trouble. Be happy you can stay here and never volunteer for anything." The other one nodded agreement.

At the midday parade after lunch, Jewish soldiers were again separated from the British companies, and from them 20 volunteers were sought to join the group of men chosen this morning. I was one of the first to jump forward. I wanted to go so badly. Kurdani seemed a dead-end street, and I wanted to go where life promised to be more exciting. It took less than a minute to reach the required number, and though none knew what we were volunteering for, we felt excited. We were ordered to be ready to move in one hour.

In feverish haste I changed from my grimy work overalls to a presentable khaki uniform. With equal swiftness I packed my gear. The dirt of the tank I had worked on still clung to my forearms, but who cared. An hour later we were 48 soldiers aboard two trucks, ready to roll.

In Kurdani I had befriended three fellows who had also come to Palestine from Vienna. Shmulik, Joshi, and Fritz. I liked Shmulik best, though he occasionally conducted himself in an aloof and patronizing manner. After work, the four of us spent much time trying to make up for the drab life in camp. We frequently visited the camp's inexpensive "movie theater" with its wooden benches and the noisy film projector on a table. It nevertheless played to packed houses in an unfinished building. We hitchhiked to Haifa on Sunday outings. Fritz then left us in the city to visit his wife, who worked as a beautician on the Hadar. Sometimes Shmulik and I sat in our tent, reading or talking, and sometimes I stayed alone in the NAAFI (military canteen) writing notes on loose sheets of paper about things past and present.

Joshi had been among the soldiers chosen this morning, and he had been upset about it. He did not want to go. When we three friends volunteered at midday, Joshi was ecstatic and stomped around like an Indian in a war dance. It was as if a weight had been lifted off his shoulders and a reprieve granted from something he dreaded.

A spirited and noisy crowd of soldiers received us at the rather antique East Railroad Station in Haifa. The building dated back to the time when the Middle East was part of the Ottoman Empire. Our travel companions, mustered from the army camps of Tira and Kayat Beach, included familiar faces, many of whom had been recruits with us in Sarafand. By then the officer in charge of our newly created Jewish company confirmed our destination as Alexandria. The closeness of the German Afrika Korps under Rommel failed to dampen the spirit and enthusiasm of most of us.

During the roll call, as we boarded the train, I became separated from my friends. We were assigned different railroad cars. Although it was October, the weather was hot. We were tightly packed into overloaded coaches. Time progressed, but we remained stationary for a long time. At 3:45 P.M. the train finally began to move.

Thoughts and notes on the train:

Alexandria, Egypt. Was something brewing? The Germans had been inactive for too long, and one wondered when they would strike again. They seemed invincible. It was no rumor that the Egyptian Arabs were prepared to be "liberated" by them. Fools. Did they really think the Nazis would accept them as equals? It was also said the Egyptians were getting ready to receive Rommel's armies when they came marching into Cairo and Alexandria. I remember Hitler's reception in Vienna. This was 1942 and the Germans were victorious on all fronts. It looked bad. I had not lost my fear of the Nazis, but I was not going to run away again. Volunteering today was not a thoughtless impulse. The burning wish to be with those transferred had several reasons. Restlessness, the possibility of adventure, and no doubt, a reckless desire to rush a confrontation with the hated enemy. I never was that way nor had I ever sought confrontation with anyone. I even was aware of a rather frightening scenario should I become a prisoner of the Germans. I could fare worse than the others if it was found out that I had been taken to a concentration camp at the outbreak of war, released with the expectation I would leave Germany for "South America" and had been caught as a British soldier, an enemy of Hitler's Reich.

The British Eighth Army in North Africa or, to be more precise, the Egypt still in British hands had a new commander: General (later Field Marshal and First Viscount of Alamein) Bernard L. Montgomery. Whatever was going to happen, we were coming closer to where it would take place. – – – –

Excursion to Alexandria

The train stopped at every railroad station on the way. Not until midnight did we cross the border from Palestine into Sinai, a trip that should have taken half the time. The night was miserable. The dim light of the overhead lamps revealed a carriage strewn with bodies and military gear. Every horizontal space was occupied. Wooden benches, luggage racks overhead, and dusty floor below. I sat on a bench next to the window, afraid to move lest I wake the man who was rolled up at my feet like an armadillo on the defense. Next morning we drew breakfast in the moving train. To carry tea with milk, hardtack, marmalade, butter, and cheese back to our seats without stumbling over packages and dropping or spilling the contents of our mess tins was a feat worthy of a juggler.

The train rolled through dismal terrain. Sand dunes as far as the eye could see, dry low bushes, and once in a while a group of camels walking single file in their clumsy-looking gait. I would have loved to see a real caravan; it would have fitted in with my sense of adventure. But the most we saw were only two or three animals at any one time. At one spot we passed an island of green, an oasis with several Bedouin tents, a flock of sheep, palm trees hanging full of red dates, but no people. Apparently they too had taken shelter from the scorching sun.

Kantara was our next stop. The place, in the middle of nowhere and just a speck on a map of the Sinai peninsular, smarted under a glaring sun. The Suez Canal, a short way to the east, was still invisible from the railroad station. The only objects of interest to me were a few uniformed Egyptians. Railroad staff, police and army personnel. After the tedious trip, and lacking anything more romantic, they presented an exotic picture on my first visit to the land of the pharaohs. Just the thought of being in Egypt was exciting. A dream of my youth had come true.

The authority of the Egyptians was restricted to the native population. Had it been otherwise, I would have suspected sabotage,

221

especially in view of the slow progress of our journey. It would have been in line with most Egyptians' hope for a German victory over the Allies in Egypt. They believed that freedom from the British would mean independence for them. Three years of Nazi conquests had taught them nothing.

As this was to be an extended stop, most of us got off the train to stretch our legs. We changed our Palestinian money into Egyptian currency and were disappointed when theirs was slightly higher than ours. Eventually we found out that the purchasing power of the Egyptian pound was greater than ours.

The official money exchange office, a little hut on sandy ground between two railroad tracks, had a long line of soldiers waiting. One needed to be patient to do business here. The queue moved only imperceptibly, and this was the worst time of the day to be out in the sun. I thought Haifa was pretty warm. When I experienced Tel Aviv's weather, I found it hot. But the heat of Kantara at midday beat both cities.

There was an alternative to the waiting line at the exchange office. Egyptian Arabs in their *galabies* ran along the train shouting: "Money change. Money change. George (every British soldier in Egypt was addressed as George), I give you better rate." Enticed by a supposedly better deal and quicker settlement, some of our men did business with those Arabs. The deal was quicker, yet not always better. A few received paper money that were no longer in circulation. I had no problem; I exchanged my money at the official station.

The only living creatures in Kantara unaffected by heat were flies. They may seem hardly worth mentioning, yet the flies of Egypt have a persistency in bothering people not easily found in other places. Those insects can not be gotten rid of by a mere wave of the hand. They always return to the place from which they had been chased. To kill them is the only solution. But Egyptian natives make only half-hearted attempts or none at all to rid themselves of those pests. Most revolting was to see the flies sit on the pussy, trachoma-infected eyes of children and adults who made no move to rid themselves of the insects. The flies here were not just annoying, they actually bit. Their Palestinian cousins, pesky in their own right, are a mild-mannered species compared to their Egyptian counterparts.

Lunch was served under the open sky. We stood in two long lines to receive our ration of bully beef (canned corned beef, jestingly referred to as "Desert Chicken" by the soldiers), dry hardtack and sweet tea with condensed milk. Kantara hosted us for 2 1/2 hours.

Half an hour into the afternoon we traveled along the Suez Canal, a ruler-straight waterway, and another half hour later our train crossed over a revolving bridge to the African side of Egypt. To be for the first time in my life on the African continent was a thrill. Alexandria, I mistakenly believed, was then just a few hours away. A delay at Ismalia, the "Garden City" near the Suez Canal did not discourage me.

The desert scenery of Sinai behind us, Egypt, on the western side of the waterway, became gradually more interesting and colorful. We steamed through a system of interlacing irrigation canals dotted with little villages, all part of the fertile Nile delta. Railroad stations were plentiful, but we were spared the tediousness of stopping at small ones. The next big city was Zagazig, and by 5:45 P.M. we rolled into Benha, an important railroad junction in Lower Egypt.

Here we were to transfer to the Cairo-Alexandria train for the last leg of our journey. To everyone's amazement, the connecting train had left Benha a few minutes before our arrival, leaving us stranded for the next six hours. This inept scheduling had governed our trip since leaving Haifa. The next train to Alexandria was not due until midnight.

I wrote about our stopover in Benha at a later date:

Always curious to see new places we asked our NCOs to persuade the commanding officer to let us visit the city. None of us was aware that Benha, like many other locations in Egypt, was out of bounds for British military personnel. Darkness had settled before we received permission to explore.

Leaving some volunteers behind to guard our gear, we left the station in big groups that later broke up into smaller ones. For an important railroad junction like Benha, the immediate surroundings of the roofless station were unimpressive. Outside the gate the aroma of burning charcoal, roast meat, spicy scents and less pleasant odors conjured up memories of the Arab sector in lower Haifa. But there most of the similarities stopped. The unpaved street we walked on had no street lighting. Illumination came from carbide lamps that lit up small stores and, indirectly, the roadway. If a blackout was in force, the general population ignored the restriction, their misconduct apparently condoned by the local administration. Storefronts, typical of many Arab cities and villages, had no display windows or doors but were simply big openings. At night corrugated roll shutters secured the businesses. Side streets, as far as we could make out, were narrow, crooked, and alley-like. To walk them, one had to contend with the proverbial Egyptian darkness. The street leading away from the station was crowded with people, and when our presence became known, Arab boys began to surround us, begging for money and cigarettes. When, with some exceptions, their pleas were ignored, the kids began to shout profanities, in which the Arab language is so rich. How surprised were those boys when many of our fellows, fluent in Arabic, replied in kind. They had never met British soldiers who not only knew a few common cuss words, but actually spoke their language, albeit with a Palestinian dialect.

After the unsettling encounter with those strange soldiers, the urchins kept away. In their place young men began to follow us. As they stayed at a safe distance they were ignored. We were not familiar yet with the warning signs displayed in all soldiers' clubs in Egypt: Never Walk Alone. British Soldier Books and Pay Books were prize items sought by Germans for their own sinister purposes. The desired documents, supplied to them through theft and robbery, earned high fees. Stealing from British soldiers was a common practice.

Eventually my three friends and I separated from a larger band of men, though we were never alone. Everybody took care not to stray from the sight of other groups. We met our commanding officer who, in the company of two soldiers with rifles, had also taken to the street. He was protected by two-thirds of our weaponry: Our unit had been issued three rifles for the trip.

In a typical Arab café we met other fellows from our company. The sweet Turkish coffee, served in the familiar small cups without handles, invoked again memories of Haifa. Our visit to the café, however, was short. We all were tired from that uncomfortable night on the train and, after finishing our coffee and cigarettes, we return to the railroad station.

After the lights of the carbide lamps in the street, the interior of the station was impenetrably dark. We felt our way to the platform, and though the route we walked was obscure, the direction was easily made out. The fellows left behind were talking and singing, and when we came closer, we found them sitting in groups on kit bags and other equipment. Many lay on the concrete floor of the platform, and my friends and I did likewise. Gas-mask containers became our pillows, the hard floor our bed, and yet, it was a pleasure to stretch out our legs.

On one side of me Fritz and Joshi had fallen asleep, on my other side lay Shmulik. For a while he and I reminisced about our youth in Vienna, just a few years back. How fate, in its twisted ways, had placed us on the platform of an Egyptian railroad station, in the military uniform of a country that our parents, a mere 25 years earlier, had faced as the enemy in World War I. While we talked, I looked at the twinkling stars above and then, overcome by fatigue, I fell asleep. – – – –

Loud talk and the noise of people moving about awakened me. The awaited train was half an hour overdue when it arrived, but at 45 minutes past midnight we moved once more. This time, in a northwesterly direction toward Alexandria and the Mediterranean Sea. The train stopped at Tanta, later Damanhur, both fair-sized cities, and then, early in the morning, we reached a foggy and wet Alexandria.

At the main train depot our cars were switched around and then, connected to another locomotive, we traveled again for a while. Our destination was Camp Sidi Bishr, east of Alexandria. We were assigned tents and, as the day had turned sunny, many sought permission to visit Alexandria. The request was denied. Being practical, we did laundry and rested up from the trip.

Next day after lunch, 49 six-hour passes (1 P.M. to 7 P.M.) were issued. As a far greater number of men were interested in a visit to Alex (the soldiers' name for the city) a drawing was held. My friends were not among the lucky ones, I was.

A streetcar took us on a 45-minute ride to the city. I had not been on a streetcar since Vienna, and the ride was fun. At Ramle Station, an open square at the end of the line, we got off. Our big group broke up into smaller bands and even individuals. Being without my friends, I impatiently took off on my own. A short block from Ramle Station was the Avenue de la Reine Nazli[24], a wide walkway and traffic artery that followed the curve of the Mediterranean Sea. With no specific destination in mind, I walked the busy thoroughfare with the expanse of the sea to my right and came to a square where, surrounded by a half-circle of columns, the statue of Ismail Pasha stood. He governed Egypt as a viceroy of the sultan of Turkey in the past century. I turned left into a boulevard of palm trees and reached another extensive plaza with the equestrian statue of Mohammed Ali, a self-made Pasha (1805) who tried to make Egypt independent of the Turkish Sultan.

A little further down was another circle of columns, and at the far end of the square stood the Bourse or Stock Exchange. I walked this district, drinking in the colorful scene and felt as if I was living an adventure.

Alexandria, as I observed on later visits, was very cosmopolitan. It could easily have passed for a French city, had it not been for men wearing red fezzes, the many Arab shoeshine boys and the street vendors selling all kinds of items including imitations of antiques. Once in a while I was approached by a man or even a very young teenager who furtively extracted a wrinkled envelope from his dress whispering, "Hey, George, wanna buy dirty pictures?"

Street signs were in Arabic and French, and so were store signs. Civilians passing me talked as often in French as in Arabic. Shopping streets, department stores, parks, many movie theaters, nightclubs, and cafés gave the place the appearance of a major city. Many of Alexandria's residents came from Europe, largely France, Greece, and Italy, as well as

---

[24] Queen Nazli. Street names of royalty and pashas abounded in the city. They were changed after the abdication of King Faruk and the army revolution in the summer of 1952.

from the Levant and Turkey. Public transportation was by streetcar, taxi, and *gharry*, a horse-drawn cab.

On the day after our short visit to Alexandria we started work in army workshops on the west side of the city. Every morning we were driven in open trucks from our camp in Sidi Bishr to the workplace. Our route led through the city and the European-dressed people on our way cheered and waved to us perhaps in the belief we were on our way to the front. Their cheers pleased us and our presence obviously comforted them. Though the Nazis were closer to us in miles than they had ever been, none of us was worried.

In the beginning we worked many hours a day, six-and-one-half days a week. But we were not too tired to spend the free Sunday afternoon and many of the free evenings in the city. Alexandria probably had never looked like this before, nor would it ever again look as it did during the month of October in 1942.

It was fascinating to walk the streets of that beautiful city.[25] It teemed with so many soldiers that one was always in a crowd. Soldiers of just about every Allied nation were present, and it was as if a future United Nations had decided to meet here. Many could be identified by their headgear. Turbaned men from India, Scotsmen wearing their woolen side cap (the Glengarry), Australians and New Zealanders with their wide brimmed hats, one side turned upward. The easiest identification was always the imprint on the narrow band on shoulder lapels that disclosed the place of origin. English, Scotch and Irish regiments with their distinctive badges, South Africans, black soldiers from East and West Africa, Czechs, Poles, Sikhs, Hindus, and more, all pushed, shoved, and rubbed shoulders in the streets.

The city also had many soldiers' clubs and hostels, some serving only specific military branches. The army had theirs, and so did the navy, the merchant marine, the air force, and the women's auxiliary. The army, least discriminating, served anyone in uniform in its clubs. The establishments of the other services were off-limit to us. Clubs were further segregated by military ranks. Additional clubs making no distinction of rank or military branch were run by Christian churches and Jewish groups. The Australian Comforts Fund, an Australian service club, had an extra line at the end of its advertisement in the "Service Guide to Alexandria." It read in bold print "Open to all Australian Personnel," meaning, Australians only.

Other clubs also stressed a particular preference, such as the New Zealand YMCA that said, "Although accommodation is primarily New

---

[25] Visiting Alexandria in the company of my wife 50 years later, I found the city to be terribly neglected.

Zealanders other members of H.B.M.'s Forces are accommodated if possible". The Menorah Club declared: "Primarily to serve the needs of Jewish soldiers from Palestine and elsewhere. It is understood that the facilities of the Club are also available to any member of H.B.M.'s Forces." The two Jewish clubs, the Menorah Club and the Jewish Club for Service Men, were organized and hosted by Jewish French ladies. Soldiers of all military branches without discrimination visited both clubs.

Clubs offered soft drinks and food at reasonable prices, had lounges and reading rooms where one could relax. Occasionally some featured classical or modern music, games, and once in a while a dance. Hostels accommodated soldiers on leave at low rates. Yet, despite the variety of free entertainment the clubs offered, a Sunday visit to Alex was incomplete if not rounded out by a visit to a cinema. Having spent one Sunday afternoon at the Menorah Club, the four of us strolled the city streets in search of a movie house. All theaters in the area were sold out. When we passed the sold-out Rialto that advertised on its marquee "They Died with their Boots on," a film about Custer's last stand with Errol Flynn, Joshi laughingly said: "I wonder if we too will die with our boots on before this war is over."

After many working hours in the big workshops where cars, trucks, Bren gun carriers (small armored vehicles), tanks, and canons were repaired in never-ending succession, we lived our life to the fullest. Or at least what we understood life in its fullest to be. We whiled away the hours with the carelessness of young men who do not acknowledge their insecure and unpredictable future. I did not worry about the future. When I sat by myself at a table in the canteen, a blank sheet of paper in front of me and tried to write a rationalization of the incomprehensible "whys" in my life, the paper remained blank. No probing in the thicket of life or searching in the maze of past events brought me an answer.

The whys of past events were puzzling, unanswerable; the happenings themselves, however, were solid enough. The distance in time and miles between my family in Vienna and me were great, and the distance created by the situation we lived in even greater. I was convinced no harm would come to them. It was almost as if I believed that time would stand still on Jägerstrasse, only to resume its interrupted flow after I returned there.

It was difficult to believe that a time of peace had once existed. It had become normal to accept war and its lunatic events. War in peacetime seemed unreal and so did a life of peace in time of war. A time without atrocities and dangers seemed unreal to those alive then. Just as unreal were references to the future. The only recognizable time was the past that stretched into the years behind me. Time ended in the present.

For a few days Shmulik had behaved withdrawn. I had felt the change in my friend's mood, but being unaware of the "Dear John" letter he had received from the girl he loved, I gave it no second thought. When the cause of his depression came to light, I was nonetheless shocked by what unorthodox means my friend had tried to cure his emotional anguish. He had volunteered for the paratroops. Luckily, things turned out well. He was refused the transfer to an airborne unit and the girl eventually married him. They lived in Jerusalem after the war.

In our camp people thought it unbelievable that a soldier had not been to Number 6 Sisters Street. The building was the official army brothel. Supervised by army physicians and controlled by British military police who were present at all times, it admitted only whites. Nonwhites had their own house somewhere else. Not having been to the brothel was symptomatic of a physical deficiency. Sooner or later, most of our men visited that celebrated establishment at least once, and married men were no exception. For a while the bachelors, who represented 90 percent of our company, made the grass widowers a target of mockery. But then defenders of those straying husbands would say: "You can't blame those married men. They are used to it and miss it." Well, it seemed that most fellows missed it, including those who had never had it. To correct the situation a pilgrimage of sorts started which the four of us joined.

It was the time of Shmulik's emotional distress, and he may have entertained the thought that by a trip to the house he was retaliating for his girlfriend's betrayal. Feeling in the dumps, he felt no compunction about the intended visit. I, on the other hand – though I never let it be known – was beset by discomfort and doubt about the impending trip. I felt an aversion toward prostitutes, and a sexual encounter of this kind remained a disquieting thought. I envied my friends' blasé manner regarding the upcoming event, and felt my behavior was unbecoming a man my age. After all, I would no longer be a teenager on my next birthday six months away. And so, in spite of my hesitation, I played along. Actually, I was curious.

Number 6, Sisters Street, was an old building in a sleazy neighborhood. The entrance hall was as plain and shabby as the outside. I would not have been surprised had I found out that the building had served the same purpose for the soldiers of the 1914-18 war. Newcomers formed a line to the left side of the anteroom where, behind a table, a military policeman sat. In front of the man was a large, open ledger in which we recorded our name, rank, and army number, all of which was checked against our Soldier Book. After a payment of 20 piasters the policeman handed us a paper stub and an Arab boy, at the end of the table, gave each of us a packaged condom and a small, soft metal tube containing a white cream. I had no idea what it was for, but felt too embarrassed to ask. Fritz later said it was to lubricate the condom.

A steady flow of soldiers, one row ascending, the other coming down, filled a staircase leading to an upper floor. Joining the climbers we reached a corridor with doors on both sides of the landing. The doors, as we later saw, led into small rooms. A bustling crowd of soldiers pushed us along. It felt like window shopping in a busy lane, but with the goods hidden and busy behind wooden barriers. Nonetheless, entrances opened and closed in irregular patterns as soldiers were received or dispatched by a variety of more and less attractive females. The instant a woman waved good-bye to one customer, another eagerly awaited her service. In front of some doors men were patiently awaiting their turn, apparently familiar with the woman behind it.

I had no intention of inspecting the rest of the building, did not even think it mattered whom I chose. I just wanted to get this business over with and be able to reply as nonchalantly as the others: "Of course, I was there."

I felt that way until I happened to glimpse a young and very pretty girl dismiss one soldier, and then lead another one into her room. In the short time I saw her, I was impressed by her appearance. Her complexion was light tan, the mouth small, the lips full and red. A crown of fuzzy brown hair haloed her black eyes and young features. She could not have been older than twenty. Several soldiers waited in front of her door, and when I disclosed my choice to my friends, Shmulik and Joshi joined my line. Fritz went next door to a woman with a pockmarked face, where no one waited. With a sheepish grin he said later that he was sorry for her.

It was strange how my aversion toward prostitutes dissipated when I finally entered the room with the girl. A feeling of being with a regular girl who would respond to my advances like a girlfriend came over me. This picture became less idyllic when she unemotionally asked for the stub of paper the military police man had handed me. My feelings were shaken some more by the entrance of a tall, skinny Arab. He poured water from a washbowl into a pail on the floor and then refilled the empty basin with fresh water from a pitcher. He pulled a clean towel from a low chest of drawers that he placed on the washstand. He exchanged a few words in Arabic with the girl and left.

The girl had taken off her light housecoat and was standing in the nude with her back to me. She was still handling something on the chest of drawers when I, slightly enamored, and attempting to get back into my previous mood, tried to touch her tenderly. She shot around and furiously shouted, "Are you crazy?" Her unexpected rage stunned me. I did not know what taboo I had violated. Her wrath completely crushed the naive and warm feelings I had entertained for a few moments in my world of fantasy. What followed was just going through the motions without fulfillment. Not sophisticated enough to see life in the light of reality, I had tried to mold it to my way of thinking.

When General Montgomery took over as commander of the Eighth Army, he at first reorganized his forces and then turned his attention to a minor evil. He closed the military brothels. Though I never again returned to Sisters Street, I felt his moral action was misdirected. Most soldiers in the Middle East had been away from home for a long time, some for years and had little choice but to seek their sexual satisfaction with native prostitutes. Being deprived of army-controlled places, they either had to look for pleasure in less sanitary localities, risking exposure to diseases or to abstain from sex. It was said that Montgomery's action was in line with his religious beliefs which, however, found little appreciation among those affected by his decree. He had soldiers miss out on the pleasures of this world for those in the great beyond; the great beyond which many of them would enter in their immediate future through the hot sands of the North African desert.

Enormous quantities of supplies, shipped from England and the USA were arriving in Alexandria. The numbers of soldiers and support services in and around the city were formidable. This huge congregation of men and materiel created, like matter compressed, a kind of time bomb that ultimately had to explode. The release was the great allied North African campaign which started October 22, 1942 and became the turning point of the war against the Axis forces. The greatest firepower ever assembled in this part of the world rained a torrent of explosives on Rommel's Afrika Korps dug in at El Alamein. In our camp, 50 miles away from the front line, the ground under our feet trembled perceptibly.

On October 26 our company was moved from Sidi Bishr to Dekeila, a deserted Arab village west of Alexandria. Our tents stood on the fringe of the village. We continued to ride trucks to our jobs. At first, we wondered if our transfer to the west might have been an indication of things to come, and we were moving in anticipation of allied advances. But this was not the case.

The first few nights in the new camp we slept on straw mattresses on the ground; beds arrived later. I was thinking about the scorpions of Kurdani, but other events made one night unforgettable for another reason. After being forced to retreat for a few days, the Axis decided to strike back at the Allies in the only way they were able. They dispatched bombers to Alexandria. By that time I had been through many air raids, none of them pleasant, but this time it was different. I described it later:

230

I awoke to a hellish concert.

The mattress I slept on lay on the ground. When I sat up, knees pushing against my stomach, feet on the dirt floor, I felt the earth shake under my feet like the hood of a motor car with a skipping engine.

All around, and separated from us only by the flimsy walls of the tent were crashing, exploding, and rumbling noises of a ferocity I had never experienced before. Flashes of light came through the narrow slit of the tent's entrance and though I was apprehensive of what lay beyond, curiosity got the better of me, and I inched toward the crack on my knees.

The dark outside had erupted into a dazzling array of fireworks, luminous and deadly. Tracer bullets of diverse colors streaked toward the sky. Some projectiles hung there for a second, only to burst into different-sized flashes a moment later. The anti-aircraft barrage seemed to tear the black firmament apart, a sight that was hypnotizing and terrifying at the same time.

After staring at this color spectacle for a while, my impression of the dark sky being attacked from below changed. It now appeared to me as if the exploding flashes probing for weak spots in the sky came from behind the heaven's dark dome.

The enemy planes were hidden by the night, but the resonance of their engines was clearly audible overhead.

Two or three more faces topped my head, looked at the display in awe, and then commented apprehensively: "Wow."

We had dug a few open trenches at the camp's perimeter after work, to be used in case of air raids, but when the moment came, none of the fellows in my tent went there. We stared at the fireworks and listened to the sounds, some of which seemed to shake the earth more than others, until one of my fellow watchers remarked with a kind of reverence: "Bet you those are the heavy guns of the warships in Alex."

I was tired and vacated my spot at the tent's opening. Rolling up on my mattress in fetal position, I pulled my blanket up to my chin, placed my steel helmet over my face, and expecting to hear shrapnel slice through the thin wall of our tent at any moment, I actually fell asleep. – –

En route to work next morning we had to skirt a few streets we usually took. But except for some isolated, unimpressive bomb craters in the middle of roadways, I saw little damage from the night attack. I may assume, however, that this lengthy air assault had done more harm to the area of the harbor than what we saw on our way to the workshops. On the trucks the conversation revolved around the events of the previous night. If a fellow dared to state that he had not been afraid during last night's spectacle, other fellows accused him of lying. I agreed with them.

If my language shortcomings were troublesome, I saw no reason to worry. Most with whom I had to conversed spoke German or Yiddish. It made life easy and supported my laziness and lack of interest in studying languages. I knew some Hebrew, slightly more English and Arabic, and wrongly assumed it to be sufficient.

One evening after a visit to an army movie theater near Dekeila, Shmulik, Fritz, Joshi and I were marching home. The night was as beautiful as a night in Egypt can be. The dark sky above was lavishly studded with stars, the air was balmy, and a light breeze swayed the few palm trees that dotted the deserted village. The absolute silence around us was broken only by our conversation conducted in German.

Next morning I was called to our C.O. "The four of you," he said, "walked through the village late last night and talked loudly in German. Don't you know you could have been taken for Germans by some English soldiers and gotten shot? Why don't you speak Hebrew when you are out at night?" — "I don't speak Hebrew," I confessed. — "Then speak English," he said. — "I don't speak English," I admitted. — "Then at least don't shout." He sounded resigned to an unresolvable situation, and I was dismissed. This exchange, of course, had also been in German.

It came as a pleasant surprise when they announced that workdays were to be shorter, and we would have Saturday afternoons and Sundays off. If the reason for the reduced working hours had been that the war situation had finally tilted our way and the extra effort at the workshops was unnecessary, this would have made sense. But with the offensive in full swing, and with vehicles and attack weapons being damaged in the progress, our technical service should have been needed more than ever. But the army's ways were as mysterious as those of God and not for us to question.

Around our camp and the village there was much open land with nothing of interest until one day a large space of it was taken up by German soldiers. We had returned from work, showered, and changed into clean clothes, when suddenly word spread that not far beyond the village German prisoners of war were arriving. Most men, who had not departed for the city before the sensational news broke, rushed to behold that unusual and gratifying spectacle. I went with Shmulik and found beyond the Arab village a sea of squatting Germans soldiers, loosely guarded by a few black African soldiers with rifles over their shoulders. I could hardly believe my eyes when I saw the hundreds of Hitler's finest, Rommel's men of the Afrika Korps, cowering in that position. They were a far cry from the warriors with the belligerent faces I had seen march into Poland and Paris on screens in movie theaters in Vienna. It seemed unbelievable that these were the same men who had instilled fear in the world they had set out to conquer. But I did not feel like gloating, nor did I have the wish to hurt them. It was just satisfying to see them defeated.

More open trucks arrived filled with more German soldiers. Sitting on the roof of the driver's cab, their legs dangling among the prisoners, were always two black soldiers, rifles slung over their shoulders. When the tailgate of the truck was dropped, the Germans, with the two Blacks among them, jumped to the ground. The prisoners joined the squatters while the two new guards just sauntered over to the sentries circling the prisoners. It was an incredible sight. The lax security seemed pure negligence, and the passivity of the supposedly stalwart German soldier was incomprehensible. Thinking I knew the Germans, I couldn't help marveling that none of them tried to overpower the few soldiers who guarded them. The opportunity clearly was there.

From ten paces away I watched two of the prisoners whisper to each other and from time to time look our way. They then took wallets from their pockets and started to extract snapshots and papers from them. One of them looked at the black guard who was watching him. He stretched the hand that held the wallets in our direction with a gesture signaling that he just wanted to walk toward us. When there was no reaction from the guard, the man hesitantly approached us.

A Buchenwald scene passed through my mind: our fellow KZ prisoner on the ground with the bullet hole in his temple, and the two SS guards, one of whom had shot the man, standing indifferently at their posts a few paces away. Still holding out the billfolds, the German prisoner haltingly said in German, "Zigarette, Zigarette."

I hesitated for a moment and then pulled a partly used pack of cigarettes from my shirt pocket and handed it to him. I refused the proffered wallets and just waved him away. I had no heart to accept his offer or to blame him for what had happened to me. I did not know what was going on in Europe. "Danke, danke," he said. I just shrugged my shoulders as if I had not understood or cared.

Nearby a group of our people stood close to the prisoners and a German corporal was talking to one of our men. When Shmulik and I joined the group, we found that the two spoke French with each other. Our man was originally from Rumania, and the Rumanian language is related to French. I knew also that our man spoke fluent German but apparently had no intention of using it. He told us later what the corporal had said and we discovered that German megalomania was not dead yet. The corporal had boasted that their retreat in Africa was temporary and Stalingrad was firmly in German hands. Both, of course, untrue. The discussion was interrupted by a British officer who angrily ordered us to leave.

233

On the following Saturday afternoon in the city we hailed a *gharry* to take us to the border of the restricted area. We decided to visit the Red Light district because of an article I had read in a magazine. The report had claimed that Alexandria was one of the five most wicked harbor cities in the world. I told my friends the story and we decided to have a look at this Sodom and Gomorrha by the Mediterranean Sea.

The off-limit districts were marked by signs every soldier was familiar with. They were fastened to corner houses of streets leading into the forbidden zone. Districts of this kind had been out of bounds to military personnel even before the heavy-handed moral policy of General Montgomery, and for good reason. Aside the danger of contracting sexual diseases, this dirt-ridden Casbah-like neighborhood was the home of some unsavory types. An added deterrent to soldiers visiting these off-limit sections was, of course, the punishment if caught.

The *gharry* dropped us off, and we walked along a narrow street. The air, saturated by what seemed to be the smell of rotting, discarded vegetables, would have been acceptable to my nose. But there were also fetid odors that lacked definition. The pleasant aroma of meat roasting on spits, often so prevalent in Arab neighborhoods, was missing here. The steady hum of many human voices was occasionally interrupted by the quarrelsome screeching of two opposing parties. A tea and coffee vendor seemed like an agitated hummingbird as he flitted from place to place.

Not only were people plentiful, but also undernourished and sickly looking dogs. Most trotted shyly, tails between their legs, obviously afraid of getting kicked for no reason by humans.

No vehicular traffic interfered, so we walked four abreast in the middle of a roadway that had no sidewalks. We were being watched. It must have been a rarity to see British soldiers in this neighborhood. The people we met ranged from almost Caucasian to Arab with Semitic features, and Negroes from sub-Saharan Africa. Color complexions ran from pale to tan, to ebony. Races of the Near East and Africa fused in this cauldron of misery. The houses were neglected relics of better times and in most cases badly in need of repairs. Fat, repulsive women sat in front of some entrance calling out to us, "Hey George, want some fun?"

Suddenly two black African military policemen appeared driving several laughing African soldiers in front of them. I thought it meant trouble. But the group just passed us, and all of them called out good natured, "Hi, George." This chance meeting made it clear that black military police of African colonies would not engage in conflict with white soldiers. Nonetheless, soon after the encounter we left this place of depravity and forgotten people.

More good news came from the War Theater. On November 8,

1942, U.S. and British forces landed in Morocco. The tide had really turned.

As unexpected as the recently reduced working hours was the order that we are to return to Palestine. On Saturday, November 14, we returned our tools to the storerooms of the workshops, said good-bye to people not of our company, and that was the last we saw of the workshop.

Sunday I spent with my friends including Joshi, in the city. I mention Joshi because he and a small group of our soldiers were ordered to stay behind when our company moved back to Palestine. Joshi had tears in his eyes when we bid him good-bye. He was killed in an automobile accident soon after we left Alexandria. He had not been killed in action, yet had died with his boots on.

On Monday, our last day in Alexandria, I went to the city by myself. Sentimental as always, I strolled the streets in a farewell mood, not knowing if I would ever come back again. I wanted to take with me the many memories that had accumulated in the short time we had spent here. The good and the not so good and remember Alexandria for the exciting and interesting intermezzo that it had been in my life. Tuesday found us aboard a train, and a scant 24 hours later we arrived in Kurdani. The trip to Egypt seemed like a dream.

Kurdani Again

I was pleased to be detailed once more to the shop where I had worked with the two Englishmen, but much had changed in our absence. The two men were gone, and so were the tanks. Huge V-twelve tank motors and radial nine-cylinder aircraft engines – supposedly also used in tanks – had taken their place. Most of the work was done as on a line assembly whereby each performed the same task repeatedly.

At first I found my job interesting. I measured the inside diameter of cylinders in the engine block for asymmetrical wear. The inside micrometer used for this purpose showed the width in thousandths of inches. If the diameter of the cylinder had lost its perfect roundness by even a few thousands of an inch, I sent the cylinder block to the next station. Here its bore was turned and reamed to a two or three thousandths of an inch oversize, giving cylinder the perfect circularity needed for high-performance motors.

After a while my job lost its novelty and became tedious, as did my daily life. The restlessness in my blood, the longing for the unknown, the exotic that forever seemed beyond the horizon again beset me. The closest I came to satisfying my appetite for change was hiking to places I had not seen before.

At Christmas 1942, most soldiers in our camp received a three-day pass. Shmulik took off for Jerusalem and Fritz to his wife in Haifa. I had nowhere to go. I saw no point in Shmulik's trip, for as far as I knew, he had failed to rekindle the relationship with his girlfriend. Yet despite the lack of progress, Jerusalem exerted a gravitational pull for my friend that I found irrational. Fritz's wish to spend the free time with his wife, made sense. I thought wistfully of our late friend Joshi who would have made an admirable partner for any excursion.

The desire to visit places not seen before made me realize that Palestine had many sites of interest. For its size it had more famous spots than any other place on our globe. Although I had been in Palestine two years, I had found little opportunity to realize my wish to explore. I had spent seven months behind barbed wire in Atlit and during the following twelve months in Haifa had worked six days a week.

Of my time in the army, the two months in Alexandria had been terrific, yet it was disappointing to have been to Egypt and not having seen the pyramids and Sphinx.

For now I decided on a trip to Lake Kineret, also called Lake Tiberias or Sea of Galilee, and as luck willed it, David, a young fellow in our company, was ready to join me. Born in Haifa, he had seen little of his native land and had never been to the eastern part of the country.

To save expenses we intended to thumb rides and use public transportation only when we had no choice. To make the most of our leave, we started early on the morning of our first free day, and I recorded later:

Because of the many three-day passes issued, the Akko-Haifa road close to our camp, had more than the usual crowd of soldiers seeking transportation. Few, I was certain, traveled for the sake of experiencing new places, but rather to visit families or friends. When we finally beat the fierce competition and got onto a truck, it took us only as far as the checkpoint, about three miles from downtown Haifa. Our road met the Haifa-Afula highway here at a 90-degree angle. We wanted to go through the Emek (Yezre-el valley) to reach Tiberias on the shores of Lake Kineret.

When a Palestinian Jew spoke of the Emek, it was with pride. This plain, almost 10 miles across and about 30 miles long, stretches from the southeastern foothills of Mount Carmel to beyond the city of Afula. Jewish settlements, orchards and fields dot its spread where, only 20 years before our visit, uncultivated land and swamps brought malaria and blackwater fever to the first Jewish settlers.

A truck took us on a little-traveled road to kibbutz Gevat. We did not mind as it was in our general direction and away from the crowded checkpoint. The slight detour even had its advantage. It was past noon and time for lunch. Though one could not buy food at a kibbutz, we did not have to worry. Boys in uniform, very much respected and catered to in those days, got a free lunch in the kibbutz's dining room. Any kibbutz in those war years was willing to feed and put up traveling soldiers for a night or two.

After the meal we hopped a pickup truck to Afula and rode from there an army truck on its way to Damascus. The driver intended to spend the night in Tiberias.

Massive Mount Tabor on our left, with its fortress-like monastery on top, seemed out of place in the flat terrain of the countryside. It looked like the hump on a camel's back. A while later the truck moved through hilly country and slowly climbed toward a mountaintop. Beyond the summit a vista of great beauty opened up far below us. Tiberias and the lake.

The late afternoon sun colored the panorama a glittering bluish-red creating the illusion of a huge two-dimensional picture postcard. Across the lake the purple mountains of Transjordan were mirrored in the blue water and in the far north we glimpsed snow-capped Mount Hermon. White houses and buildings interspersed with greenery started halfway down the mountain. This mixture of white and green stretched carpet-like to the shore of the lake. We descended a steep and winding road and passed a sign marked "sea level." Lake Kineret is 680 feet below the level of the Mediterranean.

Tiberias, like Haifa, starts at the water's edge. Also like Haifa, the built-up area of the city changes in the middle of the rise from the old section to the new. In lower and older Tiberias the exteriors of most buildings are made of square rocks, in the style established in Palestine during the past century. The new houses, built with hollow cement blocks, have their walls covered with plaster. The new houses may not stand up over time as well as the buildings of the past century, but they go up quickly, look nice, and meet the need for housing.

Our driver dropped us off in the central square. We strolled the streets and marveled at the durable crusader castle near the beach. The people around us were a mixed lot. The fez became the predominant headgear when we approached the Arab section of the city. Looking down a sloping street I saw the dome of a mosque and a thick, short minaret next to it. On the corner of that street I was pleased to read a Jewish name over an entrance: "L.Sternberg, Chemist.

Dusk came early and we decided to spend money for a bus ride to kibbutz Degania Beit where we hoped to find accommodations for the night. The kibbutz, near the southernmost point of the lake, belongs already to the Jordan Valley. Established in the first decade of this century, it is the oldest community settlement in the country.

After a friendly welcome and an evening meal in the cafeteria-like dining hall, we were taken to a guestroom containing five beds. The beds were covered with linen and it felt great to rest between white sheets. It had been a long time since I had experienced that luxury.

Saturday, December 26, 1942. I slept fabulously and at seven o'clock went with David to the dining hall for breakfast. I was anxious to get going and 30 minutes later we were on our way. A pleasant addition to our party was a girl from the kibbutz who my partner knew from his school days in Haifa. She told us of a Persian village in Transjordan (today's Jordan) on the other side of the border, and we set out to visit it.

Since no highway led from the kibbutz to our destination, we walked across multiform terrain in a southeasterly direction. In a citrus grove deep yellow grapefruits hung on trees like so many miniature moons, crescent-like when partially hidden by the dark-green foliage. When a light breeze swayed the leaves of the trees, the rays of the sun reflected in tiny lightning flashes from glittering drops of water that had been left there by the light rain of the night before. I was captivated by the freshness of the morning air, the setting so beautiful it looked like a painting come to life.

On a short stopover at kibbutz Massada we were invited to breakfast but accepted only a glass of sweet tea. Continuing southeast toward a mountain range that ran north to south, the fields of the kibbutz ended and uncultivated terrain followed.

The girl knew only the general direction to the Persian village, a circumstance that seemed unimportant at the time. And yet, we were lucky when after half an hour of hiking we met two Arab boys of perhaps ten and six. They rode an exceptionally small donkey and were trailed by a dog. I stopped them and asked in my limited Arabic where the village was. They understood and offered to take us there for 5 piasters.

Our direction changed slightly. On our original route we would have missed our target. A little later we were surprised to see a river a short way ahead. A river? We should not have been surprised. Our goal was a village in Transjordan and the word meant the other side of the Jordan. Notwithstanding I turned to the boys. "Stena shvo-ye," (Wait a moment) I said in annoyed as if the water was their fault. "Shoo hada?" (What's that?) I asked, pointing at the water. "Hada Yarmuk," (That's the Yarmuk River) the older answered.

We walked down a bushy incline and stood at the water's edge. This being the rainy season, the river was perhaps 80 feet across and quite rapid in places. It was not the width of the water that concerned me, but its depth. I was worried about the box cameras we had bought in Haifa for our trip, and though they had been inexpensive, they were right in line with our budget. Getting them wet would have ruined them even before we had a chance to used them.

While we discussed the unforeseen obstacle, the two boys jumped off the donkey and, worried about their money, gesticulated wildly toward the water, trying to impress on us the harmlessness of the river. We remained unconvinced.

Not far from where we had come through the underbrush I had spied a primitive tent. I walked over to ask the owner, a Bedouin, about the depth of the river. He pointed to his knee and said: "Hena." (To here). If he was right, the crossing was manageable, and we decided to attempt it.

The older boy wanted us to ford the water one by one on the donkey's back. Following his suggestion, David swung his right leg over the animal's back and stood with both feet on the ground. The little guide pushed my friend into a sitting position and then led the donkey to the river's edge. That was as far as the animal intended to go. It resolutely refused to enter the river. The older boy got into the water and pulled at the string around the donkey's neck while his younger brother pushed from behind. That desperate exertion by the two little fellows to get beast and rider into the river, and our partner's precariously balancing position looked so ridiculously funny, the girl and I, standing on firm ground, bent over laughing.

After a few steps into the river men and creature suddenly returned to shore. "Perhaps it's be better to forget our trip across the Yarmuk," my partner conceded, looking at the two cameras I held by their straps.

Exasperated by our last-minute decision to play it safe, the Arab boys became frantic. Then, as if a prayer of theirs had been answered, an Arab appeared on the scene. The man took off his shoes - he wore no socks - and waded into the water. As he progressed, the water reached his knees, then rose to about one-third up his thighs.

Obviously inspired by the expected 5 piasters, the two boys again tried to persuade us to make the crossing. Once more we agreed. Our friend took his seat on the donkey's back and the struggle to get the animal into the water started anew. In the river David had to pull up his legs almost to his belly, and still part of his boots got wet. In that uncomfortable position he slid back and forth and I expected him at any moment to take a bath. But he made it safely across and cheerfully waved to us.

Now it was our turn. Having witnessed my friend's balancing act, the girl and I decided to ford the river on foot. We took off our shoes, rolled up our pants and then stepped carefully into the water. It was ice cold, and the rocks at the bottom were slippery. My left hand, stretched high above my head, held the cameras and our packs. With my right I led the girl while searching with my feet for the highest points in the riverbed. The rolled-up pants got slightly wet, but we also made it safely to the other side.

We were in Transjordan near a place the boys called Adasi-e. Again we marched through bushy terrain, up hill and down, and finally came to a group of houses that we assumed to be the Persian village. Persians and Arabs differ little in their appearance. Persians (Iranians) have their own language though their writing seems to be in Arabic.

The family of the first house was in a nearby citrus grove harvesting mandarins. As we watched them, a man came over and smilingly handed us several of the fruits that were as large as a man's fist. We thanked him and continued to walk a dirt road into the village.

Between whitewashed houses people stopped what they were doing and looked at us in various stages of interest. Having gotten over their surprise, many smiled and waved a friendly greeting. Children were less bashful. They laughed and pointed fingers at us. It was doubtful if they had ever seen men in British uniforms.

We did not investigate the rest of the village for it had taken us more time to locate the place than we had planned. Our steps turned west again toward Palestine.

Recrossing the river we paid the boys their well-earned fee, and another 5 piasters bonus made them extremely happy.

On our march we rounded an extensive aqueduct, built by the Romans, then went southwest until we reached Kibbutz Ashdot Ya-akov. After lunch on the house, or in this case, kibbutz, we traveled north toward Afikim.

It was said that Afikim, also a kibbutz, had a dining room noted for its elegant interior. This point of interest aroused my curiosity, and so, on arriving at the community settlement by mid-afternoon, we went straight to this showplace. The dining hall really resembled a huge, stylish restaurant, and our admiration for the site was rewarded with coffee and a snack.

On the last stretch of our journey we passed large artificial fish ponds, operated commercially by kibbutzim, and at 5 o'clock we entered Degania Beit, tired, but satisfied. During our last night here it rained hard and in the morning the ground had turned into the mire that all kibbutzim in the Emek and the Galilee are notorious for.

After breakfast we said good-bye to the girl and the few members of the kibbutz we had gotten to know and then caught a ride to Tiberias. It rained as if another biblical flood was in the making, and we decided to take a bus back to Haifa.

How long these three days in this segment of my life lasted! So

240

much could be crammed into 72 hours in my youth. – – – –

Starting January 1, 1943 our company, and many other companies of the R.A.O.C. transferred to the newly created R.E.M.E., the Royal Electrical Mechanical Engineering. Nothing changed in the structure of the companies, only the name of the outfit, and the badge we wore on our caps.

The New Year brought additional men to our company. They were transferred from a British Pioneer unit. Three of the newcomers became friends of mine: Moshe, originally from Poland, Bubi from Berlin, and Leo from Czechoslovakia. Politically, Moshe and Bubi were on opposite sides. Bubi and Leo, however, were like two peas in a pod, when they argued with others about their political views. Both were heart and soul right-wing Zionists. In 1948 Leo joined the I.Z.L. and, as an eyewitness told me, was killed in hand-to-hand combat during an attack on Ras el Ein (Rosh Ha Ayin).

Most men in our outfit were Jews from central and Eastern Europe; many came from Germany and Austria. Jews of Middle-Eastern origin were primarily born in Palestine, though many had arrived from Arab countries. With few exceptions, all of the above were fluent in Hebrew. And still I felt not pressured to learn Hebrew. German and Austrian immigrants, a sizable part of the Jewish population in Palestine, often spoke German among themselves. Czechoslovakian, Polish and Jews from the Rumanian Bukovina knew German and used it in talks with German Jews. A German newspaper was published in Haifa by Jews and Swiss newspapers and crossword puzzles in German were also available in Palestine.

I was not so lucky in respect to English. Here I had no substitute language to fall back on and was forced, if I wanted to understand the British soldiers, to pick up what I could. Though I never wanted to sit down and study English, I bought a pocket dictionary to increase my English vocabulary. The British army personnel we dealt with, the movies I went to see (no more German translations in Haifa movie theaters), and the daily orders on the job all required knowledge of English. The Hebrew translation of the orders came printed without vowel punctuation, which made it even more difficult for me to decipher.

When I attempted to speak Hebrew, I was alarmed by its difficulty. It has many exceptions to its rules, a most complicated grammar, different word endings if one spoke to a male or female, and ornate expressions for some plain phrases. I asked Moshe, who was quite versed in Hebrew: "How do you say, 'I like you,' in Hebrew?" "To a man, it is *'atah motze chen be-ayniee'*. To a woman, it's *'at motzet chen be-ayniee'*," he said. "That seems a lot of words," I countered. "And which is the word 'like' in this question?"

"There is no single word for 'like' in this sentence," he explained. "Some Hebrew expressions come from the Bible and are flowery phrases. To translate the Hebrew, I like you, word for word into English would be 'You find pleasure in my eyes'. The Hebrew for, 'I like that box,' and box being female in Hebrew, you'd have to say: *hacufssah mozet chen be-ayniee;* translated: 'this box finds pleasure in my eyes.' As you can see, to speak the language one has to know the gender of the noun to give the verb the right ending." Our conversation, by the way, was held in German.

Even more complications await the unwary as he tries to remember that "she" in English is *he* in Hebrew. "He" in English is *who* in Hebrew, while "who" in English is *me* in Hebrew. The English word "me" is *lee* in Hebrew. Many similar sounding Hebrew words have different meanings. *Rofeh* means physician, *roveh* is a rifle. *Ssefel* is a cup, *ssevel* is suffering, and *zevel* is garbage. Because of the slight difference in a word I had an embarrassing experience soon after our return from Alexandria.

Our workshop also employed civilian personnel. Jewish men and women and Arabic men. As I was told, Islamic religion rules would not permit their women to work in a place like our shop. I had become interested in a pretty Yemenite girl named Yardena whose name derived from the Hebrew word for the Jordan river, *Yarden*. I still spoke little Hebrew, and she no German or Yiddish. She was aware of my interest and always smiled sweetly, but this was as far as our relationship went.

One day I saw Yardena talking with some of our fellows, and when I joined the group, she turned to me and said smilingly, *Mah shlomcha?* (How are you?)

I knew that the usual answer to this question is, *metzuyan* (excellent), but I had also heard the fellows answer, *mezuyan*, which I assumed to be a slurred expression of *metzuyan*. Trying to show off my finely nuanced knowledge of Hebrew, I returned her smile and replied, *mezuyan*.

The moment the word was out, I knew I had made a terrible mistake. The fellows burst out laughing, while Yardena's cute smile became forced. The soft brown skin of her pretty face slowly turned crimson and after mumbling something in Hebrew, she left.

"What did I say?" I asked dismayed the circle of still laughing faces. "You said fucked," I was told.

For a while I felt terribly self-conscious when I met Yardena at work, but once I invited her to a movie in Haifa and she accepted. Afterward we strolled the blacked-out, but moonlit streets of the city and the romantic setting of a park, yet no beauty of the night could bridge the language gap between us. My desire to learn more Hebrew faded again when Yardena moved away. Ultimately my Hebrew became more fluent, the funny-sounding words lost their comical connotations and the similarity of words their problems.

As I had mentioned earlier, Otto Margel, my Viennese school friend, had joined his father in Palestine some years back. The correspondence between the two of us had stopped after a while, but I had never forgotten the name of the village I used to address my letters to: Ramataim. During a conversation with a fellow in my company I found out that he was from Ramataim and I asked him if he knew Otto. He did indeed. Otto had changed his first name to the Hebrew Yacov (Jacob), and my friend's parents owned a small café-restaurant on what was then the only highway connecting Haifa with Tel Aviv. Their establishment catered mainly to soldiers who drove by in army trucks. With this information in mind I hitchhiked in early March the 75 miles from Kurdani to Ramataim, hoping to meet the Margels. Ramataim, about 15 road miles from Tel Aviv, is a village in the Sharon, the coastal region between Hadera in the north, Tel Aviv in the south, and bordered in the east roughly along what is known today as the Green Line. It had been, as all the rest of Palestine, a neglected region, until it was settled by Jewish immigrants. It is a most beautiful stretch of land, densely populated and rich in agriculture. Otto's father certainly had picked a most desirable spot in the *Altneuland* of the modern-day prophet, Theodor Herzl.

I found their café to be a one-storied building just a few steps off the highway. In front was a hedged-in area with tables and chairs for outdoor service. Only two people were in the room when I entered. A lanky older man, a stranger to me, and a short, slightly plump woman, whom I immediately recognized as Otto's mother. Never having met my friend's father, I guessed that this man, puffing on a cigarette, was his other parent. Wearing a British soldier's uniform, Mrs. Margel asked in heavily accented English what she could do for me. When I told her in German who I was, she remembered and seemed sincerely happy to see me. Then Otto appeared. I faced him, but he failed to recognize me in my uniform.

The effect of the nine years since our last goodbye and the surprise encounter was overcome, however, when I asked him, also in German: "Don't you remember me?" He called out: "Gustl." This was the beginning of a renewed friendship with Yacov, who I was asked to call by his Hebrew name, and I spent many enjoyable leaves with the Margels during my next three years in the army.

The café had two female employees. One was the cook, a middle aged woman by the name of Tamara, the other, a young waitress working part-time. It was good policy to have a youthful waitress, for nothing pleased a British soldier more than being served by a young female. There was much competition among the several cafés on the "strip." When one of them employed an exceptionally pretty girl, the others felt threatened when they saw military vehicles drive past their regular stop and park at a competitor's café. The girls came and went frequently in all the cafés.

On my leaves I lived in the Margels' house where a bed for me had been placed in a small room. I slept on linen, a far cry from the bed and blankets of camp life. My friend and I had our meals in the café and I especially liked breakfast. Tamara would ask us how we liked our eggs, which, in contrast to the powdered eggs in the army, were always fresh. I also got to know "catsup" which I thought tasted delicious on omelets.

The café had a record player and a large assortment of records. It introduced me to modern-day American music and the famous singers of the early forties. I fell in love with this kind of music, a love that has remained with me ever since.

Yacov and his mother invited me to spend my leaves with them, an invitation endorsed by a nod of his father. Yacov had no close friend in the village and my being there, his mother told me, did him good. The reason for this I learned later.

A Visit to Jerusalem
During the time we were apart we corresponded regularly and in one of my letters I asked Yacov if he would join me on a visit to Jerusalem on my next leave. He agreed, for he too had never been to the capital.

Some of my recorded impressions of Jerusalem are, no doubt, capricious. Colored by unfulfilled childish expectations, I wrote:

One Sunday morning in early May we started our trip. At the main bus depot in Tel Aviv long lines of people waited at individual stops for transportation to all points in the country. As a soldier I could have gotten onto the bus immediately, but since Yacov was a civilian, we took our place in line. After a wait of one and a half hours we boarded the bus.

Passing Sarafand, my first army camp, we rode through Ramle and toward a mountain range visible in the distance. Riding the bus, one does not sense the imperceptible rise from the flatlands to the slightly higher elevation, and it was surprising to find ourselves suddenly on high ground. Near Latrun we entered an opening between mountains and the ascent to Jerusalem began. Rocky formations alternated with uncultivated areas whose topsoil was still green and lush with the moisture of the rainy season. Past and through valleys the steep, serpentine way led up and down hillsides, but in the end always higher. Arab villages clinging to mountainsides produced a colorful vista that I found romantically beautiful.

At a young age I had been most impressed when reading about Jerusalem, the capital of the Jews in biblical times. When I got older and understood that this city today was as cosmopolitan as Vienna, my awe for this symbol of Jewish yearning was still hard to shed.

We arrived at our goal at noon and rented a tiny room in a small hotel across from the bus terminal. We rested briefly, and the sandwiches my friend's mother had so thoughtfully forced on us went the way of all edibles. Then we set out to see what the city had to offer.

I did not know what I had expected. Secretly, perhaps, I had hoped to be touched and led by some mystical power to an opening beyond which religious belief blossomed, a belief that had become more elusive ever since that morning in Vienna in March of 1938 when the Nazis had taken over our lives. But walking the streets of this famous city with my friend, I felt no reverence, no spiritual emotions of any kind and was disillusioned. Here, as in any other city, people strolled or rushed along streets filled with stores, window-shopped, or stopped for snacks and soft drinks at kiosks. Street vendors hawked their wares, a baby cried, and some youngsters found something amusing and laughed uproariously. Cafés and movie theaters, restaurants and bars; buses, taxis, trucks, and jeeps, this was the Jerusalem of today. The glaring sun made me blink, and with half-closed eyes I looked at the bustle around me that had destroyed a childish fantasy.

I had specific goals in mind. I wanted to see two structures that I secretly hoped would introduce me to the cabalistic aura I had expected in Jerusalem. I wanted to sense the invisible and, as yet, unfelt power of the city; like a person who for the first time tries a hallucinogenic drug and waits for euphoria. My destinations were the Tower of David and the Kotel Ha ma-aravee, the Western Wall, also known as the Wailing Wall.

In the military information office at the YMCA, another of Jerusalem's landmarks, I received a city map. Across from the YMCA the massive King David Hotel shut out the panorama behind it. The thought of our dingy hotel compared to the King David amused me. I jokingly suggested to Yacov to switch hotels. Half a night in luxury at the King equaled the monthly rate of our hotel. But even had it been affordable, the King David Hotel was for civilians and officers only.

With the help of the map we reached the high city wall and saw David's Tower. The narrow, round structure with the pointed roof had impressed me more on Palestinian postage stamps than it did in real life. But its beauty or rather the lack of it were secondary in my mind when I related it to King David. Being unaware at the time that it had been built by the Turks and not King David, I felt for the first time since our arrival in Jerusalem that something more profound than the usual curiosity was touching me.

We entered the Old City through Jaffa Gate and came to a long and narrow lane without sidewalks. It teemed with people and an occasional donkey-drawn cart found its way through the crowd. . The majority of the public wore the long outer garment of the Arabs, but western outfits were present, and bearded, religious Jews hastened along in their black coats and wide-brimmed hats, their peyot, corkscrew-like sidecurls flapping.

Hot air, permeated with the odors and noises of an Arabian bazaar, filled the lengthy canyon. Small stores on both sides of the way had the distinct windowless fronts of small Arab businesses common in the Middle East and North Africa. At irregular intervals a building bridged the lane and by connecting the opposite sides of the way it created a roofed street. Those tunneled sections were cool, but musty smelling.

We had paid little attention to where the way led and were surprised to be suddenly stopped by a uniformed man. I had never seen fatigues like these, a mixture of khaki and gray. He talked in rapid Arabic and the only word familiar to me was mamnoon, forbidden. I looked around and saw only Arab men. Some sat on tiny stools smoking hookahs, others leaned against walls of houses and doorways. A traveling coffee-and-tea vendor must have passed recently, for some of the men sipped Turkish coffee from small cups, while others drank tea from thin glasses. We had interrupted their chats, though they did not seem overly dismayed by that fact. All grinned at us, but I didn't know why. Then I saw a short distance ahead of us the Dome of the Rock, the main mosque of Muslims in Jerusalem, and their grins seemed to make sense. It was one place where Arabs had the power to refuse entry to non-Muslims, unless they carried a special permit.

"Where is the Wailing Wall, please?" Yacov asked the uniformed man who appeared to be a sort of guard. The man spoke no English but understood.

He pointed his arm in the directed we had come, and waved his hand to the left. At that moment we glimpsed a teenager with dangling sidecurls disappearing between two houses. Hoping his destination was ours, we rushed after him. The passage we entered was even narrower

246

than the original way. Unaware we were trailing him, the fellow led us through a maze of short streets so narrow our outstretched arms could almost touch the walls on both sides. After a while I began to doubt that the boy was leading us to where we wanted to go. Then, at the end of a short passage, we faced the Wailing Wall. As so often before when confronted by one of my dreams turning reality, I almost had to pinch myself to make certain I was awake.

I gazed at this remnant of Herod's reconstructed temple, the Western Wall. I wanted to touch the stones that, so long ago, had been handled by people, our people, and I did feel awe at the thought. But it was not the religious aspect of the monument that stirred me. To me this evidence of times past spoke of the glory of the Jewish nation. Of King David, King Solomon, and all the other famous figures of the Old Testament that were important to me because they were Jews to be proud of. But I was just as proud of Herzl and Einstein, Freud and Trumpeldor, and the many other distinguished Jews of the past up to this year of 1943. I came away from my experience with Jerusalem more nationalistic than religious.

The high, weather-beaten wall was made of large, square stones, and the crevices between the rocks were filled with moss and little slips of paper yellowed by age. For countless years Jews from all over the globe had made pilgrimages to this ancient wall to pray. Many had written appeals to God in their native tongues on those pieces of paper, curled them into miniature scrolls and deposited them in cracks that still had a little space left.

A narrow, open area, not more than twelve feet wide, ran between The Wall and the backs of houses opposite it. At each end of that area was a small shack; one housed a guard, the other may have been a storage facility. Nothing in its neighborhood pointed to the fact that this most sacred of Jewish relics had any standing in this world of to day. A person unaware of its significance would have thought the place a rather neglected corner of an old city.

Even the few men rocking back and forth in prayer and the single man with his forehead pressed against the stones failed to arouse any special reverence in me. These people would have behaved in the same way in any other place of worship.

Still, captivated by the picture before us, my friend and I looked silently at the scene. We had paid no attention to the clean-shaven man with a prayer book in his hands sitting on the ground. Only when he suddenly called out to us in Yiddish, Put on hats, did we look at him surprised. I had my folded sidecap inserted in the shoulder clasp of my shirt, and Yacov had no hat at all. With no disrespect intended, we said a few words to each other in English to make the man believe we were non-Jews. Yacov's blond hair and my uniform were enough to fool the man. — — — —

More of Life in the Army

Early in July my friend Erich paid me a surprise visit and we decided to meet in Haifa two days later. To my dismay I was unable to keep our rendezvous. We still lived in a time when one could never be certain of a reunion with a person to whom one had said good-bye. Erich returned to his base in Tobruk without meeting me.

The men and women who joined the British forces in Palestine had been issued two narrow sleeves of khaki fabric imprinted with the word: Palestine. The sleeves fitted over the shirt's shoulder flaps where they could be displayed. If we neglected to wear the little bands, it was not because we wanted to hide our identity — a fact that could hardly be concealed. Most of us neither looked nor talked like the fellows from the British Isles. It was simply inconvenient to put the sleeves on and take them off every time we changed shirts. Usually they were put away in one's bag and forgotten.

At certain times, however, those narrow telltale sleeves might have kept one out of trouble. Occasionally brawls broke out between soldiers from Britain and those from countries under the British crown, especially Australians. Conflicts could erupt in movie theaters, bars or on streets at night. Australians were excellent soldiers, but they were also the greatest of brawlers often drinking too much beer.

Some Britishers may have thought themselves better than people of their dependencies and resented the Jews of Palestine who refused with the subservience appropriate to colonial "natives." Friction could start when, after a free day or an evening in Haifa, a mixed crowd of soldiers waited at a bus station or tried to hitch a ride back to Kurdani. A few wrong words might lead to a small shoving match, but violence erupted when one of the Britishers said: "Fuckin' Jews." This affront invariably triggered a fistfight.

I had guard duty and Holzer, also from Vienna, was patrolling with me. It had been a special day, and we had reason to be elated. It was September 8, 1943 and it had been announced on the radio that Italy had signed an armistice agreement with the Allies. One dared to hope now that mighty Germany, having lost its main European partner in arms, would be forced to retreat from Italy and the war would be shortened. People, especially those who had families inside what the Germans called *Festung Europa* (Fortress Europe), were euphoric. Holzer even thought that hostilities would cease in the near future. I was excited too but less optimistic about the immediate demise of the Third Reich. The fervent hope of seeing the Nazi monster destroyed was still only a hope. Never having made a secret of his intention to return to Vienna after Germany's collapse, he wanted my promise now to meet him at the main entrance to St. Stephan's cathedral in the very center of the city. The time was to be midnight on the first New Year's Eve after the war. I agreed to the reunion, knowing full well that there was little chance that I would keep my promise.

As I had feared, Germany continued to fight and life proceeded without much change. I often thought about the two Englishmen with whom I had worked when I had first arrived here, and their advice to be happy with my situation. Yet I was not content. I knew nothing of the whereabouts of my parents and sister, and my hope to be sent to Europe remained unfulfilled.

Two weeks of regimental training came as a welcome change of pace. It brought relief from the monotonous life of the workshop where we had been craftsmen in uniform. Once more exposed and still unaccustomed to the rigors of military training, the familiar muscular aches plagued us in the beginning but disappeared halfway through the first week.

The emphasis was on drilling on the parade ground, the dismantling and assembly of rifles, Bren guns, and Tommy guns, and the handling of hand grenades. I loved the exercises but not the spit and polish of the brass attachments on our uniform and equipment and the mandated mirror-shine of our boots. We never seemed to please our regimental sergeant. And as much as I enjoyed using weapons at the firing range, I hated their cleaning with a passion. We also had to wear puttees again. Not the long ones anymore that came up to the knees, but the short ones around the ankles. But even short puttees took extra time to wind, as the triangle shaped end of the material had to finish exactly atop the outside of the ankle.

We marched in full battle dress, steel helmet, rifle, ammunition, gas-mask assembly tied to our chest, and big pack on our back, six miles one day, nine miles the next, and 12 miles on the third day. During two night exercises we froze, and were bathed in perspiration while drilling fully equipped during the heat of the day.

On the obstacle course we had, among other exercises, to surmount a high, wooden wall. Two soldiers, standing slightly apart, their backs against the wall and their fingers entwined, created a step for the oncoming men. This improvised step was only the first rung for the climbers. The shoulders of the men against the wall were the next step required to master the wooden barrier. On the other side we were to cling with one hands to the rim for a moment and then drop to the ground.

For one as short as I (5' 4") the climbing of that obstacle with the bulky respirator pack tied to my chest was not easy. I had climbed onto a fellow's shoulder, but my fingers barely reached the top of the barrier and were not strong enough to pull me up. The gas mask also kept me at a distance from the wall. My heavy army boots on the man's shoulders and my continued attempt to climb that cursed obstacle must have been painful, for he voiced his complaints with "oy ... oy ... oyeee". It sounded so comical that it made me laugh and the situation worse. The day was hot, sweat ran down my face and the oys from below came in ever shorter intervals. Suddenly the fellows on the ground behind me, waiting their turn, also began to laugh. We must have presented a hilarious picture as we struggled, each in his own way, to overcome our problems. He to get rid of me and I to get over the top. I could not stop laughing, and the more I laughed the lesser my chances became of getting over the wall. And then a thought struck me. The fellow wore a steel helmet. Why not use his head as another step, and get closer to the top? I did. He cried out in Yiddish, "oy, Mamme," and as I swung myself free of him, I involuntarily pushed his steel helmet down over his face. For a moment I sat triumphantly atop the barrier then slid over it and down to the ground on the other side.

I shot around to the front side of the wall again and with a face as serious as I could master, called out to the fellow: "*Slicha*" (sorry). He did not even hear me. He was busy with the next man on his shoulders trying to get over the top.

It was autumn when Yacov wrote that he was coming to Haifa to stay with his aunt and uncle for two weeks. He hinted at a specific reason for his vacation, which he would tell me when we met. The letter also contained a surprise. A cousin by the name of Dolly, one year our junior, was living with his relatives. She was their niece, and the three were from Vienna. Yacov had never mentioned a cousin before, and although I was interested in meeting her, she was not the reason for my wish to spend as many evenings with my friend as army life permitted.

I went to his relatives' address, an apartment building on Jerusalem Street, two days later. Yacov's uncle and aunt, a younger sister of his mother, their baby, and Dolly were a pleasant group. I liked them and found it nice that the aunt acted like a mother toward Dolly. The girl, however, did not see it that way, and though she did everything that was asked of her, she would have preferred less supervision. The aunt seemed to like me and I felt that I had impressed her favorably.

That first evening Dolly suggested a visit to "Woodland," a café-restaurant on Har Hacarmel, the top of Mount Carmel. The place also had tables and benches among the trees in front of the building, but because of blackout regulations no service was tended outside. If one wanted to sit in the open air, purchases had to be made in the café, and then taken out. Under certain circumstances, or with a moon above, the unlit wooded area created a romantic setting.

We took our places inside. The room had only a few guests, young couples preoccupied with each other. We ordered coffee and cake, and I supplied the cigarettes, Player's Navy Cut, the preferred brand of cigarettes in the British army. We talked for hours; often unfairly touching on subjects that occupied only Dolly and me. Yacov had come to Palestine long before Hitler had marched into Austria, while Dolly and I had felt Nazism's terror. Yacov was with his father and mother, and we were glad for him, while our parents were in Vienna. We talked of Vienna, our lives there, and time went by without our noticing it. I was reluctant to end our get together, but the way back to Kurdani was long, and it was late in the evening when we eventually parted.

I took the bus from Haifa to Kiryat Motzkin. At night this was the final stop on this route and at the station the few passengers who got off with me dispersed quickly. I walked along the main road to the edge of town. The windows of the nearby houses were dark. I did not mind walking the two miles to Kurdani by myself. It gave me time to go over the pleasant events of the evening. Only the scraping of my boots on the road, and the occasional howl of a jackal in the distance interrupted the silence around me. I thought of Dolly. I wanted to meet her again. She seemed to have liked me too, and that made me feel good. The world did not seem such a lonely place anymore. As long as my friend was in Haifa, we went out as a threesome. After he returned to Ramataim, Dolly and I met regularly.

Yacov had not mentioned the reason for his visit to Haifa, and I assumed that he wanted to talk to me alone. Yet, in all of our meetings in the city he never touched on the subject, and he finally left without having said anything. In time I found out that his mother had sent my friend on this visit to overcome "a problem." She hoped that even a short stay in Haifa would get his thoughts off a one-sided romance, and I would help him in this respect. It would have been easier, however, to convince a person that the world is flat than to redirect the feelings of this man in love. But in time Yacov overcame his infatuation and married a fine local girl.

Life is unpredictable and even a minor decision can lead to a rendezvous with destiny. The British command in Kurdani organized a tour to the Galilee for British soldiers to learn about the country. Because I loved to travel, I signed up. Two open trucks were provided for the trip, one for British personnel, the other for Jewish soldiers. Wooden benches along the sides of the truck-bed and in its center provided seating. When, in the spirit of competition, our truck moved first and took the lead, the men in the other truck roared in pretended frustration.

British soldiers loved community singing and after a while songs rang out in the truck behind us. Not to be outdone, our men followed suit with Hebrew songs. As we rolled through the countryside, a noisy, but good-humored competition was in progress.

We passed through Nazareth, which I saw for the first time, and stopped in Tiberias for a break. After the distribution of sandwiches and a drink we were ordered onto the trucks again. I took the first seat on the bench in the left-hand corner. And because the driver's cabin was narrower than the truck bed, I now had an unobstructed view of the road ahead.

This time the other truck took the lead.

By afternoon we were nearing Rosh Pina. As a leftover of the war with Vichy France in Lebanon and Syria, a short stretch of highway still had tank traps on both sides of the road we traveled. Although they did not make the already narrow road any narrower, some drivers moved more to the center out of fear of hitting the traps. The truck ahead of us entered the stretch without slowing down, and another military truck came from the opposite direction also at full speed. When they passed each other, their sides seemed to scrape lightly. Then the truck ahead of us stopped.

In the few seconds it took us to reach the vehicle, screams such as I had never heard before in my life exploded into the air. If I had thought I had seen gruesome things in my life, nothing compared to the sickening picture I witnessed. Several solid steel poles tied to the side of the oncoming truck had torn loose from their strapping when the two vehicles touched. Two of the poles penetrated the narrow metal strip between the corner of the truck bed and the driver's cabin like pencils through paper. The soldier, whose place I occupied in the second vehicle, had leaned forward at the moment of impact. His back was torn open by a pole, which also took part of his spinal column with it. He died instantly. The same steel skewered the man next to him, went through the body of the third, and wounded the fourth soldier on the bench. By then it had lost its force. The other spear-like object that had entered the truck bed flew wildly about wounding more soldiers.

I jumped off my seat and stared in horror at the scene on the other vehicle. Blood seemed everywhere, but many of the men looking bloodied had only blood of the wounded and dead on them. Terror-stricken by the sight of twisting bodies on the floor and the bedlam a few feet away from me, I grew nauseated and I averted my eyes.

Had our truck taken the lead when we left Tiberias it might have been me who got killed instead of the Englishman. The feeling of having cheated death once more never left me. I just wondered how many more times luck would hold for me. The trip that had begun in high spirits had ended in tragedy.

After several months of meeting Dolly I began to feel that my freedom was being restricted. My visits to Haifa became a responsibility, and the close friendship with Dolly was on the verge of becoming intimate. Alarmed I took the coward's way out, and wrote a Dear Jane letter to one terrific girl.

My behavior hurt her. When our company soon afterward was to be moved to Egypt and I went to say good-by to her and her family, she was cool. Despite our now detached relationship we promised to write to each other, and we did.

Tel el Kebir and Cairo

In March of 1944 our company, about 250 strong, was transferred to Egypt. Up until then I did not believe we were really going. I was happy that my wish to travel was again to be realized, but strangely enough, and for the first time, I had a feeling of leaving an existence that had become a matter of habit. Haifa, occasional weekends in Ramataim, and infrequent visits to Tel Aviv had added diversity to my life, and even Kurdani had grown on me. It hadn't been too bad, I admitted to myself, and I knew that despite my wish to travel, familiar things would be missed.

Wake-up call came at 3:30 A.M. A lively and noisy group of soldiers stowed bedding and got ready to move. Kit bags and big packs were placed outside the tents and we shouldered only the small side pack. Each man received a rifle and 50 rounds of ammunition, a far cry from our expedition to Alexandria when the armament of our company of 150 men consisted of three rifles. Following breakfast our gear was loaded onto trucks, then we climbed aboard. At Kiryat Motzkin's railroad station a train was waiting.

The trip through Palestine was uneventful. It lacked the urgency of our earlier journey to Egypt and gave the impression of a leisure junket. Two hours past midnight we stopped at Kantara, had sandwiches and hot tea, and at 7 A.M. got off the train already at *Tel el Kebir*, a place in the middle of nowhere.

It was a short ride to the camp, which had already existed in World War I. The 25 square miles of hard, dry ground without vegetation were surrounded by a double barbed wire fence. Mines designed to keep thieves out of the enclosure spiked the track between the barriers. Occasionally mines went off at night, tripped by a coyote or jackal that had strayed into the hazardous zone. The large compound was subdivided into small camps identified by letters. To our dismay our company was broken up into four units and placed in different camps. I was sent to camp B.

As in Kurdani, a network of asphalt roads connected the far-flung workshop buildings. And, as on our previous base, barracks and tents were haphazardly scattered throughout individual encampments. Shower and washing facilities in one hut, and kitchen and dining hall in another, served two bordering compounds. NAAFI (Navy Army Air Force Institute) canteens, in bigger buildings, catered to soldiers of several camps. Two movie houses provided entertainment. Tel el Kebir easily compared in size and essence to a small city.

Life in camp quickly became routine. After a few days I felt as if I had spent all of my previous military service here. Tel el Kebir, however, had the thrilling advantage of being just an hour and half away from one of the dreams of my youth: Cairo. I still remembered the disappointment of having been in Egypt without seeing the pyramids and Sphinx. But now, Cairo, one of the most intriguing cities in the world was within reach.

I was delighted to be in Egypt and nothing should have detracted from my high spirits, and yet, it seemed as if the thrill of being here was not one of absolute happiness. When clarity of mind prevailed, I was shocked to find that I was homesick for Palestine, an emotion reserved for Vienna until then. But Palestine was the country where, for the first time in my existence, I had had to fend for myself. A big step in anybody's life. It was also the source of many new experiences, which strengthened the relationship. It turned out that despite my desire to go places, as I had wished as a young lad in Vienna, it was Palestine now to where I wanted to return, and it was Palestine to where I wanted to bring my family after the war.

To overcome the confusing feelings in my early days in camp I took refuge in writing. I worked on my neglected notes and also wrote a lengthy letter to Dolly. Though not in a laughing mood, I kept the letter humorous and a short while later received Dolly's reply. She wrote how much she and her family had enjoyed and laughed at my account of our journey to Egypt. and said they all were looking forward to more letters of this kind.

Three weeks elapsed before the first group of our men visited Cairo.

We found it superfluous to be instructed about "out of bounds" sections and unnecessary to be warned about the expertise of Egyptian pickpockets. We had been to Egypt before and felt like experienced travelers. Yet the warning in "Service Guides to Cairo" to visit only bars that displayed the sign "in bounds" was more ominous when reading the follow-up: Uncontrolled establishments might use "knock-out drops" resulting in cleaned-out pockets or worse. The "in bounds" area was the modern center of the city, roughly a mile and half from north to south, and one mile across. The railroad station was in one corner of this area.

My first encounter with Cairo failed to meet my expectations. It did not, as I immaturely had envisioned, radiate the mysterious aura the dime novels of my youth had so realistically and yet deceptively described. But though Cairo may have lacked a mystical aura, it was extraordinary in many respects. The city's vibrancy and anthill-like activity contradicted my belief that no commotion of city-life could ever impress me. This exotic, bustling metropolis with its unbelievable foot and vehicular traffic, made me feel like a country lad visiting a capital for the first time. The city possessed a wealth of incomparable shapes and forms stemming from a unique past. Though French influence in Cairo's downtown seemed as pervasive as that of Alexandria, its modernistic heart was definitely Levantine. So different from Vienna, where even a discarded streetcar ticket warranted a fine if observed by a policeman. The habit of thoughtlessly dumping fruit parts, paper wrappers, cigarette boxes and other litter into the street was especially evident in quarters our truck passed through on its way to the city center.

The main transportation in Cairo was streetcars. The lines ran along the fringe of the "in bounds" section and throughout the rest of the city. Because much of the population was illiterate, pictures of objects rather than numbers or letters identified streetcar lines. Riders clung to overflowing entrances of the wagons like grapes on a vine and sat or stood on the rear bumper while the trolley was in motion. I wondered how many were injured by this reckless conduct.

Policemen and, as we also found out, railroad conductors were open to voluntary or enforced bribes. While waiting for our train to get under way at the Cairo railroad station one evening, I watched the bustle of people below my window. Soldiers arriving late hurried to get on the train before it departed and hawkers tried to make last-minute sales. A boy, not more than ten, poorly dressed and barefoot, held up several bags made of newspaper. He hastened along the train, calling out, "Peanuts, peanuts, one piaster, peanuts." He had sold some bags to soldiers leaning out of windows when suddenly a policeman appeared beside him. The officer grabbed him by the collar, took away the last two bags of peanuts still in his possession, and talked to him forcefully. I could not believe my eyes when the kid, crying by then, extracted coins from previous sales from a small cotton bag and handed them to the policeman who pocketed the money. An angry cry went up from soldiers who had also witnessed the event through the train windows. But, by then, the train was moving and so it was too late to do anything.

The rumor that one could ride an Egyptian train for less money than the price of a ticket turned out to be true. I did this only once to find out if it worked. I was traveling with a friend to Cairo one day and we neglected to buy tickets. During the ride two conductors came through the train checking transfers. Following the advice given us by other fellows, we admitted to having no tickets. One of the officials said: "Twelve piasters each," and held out his hand. We pretended to have this amount only between the two of us, and eventually the conductors without the issue of a receipt or a ticket pocketed the sum.

Cairo's street people were similar to those in Palestine and yet, they were so much more intense in their behavior. One had to put up with the aggressiveness of beggars the like I had never encountered before. Paupers, often afflicted with the eye disease trachoma, were all over the place. The trouble was that if one gave to one panhandler, the other alms seekers mobbed the giver. Street hawkers offered articles on trays, held in their hands, or thrown over their shoulders, at exaggerated prices. If an object had been offered at 50 piasters, and the buyer was willing to pay 10 or 15 for it, he had to start his bidding at five piasters.

The inevitable "dirty postcards" were offered in a stage whisper. "Hey, George, look," the seller would say, grin, and hold the pictures so close to one's nose that nothing could be seen. If one successfully caught a glimpse of the photograph he would find it to be of World War One vintage. If "George" showed no interest, the peddler turned procurer: "George want *zigzig?* (Screw) Want French girl, Greek girl, Italian girl?"

Shoeshine boys had a most ingenious approach. "Shoe-shine, George, shoeshine?" the little fellow would sing out in his childish voice. If a soldier's footwear was dusty from long strolls and he did not want a shoe shine, the enterprising youngster would dip a small brush into his shoe polish and with lightening speed smear it over the toe of the unwary man's shoe. He then moved to a safe distance to await the victim's reaction. If the soldier was angry, the boy chalked up his effort to bad business. Most of the time, however, the wet blob on the boot left "George" with little choice but to surrender.

In clear contrast to the shabby beggars and the peddlers in their well-worn, long coats, nicely dressed people walked the streets and sat in cafés and restaurants. They engaged in conversation, read newspapers or merely stared in boredom at the stream of humanity strolling past. If I was by myself on rare occasions, I too liked to sit at an outside table of a café and watch people go by. Sometimes I played the childish game of guessing if their occupations were shady or honest.

Strolling on Shari Ibrahim Pasha toward Ezbekia Garden, just before Opera Square, stood a Cairo landmark: the sprawling and prestigious Shepheard's Hotel, a place I had always wanted to visit. The Shepheard's, like the King David in Jerusalem, however, was reserved for civilians and officers only.

Another elegant spot in the city was Groppi's Restaurant and Pastry Shop. I had heard much about the place and decided to visit it. It was open to all. We were four who dared to penetrate this establishment, known for its expensive prices.

Entering Groppi's we were met by an array of crystal-clear glass showcases, filled with a lavishly display of candies, chocolates and pastries. The desire to feast on those delicacies was checked by our limited financial resources. A prosperous looking gentleman led us to a table in the inner sanctum. After the heat and glare of the outside, the dim light in this large room soothed our eyes, and the air was pleasantly cool. The place was as quiet and empty as a church during summer holidays. Well, not altogether empty. Strategically placed along the walls of the restaurant were waiters. Tall, lean men, whose dark faces contrasted handsomely with their long, white robes, drawn in at the waist by a wide, dark-red belt. A fez of the same color on their head made them appear even taller.

Only one other table in the room was occupied. Three American soldiers had just finished their meal and were smoking. Then one of them beckoned to the headwaiter: "Our check." The man delivered the bill to the table and after one soldier had looked at it, he jumped up: "What in the hell is that?"

"Your bill," the headwaiter answered coolly.

The manager, whom the Americans insisted on seeing, did not reduce the amount of the bill. Eventually the soldiers paid up and left grumbling.

This little incident had a disquieting effect on us. We had no intention of spending a lot of money in this place where service and decor, along with the high-priced delicacies, were the main attraction. We did not even try to study the fancy menus placed in front of us, the ones the Americans apparently had also neglected to check before ordering. Reading the prices hardly would have alleviated our discomfort. Too embarrassed to get up and leave, I suggested a round of milk shakes, a drink that I believed could not be overly expensive.

Our order arrived in small creatively tapered glasses. It proved that my theory about Groppi's policy of catering more to the eye than the

257

stomach was correct. When the bill came, it was 15 piasters for each of us. About five times the amount we would have had to pay in a regular café, and three times as much as an unskilled laborer earned for a day's work.

(The original Shepheard's Hotel and Groppi's were two of the buildings burned to the ground by mobs during the 1952 riots against foreigners, and especially the British.)

On a subsequent visit to Cairo I made my long awaited trip to the pyramids and Sphinx, a most memorable experience. By coincidence it took place during our first Passover holiday in Egypt. Our company had received permission to use a truck for the ride and on Opera Square, our usual meeting place in town, some of the passengers left us, preferring a stay in the city. I found it incomprehensible that one could pass up an opportunity to visit the pyramids. A sergeant major, a sergeant, and 12 soldiers, we continued to Giza.

We rode through modern Cairo, over a bridge spanning the wide expanse of the Nile, traversed an island, then a water arm, and were on the western bank of the river. By then our truck was moving too slowly for me as another dream of my youth was about to become reality. Scanning ahead to catch sight of the pyramids and Sphinx, I spotted two small triangular shapes against the horizon, and my excitement grew more intense as we approached.

We passed the city of Giza and the road curved upward. Running along the Mena House Hotel – made famous by the Cairo meeting of Churchill, Roosevelt, and Chiang Kai-shek in November 1943 – our truck stopped on a big, stone plateau just 200 feet from the Cheops or Great Pyramid.

In haste we jumped off the truck and stared transfixed at that towering monument. A guide we later hired claimed the 480-foot high giant weighed 200 million tons and its construction had required the labor of three hundred thousand slaves over 30 years. The size of those large, square blocks of stone, each weighing several tons, the distance they had to be transported, and the construction achieved without modern equipment made this story credible.

To the rear of the parking area a small restaurant catered to visitors, but more important to me was the other pyramid I had seen from afar. I found it at the end of a slowly descending dirt road on the right side of the plateau.

Returning to the center of the Cheops pyramid, we climbed up a few rows of those angular rocks and then stood before a dark opening. In front of that entrance were several Arab guides with candles in their hands, waiting to be hired for an excursion to the burial chamber inside the tomb. After the usual haggling over the price with one of them the tour started. A lit candle in his hand, the guide led our procession into a narrow tunnel. Behind him walked the sergeant major, followed by eager me and trailed by the others. After a few steps we climbed a steep chicken ladder. Because the candlelight barely reached as far as me, we walked hand in hand into the innards of the pyramid. On the way our guide explained some details of the wall impressions, but was at a loss to answer specific questions.

Higher and higher we climbed, slipped, laughed, and made foolish remarks. I was still impressed by the experience, but the millions of tons of rock around me, and particularly those above my head, made me more uneasy than reverent.

Our way led occasionally over narrow planks and when we met people on their way back, there was laughter and jostling while we crowded past each other. Climbing more slippery steps, we negotiated a low tunnel by stooping forward and landed in a fairly big room. The burial chamber of the pharaoh. Though there were two additional groups of soldiers present, the feeble light of three candles barely illuminated the place. Our guide suggested that for five piasters he'd light the room with magnesium light. We agreed, and for a few seconds the place was glaringly lit. We felt cheated. We had expected a continued bright light, but all the man had done was to burn a tiny strip of magnesium.

During that intense illumination we caught a better view of a large, hollowed stone base in the center of the floor. At closer inspection, again by candlelight, it looked like a trough whose wide rim was covered by a thick layer of wax, drippings of countless candles. The base had contained the sarcophagus, our guide informed us, adding more bits of lore to his statement. Leading us along the walls, he pointed to specific spots where torches had been secured during the burial ceremony.

Once again outside, we deliberated whether to climb the pyramid, and nine of us decided to accept the challenge. One does not just climb straight up. There are specific routes to get to the top and down, and only the guides knew them. People who had tried the ascent on their own became stuck half way up, and had to be rescued by guides. The year before, an Englishman attempting the climb had fallen to his death.

We stayed with the same man who, after a short palaver about the fee for his new service, agreed to lead the ascent. "George, you step exactly behind other. Don't go to side. Don't look down," he advised no one in particular before starting the climb. We nodded agreement and followed him single file. I learned years later that for reasons of safety the Egyptian government had forbidden the scaling of the pyramid.

At first it looked easy enough though it was not like climbing stairs. The rims and corners of the stones had been eroded. For thousands of years desert winds and temperature changes had made edges and corners crumble. Occasionally whole pieces of rocks were missing from blocks. Some exposed spots were so narrow and worn they barely left a stepping place for the toe end of one's boot. Our noses were often so close to the rock that we failed to recognize the individual layers of blocks. It left one with the impression that the pyramid had been haphazardly put together.

Our guide climbed with the steady pace of a mountain goat. From time to time he looked down on us and at one place he stopped. "This quarter pyramid," he announced. "Wanna rest?" Nobody wanted to rest, and on we went.

Halfway up the pyramid we stopped for five minutes. With the exception of the guide, everyone was sweating profusely. The smokers fished for cigarettes and inhaled deeply. The people down below had shrunk to the size of beetles, and the apex looked to be twice the distance we had come. Two men in our group had had enough and decided to remain where they were. We would pick them up on our way down. At the three-quarter stop two more of our fellows stayed behind. Ten minutes later the sergeant major, three soldiers, and I made it to the top.

We were not alone up here. Several soldiers, not of our group, had made the climb with other guides. Still, there was enough space on the apex to walk around. The pyramid did not end in a point, but had at the top an almost flat area several feet square. The view from the summit was magnificent. On three sides the desert stretched to the horizon and on the fourth, Cairo's sea of houses could be seen some distance away. The people on the ground now looked like ants. The top was covered with capital letters, carved into the rather soft stone, and we climbers followed suit. Near the edge of the little plateau, right where I looked toward Cairo, I found a small, unused spot. With the help of my pocketknife I inscribed the letters GP, initials for Gustav Pimselstein, still my name at the time.

Then we had to get back. Climbing up that man-made mountain was nothing compared to the descent. I had not noticed the zigzag trail we followed to the top or how little there was to hold on to during the climb. Coming down, unfortunately, made this abundantly clear. Some narrow spots on the rocks, often slightly rounded and polished by the touch of many hands, had seemed less treacherous on the way up than they were now on the way down. The guide's advice at the outset of our climb not to look down, was of no use during the descent. We had no choice but to watch where the man below us stepped, and in looking down we faced an abyss that made our knees feel weak. We picked up the men who had stayed behind and after safely reaching the plateau I felt childishly satisfied to have made it to the top while others had given up.

We circled the Sphinx. She had sandbags stacked from the ground to under her chin to support her big head in case bombs were dropped in the vicinity. At a pharaonic temple our guide held a lit candle under a step made of alabaster, and the light shone through the stone. To make this a full day, we visited the Cairo zoo.

At another time I spent a day at the Egyptian museum and was only one of a few visitors in the place. Because of the war, many artifacts had been taken to London for safekeeping; nonetheless, the museum seemed fully stocked with antiquities. Quite surprising were pieces of cloth that, though often threadbare, still retained their original colors after thousands of years. I walked by an endless array of tools, weapons and mummies lying and standing in showcases. Mummies held a macabre fascination for me, but one of them more so than the others. All bodies were wrapped in cloth-tape; the one that had aroused my morbid curiosity had part of the material missing from the front of its foot. Exposed were toes covered by dried, almost black skin. A skeleton was just an assembly of bones for me, but this was the skin of a person who had been alive millenniums ago.

On April 29, 1944, a Jewish R.E.M.E. company arriving from Tripoli boosted the Palestinian R.E.M.E. in Tel el Kebir to more than 400. The new support company was also dispersed to different camps. The colonel in charge of Tel el Kebir may have felt that a group of more than 400 Jews dispersed over several camps was a better arrangement then to have all of them concentrated in one place. With years of unrest in their colonies, one might expect the British to distrust "natives." Especially when those people wanted to have their own nation in what the British considered part of their Empire.

While still in Palestine I had visited the offices of Hitachduth Olei Germania (Association of German Immigrants) in Haifa, hoping they could help me find out about Jews left in Nazi Germany. They could not. To an inquiry about my parents and sister, mailed from our camp in Egypt to Hitachduth Olei Austria, (Association of Austrian Immigrants) in Tel Aviv, I received an answer dated May 30, 1944. They said that their Swiss agent had informed them of the following: "In our Theresien-stadt files is a Mrs. Anna Pin(m)selstein. However, without further leads there is no 100 percent guarantee that this is so." I had no doubt that this person was my mother. The association went on to say that they had repeated the Swiss agent's letter verbatim and had asked for more information. They promised to inform me of any new developments. That was the last I heard from them.

I was detailed to a shop that worked two shifts. I worked the second shift from 5 P.M. to 2 A.M. with a one-hour break. Our job was to run-in overhauled motors. A job is a job, but I disliked the night hours. When the other fellows spent the evening at the movies, sat in the canteen or in the huts to talk, read, or played cards, I was in the shop with a few other soldiers listening to the deafening roar of thirty engines that made normal conversations impossible. I requested a transfer to the day shift and it was granted. I was transferred to another workshop, but also moved from camp B to camp D.

As there was no space for me in the two Jewish barracks in camp D, I was billeted in a hut with soldiers who came from different parts of the British Isles. It was like being moved to a foreign country. Some of their English was hard to understand, especially the Irish brogue and the Cockney accent of some Londoners. I never developed a real rapport with the soldiers in the hut and, no doubt, this was partly my fault. I felt like a stranger among them. I lived in the hut, the only Palestinian, for about six months. The men were nice to me and our discussions about Zionism and Palestine helped improve my English.

Our wish to be united in one camp was finally realized. The Palestinians were consolidated into camp S. The two workshops for the repair of motor vehicles assigned to our companies could not employ all our men. Many continued to work in shops dotting the wide expanse of Tel el Kebir but lived in camp S.

We met soldiers other than Palestinians at the canteen, camp movie theaters, entertainment shows, and at league soccer games, where our team represented camp S, the only Jewish compound. To the chagrin of the other camps, our team made it to first place in a short time, in the standings of the Tel el Kebir league.

The only time a member of our team was cheered by non-Palestinians was when a select team of Tel el Kebir played against the Wanderers. This outstanding British soccer team toured camps of the Near East and played exhibition games against select camp teams. To meet the Wanderer on the soccer field, the best players of the teams of Tel el Kebir were chosen, and Meir, one of our men, was selected too.

Meir was a terrific soccer player and played right forward. He meant trouble for the opposing group once he received the ball, something the Wanderers did not know. During the game his teammates, the Britishers, being aware of his forceful attack, kicked the ball to Meir at the first opportunity. True to his fashion, he then stormed forward, past the unprepared Wanderers players, and in the first five minutes shot the first goal. It was one to nothing in our favor. The howl of appreciation that arose from the spectators was deafening, but that breakthrough by Meir happened only once. From then on he was guarded by opposing team members who, so much better than our select team, won the game five to one.

In the summer of 1944 part of our company was taken on a 14-day regimental training exercise. The training camp was near Ismalia, close to the Suez Canal. Though we were strictly regimented there, it was a vacation from work. The exercise required swimming in the Suez Canal, and non-swimmers had at least to get their feet wet. I am not a terrific swimmer, yet when a group of our fellows decided to swim across the waterway, I was game. We looked out for passing ships and when none was in sight, we began our swim. I handled the crossing pretty well, though the other shore had looked closer than it was. After a short rest on the east side of the canal we got into the water for the return swim. Asia to Africa. The distance between the shores of the two continents appeared twice as great as before. I was a bit worried when I began my swim, but managed it all right.

With the battlefront out of Africa it seemed unrealistic for the British to teach Jewish Palestinians how to dismantle mines, handle explosives and set booby traps. The British officer who instructed us in those crafts explained: "Different mines have different objectives. There are mines against soldiers, against motor vehicles and against tanks. Though all are buried, different weights will detonate them. If I place an anti-tank mine in the ground, I don't want it to explode when you step on it. You are too easily replaced. I don't even want a truck to be blown to bits because compared with a tank it's a cheap vehicle. If it's an anti-tank mine, I want it to blow up a *tank*. To accomplish that, the trigger mechanism of the mine will only detonate if something as heavy as a tank rolls over it."

He told us that the Germans sometimes connected one mine to another below. "If the top mine is found, exposed and deactivated, you better make certain no 'strings' are attached. Carelessness will end your career. Germans also like to kill or maim unwary soldiers by placing booby-trapped fountain pens or other items on dirt roads. Those objects, if carelessly picked up, trigger explosives that can blow off fingers, a hand or even kill. The Germans use those dirty tricks now in Italy. The trouble is that sometimes kids or grown-up civilians find these booby trapped articles first, with devastating results."

The officer displayed several mines, the last of which was the anti-personnel mine. "A nasty thing," he declared. "Its cylindrical body, filled with steel balls, jumps chest-high before it explodes. Can you picture what happens when this device blows up among marching soldiers? Once you step on it, it's activated. You can't escape by lying down or outrunning it. Don't even try. The only way you can save yourself and others, is to keep your foot on that damned thing, and not let it come out of the ground. Lean to the side. It'll blow off your leg, but you'll probably live."

With a sketch on a blackboard he explained how to cross a minefield. Supplied with those instructions we were taken the next day to a prepared area, and told: "This is a 'mine field.' Make it safe for your convoy to pass."

In principle we did exactly as taught; yet some of our men would not have made it in a real situation. One picked up a hammer that he thought somebody had forgotten. We heard that distinct little bang signifying he had been blown up by a booby trap. Another man forcefully probed the ground with his bayonet and set off another mini-explosion. A few more small detonations here and there were heard during the course of the exercise, and then happily the show was over. A poor performance by us, but after all, we were craftsmen and novices at this special kind of exercise.

Six months after our arrival in Tel el Kebir I was granted two weeks leave which I wanted to spend in Palestine. The thought made my heart beat faster. A week before leaving, I went to Cairo with Werner, a fellow Viennese, to buy gifts. Werner's parents lived in Haifa where his father owned a Viennese-style Café on Herzl Street. Cairo had innumerable souvenir shops, and I remembered one on Opera Square that was the closest to the railroad station.

Inside the shop a young man dressed in Western fashion, but unmistakably Egyptian, came forward to assist us. The souvenirs on display had no price tags. The price quoted, in those cases, depended on the origin of the buyer. In our case the prices were high. Questions and answers with the sales person had been in English, but then Werner turned to me and said in German: "It's too expensive. We don't have to buy here, we can get gifts cheaper at home." To our surprise the Arab switched the conversation to German. He told us that he had studied the language at the university in Istanbul, Turkey. We bought a few items at a reduced price, but communicated then between us in Hebrew, convinced it was a language he did not understand.

On Leave in Palestine

In a scene in the movie "Flesh and Fantasy" Barbara Stanwyck and Charles Boyer reminisced about places in the world they had visited. Barbara Stanwyck said: "I remember the perfume of orange blossoms in Palestine." Her words came to my mind as I stood at the open window of the train while it steamed past citrus grove after citrus grove. The blossoms of the trees were long gone, but the air still felt like perfume. Before we reached the green stretches of groves, we had passed hours of monotony. Egypt was long gone, the Sinai peninsula had been left behind, and we had passed the Arab cities of Rafah, Khan Yunis, and Gaza. As we traveled north, evening settled over the landscape to the east. The sun, very low on the horizon in the west, seemed to be making one last effort to escape the waters of the Mediterranean before disappearing into the sea for the night.

I got off the train in Tel Aviv and took a bus to Ramataim. How wonderful it felt to be on leave with freedom to choose. Getting up in the morning when I felt like it, not on schedule. Breakfast ordered and served at the small table I shared with Yacov in the café, and days and evenings independent of army regulations. Well, not completely ungoverned by army rules. I did not own civilian clothes, but would not have worn them anyway. Members of the British military were not permitted to wear civilian clothing even when on leave. There was little chance I would be checked for identification papers in Ramataim, yet I preferred to observe this standing order.

Enjoying the pleasures and freedom of vacation did not mean I disliked army life. In fact, if my friend's house was home away from home, I still felt that the army camp was my actual home. The people of the unit were my family. Close friends were like brothers, speaking acquaintances like cousins, and other soldiers of our unit like distant relatives. There was a feeling of belonging that most of us shared, especially those with no real family ties in Palestine. I had become so used to army life it was difficult to imagine any other way of living.

That first leave to Palestine was followed by many more, and most of those leaves were spent in Ramataim. I was drawn to this village because I liked Yacov's company and his parents. I was grateful for their hospitality, the comfort of their home, and the feeling of being near a man and a woman who were parents, if only to my friend. I also appreciated Tamara's home cooking.

An additional attraction developed a few leaves later when Yacov introduced me to a pretty girl named Shoshana. She lived with her mother and younger sister in a small cottage just off the main highway in Kfar Malal, a village north of Ramataim. They were immigrants from Germany.

When I was on leave from Egypt, we went to the movies and on walks. Her boyfriend was in the army, and she was true to him. I sometimes dropped in at her home, and the visit started with the inevitable coffee and cake and a chat with her mother. The elder lady, a nice but possessive matron, apparently enjoyed my company and our conversation. When I shared her table, she'd keep refilling my coffee cup and placing another piece of cake on my plate. We talked in German, the language both of us were most comfortable with. While we talked, Shoshana was doing little jobs in the house that, as far as I could tell, could have waited to be done later. When, in the course of her activity, she passed our table, she seemed unaware of my mute pleas to rescue me from her mother. When we finally escaped to the outside, she played innocent. I may have believed her, had her mischievous eyes not belied her innocence. Eventually she laughed and defended her behavior: "Don't be angry. My mother likes you, and loves to talk to you."

Occasionally on a Saturday nights Yakov and I picked up the sisters and proceeded to Ra'ananna, another village in this cluster of settlements. Here we met the girl who refused to return my friend's love and her brother. The siblings and their parents were also immigrants from Germany.

At the table near the front window of Margel's café sat a man by himself. He was slim, his face gaunt, and the clothes he wore were too large for him. I guessed him to be in his early forties. Though he never ordered anything on his occasional visits to the café, he occupied that seat near the window with the Margel's apparent blessing. He struck me as unusual, for he always seemed lost in thought or absorbed in daydreaming. His starry eyes focused generally on the top part of the empty chair across the table. Sometimes he peered to the outside, and though I was unable to see his eyes then, something in his demeanor made me feel that they were unseeing.

Late one afternoon I again watched the man. There seemed little chance he'd become aware of my attention. As always, he appeared oblivious to the world around him. Outside dusk was settling, yet things were still easily recognizable. On the road beyond the garden hedge traffic, mostly army trucks, rolled by. From time to time when a vehicle had a glass window on its side, the setting sun flashed momentarily in its pane. A little later Yacov took a seat beside me. I asked my friend about the man's bizarre behavior. "He can sit like that for hours," Yacov said. "Come, I'll show you how strange it is to talk to the guy."

I was reluctant to disturb the man, but Yacov assured me he would not mind. Greeting him with shalom, my friend sat down beside the stranger, gesturing to me to take the chair across from the fellow. The man neither moved nor answered Yacov's greeting, and after a while I found it weird to sit with that stationary figure. The stranger seemed unaware of our presence, and continued to stare straight ahead. But now his gaze was fixed on my chest.

A minute or so had passed when unexpectedly the man said shalom to me, and then: "Shalom, Yacov." While the sudden change in the stranger's conduct surprised me, Yacov behaved as if nothing unusual had occurred. "How are you?" he asked his neighbor, but the man had again retreated into his former silence. After a considerable time lapse he answered: "All right." The two went on in their exchange this way for a while, and then we left. "Well, what do you say?" Yacov asked me before we were out of earshot. I whispered: "Quiet, he'll hear you." "No," Yacov said, "he is gone again." My friend was right. The man was frozen once more into immobility, his eyes fixed on the empty chair behind the table.

"What is wrong with him," I asked. "Nobody really knows," my friend said. "The man is normal in the sense that he is not crazy. People who knew him in Germany said he was all right there until he was arrested by the Gestapo and taken to a concentration camp. The incarceration must have had a traumatic effect on him. When he returned from the camp, he was like that.

"Traumatic experiences?" I thought. I knew them well. But how terrible when one's mind cannot cope with a situation and looks for a way out. I thought of the men who had committed suicide in Buchenwald while I was there. Or those who had given up the fight for life and just withered away and died. And men who, as a result of their experiences in horror, retreated into a world of their own. Sometimes only periodically; like the man in Margel's café.

On my leaves to Palestine a visit to Susi was a must. She was the girl my friend and I had strolled with in Vienna and the one I had visited on the evening before I joined the British army. She had married Jo (pronounce Yo for Yosef), a fellow soldier in my outfit. Susi, like Erich and many other young people from Vienna, had left the kibbutz for a life in the city. Many had joined the British army.

Susi had a sizable circle of friends and acquaintances that visited her when on leave from their army units. Some, like myself, stayed in touch with Susi also by mail although she was never in a hurry to answer a letter. If one wanted to know the whereabouts of a friend in the army, a visit to Susi's home was the way to find out. She usually knew if Moshe, Chaim or Mordechai (Tom, Dick, or Harry) was in Palestine, Egypt, the Cyrenaica, or Italy, and where a letter would reach him at his military address.

As a soldier on leave I was permitted to purchase certain rationed grocery items at the military canteen. I had no need for them, and neither did the Margels. I bought them for Susi and her father, but was always reimbursed for the money spent.

After a few days in Ramataim I informed Yacov of my intent to spend a day or two in Tel Aviv. The city would be hot and the central bus station, with its multitude of people, really sizzled in dust and heat when I arrived. The walk to *Beit Hadar* (Citrus House), where the military canteen was located on the ground floor, was not far. I purchased butter, eggs, chocolate, sugar, and other rationed items at slightly reduced prices, and then boarded a bus to Susi's place.

Once aboard, trouble began. The canteen supplied no carrying bag and I had to transport the purchased items under my arms and in my hands. The bus was crowded, the day was hot, and while the butter and chocolate began to get soft, I tried to hold on to the rest of the groceries, especially the eggs.

Since only a fraction of the population owned telephones, and Susi was not one of this select group, I was unable to inform her of my impending visit. If she was not there, I could always bank on her father being home. On one occasion this assumption proved to be a mistake. I climbed to the third floor and unceremoniously kicked with my foot against the door to their apartment. No answer. I kicked again and a third time and was finally confronted with the annoying fact that nobody was home. The dream of ridding myself of those packages and savoring a glass of cool lemonade, melted in the stuffy air of the third floor landing like the butter in my hand.

Unfairly irritated at Susi, I felt like leaving the groceries to their fate in front of the door. If a chance passerby removed some of the abandoned goods, too bad, I did not care. But then a friendly neighbor saved the situation and, alerted by my unorthodox way of getting Susi's attention, opened her door. Recognizing my predicament, she offered to keep the groceries until my friend's return.

I failed to see Susi during that leave and once back in Egypt wrote her about my experience. By that time my feeling of chagrin had dissipated and my description of the event and my absurd actions was humorous. For years Susi recounted my plight and laughed heartily about the melting butter, the soft chocolate, and the rescued eggs.

If more friends were on leave at the same time, we spent an evening on the flat roof of Susi's apartment building. Sitting on blankets and wooden boxes, we talked or sang until late. When this happened I stayed overnight in a hotel.

If we were a large group, we would meet at Café Noga on Pinsker Street, near Allenby Road. The café was usually crowded, and a small band played popular music. The conductor, a Rumanian Jew, often played Viennese music, operettas, and Hebrew songs for our table, and at times we would join in. It was strictly a scenario for Palestine. Anywhere else in the world, the singing of Hebrew and Viennese songs during the war, and this by soldiers in British uniforms, would have been inconceivable. But most of those British soldiers in our group were born in Austria and Germany and had tasted the spirit of Eretz Ysrael.

In spite of my bond to Palestine and the thrill I felt when thinking of specific places and persons there, my daily existence centered on life in Tel el Kebir. On the other hand, my acceptance of our bland camp life only masked my fervent wish to be reunited with my family. They were always in my mind and often played roles in dreams at night and thoughts during days. I made several attempts to find a way to make contact with my family or at least to find out about them.

When the Jewish Brigade was created and moved to Europe in 1944, the opportunity I had been waiting for seemed at hand. I asked for a transfer but my request was denied. Other members of our unit, not all in favor of being sent abroad, were shipped to the continent and attached to the newly formed Brigade. Disappointed but not discouraged, I submitted two more petitions with the same negative results. And so, with little choice for the moment, I settled down again to life in Tel el Kebir, still confident that eventually my time would come.

Life in camp was not as tedious as my previous paragraphs may have suggested. Decisions about what to do after work and where and how to spend a weekend were important enough to provide life with a sem-blance of meaning. But decisions, their scope insignificant in retrospect, befitted our individual physical and mental needs. I still was crazy about movies and two or three visits a week to the base movie theater were not uncommon. I spent more time reading and writing.

One of my friends could not wait for work to end on Saturday afternoon when he and many others settled on beds to play cards uninterruptedly for 18 to 20 hours. Lights-out in barracks was not enforced in Tel el Kebir. Up to a certain time in the evening the players would ask friends and kibitzers to get them sandwiches and coffee from the canteen. When the food arrived, the chain-smoking men were so absorbed in their games, they hardly were aware that they had accepted and consumed the food and drink supplied to them.

I still enjoyed roaming Cairo. Drifting with the throngs of people, having coffee with friends at Café Brazil, and when the heat of the afternoon got too oppressive, take in a film at the Metro Movie Theater on Shari Soliman Pasha. The theater showed only MGM movies and seemed the coolest place in town.

One evening I attended "The Mikado" at the Royal Opera House. It was a benefit performance aiding the British War Fund. King Faruk was not present, though the empty royal box with its elaborate gilded designs caught everyone's eye.

We traveled to Cairo mostly by train, a mode of transportation that had its drawbacks. Since no late train ran on this line, we had to return to camp early. The distance from the Tel el Kebir railroad station to camp S may have seemed short when traversed by motor vehicle. On foot, however, the three miles or so were a long walk. When permitted to use one of the workshop trucks, we met as late as midnight on Opera Square and had a ride back all the way to our barracks.

The route to Cairo led over stretches of desert, past little villages with their greenery and tall palm trees, and along and across narrow canals that supplied precious Nile water to cultivated fields. I watched and felt sorry for the little donkeys that in many places trotted blindfolded in endless circles, turning tall, upright wheels with attached receptacles. The containers scooped water from canals and emptied them into irrigation channels. I glimpsed men and women work in fields with primitive hoes and wooden plows; tools that had not changed since pharaonic times.

Riding our truck, we'd stop halfway through our journey at an Arab roadside café to buy cold drinks in bottles. Foreign military forces in Egypt had been warned not to drink water or soft drinks dispensed from jugs.

My friends and I enjoyed occasional excursions to the garden city of Ismailia and a swim in lake-like water there. Nostalgia may have inspired our visits, for we surely had experienced similar situations in our youth in far away Europe. We settled on a beach among local folks and their children, and since we all wore bathing suits, we almost felt as if we belonged. When the late afternoon sun dropped behind the trees, the families packed up and left for home. Home! A residence in Ismailia or surroundings. My address was 2 Base Workshops, (S Camp) REME, MEF (Middle Eastern Forces).

To what drastic measures the wish to be with one's spouse could lead I saw in the action of a friend. Working as a welder, he stared into the brilliant light of the arc, foolishly ignoring the damage it could do to his eyes. When they got swollen and lobster red, he received a few days sick leave; enough to go home to his wife in Palestine.

Every two to three weeks each of us had guard duty at night. One evening a man in my guard detail became sick and had to be replaced. The young corporal in charge of our group had no problem picking a replacement, even though he knew that in general any soldier suddenly put on guard duty would be madder than hell. The exception to this rule was one elderly soldier. The corporal felt embarrassed to inform the man of his unexpected duty and asked me "Please, go and tell my father he has guard duty tonight."

Abe, a fellow from Germany, had his fun with British soldiers working with him. He'd drive them batty with his English. He'd pick a little-used word from an English dictionary or a short elaborate paragraph from an instruction book and use them indiscriminately. With a serious face he would say to a soldier standing next to him in chow line: "Mutton. Mutton again? Did you know that all the structures of a quadruped that lie posterior to the attachment of the hind legs to the trunk have nothing to do with elephants?"

The addressed soldier would look at our man perplexed, and then let go: "What in the bloody hell are you talking about?"

Abe played hurt: "Don't you understand English?"

Or he'd put together sentences that even if they made sense, were too complicated to be understood by mere soldiers. Talking to one or several soldiers in the workshop about an engine, he would say: "I want to postulate that this engine circumscribes a multiformity of parts. Notwithstanding its relative simplistic manifestation, it expresses an insipidness of its epiphany."

Bubi was our group's dandy. He was the first to convince the Arab tailor in camp that it was permitted to take in the back of his shirt so it would fit him snugly and not like a half-filled balloon. He had his khaki army shorts shortened to above the knees, in contrast to the British soldiers. Theirs almost covered the kneecaps, which gave the impression they were losing their pants while walking. In winter Bubi even had his battle dress jacket taken in the back, which gave his uniform a smart look. Surprisingly he was never confronted by anyone of rank and told that it was against army regulations to alter uniforms. Nobody seemed to notice and eventually all of us copied him.

Uri is the last of the people in my company I will describe. Uri was a vulcanizer. He helped fellow-soldiers, free of charge, to spend weekends at their homes in Palestine. He created a rubber stamp that he used on blank passes made out for a vacation in Palestine. Those passes, however, were only to be used by fellows off work or those with a sick leave too short for an official trip home. He made such a perfect stamp that when eventually the Military Police was informed there were too many soldiers going on leave to Palestine, they took protesting British soldiers off the train whose genuine passes they thought were counterfeit, while accepting Uri's faked ones.

Uri lived in a tent and had hidden the rag-wrapped rubber stamp in the sand under his bed. When he became a suspect, perhaps because of his work as a vulcanizer, and the Military Police, after an extensive search of his things, finally found the cache in the sand, he was taken in for interrogation. Suspecting a possible sinister conspiracy behind Uri's work, the military policeman lifted a wooden club off a hook on the wall to encourage him to confess. Holding it in his right hand, he threateningly tapped the hollow of his left hand with the stick.

Uri was not impressed or intimidated and boastfully, though without justification, claimed: "The Gestapo got nothing out of me, and neither will you." Whether it was his gall, or their unwillingness to press too hard for his ownership of the stamp, he was released with a warning.

1944 was a year of momentous events. From the Allies' point of view the war was progressing well and with unparalleled intensity. The landings on the Normandy coast in June lifted our hearts, and the initially slow, but eventually irresistible advance toward Germany filled us with jubilation. The invasion of southern France in August and the German retreat before the advancing Russians in the east throughout the year were further glorious developments. Only on one frightening occasion in mid-December did the Germans appear to have regained the upper hand in their fight against the Allies. Their powerful offensive in the Ardennes Forest clouded the picture of general progress, and it took a long month and half to drive them back.

VE Day, VJ Day, and a Letter

When Hitler, shirking responsibility for his crimes against humanity, the murder of millions, and his disregard for the welfare of his own people, committed suicide, and his "Thousand Year Reich," lay in ruins, the German military command was forced to call it quits on May 7, 1945.

The moment of their surrender found me on my last day of leave in Palestine. Though everybody had known that Nazi Germany was near its end, the announcement of the surrender did something to me. I felt as if I had stepped through a door that led from the gloom of the past into the brilliant light of a new future. It was like an awakening from a nightmare. In my state of happiness I naively believed that with the end of the war all problems had been solved, and I only had to find my family to resume life the way it had been. Another request for a transfer to Europe to look for them could hardly be rejected at this juncture, or so I assumed.

But first I had to return to camp. When several fellows of my unit and I wanted to buy tickets to Tel el Kebir, we were informed by Military Police at the Tel Aviv railroad station to report to Sarafand and await instructions. For a moment this unexpected order brought a ludicrous notion to my mind. Was it possible that with the cessation of hostilities and the war over in Europe we would be unceremoniously discharged from the army right now? Once in Sarafand, and still in the dark about our future, we asked for an extension of leave. The request was rejected, and even a 24 or 48 hour pass to town to celebrate V-E Day was refused.

After lunch we were informed that we'd be transported the next day to Haifa, placed aboard a troop ship destined for Port Said, and then dispatched to Tel el Kebir by train. Now their refusal to grant us leaves for the evening made more sense. To the British way of thinking, anyway. They may have believed that in celebrating we might get too drunk to return to camp on time and so miss the boat. Their premise was wrong, of course. Jews in Palestine drank alcohol in moderation, and if they did, it was mostly wine. We surely would have been back on time. Next day we arrived in Haifa by train and boarded a ship crowded with British soldiers on their way to Egypt. While we sailed the Mediterranean Sea, Churchill's victory speech came over the ship's intercom on deck. From Port Said, again by train, we arrived late at night at Tel el Kebir.

Victory in Europe changed absolutely nothing in our way of life. Everything went on as if nothing unusual had occurred. My request for a transfer to Europe was again refused. A large percentage of the more than 20,000 Jewish male and female soldiers having relatives in devastated Europe wanted to go there. With no mail service between the civilian population of Central and Eastern Europe and us, I continued to be in the dark about my family's whereabouts.

We had had no real friction with the British for a long time though an occasional "fuckin' Jew" still led to fistfights. Some time back a fight between one of our Sabres and an English soldier had occurred in front of the camp movie theater. Bogard, our man, had bought a ticket at the box office window and was picking up his change. The man behind the window commented something about Bogard's slowness. Words were exchanged, and then the ticket seller said: "fuckin' Jew." Our fellow challenged the swearer to step outside, which the man did. Both were tall men, but Bogard belonged to our sport-boxing group and thrashed the man thoroughly.

Outside the theater a long line of soldiers was waiting to buy tickets. We Palestinians may have made up 20 percent of that group. Though we were in the minority, it was obvious to anyone present, that had Bogard been on the losing side, we would have intervened on his behalf. This incident later became the topic of a conversation between a British Tommy and me while we pushed guard at night. At first it was small talk, but eventually the subject of a fair fight came up. "You Jews are like burs. You bunch and cling together when someone tries to touch one of you."

I explained to him that Jews had been on the receiving end for hundreds of years, and had rarely dared to fight back against all the misery and degradation heaped onto them. But as could be seen in

Palestine, times had changed. Now if Jews were attacked, they fought back, and other Jews came to help them.

He disliked my reference to Palestine. He was, after all, British and even the lowliest British soldier felt like a master in what was to him a colony. The British presence in Palestine, my partner argued, was beneficial to its inhabitants. The British kept order, and developed the economy. Apparently he was unaware that it were the Jews who developed the economy. And as for keeping order, when trouble between Arabs and Jews was in progress, British policy always favored the Arabs.

Accepting the futility of our debate I hoped to end the topic with an unanswerable – I thought – parting shot. I said: "As Palestine is only a mandate, and not a colony, it actually puts the British on the same footing with the rest of the population. Why don't you learn Hebrew or Arabic, so you can talk and do business with the population as equals?" To this he replied with the pure arrogance of an overlord: "Anybody who wants to talk or do business with us should speak English."

In the Pacific the Americans fought bloody island and sea battles against the Japanese. The British, principally with the help of Indian and Chinese forces, were pushing the imperial Japanese armies out of southeast Asia. To shorten the war the Americans dropped an atomic bomb on Japan. As this failed to bring the Japanese to their knees, a second atomic bomb followed, and Japan signed the surrender on September 2, 1945, VJ Day.

Not all camps in Tel el Kebir had common borders. Camp S and camp R did. They lay side by side, and shared a canteen. Some stretches of low barbed-wire fence defined the border. The barrier actually had no purpose. Closer than the British soldiers of camp R was a group of Tommys in our midst. Among the dispersed huts and assorted tents of our compound they occupied one billet. Nobody knew the reason why they were forgotten inside the Palestinian camp, but as those men in our midst were unobtrusive, nobody even thought about them.

With the war over celebrations were again in order. In camp S everyone was elated. Some danced the hora, and even the non-dancers smiled, for hopes of an early army discharge were high. The two theaters in camp showed movies free of charge that evening, and some of us decided to go.

Before we left for the theater, which was about two miles from camp S, we bought a few things at the canteen. Our neighbors of camp R, hardy British soldiers, sat around small tables drinking beer. Everyone was familiar with their weekend ritual that normally started later in the evening but because it was VJ Day had begun earlier this time. On these

274

occasions, the soldiers covered the table with bottles of beer, drank, talked, went to the latrine to relieve themselves, came back, and guzzled some more. Filled bottles replaced empty ones, as the situation required.

At the theater we met more of the fellows from camp S but kept to our own group. It was near midnight when we again approached camp S. The night was dark but from the direction of our camp and still some distance away, two dazzling headlights of a truck blinded us. As we advanced I saw human figures pass occasionally in front of the beams. Something is wrong, I said.

The road led through camp R and here everything was quiet. Getting closer to the truck, parked on the border to our camp, we were stopped by military police. Asked where we were going, we said camp S. They wanted to know why. After identifying ourselves we were permitted to continue. There were at least another 20 of the red-hats in the vicinity.

We entered our area of scattered huts, each of us intending to seek out his own, and saw some of our fellows running between the buildings. They stuck their heads through the doors of huts, and screamed into the dark: "Come on, get up. Let's kill 'em." I tried to ask one of them what had happened, but his answer was too incoherent to make sense.

On the following day our camp was still in a bit of an uproar. Now I learned the reason for the rage of the night before. In celebration of the victory our office hut, next to the road, displayed two flags. I believe no insult was intended, but the blue and white flag was on the roof, and the Union Jack fluttered obliquely over the office entrance. An officer of camp R ruled that the Union Jack was not to fly lower than the Jewish flag and the situation was corrected. Both flags stood upright on the same level at opposite ends of the roof of our office building.

That might have been the end of the story had not word gotten around camp R that the Palestinians had slighted their banner. That night some drinking buddies of camp R decided to avenge the insult to the Union Jack. One of them was to steal the Jewish flag off the roof and destroy it.

The English soldiers living in our camp happened to hear the plot and reported the fellow's intention to the sergeant of our guard. The man on the roof was caught with the flag in his possession and placed under arrest in our guardhouse, a room in the office building. Our commanding officer that was told of the incident was rightly concerned for the safety of the culprit. He transferred him immediately to the main prison in Tel el Kebir. Had a certain group of our men found out what had taken place, the man's life would have been in jeopardy. Our guards would have been powerless to prevent an attack on the prisoner without shooting at our own people.

After the transfer of the perpetrator, the news of the thievery spread in our camp. It brought together a crowd of angry fellows who were ready to avenge the intended desecration of the symbol. Furious that the thief had escaped their wrath, they learned of the soldiers in camp R who had conspired with the culprit and went to confront them.

Meanwhile, in the canteen, the schemer waited in vain for their hero. When he failed to return, they went looking for him. More British soldiers joined the group when they learned the reason for their search. When the two opposing forces met, the ensuing clash developed into a fight with clubs, pipes, beer bottles, and, in some cases, knives.

As I was told, Sergeant Major Shimshon (Samson) worked like Samson among the Philistines. He alone sent a score of opponents to the hospital. One British soldier, about to hit him on the head with a steel bar from behind, was prevented from doing so by an elderly chap of ours. The fellow, a man from Russia, stepped in between the two and, in trying to divert the blow, was hit on the chin instead. He needed stitches, which he proudly displayed from then on. Only two of our men were taken to the hospital but required only first aid.

Incensed by anything British, some of our political right-wingers broke through the entrance of the hut the Englishmen occupied in our camp. It must have been a frightful experience for the British to face that wild-eyed band. They crowded together, one of them training a Tommy gun at the intruders. My friend Bubi, enraged, tore open his shirt and exposing his chest screamed: "Shoot. Shoot. Why don't you shoot." Only after our men found out that it was thanks to those soldiers the theft of the flag had been prevented, did the aroused Jews apologize for their behavior. The entire military police force of Tel el Kebir turned out to separate the combatants but no arrests were made. The police we saw when we came from the movies were just a remnant of the original force.

The story had a sequel the next day. A group of our soldiers connected pipes to a length of about 40 feet and fastened the improvised flagpole to a hut. The maligned Zionist flag was hoisted to the top. Let them come, the word was, meaning the soldiers of camp R, and try to get our flag.

They even wanted to illuminate the fluttering banner by night. An array of car headlights, fed by car batteries, would be trained on the Jewish symbol after dark, but our own officers refused to go along with that scheme. We were after all in the British army and on the following day the mast had to be dismantled and the flag brought down. There was at least the satisfaction of victory for one day.

And then, a most wonderful thing happened. A letter arrived. It reached me in October of 1945. Frau Lewin, the lady from Bat Galim, had received the message from my sister Berta and, being in touch with me through our yearly New Years greetings, had forwarded it to me. It was the first sign from a member of my family. It was astounding that the letter had found its destination. It had the name of the person, the city and the country written on it, but no street address. The Lewin family had no phone, so they were not in the phone book, and though Bat Galim was not very big, people knew only the people in their immediate neighborhood. The feat of finding me can therefore only be attributed to the diligence of those fine people at the post office in Bat Galim.

Any attempt to describe my emotions would fail as I held that small Red Cross form in my hand. My hand trembled and my heart beat furiously. I stared at the writing, still not believing my eyes. In the limited space assigned to correspondence, my sister's short message meant volumes to me. I knew at least that she was alive. My great concern now was our parents. This may be the right place to insert their story, related to me by my sister an eternity later.

After I had left Vienna, my parents and my sister remained in the city for another two years. In 1942 the three were deported to the Theresienstadt ghetto in occupied Czechoslovakia. It was not too bad there. It was the Nazis' showplace when they wanted to prove to the Red Cross, and the world in general, how humane Jews were treated in a camp.

In October 1944 my parents and sister were selected for a transport to Auschwitz. My mother begged Dr. Murmelstein, the elder of the Viennese Jews in Theresienstadt, to postpone their deportation. She trusted that Murmelstein, who was the former rabbi of the Klucky Temple, the synagogue in our neighborhood that was destroyed by the Nazis in the "Kristallnacht," November 1938, would intervene on their behalf. She hoped that being the daughter of Seidler senior, one of the elders of the synagogue, and a steady financial contributor to this beautiful house of worship, would influence Murmelstein's decision. It did not work. My parents and sister were transported to Auschwitz.

The Jews on the train to Auschwitz had been ordered to keep away from the windows. All windows were closed, but where my sister sat part of the windowpane was missing. At one point while the train was in motion, she stuck her head through the opening. One of the guards on the train, who was watching the outside to prevent escapes, fired two rounds toward her. She heard the bullets whistle past her head, and one grazed her hair.

At the railroad station in Auschwitz, men had to assemble on one side of the train, women and children on the other. My sister and mother, trying to keep together, held hands when the mass of people moved forward. Suddenly a boy of about 14 appeared among the women, asking them their age. Reaching my mother and sister, he hastily whispered: "How old are you?" "Eighteen," my sister replied. "Say 19." He turned to our mother. "Forty-four," she answered. "Say you are 39," he hissed, and continued his dangerous mission to warn people that being too old or too young could be fatal.

Still holding hands, the two reached a single SS man who, with a slicing downward motion of his hand broke their clasp. His action sent them to two different sides of the platform. The haggard face of our mother and the youthfulness of my sister made the question of age unnecessary. Mother was doomed, and father was not seen again either. Berta was spared.

On the same transport was Vera Korkus, a friend of my sister. They were friends from Vienna. At Auschwitz Vera and her mother were separated from each other the same way my family was. Later at the camp, Berta and Vera met Vera's older sister, Ruth. Ruth had been a laborer in Auschwitz already for a year. Ruth asked Vera where their mother was, and when she was told of the separation, Ruth, having seen thousands of cases like that, said there was no chance the parents were still among the living.

By Ruth's account, the procedure for new arrivals never varied. Being in the wrong age group, or looking weak or sickly, the doomed were handed a piece of soap and led straight to the so-called showers. Instead of water, the showerheads emitted poison gas.

By 1944 Auschwitz was working at full capacity; German industry had produced a cyanide gas that efficiently murdered thousands of Jews a day in most of the extermination camps. Yet, according to Ruth Korkus, the methods used in the Auschwitz gas chambers were not altogether foolproof. What had not been taken into account, and none of the perpetrators really cared about this, was that at times victims survived the lethal fumes when they lay buried under the bodies of those who fell on top of them. But because the killing machine under Hoess's command was not permitted to slow down, no time was wasted looking for Jews who still had life in them. But escape from the gas did not save their lives. It delivered them to an even more horrible end when they were thrown into the inferno of the ovens with the bodies of the dead.

But for Rudolf Hoess the gassing of Jews was not a new method to kill them. At his trial he admitted that long before he became commander of Auschwitz, he had Jews killed by gassing and suffocation. He accomplished that by having a hose connected from the exhaust pipe of a truck to the securely encased and insulated truck-bed. The inside of the truck-bed was closely packed with Jews.

When he was told that the motors did not always perform uniformly well, and the exhaust fumes were not strong enough to kill everybody, but left many just unconscious, he ordered the survivors shot afterwards.

On October 27, 1944, after twelve days in Auschwitz, my sister, and others like her, were shipped by rail in open cattle cars to the concentration camp Kurzbach near Breslau (today Wroclaw, Poland). In Kurzbach they were held for three months. In anticipation of the advancing Russian armies, all prisoners had to dig defense ditches. Berta told me that the two women SS guards in charge of her group were quite different. One was relatively nice, the other a sadistic beast. One day my sister tore a piece of cloth off her coat, made a little dog from it, and gave to the friendlier guard. Asked by that guard if she could make a bigger dog, my sister said she could if she had enough material. It was close to Christmas, and apparently more guards wanted those hand-made animals for gifts. Berta was excused from hard outdoor work for the next two weeks. She was permitted to stay in the barn where they lived and make those animals. As an added bonus she was given raw cabbage and bread. The stay inside the enclosure also helped heal a puss-filled sore on her foot, which had come from wearing wooden shoes.

When they were force-marched from Kurzbach in January of 1945, the 1,000 women prisoners had to drag themselves along icy roads in the harshest of winter weather. They walked from sunup to sundown. On the eighth day the survivors of the march reached Gross-Rosen, another concentration camp. During the first four days of the march my sister saw people, who could not walk anymore, stay behind. On the fifth day she also considered giving up in hope that the advancing Russians would take care of her. On this day the mayor of a town they were passing through said to the SS commandant: "I don't want anybody left behind. Here is a horse and wagon, put the people who can't walk on it, but take them with you." My sister decided now to continue the trek on foot, and this was her salvation. When they arrived in Gross-Rosen, they learned that the SS had shot the people who remained behind.

After ten days in Gross-Rosen they were once more on their way. Transported again in open cattle cars, they arrived at the railroad station in Dachau, near Munich. The commander of the concentration camp there refused them entry. The camp was filled to capacity. They were sent on to Buchenwald, but this concentration camp did not want them either, and so their final destination became Bergen-Belsen.

Having gone through hell and survived the sadistic excesses of SS guards, my sister was barely alive when the British liberated her on April 15, 1945. She weighed 60 pounds, could not walk, and had to crawl on all fours. The liberated prisoners craved food. The British had reached Bergen-Belsen in the early part of the day, and by afternoon all prisoners held a loaf of bread and a can of spam in their hands. But the prisoners could hardly swallow a thing. Their throats were dry and their stomachs unused to solid food. Most of them contracted stomach typhoid and some died just from eating too much too fast.

Our mother, born in 1900, was 44, and our father, born in 1893, was 51 years old when they were murdered in Auschwitz in 1944. Where was our God, the God of Israel, when all this happened? He would have spared Sodom and Gomorra had there been 10 righteous men among the inhabitants of the two cities. Were there not 10 righteous men or women among the millions murdered in the holocaust, a crime unparalleled by anything the world had ever witnessed? No scourge in history achieved what the Nazis meted out to humankind in the few years of their reign of terror. Did He feel no compassion for "his people" when they cried out to Him while being tortured and put to death in horrible ways? When their last breath was: "Shmah Israel," "Hear Israel?" Not a call for help anymore, but a question: Why?

With Berta's letter in hand I could hardly contain my excitement. Knowing that she was alive, I had to find my friends and tell them. They surely would rejoice with me. While searching for them, I told everybody I knew on the way about my sister's rescue. I found Bubi and Moshe in the mess hall, and holding out the letter to them, I could only stammer: "She is alive, she is alive."

When the emotional turmoil finally gave way to reason, my first decision was that if I could not go to Europe, I would try to bring my sister to Palestine. I wrote the Margels and informed them of my sister's survival. Yacov's reply came quickly, and the letter started wonderfully: "Get in touch with the Sochnut (Jewish Agency) right away and ask them to get your sister a certificate permitting her to immigrate to Palestine. Let them know there is a family which would love to take her in." But my spirits sank as I read on: "Unfortunately you can't mention our name to the government because we are illegally in the country." It sounded incredible. Living in Palestine for over 10 years, owning a house, running a business, and catering to the British, the Margels were still illegals! Having entered and settled in the country without a certificate, they would have been deported, had they filed for permanent residency with the British government of Palestine.

On the Red Cross form on July 22, 1945 my sister had given her address as Goethestrasse 15-17, Linz, Oberdonau, Österreich (Austria). The message had taken two and a half months to reach me. I immediately tried to answer but was distressed to find that postal service with Austria had been interrupted. It stayed that way for more than six months.

I was contemplating my next step a few days later when another letter arrived. It too was forwarded by Frau Lewin and contained a telegram from my sister. Strangely, the message was in English and had been dispatched from Prague.

To compound the confusion, a third letter arrived less than a week after that. It had also been mailed from Prague, and the envelope bore Czechoslovakian stamps. It was addressed to me in care off Frau Lewin, and though my sister had written the letter inside, the handwriting on the envelope was not hers. Both letters from Czechoslovakia had no sender's address. This mail from Czechoslovakia remained a puzzle. My sister later insisted that all the mail she had sent to me was from Austria. There may, however, be a solution to the mystery. Because the mail service between Austria and the Middle East was interrupted, my sister may have entrusted her letters to somebody who was going to Prague and asked that person to mail her letters to me from there.

My most earnest wish was to get in touch with her and make certain she knew her messages had reached me. I was convinced she was as anxious to hear from me as I had been to hear from her. And also I had to determine whether my sister was in Austria or Czechoslovakia. A correct address was essential.

I learned of the "Council of Austrians in Great Britain" at Austrian Center, 124, 126, Westbourn Terrace, London, W.2 and sent them the letter I had written to my sister. I asked them to mail it to her address in Austria. Their reply was prompt and in German. They wrote: "We forwarded your letter to Austria, and hope you won't have to wait too long for an answer. We hope regular mail service will be restored soon and you won't have to use this roundabout way."

This encouraged me. At least they had forwarded my letter, and if things went well, an answer from Berta with her correct address would be forthcoming. This was extremely important also for another reason; I needed to gain permission to go to Austria. With my sister alive and her letters in my possession to prove it, I thought I had enough to convince the army bureaucracy of my need to go to Europe.

How wrong I was. Nothing changed. When, at certain times, I believed myself close to my goal, a new disappointment frustrated my hope. There was talk of our companies being shipped to Europe, yet nothing happened. Another of my requests for an individual transfer to the Jewish Brigade was denied. What else could I do to see my sister? To try and find our parents? At moments like that the world around me seemed made of rubber walls, giving way but resisting penetration.

The Council of Austrians in London, which had records of survivors, informed my sister of my address. Her next letter reached me in June of 1946 at my army base in Egypt.

Meanwhile, Bubi had recently returned from Belgium where he had been on compassionate leave to see his parents. They had survived the Nazi scourge and had been able to get in touch with their son. They had furnished certificates attesting to their poor health and my friend had been granted leave for the visit. In my friend's case, however, there may have been an additional circumstance that expedited the granting of his leave. Bubi's brother, captured in Greece with the British Expeditionary Forces in 1941, had been a POW of the Germans until they surrendered. He too went to see their parents.

Attempts to Meet My Sister

Bubi, aware of my frustration, suggested I should apply for leave on compassionate grounds. He cautioned me, however, that the process generally took months before a decisive positive or negative answer would be forthcoming. Hundreds, if not thousands awaited decisions by army authorities on similar petitions. Those were bleak prospects indeed, and I wondered if there were any avenues that would produce faster results or perhaps, bypass the slow-moving army bureaucracy altogether. Army regulations required that requests be submitted to the company office where, I assumed, it would go through channels until it reached the commander of Tel el Kebir. And then?

My disappointment grew by the day, week, and month. While I was pondering how to cut through army red tape, an unobtrusive little press item provided me with a clue that could help me solve my problem. It was a short notice in a London newspaper that someone had left on a table in the canteen. It told of a Scotsman in the British Army stationed somewhere in Europe who had applied for special leave. His wife had recently given birth to a baby, and he wanted to see his family. After requests for leave were denied because there was no apparent emergency, the frustrated man, acting contrary to army regulations, mailed a letter to his Commander-in-Chief, King George himself. The article omitted, however, how the letter was conveyed to the addressee. The king, or whoever represented His Majesty, presumably received the plea and intervened on the soldier's behalf whose leave was then granted.

Although I believed my reasons for a transfer or leave to Europe were at least as urgent and important as that of the Scotsman, I assumed that a letter of mine addressed to the king had little chance of reaching the monarch. Tel el Kebir was a great distance from Buckingham Palace, and not only in miles. A letter sent by me to the king would have had to pass through several stations and inspections as it got closer to its intended goal. I planned to follow the Scotsman's example – up to a point. The targeted person had to be very important, yet someone closer to home. This appeared a sensible decision in a senseless situation. So I composed a letter to General (later Sir) Bernard Charles Tolver Paget, Commander in Chief of all military forces in the Middle East. In the British style of correspondence, I started with "Sir," and ended, "your obedient servant."

My problem was how to get my request to the C-in-C without it going through the chain of command as required by army regulations. A letter mailed from an Egyptian post office might have succeeded; yet, unreasonable as it may seem in retrospect, I was reluctant to violate the military code that prohibited the use of civilian mail by members of the armed forces. I had no qualms about doing what I was about to do, but it was to remain an internal army matter. The letter had to go by military mail, carrying my address, and had to originate from our own regimental post office. If it passed our postal station, I hoped it would continue unimpeded until it arrived at its destination in Cairo. But what army postal clerk, considering the trouble he might find himself in, would dispatch my letter?

Efrem was a clerk at the camp S post office. He was a nice guy, though quite easily aroused by anything contrary to his political views. He adhered to the right-wing theories of Jabotinsky, and though I did not share his political view, I respected his opinion and had often sympathized with them to some extent. We were not friends, but having been in the same army unit for a long time, we shared a sort of comradeship. Nonetheless, it was not easy to take somebody into my confidence that I knew only superficially.

Efrem had joined the British army, like many others, to do his part in the fight against the Nazis. He felt no love for the British who, in his view, occupied Jewish land and kept Jews from making "Aliya," i.e. from coming "home." I felt if someone was to be trusted with my letter, he was the right person to approach.

I was right. Efrem agreed to send the letter on to GHQ Cairo as if it was the routine thing to do. He did not seem worried that it made him a co-conspirator in an act considered unlawful by army standards – an act that might have gotten him also in trouble.

In my letter of January 3, 1946, I requested compassionate leave. On January 14, GHQ Cairo replied! The letter, addressed to me, was marked registered and confidential. It was not what I had hoped for, but it was an answer. The Commander in Chief, I was informed, was out of Egypt at present. News in the Egyptian Mail, Cairo's English newspaper, placed General Paget in Syria. Two items in their letter were meaningful to me. The first was the permission to write to GHQ again if I wanted additional information – access to an otherwise almost unreachable army station. The second was the request for a certificate proving my sister's poor health before I "might" be considered for compassionate leave to Europe. The interrupted mail service with the continent made this last requirement unattainable for me. At least for an unknown length of time.

I had no doubt that my sister – after all she must have gone through – could obtain the paper Cairo required. But this was of little help to me when all my attempts to get through to her were in vain. In an effort to explain my problem to the proper officer at GHQ I wrote another letter which I mailed, again with Efrem's help, on March 1, 1946. Two days later I was instructed by our camp S office to appear before the commanding officer of Tel el Kebir, a British colonel. This meant trouble, and the obvious reason had to be my latest letter to GHQ Cairo. On the day of confrontation I wore a freshly pressed battle dress, our winter uniform, the brass parts of my army belt, and boots were polished to a high shine, and I carried the reply of the GHQ in my pocket just in case. While facing the closed door to the colonel's office, the British RSM (regimental sergeant major) straightened the beret on my head, the rim of which had to be exactly two fingers above the eyebrows and then hissed: "Salute smartly in there." He pushed open the door and quick-marched me into the room. His staccato, left, right, left right, left right, was speedy, and his "halt," a short bark. I stopped at attention one step from the colonel's desk. On the desk lay my letter.

A colonel in the British army was, and perhaps still is, a no-nonsense person. The man behind the desk, the epitome of the senior British army officer, glared at me in anger. He was confronting a soldier whose offense had been severe enough not to be handled by a regular officer of his unit but by the commander of an army base. He seemed a career man of the old colonial school and had without doubt served in "Indsha."

"Who gave you permission to write to GHQ Cairo?" he asked sharply. – "GHQ Cairo, Sir!" I answered smartly. And, contrary to military conduct, pulled the envelope with the letter from my battle dress front pocket, and placed it on the table. The RSM snarled at my sudden move but was too late to stop me. As I had hoped, the letter changed the situation somewhat. The colonel could not confiscate it, for I had mailed it to GHQ with their permission. Dismissing with the warning never again to ignore army protocol, I was relieved that he had not inquired how it came that GHQ had written to me in the first place.

Headquarters Cairo also answered my second letter. But it too was disappointing and no help to me. They again asked for proof of my sister's poor health, which I could not provide. I had to look for other ways to get to Europe, and another opportunity seemed to avail itself a while later.

"If I can get on a plane, I'll just go. The 20 Egyptian pounds the captain of our soccer team has handed me, I'll use for my own purpose. When it's over and I come back, I'll return the money."

These, and related thoughts occupied me as I traveled by train to Cairo one early morning. The money mentioned was for the purchase of a trophy for the top team of Tel el Kebir's soccer league at the end of the season. The award, however, was the least of my concerns on this trip. I went to Cairo primarily to seek either a plane ride to Europe without proper papers or the permission of the army. An unusual undertaking under any circumstances, foolish perhaps, and yet not too crazy for me to attempt at the time this narration took place.

When my friend Ariye, also from Vienna, told me in detail of an offer he had had in a Cairo bar, the possibility of my dream becoming reality fascinated me. The offer may have been extended frivolously, influenced perhaps by too many drinks, but it seemed like an ideal way out of the quagmire that had haunted me ever since I had first requested a transfer to Europe.

Ariye was no drinker, yet he happened to sit on a barstool next to members of the American Air Force. In due course my friend and an airman started a conversation and as time progressed they became buddies. Ariye told the man that he was from Palestine whereupon Allen, the friendly airman, exclaimed: "Ah, that's only 200 miles as the crow flies. You're probably home every week." Before my friend could set the record straight, his new acquaintance, while trying to keep his balance on the bar stool, continued sorrowfully: "I'm so far from home. No chance gett'n to visit my folks." To console the sentimental airman, my friend confided that he could not go home every week but only every six months when his leave came due. "So close to home, and you can't get home?" the American wondered. "Tell you what. Any time you want to go home to Palestine, look me up. We have planes flying to Palestine all the time. I'll put you on one, and you'll be home in no time."

Ariye laughed when he recounted the conversation. But his story fascinated me, and I saw no humor in it. To me it seemed to offer a way to get to Europe I had never thought of. Hitching a ride on a plane! Hiding my intense interest, I casually asked Ariye at what airfield Allen was stationed. He did not know.

I was hooked and decided to search for Allen and his airfield in and around Cairo. Though it was clutching at a straw, I was almost convinced that if I located the two, my problem would be solved.

My search, however, had to be postponed. All of Egypt's cities were out of bounds to foreign military personnel. The native population had taken to the streets to vent their frustration with their government and the reigning monarch, King Faruk. But intrigue turned the rampaging mob's anger against the British and their forces. In many places British personnel were attacked and in Alexandria's Ramle station, so well known to me from back in 1942, I was told that British soldiers had been decapitated by a band of frenzied Arabs. When things finally quieted down and the off-limit order was lifted, I asked for and received a one-day pass to Cairo. Our office thought I was going to purchase a cup for the soccer game finals.

And so I was on that early morning train to Cairo, and as it rattled on so did my thoughts. I tried to envision a meeting with Allen, provided I found the right airfield and the right Allen. I wondered if he'd remember my friend Ariye or, more important, his promise to him. If he remembered, would he be willing to help me after listening to my story and the drastic change of destination? Would he consider me nuts, for wanting to be stowed away on a plane to Europe to see my sister?

Beside the 20 Egyptian pounds of the soccer league, I had 10 of my own, a few Palestinian pounds, and seven American dollars, a currency forbidden to own. I had received the dollars in letters from grandma in New York. But since she did not know how to write, it was her daughter, my aunt, who wrote in her name and added the occasional one-dollar bill to the letter. These were meager assets for a junket to Europe, yet I wasn't worried. All I wanted was to get on a plane.

Cairo at first looked its old self. Throngs of people milled about the railroad station, the adjacent Bab el Hadid Square and Ibrahim Pasha, the street leading to Opera Square. Then I noticed that the crowd I felt most comfortable with, British soldiers, was almost nonexistent. Evidence of the recent riots was still in the streets. Conspicuous was the unusual number of policemen everywhere. Many big department stores like Cicurel and Ben Zion (owned by Jews) were still closed. Egyptian police with rifles over their shoulders guarded the properties, making it apparent that the Egyptian government still considered the situation unstable and feared break-ins and looting.

Since I did not know an American airfield around Cairo or anywhere else for that matter, I visited an army information office across Ezbekiya Garden. The lady was nice, but her directions to John Payne Airfield were rather vague. She told me to take the "electric train" to Heliopolis and then ask for further directions.

Heliopolis, a suburb of Cairo, was one of the nicest neighborhoods I had seen around this city. The streets were clean, and the houses looked like residences of well-to-do people. I stayed only long enough to inquire of the airfield's location and was directed to a road leading out of the district and into a region that seemed like the beginning of the desert.

A hitched ride brought me to a crossroad. The driver pointed to one road leading away from the junction. "This is the way to the airfield," he said. – "Can I walk?" – "You can, but better wait for transportation," he said and took off without an explanation. The wait at the crossing was lonely. The absolute silence of the place felt as oppressive as the vibrating heat over the surrounding barren hills. Though the rises were not high, they hid anything that suggested a human habitat behind them.

I heard the engine of a vehicle long before it came into view. The driver of the Jeep, an American sergeant, stopped for my hand signal and, learning my destination, motioned to the empty seat beside him: "Jump in." In the back of the Jeep sat two other hitchhikers – tall, scrawny Sudanese soldiers.

While we drove in silence, I wondered whether I should confide in the sergeant. He looked like a decent fellow who would keep to himself anything I'd say. And I was dying to tell my story to someone. I asked him if he knew a flier by the name of Allen on the base. He did not but said he'd find out for me.

Near the camp's entrance the two Sudanese soldiers got off the Jeep. The military policeman at the gate let us pass when the sergeant said I was with him. We drove to an office barracks where a few soldiers and several Arab civilian clerks were working. The sergeant called a civilian clerk over and told him to look for Allen in the files. He then turned to me: "Do you know his first name?"

I had not known that Allen was also a last name though it really did not matter. I had never expected to find that particular Allen. I had not even found out from Ariye if the man he had talked to in Cairo was a flier, a crewmember, or just someone on the base who had connections. "It's his first name," I said. The sergeant looked at me in disbelief. "That's his first name?" He then continued: "How do you expect me to find somebody whose first name is Allen on a base of several thousand men?"

I decided to confide in the sergeant. "May I please speak to you in private?" Somehow I felt that Americans could do anything, and so I told my woes to the man, hoping to hear him say: "All right, I'll get you on a plane." It was not that easy. What he said was: "I can't help you. But I'll send you to someone who may be able to do something for you. He is the traffic officer and puts people on planes." That sounded promising, and in my mind I saw myself on a plane by that night.

The sergeant told a soldier to take me some place. We walked among the barracks, and then entered one of them. Considering the prevailing heat, the several men in their underwear taking it easy on their beds were properly dressed. My guide asked for a particular person, and was told he was in the shower.

On we went to the showers. Inside, near a shower stall, stood a naked young man toweling himself. The first thing I became aware of was a small golden Star of David he wore on a chain around his neck. *He is Jewish*, I exulted in my heart.

"Someone's here to talk to you," my guide informed him, and left.

The young man looked at me curiously. "Yes?"

I introduced myself and again told my story and wish. I felt so confident of his reaction that I was taken aback when he too said: "I can't help you."

Noticing my disappointment he continued defensively: "I can put you on a plane that stops in Athens, Rome, and Germany. But in each of those places papers are checked. When they see you in your British uniform and with no papers, they'll check back to find out who the traffic officer was who put you on that plane. They'll get to me, and I'll be in trouble."

He looked at me, hoping I'd understand his predicament. He found no understanding in my eyes. Nothing he could have said would have eased my disappointment. He tried anyway. "Look, I am a long time away from home and should return to the States in a few weeks. If I get caught helping you I'll land in jail, and you don't want that, do you?"

By then I was aware of the hopelessness of the situation. I knew he was right and yet, my frustration was so deep-felt that nothing could calm me down. Not even his right to go home. I felt betrayed when all that man before me defended was his own good fortune.

He sensed my unforgiving attitude and made one more attempt to mollify me.

"I promise you one thing," he said, "if you get a furlough, come back to me. There is a Jewish major in our outfit who will put you on a plane to Europe for certain. You won't have to take a long sea trip to get there."

I thanked him, but my heart was not in it. I thought that if I received a "furlough" to Europe, going by boat wouldn't bother me.

The Toulon Caper

Despite the early time of the year, the Egyptian sun had burned the ground of our camp dry and dusty. It made powder of the earth that once had been a solid surface, and what little greenery had come to life during the sparse winter rains had shriveled and dried up in the heat. April was nearing its end, and talk of men being discharged was making the rounds. I did not know when my turn would come, yet on the other hand, saw no chance to visit my sister in Europe once I became a civilian in Palestine. The pay in the British army was far from generous, and I had saved little. Even were I able to acquire the money for a ticket, two additional obstacles might still have confronted me. Would the Allied

288

authorities let me enter Europe? And if they did, would the British permit me to return to Palestine afterward? I had no intention of remaining in Europe after seeing my sister but rather wished to bring her eventually to Palestine.

Since my fruitless attempt to hitch a flight to the continent I had searched unsuccessfully for other options. Nearly six months had passed since the wonderful letter of Mrs. Levin that had brought me the news of Berta's survival. My initial euphoria, however, became frustration when the mail connection with Europe remained disrupted, and I did not know exactly where my sister lived. It also increased my anxiety about the fate of my parents of whom I had heard nothing.

My resolve to reach my sister while still a soldier became more urgent as time progressed. The final attempt to meet her developed into my strangest exercise yet. A thought that had occupied me since Bubi's return from his compassionate leave to Belgium. I decided to try my friend's route without the blessing of the army. It wouldn't be a simple plane ride to Europe with the Americans, but rather travel with complicated hurdles to overcome and contacts with people I would have preferred to avoid.

Just three days before setting out on my adventure, I was still undecided about my starting date. Soldiers on their way to the continent were provided with several travel documents. A fact my friend Bubi had neglected to tell me until those three days before I left. Of the various documents in question I obtained only one special blank pass that would, in time, have to display the red stamp of British Military Headquarters in Cairo. To achieve and transfer a facsimile of that stamp onto the pass, I worked most of my last Sunday in camp in the canteen. Though I intended to avoid using the document and rather depend on intuition, luck, and my agility in awkward situations, it gave me a sense of security.

Bubi supplied me with the original red stamped pass he had used, and this was the model for my forgery. I had talked with my friend on several occasions, inquiring in detail about his journey from its beginning at Tel el Kebir to his arrival in Brussels. But as he had traveled with legitimate documents, he had experienced none of the problems I anticipated. Nevertheless I made notes of places and specific moments during his travel days, and when I had memorized the details, I disposed of what I had written. In Bubi's view I had nothing to worry about if I followed his instructions. Maybe.

Against the heat and glare of the outdoors the canteen felt quiet, cool, and comfortable. I chose the place because few soldiers visited the NAAFI during daytime on weekends, and I hoped to work undisturbed at my task. I had several blank passes of the sort needed for travel to Port Said, but only one I thought I might need for Europe. Earlier I may have asked Uri, the vulcanizer, to make me a rubber stamp, but since his brush with the British military intelligence he was keeping his nose clean.

A small bottle of red ink, and several pages of scratch paper, all "borrowed" from our company office, were tools for the forging of the stamp. The big room of the canteen remained empty most of the time, and nobody bothered the lonely guy at a corner table who was nursing Coca Colas and smoking innumerable cigarettes. For hours I measured in millimeters the height and the width of the letters of the original stamp, the space between the lines, the distance between the letters, and the distance between the words. I used the sharpened point of a wooden match for a pen, and created stamp after stamp on plain paper. One of my problems was the bright red of the ink that looked spurious on the scratch paper. I tried to dull the color of the ink by mixing a drop of it with dust from the floor, dirt from the outside, a minimal amount of black ink from a fountain pen, but nothing gave it the shade I thought I needed. The results of my experiments were frustratingly inadequate, and I grew tired. Bubi brought me a sandwich and coffee, just as I had done when he played cards for hours. Then I started again.

In the afternoon I tried to transfer my counterfeit creation from one piece of paper to another. I once had heard that the surface of a raw potato cut in half would transfer an image like the stamp of an inkpad. I got a potato from the kitchen and tried it. All it did was leave wet round spots, the size of the vegetable, on both of the papers. The spots failed to disappear even after they dried.

I tried other ways, and suddenly I hit it right. I had rolled my handkerchief into a ball and, licking it until it was moist, I pressed it against the image of the stamp I had made. When transferred to a piece of scratch paper, the result was encouraging. It seemed that I had hit on the right method, and yet I hesitated for a long time to transfer my artwork onto the pass. The deed was irreversible.

I smoked another cigarette and got up my courage. On the grayish paper of the pass the stamp looked real.

April 30, the day before my journey, was my twenty-third birthday, a day on which normally a young fellow looks forward to a good time. I spent the after-work hours of that birthday shopping for a few things in the canteen and packed clothing for the trip into my knapsack and the small carrier bag on a strap. I tried to do this inconspicuously, for the fewer people were aware of my intention the better. My immediate circle of friends knew of my plan, and so did that exceedingly reluctant lieutenant whom I had made a co-conspirator against his will.

I had known this officer for almost four years and long before he had received his military commission. He was from Germany, and our conversation was in German. We addressed each other by our first names, but this familiarity was not the reason for including him in my scheme. He was the officer in charge of the shop where I worked, and rather sooner than later would have known of my absence. Somebody else answering for me at morning roll call would have been the giveaway.

Poor guy. When I asked him not to report me absent until Ariye gave him the go-ahead, he tried to dissuade me from my resolution for my sake as much as for his. By that time, however, my mind was made up. I had decided to go ahead with the trip to Europe by boat, and nothing would deter me.

May 1, 1946, was a workday. When the fellows of my hut went to work that morning, I procrastinated and stayed behind. Nobody paid attention. Eventually I was by myself in the empty barracks, waiting for Ariye to show up with a truck borrowed from the workshop. I had to be careful not to be seen or recognized by anybody of rank in camp S. Wearing a clean battle dress instead of overalls would have been difficult to explain at this hour of the day. But no problem arose. When I heard the expected vehicle outside, I hurriedly left the hut and slid into the driver's cabin with my gear.

Ariye dropped me off near the base's main entrance and wished me good luck. I would need it. It was a long way from the center of Lower Egypt to Europe under those circumstances. If I were caught, the army would call it desertion, and though I did not think I'd be a candidate for the firing squad, the possibility of an extended stretch of field punishment in a British prison was an uncomfortable thought.

I shouldered my big pack like a Rucksack and slung the haversack over my right shoulder. The MP guard at the gate checked my five-day pass to Port Said, then waved me on. I had filled in the needed information on the pass and Bubi had forged an officer's signature to the document. The road from the base sloped down toward the main highway. A short distance down it a military truck stopped for me and gave me a ride. It dropped me off at the railroad station, well in time for the train to Port Said.

The Tel el Kebir railroad station was a small, open-air depot consisting of a platform and a few small huts that smarted under a merciless mid-morning sun. Since I had opened my eyes that morning I had felt high-spirited, and my senses seemed keener. Though I realized that I'd be a soldier on the run, a fugitive from the army, I was elated by the prospect of seeing my sister and thrilled by the cat-and-mouse game ahead of me.

The station was almost deserted. A group of Arabs in their tattered clothing were crowded into the narrow shade of one of the huts, and when I passed them on my way to the ticket window, they paid no attention to me. With the ticket in my pocket I too looked for shelter from the sun. I hoped to avoid being spotted by the army's R.T.O. (Railroad Transport Office) personnel whose job it was to assist soldiers in transit, but also to check their papers. I placed my big pack in the shade of a hut and settled on it as on a hassock. The next step was the inevitable cigarette. The first phase of my journey had passed smoothly, and I was almost ready for what was to follow. I say "almost" because an important provision for success was missing at the railroad station. The presence of soldiers, preferably those wearing the R.E.M.E. badge on their berets like me. This frustrated for now my hope not to attract attention.

In my mind I went over Bubi's directions. According to my friend, the station should have been teeming with soldiers and the train to Port Said packed with army personnel. After his first prediction had proven wrong, I hoped his second would be more accurate. He had further assured me that outside the railroad station in Port Said several large trucks would be waiting for soldiers to be taken to the transit camp. When they boarded the vehicles, I was to follow suit.

In the general confusion of our arrival at the transit camp I was to distance myself unobtrusively from the men. While they waited in a long line in front of an office to be processed and assigned accommodations, I was to walk down the main road toward camp C. And again according to my friend, camp C would be crowded with soldiers, making it easy for me to disappear among them. Settling on an empty bed in a tent I was to wait until a ship sailed for Europe. Should a soldier claim to have been assigned the spot I occupied, I was to say sorry, and move to another bed. Bubi had no specific instructions on how to get aboard the ship, how to behave once I had boarded her, or what to expect in Europe. He dismissed those so very important situations with: "You'll find a way."

Trying to think ahead and assuming that everything would go well with the voyage, I decided that once in Europe, I would look for an army chaplain, Jewish or any other faith. I would tell him my story, and I felt certain that with his influence, he could arrange for me to see my sister, since I had traveled so far.

At this point my thoughts were interrupted. A large contingent of soldiers appeared on the platform. Though they did not belong to my branch of the army, I got up and slowly approached them. British soldiers were often reserved with people they did not know, but here was a chance to be absorbed into a group, an opportunity I could not pass up. When I started a conversation with one of the soldiers I was disappointed to learn that they were going only as far as Ismailia. It was not to be the only disappointment on my journey. More situations were to confront me that had been missing from Bubi's coaching.

A freight train pulled in. German POWs crowded the open doors of the railroad cars, and out of nowhere ten or twenty Arab boys and men appeared and rushed along the stock cars trying to sell souvenirs to the prisoners. The train departed, and ours, long overdue, still had not arrived. My restlessness increased. While I silently cursed the unreliability of the Egyptian railroad system, the train arrived. Searching for a carriage with army personnel, I passed quickly along the cars and finally picked one with at least some soldiers. In Quassasin six more came aboard and, to my delight, they wore R.E.M.E. badges on their berets.

They took seats across the aisle from me, and one came over to my window to view the passing scenery outside. We steamed past fields of the rich Nile delta, but my interest lay in a conversation with the man. A little later the opportunity arose. We had stopped for a short time at a little station, and as always, Egyptians hurried along outside with souvenirs, peanuts, and dates for sale. Just before our train began to move I watched a group of boys getting ready to express their feelings for the British. The fellow next to me was unaware of the preparations in progress. The kids were picking up small rocks that would become projectiles once we were moving. The stones, not life-threatening, would be painful and could even lead to serious injury if they struck an eye. "Be careful," I warned my neighbor, and when I pushed him from the window, the first missiles hit the side of the moving railroad car.

Out of reach of the attackers, we stood together at the window and talked. I asked the question closest to my heart. Where are you headed? Hallelujah. The group was going home to England! When he asked my destination, I said: "156 Transit Camp, Port Said." The rest of the journey was uneventful.

At Port Said I happily observed that many more soldiers had been on the train than I had assumed. The mass of people leaving the carriages moved forward in a steady pace on the platform when suddenly a voice ahead of us called out: "Show your passes." A little further down four military policemen, standing across the platform, glanced at documents soldiers held out to them. No one was stopped. Apparently the MPs were only looking for soldiers who had no pass. I flashed mine and was safe.

By then my first attraction to the R.E.M.E. group had waned. The group was too small to disappear in, and if I stayed in their company, they would expect me to participate in functions I could not afford. Consequently, after leaving the station, I distanced myself from the six by feigning interest in stalls selling souvenirs. What I really was looking for were the "several trucks" that were to take the "many soldiers" to the transit camp. But of the mass of army personnel from the train only about 15 men remained near a lonely truck, and as that group included my sextet of R.E.M.E. men, I could safely assume it was destined for the transit camp. Confounded, I thought, that's it? Bubi, what kind of stories have you been telling me?

When nobody else joined the group, a staff sergeant ordered the men onto the vehicle with their equipment. At the last moment I rushed from the stalls to climb aboard. No benches were provided and I made my way forward to an opening in the front, partly because I wanted to see the city we'd be driving through and also to avoid having to talk to anybody.

It was a bad situation that could have been worse. Had the staff sergeant read names off a list for the men to board the truck, I would have had to abort my trip to the camp for the time being. And such delays always increased the danger of getting caught. To enter the camp on my own at a later time I would have to depend on a chit Bubi had handed me before I left Tel el Kebir. It was two inches square, dark green, and was hand-stamped: "156 Transit Camp, Camp C." It was the permit given to soldiers who wanted to visit the city. The paper had come with my friend's warning that it may have been replaced by a more substantial document since he had last used it.

As the truck rolled toward our goal, the man on my left offered me a cigarette. He was a young officer who was apparently happy to go home and was in a chummy mood. I thanked him but, though it may have seemed impolite, made no attempt to converse with him. His next question assuredly would have been about my destination.

We drove through Port Said, and a small boat ferried us across a stretch of water to another part of the city. After a while we entered the transit camp. The staff sergeant who had ordered the men aboard the truck told us to get off. When the vehicle pulled away and we stood on an open road in the bright sunshine, I felt extremely vulnerable. "Put your gear down and leave it there. Then go over to that office and queue up along the wall," the staff sergeant ordered. He pointed to a hut slightly ahead and about 50 feet to the left of the road. I hoped it was the road that led to camp C, and I intended to walk it when the opportunity arose. For now I put my gear on the ground and followed the others. Walking slowly, I was the last to make it to the line, which had been my objective all along. I had to get away from here. I could never enter the office without being found out. In the distance I saw tents with their walls rolled up, an indication that they were not inhabited.

The staff sergeant took the first man into the office and I checked my watch to see how long the processing lasted. A few minutes, long enough to get away from here. "Where is the latrine?" I asked a passing soldier. He pointed to a small building across the street.

I strolled to the other side. From the entrance I watched the people near the office. When the staff sergeant took the next man in, I decided:

"Now or never." I walked to my things on the road and picked them up. Shouldering my big pack, and slinging my small pack over my shoulder, I looked straight ahead, and started to walk. The soldiers already processed stood in small groups near the office. None had paid attention to my departure, and nobody missed me.

Camp C looked like camp A. With a few exceptions most tents had their sidewalls rolled up, providing an unobstructed view of the camp. Here I was to have disappeared among masses of soldiers who were being channeled to destinations in the Middle East, re-deployed to the continent or on their way home to England. But there were no masses. I entered a large double tent and found that most cots had equipment on them; some seemed unoccupied.

At the moment the tent was almost empty except for a group of men in shirts and undershirts playing cards on a bed across the aisle from me. On the bed next to where I stood a soldier was stretched out and he was reading a book. I pointed at an unoccupied place. "Anybody sleeping here?" I asked the man with the book. He shook his head. "I'll take it," I declared. "Sure," he said. I put my baggage on the bed and relieved sat down next to it. During the short exchange of words the card players had looked briefly in my direction, then resumed their game.

What now?

Suddenly I sat up straight. I could not believe my ears. I heard dear, familiar sounds. The card-players were speaking Hebrew. Had I hit the jackpot? If those were Jewish soldiers on their way to Europe I could go with them. Delighted by so much apparent luck I went over to them and said "Shalom." I continued in Hebrew: "Are you going to Europe?" They looked at me, and a few seconds passed before one answered "No. We are with the Jewish Brigade and are on our way home."

That was disappointing. Nonetheless, the surprise made me throw caution to the wind. They had been in Europe. If they told me of the situation there I might be able to use their knowledge to my advantage. Without holding back I told them my story and the reason for being here. When I finished, they sat without comment. Was something wrong? Then came their advice. "Don't try. You can't do it. Go back to your camp before you're in serious trouble."

I was deeply discouraged by their remarks. I never expected, nor had I wanted to hear, advice of that kind. Later I found out that they had distrusted me in the beginning. I had spoken English when I first came into the tent and then told them a crazy story. Trying to go to Europe on a troop ship without necessary papers? I just did not seem kosher to them. The Jewish right wing underground in Palestine gave the British trouble. The Haganah, of the center and left was attempting to smuggle Jews into the country. The British had their hands full trying to catch "terrorists" or people working for the illegal Aliya. Now I showed up. A fellow they did not know from Adam. And this someone, apparently with no fear of betrayal, told of an escapade so risky, one would not tell an acquaintance, much less a stranger. They suspected me of belonging with the British and of being an agent provocateur.

It had of course been naive and foolhardy to tell strangers my intentions, but since they were Jewish soldiers, I felt happy and had no doubt that I could trust them. I managed to convince them of my sincerity yet their original advice did not change: "Don't."

In the tent was also a young man who was on his way to visit his sister in England. He promised to tell me a day in advance of his ship's departure. He borrowed two Egyptian pounds from me that he promised to mail to Ramataim. He never did.

To eat in the dining hall one needed coupons supplied by the camp's office. I had none. Since there was no restaurant on the base, I ate mostly cold sandwiches in the canteen or, once in a while, when a fellow did not feel like eating, he gave me his coupon.

I had to go to Port Said.

Bubi had said to buy European currency before I left. Because he traveled to Belgium, he advised me to get French and Belgian francs. He also told me to get two or three English sovereigns. Gold coins were worth double or triple their face value in postwar Europe. I also needed a picture postcard which I intended to mail to Ariye on the day I attempted to board a ship. The previously agreed code: "I am visiting Aunt Rose," would confirm one of two things: either I had succeeded in boarding a ship, or had been arrested while trying. My friend would then inform the officer of the shop who, now released from his silence, would report my absence to the military police. The MPs actually came looking for me in Ramataim. Yakov, of course, knew nothing of my whereabouts and could not understand why the police were looking for me.

Now I had to try Bubi's little pass. I had shown it to the fellows in the tent and asked if it was still in use, but never having left the camp, they did not know. With little choice I would soon find out if the paper meant a trip to Port Said or one to a jail. It worked, and I hiked to Port Said. In the bazaar of the moneychangers I bought French francs and two sovereigns. The Belgian francs I found too expensive and did not think I would need them. The gold coins, tied into a corner of my handkerchief, I placed in my trouser pocket. In an Arab restaurant I made up for my diet and then returned to camp without being bothered by military police.

On the third day after my arrival the young man informed me that a ship would leave for Toulon, France, the next day. Because he was to go to England, and I knew of other soldiers with the same destination, I hoped the ship would continue to an English port after the stopover in France.

Camp C had not received new soldiers, but camp A was fully occupied. On the day of departure I mailed my postcard to Ariye, collected my belongings and bidding the fellows of the Jewish Brigade good-bye, I furtively made my way to the canteen in camp A.

The place was filled with noisy soldiers and their gear. I settled on an empty chair, waiting for things to develop. Time passed slowly. Then, without apparent instructions, the soldiers began leave the room. Joining the exodus that moved toward camp A's parade ground, I found the square covered with several hundred soldiers. I knew a roll call would follow, and because the officers and NCOs were keeping close to their units and individual groups, it was time for me to disappear. Again I chose a latrine as a lookout and from its relative safety observed the proceedings.

The day was another hot one and for now the soldiers just stood on the square exposed to the sun, waiting. After a long time the roll call started. It was noon before it was over, and the departure of single groups and military companies began. All moved in the same direction. But what had started out as an orderly procession turned into a disorganized mob a short while later. Nobody tried to control the march, and the greater the confusion, the safer I felt. Bolstering my confidence was the fact that none of the soldiers carried travel papers in their hands. It led me to assume that no inspection was forthcoming. Groups and units broke up when some of the men moved faster than others. Many of the soldiers, having spent years overseas, had collected personal things to which gifts had been added. Here and there a package was dropped, and the owner, his equipment hanging from his body and packages filling his hands, had a hard time picking it up.

I had looked for and recognized the band of R.E.M.E. soldiers from the train. I had a change of mind about them. I tried to convince myself that the one soldier of whom I had been wary could never guess that I did not belong with the travelers. It made sense to join them since we wore identical badges and insignias.

But again I change my mind about sticking with the group when the soldier in question, walking beside me, said: "You did not say you are going to Europe." "Certainly," I replied, feigning surprise at his misunderstanding. He seemed to have a problem with my answer but did not pursue the matter. That little intermezzo finally made me decide to avoid the group if I made it safely onto the ship.

We reached water and a ferry. Others from the parade ground assembly had been shuttled to their destination before we arrived, and now we had to get aboard a little watercraft to the last man. We stood as close to each other as sardines in an upright can. While we moved toward the ferry a man with a movie camera stood off to the side and filmed the boarding soldiers. Apparently some newsreel company was photographing soldiers on their way home, and it was ironic that I, who had meticulously shunned attention, was forced to march past that lens. Eventually, I assumed, my image would be projected onto some movie screen in a theater, where I would be thought of as one of the homecoming British heroes.

The ferry brought us to a long, wooden float and towering over it was a large, sleek vessel. The Devonshire. Crammed together on that platform, we advanced slowly toward a distant gangway that soldiers climbed in single file. At the top a uniformed man of rank, leaning against the ship's rail, watched the men come aboard. This was, as I later found out, the ship's regimental sergeant major. As we progressed, I became painfully aware of my inadequate travel equipment. All the men around me were overloaded with baggage while the knapsack on my back and the small side-pack hanging from my shoulder were hardly the amount of gear a soldier carried with him on an extended move. The officer at the top could hardly fail to recognize the anomaly.

Heaven sent me a Scotsman. This soldier next to me was literally dragging himself along. He was perspiring profusely, for he carried so much baggage it was surprising he did not go down on his knees. It included a huge suitcase. For a moment I remembered the lady with the suitcase at the railroad station in Jena. "Let me help you," I suggested here too, and took the suitcase from him. The appreciative "thank you" came from his heart and now both of us felt better. I carried a suitcase that was as heavy as if it was filled with rocks, but I had no complaints.

Just a few men away from the gangplank I caught sight of an officer standing next to it. He handed something to every soldier who passed him. Whatever it is, you can't take it, I decided. For all I knew it might have been to check the number of soldiers boarding the ship. Any discrepancy would lead to a security check, I thought. I reached the gangplank and, acting as if I was unaware of the officer's function, moved speedily past him. I had barely taken two steps when I was pulled back by the officer. A little card was pressed into my hand. I dared not look at it, but continued my climb to the ship's deck. My head bent low as if pulled down by the weight I carried, I avoided the glance of the uniformed man at the rail and followed the stream of soldiers before me. The grateful Scotsman relieved me of the suitcase as we descended into the vessel's interior.

We arrived in a huge, brightly lit room filled with long wooden tables and benches. Everybody was by then checking the chit received, which turned out to be a table assignment. Steered in the right direction by a corporal, I reached the assigned spot and sat down.

So far so good. Now if the number of soldiers aboard the ship was not questioned, then the card received from the officer benefited me. It relieved me of my worry about where to sleep, and how to feed myself.

It was past noon when I had boarded the Devonshire, and during the first few hours I had mixed feelings, the least strange of which was insecurity. No one was permitted to leave the hall, and speeches and instructions came in quick succession over a loudspeaker system. As time dragged on, my restlessness grew. Yet mine was not more noticeable than that of the others who, though for different reasons, were as jumpy and impatient as I. An inconspicuous inquiry as to the time of departure brought no answer. We were to have left at one o'clock, two o'clock, three o'clock, and as the hours passed, my suspicions about the reason for our delay grew. Was it I? After all, if the count of passengers did not square with the one in the office, an unknown person had to be aboard. The safety of the ship depended on its security and, with unrest in the Middle East, it was very important to investigate such a discrepancy.

At four o'clock an officer passed from table to table and ordered the ranking NCO to make a list of the men present. I had almost expected that, though not for the reason it was being done. I debated with myself whether to give my real name and serial number or a phony one. I thought it would make no difference, and I supplied the correct identification. Nothing disagreeable happened. Half an hour later we were permitted to leave the hall. Everyone went up on deck.

At 5 PM the Devonshire moved away from its mooring and turned toward the open sea. I stood among hundreds of soldiers along the ship's rail, gazing first at retreating Port Said, then at the disappearing Egyptian coastline. When land was out of sight, most men left the deck. I stuck it out, fascinated by the water around me and my success up to then.

At dinner, two men from each table were chosen to bring food in containers from the galley to the table. In the days that followed, the service rotated. I had my first meal with my unsuspecting table partners. We also had kitchen duty, and I was called up. I could not believe it. I did duty by name and military number.

My first night in a hammock turned out to be unpleasant. The sea was choppy, and the vessel moved not only forward, but up and down. My hammock swayed and banged against neighboring hammocks. The next night I spread blankets on a table and slept on it.

In the afternoon of the second day we arrived in Valetta, Malta's main harbor and capital. Only 58 miles south of Sicily, the island of Malta, and particularly Valetta, had been attacked almost daily by German and Italian bombers during the war. The people of the island had suffered cruel hardships but had survived the bombings. Also the expected invasion by Axis forces never took place. The attacks stopped when the Allies invaded Sicily in the summer of 1943.

At 9 A.M. the next morning, a beautiful, sunny day, we steamed out of Valetta. The morning after that it became cold and the sea got rougher. We were nervous about anti-ship mines that might still float in the Mediterranean.

On the evening before we reached Toulon orders were posted on bulletin boards. After docking, officers or NCOs were to accompany their groups of men off the ship. I could not attach myself to any group because the man in charge would recognize me as not belonging. Compounding the problem were the different insignias soldiers wore on the sleeve of their battle-dress jackets. The sleeve of my jacket had only a narrow bar that showed the three colors of my army group. But even as an R.E.M.E. man I failed to show a square blue patch of material into which the yellow letters "R.E.M.E." were embroidered. I had not known that R.E.M.E. soldiers wore those insignia in Europe. It was an unexpected situation, but it did not particularly bother me. I was going to proceed with an alternate plan to get off the ship, and onto European soil.

For some reason I believed that the Devonshire, after leaving Toulon, would sail for the British Isles, a place I did not want to go. My alternate plan was to give myself up before that happened, for I did not believe that I would be held prisoner aboard ship and taken to England. I hoped to be put ashore and imprisoned in a military jail. Once there I planned to ask for the help of an army chaplain to see my sister. Next morning, while soldiers disembarked, I went to the ship's office. A lonely staff sergeant sat behind a desk. I went up to him, and said: "I'm aboard without permission."

It took the man a while to comprehend my statement. Once it sank in he asked for my name, rank and serial number. He then picked up the phone and talked excitedly into it. The only word he said that registered with me was "stowaway." A short time later the sergeant major stormed into the office. With a glance he took in the room, and when he saw me standing beside the staff sergeant's desk, he shot over to me. He looked as if he was going to attack me or have a fit of apoplexy.

"What's that?" he shouted angrily at me. "You are a stowaway?"

"Not really," I said.

I had never seen anybody in the army lose his temper like that, and least of all a feared regimental sergeant major. He knew I was Palestinian, the PAL in front of my army number disclosed that, but he did not know the why of my action. For all he knew I could have been a Jewish saboteur, who had brought explosives aboard to blow up the ship with a

300

time device after I had disembarked. The British were having enough trouble with Jewish "terrorists" in Palestine at the time. Several months after my escapade on the Devonshire I read in the paper that the ship had been warned about bombs aboard. The vessel was searched, but no explosives were found.

"What do you mean, 'not really'?" he fumed.

"I had a place at table...," and I gave him the table number. "I also did kitchen duty."

That seemed to make his situation worse. Had I been a stowaway and hiding during the trip, it would have reflected badly on him. But that a soldier, who did not belong aboard, was assigned duties, was more than he could bear. His only hope was that I was a Palestinian who was being sent overseas but did not want to go, a soldier who, by telling a weird story like mine, hoped to be sent back home. Soon enough he was confronted by the truth. Except for the table roster, my name did not appear on any official list of transferees.

I was taken below to the ship's brig, which consisted of a small guardroom and a few cells. I was placed in one of the cells, and the door, with one small window at face level, was locked behind me. The room had little light, and I sat down on the lower of the two bunk beds in the semi darkness. Now I had to wait. I hoped it would not be for long. Having been relieved of my baggage I had nothing to read, no paper to write on. The military policeman that guarded me was unfriendly. I apparently had delayed his disembarkation.

Fresh troops came aboard in the afternoon, and with them new military police that took over the jail. Except for their corporal, all these men were very young. As I found out later, it was the first time in their lives that they had left the British Isles. They wanted to know the reason for my being in jail, and when I told them, they did not seem to condemn my escapade or think I had acted like a criminal. They became friends of mine right from the beginning.

On that afternoon one of them took me on deck for one hour. We walked and talked, and I caught a glimpse of Toulon, if only from the Devonshire. I also saw the scuttled and capsized French warships the French had sabotaged so they would not fall into German hands.

Next morning I was returned to the office. I was marched into an adjacent room where, behind a desk, the ship's military commander, a colonel, was sitting. To his left stood the sergeant major, and to his right a staff sergeant who started to read from some papers. It was obvious he had a problem pronouncing my name.

"PAL 6585, Craftsman Gostav Pim... Pims...

"Gustav Pimselstein," I volunteered, and the sergeant major barked: "Shut up. You only speak when spoken to!"

After the charges had been stated, the colonel spoke. He too was very angry with me for the situation I had created. "You are a deserter," he hissed at me.

He was wrong, and I dared to contradict him. "I am not a deserter. I have voluntarily given myself up, and I had a reason for doing what I did."

Surprisingly, nobody interrupted me. Then the colonel said: "What have you got to say for yourself?"

I told my story from the very beginning.

I must have impressed that officer, for when I finished, he thought for a while and then said: "The Devonshire returns tomorrow to Alexandria. You will be returned to confinement for now. If you will give your word of honor not to attempt escape while we are underway, you'll be released from prison 24 hours after we leave Toulon. You will be free aboard the ship and will stay with the other soldiers. 24 hours before we reach Alexandria you will report back to the guard room where you will wait for further orders."

I felt devastated. Not because of the prison, but because of the ignominious end to my undertaking. The Devonshire was returning to Egypt, and I had failed miserably in my mission. The thought that it had not been for lack of trying failed to comfort me. I asked to see a chaplain. None was provided. Our stay in Toulon was too short.

Not 24 hours after leaving Toulon, but immediately after departure, was I told to leave the brig. I was assigned to the same hall in which I had been before. Again it was filled with soldiers and in one part of the room a large contingent of returning Jewish Brigade soldiers had settled.

I was placed at a table of British soldiers who had no idea that I was a prisoner and a Jew to boot. They talked freely, and I found it interesting to listen to them. Their main concern was Palestine and the deeds of the "terrorists" there. They considered every Jew a terrorist, out to kill British soldiers. Not surprisingly, they were afraid to be sent to Palestine. The topics of their conversations changed, however, when I tried to explain the situation of the Jews in that country and they found out that I was a Palestinian, a Jew.

Three times a day I had to report to the military policemen in the guardroom. In fact, I spent more time with them than with the fellows at my table. Most of the MPs got seasick and quit eating. As their food was delivered to the guardroom I took my meals at their table. I picked what I liked and ate more of the things that were to my taste. The sick military policemen lay in the cell bunks, and those who felt reasonably well told me jokingly that I would have to take over their guard duties; they were too sick to handle them. The new found friends in the guardroom were curious about life in Egypt and Palestine. I told them much about both countries. I especially described the number and variety of the Jews in Palestine and their goals. They were much more receptive and understanding than the British at the table upstairs.

The ship's sergeant major, whom I had pegged a brute in the beginning, became friendly after a day at sea. When we met on my strolls through the ship he'd always asked me: "How are you?" which was less of a question than a greeting.

Every afternoon the soldiers played tombola (Bingo). British soldiers were crazy about the game, and I occasionally liked to play it too. The money used aboard the ship was French francs. I did not have too many francs to begin with, and having spent some of them in the ship's canteen, I had not many left when I started playing. After a short while I ran out of francs. Being aware that sooner or later I would be using Palestinian and Egyptian pounds again, I wanted to exchange the few American dollars in my possession. As there was no moneychanger aboard, I had the chutzpah to ask the sergeant major where I could change my dollars into French francs. He looked at me surprised and then said in a stage whisper: "Go away. You're not supposed to have dollars."

We steamed between the islands of Sardinia and Corsica, and eventually past Stromboli, a live vulcano of the Lipari Islands. Thick white steam escaped its crater, rolled down the mountainside and into the sea. We passed the Straits of Messina between the end of the Italian boot and the island of Sicily and, as ordered, I reported to the guardroom 24 hours before we were to arrive in Egypt. "Come back before we land," I was told.

Alexandria. What a different arrival from the last time I was stationed here almost four years ago. I bade my friends, the policemen, farewell before my gear and I were picked up by two different military policemen. A jeep took us to the military jail in the city, the Mustapha barracks. The prison was a square, two-storied building with a yard in its center that had the open sky for a roof. In the office my particulars were taken down once more and before I was taken to my cell I was relieved of my big and small packs. I kept my wallet and money and the two hidden gold sovereigns in the knot of my handkerchief.

I was led to the second story where a railed walk surrounded the yard below. Off this walk, and for the whole length around it, a large number of doors, made of crossed bars, separated the small cells from the relative freedom of the outside. Once a day the prisoners had to walk for an hour in a circle around the yard. During the days I spent here I became acquainted with the unbelievable assembly of my fellow prisoners. There were Englishmen, two blacks from East Africa, an apparently crazy soldier from India who had killed another soldier, two

German POWs who had committed a crime, and myself. Being from Vienna — it is a mystery how they found out — I was labeled "the Austrian-Palestinian." The cooks of the prison were two disgustingly dirty Arabs, and the guards were Scottish soldiers.

The days were hot and boring and the feeling of uncertainty about the length of my stay here was disturbing. On the second day I felt already as if nobody outside the prison had been informed of my presence here. To overcome that disagreeable sentiment I requested, and was granted some blank papers and a pencil by the NCO in charge of the guards. I spent most of my time writing about my latest (mis)adventure from then on.

On the fourth day a British corporal and a soldier arrived from Tel el Kebir with the order to pick me up. Both carried rifles, which seemed ridiculous. At the railroad station in Alexandria my two chaperons wanted to buy something in a shop and, apparently uncomfortable entering the store carrying rifles, handed me the weapons with the request to keep an eye on them. It seemed like a farce on a stage.

Late at night we reached Tel el Kebir. The HQ building to which we were supposed to report was deserted but not unguarded. Two German POWs, carrying long sticks for weapons, were ready to defend the British HQ building of Tel el Kebir, which seemed another scene out of a comedy with an improbable plot.

I suggested to my escort that, to get rid of me, they should take me to the guardhouse in camp S where the NCO in charge certainly would sign for me. They agreed, and I spent my first night back in freedom on my own bed. I knew our men would not imprison me. The next day I went to our office, and told them I would report to HQ Tel el Kebir on my own. That, however, would have been too much freedom. To give it the right appearance, I was taken to Headquarters by one of our soldiers in a jeep and from there to the main jail of the camp.

The jail was a small one-story building surrounded by a barbed wire fence. From the guardroom led a door to a short corridor and four small cells secured by heavy doors with little windows. A cot and some blankets were the rooms' inventory. The jailers were a British corporal and a few Egyptians in British uniforms. Not that it mattered, but I was surprised to learn that the Egyptians were Jewish. To the corporal's regret, they spoke fluently Arabic and French, but only minimal English.

I was the only prisoner and apparently not considered dangerous, so the doors to the empty cells, including mine, and the door leading to the guardroom were always open during the day. Bubi, Moshe, and other friends came to visit and the corporal in charge of the guardhouse permitted me to smoke though the standing order was no smoking inside the cell.

Several days passed before I was taken before the commanding officer of Tel el Kebir. He was an older man, also a colonel, but not the nasty officer I had encountered on my previous escapade a few months earlier. Beside the colonel's desk stood the commanding officer of my unit, Major Creuden who, though in the British army, was American by birth. The colonel studied some papers on his desk and then said to me: "Do you understand English or do you want the major to translate?" I said I spoke English.

The colonel continued. "I cannot judge you. I shall have to leave the judgment up to a higher council." I was disappointed. I had hoped to know where I stood, but on the other hand, his indecision came also as a relief. Had he convicted me, who knows where I would have spent the next night, the days after, and the weeks or months following. I was returned to jail.

Being the only one who spoke English, the guard corporal often sat with me on my cot and our talk touched on a variety of subjects. He knew why I was in jail, and eventually and unavoidably our conversation turned to politics. We had some heated discussions about the Jews' goals and the British policies in Palestine. When he was losing an argument, he would shout: "Oh, shut up!" and run out of my cell. After he had thus expressed himself several times, I warned him: "If you say once more 'shut up' to me I won't talk to you anymore." But he laughed. "If you won't talk to me, you won't take a shower every day either." — I had insisted on showering daily, for which the corporal had to take me to the nearest camp. I was well aware that by army regulations he had to take me to the showers only once a week.

I seemed to have become a celebrity in Tel el Kebir. A journey, without permission, from Tel el Kebir to France seemed an impressive accomplishment. Soldiers not of my company came to look at me when I walked behind the barbed wire fence of the jail's compound.

I awaited the decision of the higher court with mixed emotions, wondering how a military judge in Cairo would pass sentence in an unusual case like mine. To my surprise I was brought back before the same CO of Tel el Kebir, the colonel who had refused to try me earlier.

My commanding officer, Major Creuden, was present, but again strictly as a spectator. This time, in my defense, the colonel wanted me to tell the reasons behind my actions. Once more I related how, after so many years, I had received the first sign of life from my sister, but still nothing from my parents. I told of my unsuccessful legal and finally illegal attempts to see her. I wanted to get everything off my chest and did not care anymore what the man thought of my "crime" and me. I told about the letters to GHQ Cairo, the encounter with the American Air Force officer at John Payne Airfield in Heliopolis, and finally my miscalculated trip to Europe. I narrated my story standing at attention, and when I finished, I fell silent.

The colonel sat motionless behind his desk, and an eternity seemed to pass before he moved. Perhaps he was thinking about the terrible things that had happened to the Jews in Europe, or maybe he was impressed by my unusual and desperate attempts to see my sister. Perhaps both considerations influenced his decision.

He then read the charges:

1) Leaving a military compound without permission.

2) Absent without leave.

3) Unlawfully boarding and staying aboard the H.M.S. Devonshire.

He did not mentioned desertion. It felt like a movie script when he cleared his throat and announced the sentence: "Nine days pay stop. Eight days royal warrant." The pay stop was for my days AWOL, but, of course, the judge knew only of the official time I was reported absent. The royal warrant was the penalty: No service pay for eight days. When the sergeant major marched me out of the office he whispered fiercely at me: "You lucky fellow." It sounded more like a compliment. It was my first and last punishment in the British Army, and some weeks later I was honorably discharged from the service.

Before my discharge, however, a fellow soldier in my unit by the name of Manuel Wiznitzer approached me. "Tell me," he begged, "tell me how you did it. My mother is alive in Rumania, but I can't get leave. I want to try your way." I sat with Wiznitzer for a long time and told him all I knew. I warned him of places that could mean trouble, and what to expect, and how to behave in certain situations. I painstakingly went over every detail that I remembered. I put my whole being, my soul into what I told him, and when I finally believed I had explained it all, I wished him luck with all my heart.

Almost a year later, in early June 1947 I received a letter from Wiznitzer. It was mailed from No. 1 Camp, Holding and Mob. Center R.E.M.E., Farnley Park, Otley (Yorkshire) Great Britain. In it he wrote that thanks to my instructions he had succeeded in reaching Rumania. He said he was surprised about my achievement, considering my lack of experience and lack of knowledge about many things. He wrote, "Bravo, Pimselstein," and, to be honest, I am so very proud of this fellow's compliment that I still have and treasure his letter. It somehow made me feel that my effort had not been entirely in vain.

Unrest in Palestine or Between Two Wars

At the beginning of 1946, several months before my discharge from the army, I joined a cooperative made up of fellows and girls, all more or less my age, and all from the British army. In time I had convinced my friend Erich to join us. We wanted to establish a new settlement, and were provided by the Jewish Agency with a loan for the land on which to settle and agricultural equipment needed. It contained a condition our benefactors insisted on. Our main activity had to be agriculture. The trades we were familiar with were to be only a sideline. We needed the loan. So that left us no choice but to accept their demands.

I still wanted to bring my sister to Palestine, though my chances were slim by then. For several months now she had been engaged to a Holocaust survivor from Poland who wanted to go to the United States, not Palestine. I did not blame him. Life in the Middle East was tough.

Troublesome incidents between the British civil authorities, Palestine police and British army on the one hand, and the *IZL*[26], the *Hagana*[27], *Palmach*[28], *Stern Gang*[29] and the general Jewish population on the other were almost daily occurrences in Palestine. Newspapers reported the activities of the political "gangs" and the daily searches and counteractions by the British. The back and forth went on as steadily as the ebb and flood of the Mediterranean.

Headlines in June 1946:

"Stern Gang youths arrested. One aged 22, two others aged 18 admit in court membership in illegal organization." -- "Girl caught broadcasting over clandestine radio station for the Stern Gang is sentenced to seven years prison." -- "Gang members receive instructions at a kiosk on Allenby Road" (Tel Aviv). *-- "At a Paris conference the British vow never to leave Palestine." -- "Five British officers kidnapped. Curfew imposed on Tel Aviv. Just before the actual curfew, long queues form outside shops. People try to stock up on food." -- "All Jewish premises, restaurants, bars, cinemas, hotels 'Out of Bounds' to British forces until British officers are released."*

Those restrictions were to put pressure on the Jewish population and their economy. The British hoped it would force the underground to relinquish their prisoners. There was little that could be done, how-

---

[26] Irgun Zvai Leumi, National Military Organization. The major right-wing Jewish underground.

[27] Hagana, means Defense. The largest of the underground organizations of the Labor party and the left-wing Hashomer Hazair party.

[28] Palmach or Striking Unit. An elite group of the Hagana.

[29] Stern Gang," so dubbed by the British. For Jews of the political right, they were the Stern Group. A small, right-wing faction whose actions were as potent as the sting of a scorpion.

ever. The right-wing underground never let its actions be influenced by outsiders – not even by fellow-Jews.

Newspaper excerpts:
June 20, 1946. *"Haj Amin el Hussein, the ex-Mufti of Jerusalem, who was Hitler's guest in Berlin during the war and the organizer of Moslems to fight on the German side, is now a guest of King Faruk of Egypt."*
In Egypt too, there was no peace between the British and the Egyptians. A newspaper noted: *"British soldiers attacked on their way back to their base in Sidi Bishr. One soldier wounded. Three hand-grenades thrown from a passing car miss their target."*

The British focused their attention on settlements and kibbutzim of the Labor party, and Shomer Hazair. -- *"Kfar Giladi surrounded and searched for eleven hours. Farmers from Hulata and Ayeleth Hashachar waving white handkerchiefs are challenged by British soldiers. Two farmers are killed, six wounded."*
More searches in Tel Aviv, Ramat Gan and Kiryat Meir. Nothing found.
June 29, 1946. *"The British occupy the building of the Jewish Agency and confiscate secret files."* -- July 2, 1946. *"British arrest Jewish leaders. Close to 3,000 Jews detained. Search 25 settlements, with the result that 4 Jews killed and 80 more injured. In kibbutz Yagur the British find and confiscate large quantities of ammunition and explosives."* (A bad blow for the Hagana and the Yishuv at large.)

Events of this kind were happening when we finally returned to Palestine to be discharged from the British army. To celebrate the occasion, all Egyptian employees who had worked with the men of our two companies were invited to a luncheon in the now empty building of workshop number 122. The office personnel wore suits; the unskilled laborers, like the little fellow who had helped me when I ran the store room of our workshop, came in *galabies*, robes. I felt sorry for my assistant who now had nobody to bring him a little extra food as I had done. It was inevitable that because of the reduced number of active workshops in Tel el Kebir, he and many others would be laid off. The atmosphere was amiable; our Egyptian co-workers· enjoyed the attention and the food on the tables, and finally speeches were made.
Major Creuden thanked the Egyptians for their help, and stressed how well we had gotten along with each other. He wished them the best for the future, and hoped they would always remember the good spirit that had prevailed between us. An Egyptian office worker replied in a similar vein. He added: "We wish you a happy life in your homeland, and

we know that our people and your people will always remain friends." About two years later, when Egyptian forces invaded and Egyptian planes bombed the newly founded State of Israel, I was thinking of that speech.

On the day before our discharge, July 4, 1946, a truck convoy took us to Quassasin, a huge British military base north of Tel el Kebir. Here we returned part of our equipment and then boarded a train for Palestine. It should have been an uneventful ride, but it wasn't. I had made myself as comfortable as possible – the train again being over-loaded with soldiers – and had slept well, when I was awakened by the rippling effect of the carriages as we slowed down. The dimmed lights inside the car were fully lit by then and drowsy-eyed fellows asked what was going on. Outside it was dark. When the train came to a full stop, the outside was suddenly bathed in the glaring light of strong lamps.

Red-capped military police surrounded the train. Over a loudspeaker we were ordered to leave the cars with our equipment. Outside we had to form a row along the carriages, our gear in front of us. I saw military policemen go through the carriages while others on the outside, in groups of two, went from soldier to soldier to check the baggage. They searched for contraband weapons and ammunition which, the British feared, might end up with the Jewish underground in Palestine.

Nothing of consequence was found, except that one foolish fellow had in his pack three rounds of 303 ammunition; bullets used in British and Canadian rifles. He insisted that he had forgotten about them, and even the British did not believe that he had wanted to smuggle them into Palestine for a sinister purpose. We were dismissed and continued our journey. In trucks we transferred from the Rehovot railroad station to Sarafand. The last of our military equipment was taken. We received a set of civilian clothing and ten Palestinian pounds. Seventy pounds, still due, were mailed to my new address a few weeks later. After four years as a British soldier I was discharged from the army July 5, 1946. So much had happened to me in those years and yet, it seemed only recently that I had volunteered my services to King George VI.

Our settlement in *Gush Tel Mond*, Tel Mond, was named *Dror*, Freedom – and later, *Bnei Dror*, Sons of Freedom. When I arrived, two large and one small wooden barracks and two short rows of two-man tents had been erected. Within a short time two more huts went up. The main structures contained the kitchen, the dining area, small rooms for married couples, and a storage facility. The tents were for single people who had to double up, and couples who had found no accommodations in the huts.

The district, a cluster of villages 22 road miles north of Tel Aviv, consisted of the villages Tel Mond, Kfar Hess, Herut, Ain Vered, and a small Yemenite settlement. The communities, about one or two miles apart, formed a loosely oblong ring that, in case of attack on one, made quick help by the others possible. An exception was the newly founded Dror. It was just a stone's throw away from the last house of Tel Mond, the village.

That group of Jewish localities was close to one side of the "Arab triangle" which consisted of the cities of Jenin, Tulkarem, and Nablus (Shchem). Our district's closest Arab neighbor was Tira, a large village. Since Arabs and Jews lived in peace with one another, the nearness of Arab areas created no uneasiness. In many places a business relationship existed between the two communities.

When it had become clear that agriculture was to be our main occupation, I first toyed with the idea of leaving the group and moving to the city. I had no taste for farming and had hoped to work in a shop in our settlement after my arrival there. But too many of us had the same wish. Since I had never farmed, I decided to give it a try. Although a great many of the returning Jewish soldiers had gone back to their villages and occupations, thousands of others had exhausted the labor market. The Jewish Agency's warning about the many unemployed in the country had merit. Being in Dror we had at least the safety of a secure economic existence. Still, disappointed at the kind of work awaiting me, I decided to postpone the inevitable by a week's stay at the Margels' in Ramataim.

As on so many occasions before, it was a pleasant experience. The weather was warm, the café's business brisk - British soldiers were again permitted to frequent Jewish establishments - and the phonograph played the music I loved.

Though the usual customers, British soldiers, took up some tables in the hedged-in square in front of the café, I always found a seat in this area. I read, wrote and daydreamed, not bothered by the immediate future. The trouble with the British continued, but at least the war was over. No more worries about an advancing enemy or bombs being dropped in one's vicinity. It was time to relax. Life at Dror promised to be removed from all hassles. It meant a six-day workweek, Saturdays off, an occasional movie, or maybe a short trip to the outside world, called Palestine.

The waitress interrupted my writing. Somebody wanted to talk to me. She pointed to a large group of soldiers and military police sitting around two tables placed next to each other. One of the military policemen beckoned to me with his hand and I went over to him. The soldiers around the tables looked at me curiously. The policeman was a corporal and I starred at him blankly. "Yes?"

"Don't you remember me?" he asked. Then I recognized him. He was the NCO in charge of my friends, the military police, aboard the

Devonshire. I felt slightly embarrassed. He had recognized me as a civilian, while I had failed to do so, even though he was in uniform. But I was really happy to see him and greeted him warmly. Now I understood the other soldiers' stare. He probably had told them about my unconventional trip to Toulon. "What happened to you after you got back to your unit?" he wanted to know. When I told him the verdict, he too exclaimed: "You lucky fellow."

Two days after my return from Ramataim to Dror something came up. A group of ten fellows, including me, were called to one of our little tents. Inside we were introduced to a man of about 50, easily recognizable as a veteran *Sochnutnik*, an old hand of the Jewish Agency. He came straight to the point. Some Jewish soldiers stationed in Europe with the British army worked for the *Bricha*[30], Escape. The men of their company, eligible for discharge from the service, had returned to Palestine. 10 men of that outfit, engaged in covert activities for the *Bricha*, had become "civilians" and remained in Europe. To equalize the needed number of returnees, 10 holocaust survivors were substituted for the missing men and had arrived "legally" in Palestine. But that was as far as the newcomers could be trusted to play their role. To go through the actual discharge procedure, soldiers or ex-soldiers would have to be used to avoid arousing suspicion of the British at the demobilization camp. That's where we came in.

"I admit," this visitor granted us, "it may mean prison if any of you were to be recognized by a British soldier who knew you before under a different name or was aware of your previous discharge from the army. But the chance that this will happen is almost nil." Considering my recent meeting with the military police corporal at Margels' café in Ramataim I could have contradicted the man. The world seemed such a small place after that incident. I said nothing and, in spite of the chance we were taking, I was among the 10 who volunteered.

The next day a pick-up truck drove us to a Drom Yehuda bus company office in Rehovot, a city about 40 road miles to the south. Soldier and pay books of the men we were to replace were matched as well as possible with our appearance. I became a corporal with a Polish name, which I tried to memorize, and spell. To be on the safe side, I also studied a few details marked in his soldier book. After that we were taken to a small storage room to receive the military equipment to be

---

[30] Bricha, a clandestine organization that smuggled Jewish survivors of Nazi concentration camps over the border from Austria to Italy, with their final destination Palestine. Those refugees, too, would try to run the British blockade of Palestine aboard little ships; a situation quite familiar to me.

returned. From a cardboard box filled with an array of British khaki uniforms and berets we picked the appropriate attire. It felt funny to be in uniform again.

With counterfeit passes we entered familiar Sarafand, the place of my discharge only two weeks earlier, and somehow I felt at home. Before returning our uniform and equipment I bought cigarettes at the canteen. As during my real discharge we received a civilian outfit and money, and returning to the pickup outside the camp, we were driven to Rehovot.

At the Drom Yehuda office we left the things received. After changing back into our own clothes and being thanked by the men in the office, we boarded a bus to Tel Aviv and then Dror - civilians again. This was the only time I aided the intricate mechanism of illegal immigration of other people to Palestine. Our participation in that important undertaking was only one thread in the fabric that eventually became the State of Israel, but every thread counted.

The situation in the country continued to be critical. On July 17, 1946, the entire Jewish community in Palestine ceased work for a day to protest the continued incarceration of 1,650 Jewish men at Rafa detention camp.

One wing of the King David Hotel in Jerusalem had been taken over by the British army. It became the General Headquarters of the military, as well as the seat of government institutions. On July 22, 1946, the IZL cautioned the government by phone of an impending explosion at the King David Hotel, giving them ample time to evacuate. The British chose to ignore the warning. The destruction of one wing of the hotel took the lives of 91 persons. 13 were missing and presumed dead, 45 more were injured.

The British imposed an indefinite curfew on Tel Aviv, suspecting the brains of the IZL to be in that city. Tel Aviv was cut off from the rest of the country. Telephone connections were disconnected, and two divisions of soldiers checked 200,000 inhabitants. The extended curfew was temporarily interrupted for two hours each day to enable citizens to buy food. Curfew breakers were bullied and beaten and in some cases arrested.

The British had to contend with another headache. A continuous flow of immigrant ships appeared along the coast of Palestine. The refugees who got caught were sent to newly erected detention camps on Cyprus. Newspaper headline: *"Haifa under curfew, and curfew breakers protesting the deportation of immigrants clash with troops. Three civilians are killed, and seven wounded."*

My friend Erich had been discharged from the army at an earlier date and had settled in Dror before I arrived. True to his style, he already had an eye on a girl. As boys and girls then rarely moved in with each other before marriage, Erich and I shared one of the small tents. It was Bat Galim all over, only smaller.

As expected, life at Dror was placid. Owning no fields or orange groves that produced yet, the men and women of our settlement were hired out to farmers of neighboring villages on a daily basis. Money had to be earned from the start. The kibbutz-like life of the beginning was to change when Dror became self-supporting. Fields and properties were then to be evenly divided among its members, and after each had built a house on the allotted land, we were to become individual farmers. It was agreed, however, that this arrangement lay in the far future. For now, members had handed to the *Wa'ad* (committee of the settlement) the 80 pounds received from the army. The money was needed to run the community because the income from outside sources was as yet inadequate to cover expenses.

Under the work arrangements, only five or six men work steadily in a little workshop. They built, among other things, two wheeled platforms to be pulled by donkeys or horses, transport vehicles farmers in the neighboring villages needed and bought. The rest of us worked at all kind of jobs. We trimmed citrus trees, including lemon trees whose branches were thorny, fertilized and irrigated citrus groves and picked fruits when they were ripe. Occasionally, when needed, we helped at the workshop. Besides that we did plumbing and paint jobs, dug ditches for large water pipes and assembled them in the trenches. We even worked sometimes in our community kitchen and laundry. Women cooked and also worked at outside jobs, though never at physically strenuous ones.

As our money was in the community treasury, we received articles of toiletry and one Palestinian pound per month for personal expenses. Later, when the allowance was raised to one and a half pounds, we had to cover the expenses for toiletries, the repair of work boots, as well as the purchase of clothing.

At one of our periodic membership meetings it was proposed that a young woman and I should run the small canteen in our settlement. It was the place where members purchased items of personal hygiene, writing paper, envelopes, stamps, and so forth. We were also asked to handle the monthly payments to the individuals in the group. It meant responsibility, extra work in the evening, and work for two hours on days off. But since there was little else to do in our free time, we accepted.

The tent that Erich and I shared had just enough space for two beds, a short, narrow table that fitted snugly between them, a small wooden locker on each side and a single light bulb hanging on a short cable inside the tent. There was no feeling of insecurity, and safety measures seemed unnecessary. No fence surrounded the settlement, and no special lighting illuminated the area at night, for we were almost an extension of the village of Tel Mond.

One night an event changed our perspective about our security. I awoke to the cry of a female voice. "Arabs," she screamed, "Arabs." The woman who had sounded the alarm lived with her husband in a tent separated from ours by a narrow path. Her cry gave me a creepy feeling. I had not thought of trouble with Arabs, and for now did not know what had happened. It took me a moment to turn on the light, jump into my overalls and shoes and, grabbing my flashlight off the table, I shot through the tent flaps. Others were just as fast and then we listened to the woman telling in haste of the Arab in their tent. He had robbed them of their suitcase, and a few other things. We later learned that three Arabs had been in our encampment.

Uncertain of the direction the robbers had taken, a group of about 15, we spread out and ran toward the west where, about a mile away, we knew of an Arab village. The distant stars radiated little light and the moon had not risen yet as we hastened over sloping, uncultivated ground. The accursed flashlight in my hand refused to stay lit as I ran over the unfamiliar terrain. Ignoring caution we covered about half a mile and came to a spot known as *Gan Eden*, Garden of Eden, a large assembly of cacti, growing here taller than men. We stopped in a clearing among those giant plants and considered the situation. Nobody had thought what would happen once we reached the Arab village. And worse, it made sense that the robber was not alone, and what would happen if we met them? They certainly were armed while we did not even have a knife between us.

Abandoning this hopeless chase, we returned to Dror with the intention of calling the police next morning. Unarmed guards were posted, yet, it was the umbrella after the rain.

During the chase I hadn't thought of Erich. It was too dark even to recognize the third guy away from me, and I had taken it for granted that my friend was among those rushing down the slope. Without looking for him among the people standing around in the dark and talking about the events, I returned to the tent.

To my surprise, Erich was in bed. "What's the matter with you?" I asked, slightly disgusted over so much unconcern. "They stole my overalls," he complained with a face so comical I burst out laughing. We kept our work clothes on the table, and one of the robbers had just reached through the tent flap. He had gotten hold and taken Erich's overalls.

Next morning a Palestine policeman arrived in the company of a Jewish policeman and an Arab tracker. The trail of the robbers led exactly in the opposite direction we had taken the night before. It went

314

past Kfar Hess, toward the foothills of the mountains to the east, and into Arab territory. On the way the search team found two empty suitcases and a few pieces of clothing. The search was suspended. In those days Arabs came to steal, not to murder.

After this episode it took no time before a fence surrounded our encampment and lights arose on poles on four corners. It still left some poorly lit spots around the perimeter, but more lighting was expensive, and it was hoped that a two-man patrol at night (on a rotation basis) would compensate for that deficiency. The only firearm at Dror was a small "illegal" pistol that the driver of the tractor carried with him when he went out to work in the fields at night.

To improve security Erich suggested a dog.

Lavan, white in Hebrew, was a huge dog. He was frightening to look at but was so tame, or perhaps lazy, that if stepped on by mistake he wouldn't even move his tail. Some watchdog! He and the poor guy who had brought him to us were the joke of Dror.

The youth group in Vienna to which Erich and I had belonged (and which I had refused to join when it left for Palestine) had been sent to Na'an, a kibbutz southeast of Rehovot. The kibbutz trained watchdogs as a sideline. Erich believed he had observed enough of the training of dogs to be able to make Lavan a member in good standing of the night guardians protecting Dror. Lavan became a fellow lodger in our tent. The rope around his neck was tied to one of the two poles that kept the tent in an upright position. It made it possible for the dog to be inside and outside our abode at any time.

Erich began his training. He fed the dog raw meat. It made the dog fierce but also prevented the guards from waking us in the morning. Lavan showed his teeth and growled menacingly at anybody who tried to come near our tent. Because the danger stemmed from Arabs who came as thieves in the night, Erich used an old garb of an Arab to nettle the dog. He rolled the garment around his left arm and pushed it provokingly toward the dog's face. The dog, angered by the action and the smelly material, began in time to react viciously. He locked his teeth on the arm covered by the garment and released his grip only after Erich spoke soothingly to him. Lavan had turned from a lovable Dr. Jekyll to a dangerous Mr. Hyde. The rope tying him to the pole, too flimsy now to restrain him, had to be exchanged for a chain.

One morning we were awakened by the angry growl of Lavan and a moment later the tent collapsed on our heads. The dog, trying to get at the guard who had come to wake us, had pulled the tent pole out of the ground. After that the guards refused to wake us even though a special strong pole had been driven extra deep into the ground. We had to buy an alarm clock to get up on time in the morning. Tied to the pole most of the day, Lavan tolerated nobody near him but my friend and me. As he could not be made to accompany the patrol at night, he became useless. Failing to perform his duty (perhaps faulty training was the reason) the dog was given to a kibbutz, who would train him properly. He would not be returned to us, and once again Dror's safety depended on its inhabitants.

Since my discharge from the British army I had little opportunity to use my English. Many of the men and women who had served in the military did not necessarily know a lot of the language and could converse only in a primitive way. Even those who were more fluent in English did not speak it at Dror. It would have seemed snobbish. Hebrew was the common language or, with some of my friends, German.

One exception had to be made as far as the English language was concerned. A young Italian woman, wife of a member of our settlement, spoke only Italian and English. She had met and married her husband while he was serving in the British army in her country. For me her presence at Dror was a blessing as it gave me the chance to converse in English, an opportunity I utilized to the fullest. Several years later, and after leaving Dror, I recognized her at a bus station in Tel Aviv. Delighted by the meeting and the opportunity to speak English once more, I approached her. Greeting her with shalom, I continued in English. To my surprise she answered in Hebrew and refused to speak anything but Hebrew. Being Christian by birth, she had become a fervent Israeli.

Having been officially in Palestine since November 25, 1940 (though not with the blessing of the [British] Palestine government), I wrote a letter to the Department of Migration in Jerusalem on January 25, 1947, Requesting the status of citizen. I believed that my four years in the British army qualified me for that privilege. Their answer seemed the extremity of red-tapeism. The Palestinian Citizenship Orders 1925-42 required that one had to have lived in Palestine for a period of not less than two years out of the three years prior to application.

I was stunned by the government's reply and felt exasperated and bitter about British fairness. Had I remained a civilian in the country instead of serving four years in their armed forces I could have become a citizen of Palestine. Now I had to wait two years before I would be able to apply for citizenship.

316

Jobs in the City

Occasionally I acted impulsively and sometimes landed in situations that were unpleasant or downright dangerous. But my departure from Dror, in the early part of 1947, was not based on impulse as my friends suspected. It actually had taken me quite a while to get up enough nerve to move from wishful thinking to action and from the financially secure Dror to the rather unstable working conditions in Tel Aviv. I had grown progressively restless in the settlement, and my reasons for the transit were threefold: though not necessarily in the order noted. One: I had grown up in a big city, and life at Dror seemed restrictive and tedious. Two: I could not adjust to the type of work allotted to me, and also could not see myself becoming a farmer for life. And three: I still wanted very much to see my sister in Europe, even if only for a short time.

Unaware of my long inner struggle, my friends at Dror, and especially Erich, were shocked by my apparent sudden, and seemingly foolhardy decision to move. Their effort to change my mind fell on deaf ears. Their warnings about the constant trouble with the British, and the economic effect it had on the country, especially the cities, failed to change my mind. They correctly pointed out to me the rather peaceful life in the district of Tel Mond. And yet, what appeared to be an unwise move at the time may have saved my skin about a year later. In the Israeli army by then, and on a visit to Tel Aviv, I met an acquaintance from Dror. We exchanged news about ourselves, and then I asked about certain fellows I knew more closely in the settlement. I was shocked to hear that several had been killed on one occasion. A commander in the district decided to attack and capture the Arab village of Tira. He assembled men from the district, some of which came from Dror, and ordered the attack during daylight over open fields. The Arabs were on guard and had a turkey shoot.

While listening to the man a creepy feeling came over me. I could easily have been one of the fatalities had I stayed on in Dror. I had little doubt that I would have foolishly volunteered to join the group of men who had been chosen for the raid.

I felt elated as the bus carried my two suitcases, bought at the leather bazaar in Cairo, and me toward Tel Aviv. Once more I was on my own but, in spite of the good feeling, I had conflicting emotions as I traveled toward a destination that promised neither tranquillity nor assured employment. The only positive ingredient in this mixture of uncertainty was the promise of a place to stay in the city and this free of charge. This most generous offer which relieved me of a great financial burden came from Ruben Fink, a friend from the British army and a

317

member of Dror. He had arranged my accommodation in his parents' home.

The Finks, immigrants from Nazi Germany, lived in a nice Tel Aviv neighborhood. Their apartment, on the second floor of a building on Gordon Street, was just a block-and-half away from the main thoroughfare of Dizzengoff Street, and only a short distance from Dizzengoff Circle. The family consisted of five persons. Father, mother, and a daughter, slightly my junior, who lived with her parents. Ruben, their son, was in Dror, and his younger brother in a kibbutz. The family owned a little factory south of Tel Aviv that produced a chocolate spread, the quality of which the father, through continued experiments in the kitchen of their apartment, always tried to improve.

For lack of a more convenient spot in their home, my bed was placed below a window in the living-dining room. I was so happy to be in the city that even a spot in the bathroom would have sufficed. My sleeping quarters in the midst of their apartment had to inconvenience them a great deal, yet they never made me feel that it did. With the exception of meal times the room was mine. The Finks were the nicest people, always friendly, and the Ruben I knew in the army and at Dror mirrored these characteristics.

The family was traditionally religious, and Friday night dinners, which I had to attend, were the way grandma used to prepare them for the Seidlers in Vienna when grandpa was still alive. After dinner the three Finks sang *smires,* songs in honor of the Sabbath, while I sat on pins and needles, waiting for an opportunity to depart. I was dying to smoke a cigarette that, during the Sabbath (lasting from early Friday evening until Saturday night), I could not do in their home. Mr. Fink, also a smoker, never lit a cigarette during those hours. It became routine that after the meal, and having listened to their singing for a while, I lamely excused myself for want of a breath of fresh air on the flat roof of the building or a stroll on the street. They were aware of the reason behind my exit but were tolerant enough never to mention it.

On my first day in the city, I explored the neighborhood. I felt as if I were in a dream. Main thoroughfares in Tel Aviv, lively during the day, were even more so in the evening. I soaked up the life around me, the traffic, the illuminated store windows, the crowds in the street and at tables of sidewalk cafés, the restaurants, and the movie theaters. It was not that I intended to become a regular patron of those establishments, but an occasional visit to one of those places would add spice to what I considered city life. After the silence and solitude of Gush Tel Mond I relished the bustle like long-missed nectar. I sniffed the perfumed scent of girls passing me on the street and this for no other reason than that it emphasized the atmosphere of the big city. The experience made my blood tingle and my brain intoxicated. It had been too long since I had last lived in a city.

Two days later I found a job at a lumberyard just outside Tel Aviv. With others I moved and stacked different-sized boards in the yard, loaded and unloaded trucks, carrying the wood on my shoulders. For a few days my shoulders hurt dreadfully. Checking them in the bathroom mirror in the evening, I found the skin to be of a deep red color and extremely sensitive to the touch. For obvious reasons it brought back unpleasant memories of Buchenwald though the circumstances were as different as heaven and earth. But the pain, which made me clench my teeth during the first few minutes of work every morning, grew less as the day wore on. After two weeks, when I had adjusted to the job, business slowed, and being the last one hired, I was laid off.

I acquired my next job by coincidence. One evening I was strolling along Allenby Road and recognized an acquaintance behind the sales counter of a store. The man's name was Altman, and we both had served in the same unit in the British army. Since I had not seen him since our discharge and was curious to find out how he had fared after the army, I entered the store to say hello.

My interest paid off when I discovered that Altman and his cousin owned the business. I inquired about a job, and by another coincidence, they needed a sales clerk for a new store they had opened on Shenkin Street. I was hired. I liked the job. Altman worked with me while his cousin ran the store on Allenby Road. Business fluctuated, depending often on the operations carried out by the underground or the British reaction to it. We sold over the counter, and I handled locksmith jobs. At one time, sent out on an errand, I had an unexpected, pleasant encounter.

Beit Hadar, Citrus House, looked at the time like a fortress. A tall barbed wire fence along the curb surrounded the building. People passing were forced to skirt the enclosure by walking in the street. The stronghold was guarded by military police that patrolled the inside of the fence with Tommy guns at the ready.

I was walking past the barrier when suddenly someone from behind the fence called out: "Hey. You there!" I turned toward the caller, and recognized the man. He too had been one of the military policemen who had guarded me on the Devonshire. I was glad to see him, but felt uncomfortable about the way we had met. His interest in the outcome of my adventure trip, as he called it, was amusing, and his exclamation: "You lucky fellow," predictable. We talked for a while and parted on friendly terms. No rancor on his part about the situation he was in.

One evening Altman had me deliver merchandise to the other store, which led me past Barclays Bank on Allenby Road. Just before returning to Shenkin Street, bursts of automatic gunfire were heard. The sounds were clear enough to establish the trouble spot as not too far from the store. Reacting by instinct, all those present in the place took shelter behind the counters. We hoped that the stored metal items on the inside shelves and drawers would afford us safety, should errant bullets enter the shop. To exacerbate the uneasiness, the lights went out a little later in our store, and also along Allenby Road. "They must have hit electric cables," someone said. "It's probably the IZL or the Stern Group that is trying to rob Barclays Bank," another person commented.

We continued to squat and listened to the exchange of fire. After a while it grew quiet. More time passed. Eventually it became clear that our continued stay in the store was useless. No customers could be expected. The insecurity of the neighborhood would deter people from purchasing anything but food, and this only if there was fear of an impending curfew. After a phone call to the Shenkin store, Altman's cousin informed us that whoever wanted to go home was free to do so. A young fellow and I left the store. By then I, too, believed that an attack on Barclays Bank had taken place - the bank I had walked past just a short while before. Perhaps I had been lucky again. Innocent persons easily got hurt in shoot-outs of this kind.

Despite the darkness, the canyon of Nachlat Benyamin Street looked like a night scene in a silent movie. Things could be recognized. "Let's not hurry, but walk at a regular pace," I suggested. "If we are spotted by British Palestine police or an army patrol, at least we won't appear suspicious." Young Jewish people were always suspect when found near a trouble spot.

Barclays Bank, on the corner of Allenby Road and Achad Ha'am Street, seemed the closest point of danger we had to pass on Nachlat Benyamin. But a little further down the street, an armored car turned a corner and moved in our direction. Its appearance was as unexpected as it was shocking, and in the existing situation could have spelled trouble. Uncertain if we had been spotted we dared not retrace our steps lest we looked suspicious. With no place to hide we continued on our way, hoping the British police or military in the car would not be rash in their conduct once we came face to face with them.

The vehicle's searchlight, dark until then, suddenly came to life. The beam moved back and forth along the front of the buildings on one side of the street, then switched over to the other side following the same pattern. Sometimes the finger of light shot slightly ahead of the slow-traveling vehicle then changed to the rear, from where men in the car may have expected hostile action. It was apparent by then that we had not been detected yet, and I wondered how the men in the armored car *would* react once they had us in the beam of their searchlight. The recent

320

exchange of fire only two blocks away from where we met the armored car had to have made the men in the vehicle edgy.

In a few seconds we were caught up in the blinding beam of the searchlight. My stomach felt queasy as the car coming toward us slowed to a crawl; the erstwhile inquisitive light was now riveted on us. Step after step, and closer and closer, we came to that steel monster, our well being depending on the mental state of the man behind the machine gun. Soldiers and policemen near the scene of conflict with the underground occasionally used their weapons first and investigated later.

We advanced toward each other at what felt like a snail's pace. Then we were level with the armored car, we passed each other, and for an unreasonable length of time the unrelenting beam of the searchlight followed and remained focused on us. When it finally let go, and moved away, we both exhaled a sigh of relief. It could have been a disaster. We never looked back.

The assault on Barclays Bank was one of the lesser operations of the right-wing underground. Prevailing conditions in Palestine at that time are best mirrored in newspaper headlines, which invariably told of actions by clandestine groups. March 1, 1947: *"IZL, attacks a dozen British installations throughout the country."* – April 1, 1947: *"Stern Gang claims responsibility for attack on oil refineries in Haifa Bay. Oil tanks are ablaze, and Haifa is almost blacked out under a pall of thick smoke."*

In the spring of 1946 the Ramat Gan police station, a Teggart Fortress, had been attacked and robbed of great quantities of weapons and ammunition by members of the IZL. One of their men, Dov Gruner, was wounded and captured by the British. On the morning of April 16, 1947 Dov Gruner and three members of clandestine groups were executed by hanging. It worsened the situation in the country.

The British authorities placed Jerusalem and the Tel Aviv-Petach Tikva area under martial law for 15 days. During that time forces of British Palestine police and army fine-combed in vain the affected territories for the leaders of the right-wing underground. People were permitted out of houses during specified hours to buy provisions. During subsequent months headlines rarely varied: *"Attacks by Terrorist Groups intensify. - Trains derailed. Attack on Cairo-Haifa Railway Lines. 8 killed, 27 wounded."*

And during all that turmoil immigrant ships carrying Jewish refugees continued to arrive at the shores of Palestine. The British caught most, and their human cargo was forcibly deported to prison camps on the island of Cyprus. By April of 1947, these camps held over 11,000 Jews.

After two months at the hardware store I was let go. The continued curfews and other penalties meted out to the Jews by the British reduced business drastically. I started to work for a locksmith who had a tiny place in the backyard of a building on Levinski Street in the Neve Sha-anan district of Tel Aviv. The man had to fill an order for a complicated clamp system for bookkeeping papers and the work lasted for a month and half.

Like so many small businessmen, my boss barely eked out a living and was occasionally late in paying me my wages at week's end. One day he was very upset, and when I asked for the reason, he told me a bill for 50 (Palestinian) pounds (the equivalent of at least $500.00 today) was due for the materials we worked with. I lent him the money without signature and he returned it when he was paid for the job. Unfortunately he found no additional projects for his business and I was once more out of work.

Arabs began to assault Jews. Driving through Arab villages and cities became unsafe for Jews. The press had additional news items to report. *"One Jew died and four were wounded in stabbings near the Tel Aviv-Jaffa border."* - *"Three Jewish drivers killed by Arab mobs as their cars approached Tel Aviv from the south."*

More searches, arrests, and curfews for Jews followed confrontations with the British, and Palestine became a police state. Some curfews brought life for the Jews almost to a complete standstill. Because nobody knew how long restrictions would last, the chance of finding work in the city became more and more remote. When I learned that the British army would hire ex-soldiers who had gone through an automechanics class organized by the *Histadruth*, the labor union, I joined the course. The training was to take one month, but lasted six weeks. Most of us became infected with the same affliction: malnutrition of our purses. Sadly I watched the rapid disappearance of my money.

Of the slightly more than twelve participants in our class, only one other fellow and I passed the final test. As third-class mechanics we were to go to Haifa to work for the British army. In the end I went alone. The other man had found work in a village, which he preferred to camp life.

I left one suitcase packed with clothing in care of the Fink family and gratefully said good-bye to them. Without their kind extension of free shelter, my stay in Tel Aviv would have been of short duration.

Haifa, you beautiful, I return to you like the prodigal son. - Or so I thought.

For lack of opportunities elsewhere, men came from distant areas to seek work on British military bases. Civilian workers employed by the army in Kurdani, who were not from nearby areas, lived eight to a tent in a small camp on the outskirts of Kiryat Motzkin. Each of us kept his little stock of belongings in a suitcase, a box or a bag under the bed, and

322

larger garments fastened in some fashion to the walls of our housing. During my short stay there I never heard of anything being stolen. Living conditions were primitive, and to an outsider we may have appeared a band of displaced persons awaiting resettlement. I found nobody in our tent I particularly cared to befriend and the painful sense of loneliness, experienced in that room of rented beds in the German Colony some years back, returned. I was again a stranger among strangers.

Military trucks drove us the two miles to the workshops inside the army base every morning, and returned us to our camp after work. The atmosphere at the workplace was cheerless, and the job I had to handle mentally unrewarding. Evenings in our tent city were worse. The drabness of the place intensified my discontent and even the proximity of Kiryat Motzkin and adjacent Kiryat Haim, two small Jewish towns, failed to improve my disposition. They offered no social activities and were quiet when evening fell.

Perhaps my failure to adjust to life here was partly due to the still vivid images of my past experiences in this area. It was not that I yearned for army life, but conditions between my time as a soldier in Kurdani, and now as a civilian were so drastically different they were depressing. In my frame of mind the present seemed without design, and the future without purpose.

Unhappy with the way things had developed I reluctantly began to toy once more with the idea of moving to America. Leo, the cousin who had escaped from Vienna to Switzerland, to Belgium, and finally to New York, lived there, and my sister would eventually also emigrate from Austria to America. I had uncles, aunts, and cousins in the New York area and cousins of my father in Canada. And though I had never met any of them, I believed that being a relative would carry some weight in their feeling toward me.

But then optimism returned.

I disliked the idea of leaving Palestine and felt confident that this disagreeable situation would improve with time. There was also the nearness of Haifa, the city I had come to love from the very first steps taken after my release from prison camp Atlit. It was in Haifa where I again had learned to walk as a free person after oppressive Nazi Germany, the restrictiveness of the ships that had brought us here, and the restraining barbed wire fence of British policy in Palestine. The city in which, despite the difficult time of adjustment to the new country, I had experienced a romanticism found only in books. Though I tried to be clear-headed and realistic about my renewed acquaintance with Haifa, I yearned for, but missed, the titillating and intriguing emotions of newness and adventure that had once been my companions in this charming city.

323

On my first day off after my arrival at Kiryat Motzkin, I went to Haifa. I felt it necessary to visit Dolly and her relatives and yet, was reluctant to do so. I had not written to them in a long time and had inquired only incidentally about their activities in my letters to Yacov in Ramataim. When I finally went to their place and nobody answered the door, I felt relieved. I did not try again to get in touch. I strolled the streets of the city, visited places that held memories, but the magic was gone. It was like eating a cake I once had loved only to find out that it did not taste the way I remembered.

On the return trip that evening our bus was stopped at the "check post" by the feared *Kalanioth*[31], the Red Beret, the commando branch of the British army. Two of them came aboard, Tommy guns in hand, and each passenger had to present identity papers. I handed him my soldier book, which caused him to ask: "You're in the army?" Before I could answer he had opened the book and saw the inside pages stamped: "discharged."

"Why is the corner of your soldier book missing?" came the next question.

The book's upper right hand corner had been cut off at my release from the army, identifying it as not in use anymore. I explained the mutilation, and he returned the book to me. He went on to the people in the last row of the bus, the row behind me. Here he checked only four persons. The fifth passenger in the middle of that row and facing the aisle was a soldier. A Red Beret.

My seat being next to the aisle, I had watched the man come aboard the bus in Haifa and make his way to the row in back of me. I had paid attention to him not only for what he represented, but also for his face. It was rectangular and seemed the size of a large shoebox. The narrow crown of fire-red hair that haloed his head below the beret made him look Irish. His ears were big, and so was his mouth. Despite the freckles and a well-proportioned, fine nose, he looked mean. My assessment of him, no doubt, was influenced by the sometimes villainous behavior of his army buddies.

When the two Tommy gun-toting soldiers had left, and the lights inside the now-moving bus had been turned off, I was tapped on the shoulder from behind. I turned to see who wanted my attention, and recognized the silhouette of the soldier and his beret against the dark sky outside. His features were indistinguishable.

---

[31] Kalanioth is plural for the poppy flower in Hebrew. The flower's red petals and its black center were a synonym for the soldiers' red berets and, supposedly, black hearts. Their action against the Jewish population was the source of their ill repute.

Before I could say anything the redheaded commando asked: "*Red ihr eppes Yiddish?*" (Do you speak Yiddish?) He was a Jewish tailor from London who, stationed in Palestine, wanted to spend his leave with his relatives in Kiryat Haim. His disclosure confirmed the axiom not to judge a book by its cover.

After only two weeks I was fed up with Kurdani, Kiryat Motzkin, and the Haifa area and returned to the district of Tel Mond. I could again have joined the community of Dror, but their kibbutz-like life, and their future goals still failed to attract me. I had come back to the farm district out of necessity, and was willing to work as a farmhand as long as I was independent and had hopes of returning to the city once things improved.

Events Preceding the Establishment of Israel

Uri, the vulcanizer of our company in the British army, had become a farmer in the district. He was married and his wife was pregnant. Though she was active in and around the house, he needed help with his work. We talked and he hired me. For eleven days of work on his farm I received room and board for a month. On my days off I found occasional jobs with other farmers through the labor exchange in the village of Tel Mond, and for those services I was paid cash. After working for Uri a month and half, a cousin of his moved in and I moved out. I transferred to another farmer with arrangements identical to Uri's.

Uri, by the way, came to an ignominious end. After the creation of Israel, in the no-man's land between Kfar Hess and the Arab village of Tira stood an abandoned two-wheel platform that Uri said he would pick up one day. Warnings by neighbors failed to sway him from this foolhardy intention. I could clearly envision him in my mind as he stood there with the pipe between his slightly crooked teeth and his devil-may-care grin on his face, mocking the alarmists. The bullet that ended his young life in the no man's land came from an Arab sniper out of Tira.

Besides being a farmer, my new boss Abe was a night guard in a tiny workshop hidden away in an orange grove. The activity there had to do, as he confided in me, with weapons.

On several occasions I had seen a young Arab ride through the village, and on one occasion I asked him if he would sell me his donkey. He refused, but promised to bring me another animal.

Being green in respect to donkeys, I acquired a tall, skinny and shaggy animal for two Palestinian pounds. That poor beast, because of its age, moved slower than I walked.

When I met that young Arab again a few days later and complained about the animal, he showed me something I would have been better off not to know. He jumped on the animal's back, the donkey let out a terrible cry of pain and started to run. When he came back and showed me what had made it run, I felt sick. Near the animals neck, partly covered by hair, was a deep, open wound I had not seen. The boy wanted me to insert a twig into that injury and jab and twist it around[32].

I gave the donkey to a family in the village who promised not to work it, but to keep it until it died.

I had worked in the field for half a day, and then sat down on the ground to eat my sandwich. The countryside simmered peacefully in the hot sun, and the silence was only interrupted by humming flies attracted to my food. When by myself, I tended to look forward to the relaxing atmosphere of a short break after my meal. With a cigarette between my lips I'd stretch out on the ground and my mind started to fill pages of my narrative that was still missing from my then partly written biography.

This time, however, the envisioned activities were not realized, for before I took the first bite out of my sandwich I caught sight of a tall man walking toward me from across the field. He was an Arab, but his appearance held no menace for me. The relationship between Arabs and Jews in our area was still an agreeable one. Once we faced each other, I saw an alarmingly lean old man with a single tooth in his mouth. After the customary greeting, he unceremoniously squatted down across from me. Believing that the rule of hospitality required the sharing of my sandwich with this stranger, I divided the bread, offering him half. He accepted with *katacherak,* thank you, and then we ate in silence. At the end of the meal I reached for my cigarettes, but he placed his hand on mine and stopped me from extracting one. He pulled from his coat a little folder of cigarette papers and a small bag containing tobacco, and deftly prepared a cigarette. His tongue wetted the inside length of the rolled-up paper, and after it stuck to the outside, he licked the seam to make it smooth. That cigarette was for me.

I felt cornered. My brain ordered my stomach not to rebel, for with the occasional eye contact during our meal I had seen how my guest had chewed the sandwich in his open mouth, moving the food from place to place with his tongue, his one tooth joining the melee from time to time. Had I been able to reject his offer tactfully, I gladly would have done so. But I had reached for my cigarettes and could not claim to be a non smoker. As no other pretext came to my mind that would not seriously bruise the man's pride, I accepted his offer. I waited for him to roll his own cigarette, then lit both.

---

[32] I hope it is not a cruel village practice for donkeys that have gotten old.

The political and security situation in the country, in this summer of 1947, continued to worsen. Of the many refugee ships that tried to break through the British blockade of Palestine, one especially attracted worldwide attention.

The vessel Exodus.

The Exodus, in appearance and seaworthiness almost identical to all other dilapidated refugee ships arriving at the shores of Palestine, had reach its destination with 4,500 men, women and children aboard. With the exception of the very young, all travelers on the ship had survived Nazi death camps. Caught by the British Navy they were not interned but returned to, of all places, Hamburg, Germany. Hundreds of British soldiers, equipped as if for battle with a superior enemy, were on their most brutal behavior and overcame those people who refused to be sent back. The refugees were no match for the combat-trained soldiers and the uneven contest ended with their return to Germany.

Meanwhile Arabs openly proclaimed their intention to cut the Tel Aviv-Jerusalem road to starve the Jewish population of the capital. Arab gangs, which fired on Jewish vehicles from hill tops bordering that important roadway, were never apprehended and brought to justice by the British. As the number of Jews killed on that road increased, the Arabs in November of 1947, and with the apparent tactical consent of the British, laid siege to Jerusalem.

In other unprovoked aggressions and murders of Jews by Arabs, the British government never tried very hard to find the culprits. They were openly on the side of the Arabs. Jewish settlements had permits for a few rifles that were assigned to official guards by name, a fact I discovered a few months later. If the restricted number of weapons allotted to the Jewish population by the British was meant to keep them out of the hands of the Jewish underground, it was an illogical assumption. The Jewish underground hardly needed the good will of the British-Palestinian authorities to arm themselves. They raided army locations, to be sure, but otherwise had their own sources and ways of bringing small weapons into the country.

Compared to most of Palestine, life in our district was tranquil. I should have had no complaints about living here, and yet, as always, I missed the animation of the city. On rare occasions I took a bus to Tel Aviv to exchange or replenish my collection of light reading material in English. Paperbacks by Erle Stanley Gardner, Ellery Queen, Max Brand, Damon Ranyon, or The Saint. I took time out for a cup of coffee and a slice of cake in a café on Allenby Road, and later walked the promenade of Tel Aviv's waterfront. Then it was back to the monotonous life of

Kfar Hess; agricultural labor during the day, reading, writing, or just idleness in the evening.

The behavior of the British military during security operations created a tense atmosphere. About two kilometers of orange groves lay behind me and, stepping out into the open, lonely stretches of fields sloped toward the main road ahead, I became uncomfortably aware that in a not-too-distant grove soldiers were moving about the trees. Not just soldiers, but Red Beret.

For a few seconds two thoughts raced through my mind. Should I retreat quickly into the grove behind me or continue my walk? I had nothing to hide but ugly stories made their rounds among the *Yishuv,* the Jewish population of Palestine. It told of cases where British security personnel, after battling the underground and sustaining losses, apprehended innocent Jewish civilians and released them in an Arab city. Which was tantamount to dropping a fly without wings onto an anthill. A death sentence of the worst kind. One could also be 'shot while trying to escape,' or be beaten up for the same supposed reason. One just never knew what to expect.

I was reasonably certain the soldiers had observed me when I had stepped into the open, and so I abandoned the thought of running. The grove behind me was no place to hide with soldiers at such close proximity, and the nearest Jewish settlement was too distant to provide safety. Had I disappeared, the soldiers would have combed the grove until they found me, which could have proven worse. As suspicious as I was of their intentions, they surely regarded me with equal distrust.

I walked toward them, but every fiber in my body wanted to resist the advance. A misguided wish for self-preservation appealed to my senses: run, avoid an encounter that may have grievous consequences.

I had not stopped for a second after emerging from between the trees and hoped that my unhesitating walk gave a reassuring impression to those men below, namely, that I had nothing to hide. Several steps before I reached the "hidden" soldiers, a few of them stepped onto the road, Tommy guns trained. I could hardly ignore the group and stopped.

A sergeant asked for identity papers and then interrogated me. Where do you come from; where are you going; for what purpose, and finally, like the soldier at the check post near Haifa, why is the corner of the soldier's book missing? During the interrogation I tried to read their faces. Why were they here? Had something happened? Was there any reason for me to worry? It was hard to tell. My soldier book returned, I was told to move on. To my taut nerves it sounded more like a threat than just a harmless order to get going. A Tommy gun fires accurately for up to eighty meters; I counted ninety long steps before I began to relax. Nothing happened.

I wrote in my diary:

Kfar Hess, Wednesday, October 1, 1947

The slogan of the Jews during the Arab riots of 1936-39 was "Havlaga," restraint. They did not retaliate for murderous attacks on Jews by Arabs, which made the Jews appear without backbone, and the Arabs stronger than they were. Not to retaliate was to defuse the situation and prove to the world that the Arabs were the aggressors. As if the world cared. Things have changed, and though some of the Jewish underground groups are still restrained in their response to cold-blooded murder, they occasionally hit back.

I have heard a lot about the 1936-39 Arab riots and have forgotten nothing. Too uncomfortable is the thought that danger may lurk behind any encounter with an Arab. Two months ago, a situation reminiscent of the thirties had all the makings of renewed Arab riots. In 1936 a Jewish cattle dealer who did business in Arab villages was found murdered near the Jewish town of Petach Tikva. Since the victim was not robbed, it clearly was a political assassination. That murder followed more killings of Jews near Arab villages with the same modus operandi. Nothing was stolen. Two months ago a Jewish cattle dealer was murdered close to the Arab village of Fodsha, near Petach Tikva. As if following the scenario of a decade ago, one Jew was shot and killed near Petach Tikva every night for a week. Though the victims were now robbed, there were too many killings in a short period of time and too close to the same sector to be dismissed as just criminal robbery and murder.

The Hagana traced the murderous gang to a notorious Arab café near Fodsha, and one day a party of armed young Jews appeared in front of that building. Acting recklessly, the leader of the group entered the café and asked for a specific Arab, the suspect. The answer was shots that killed him. In the following exchange of gunfire several Arabs were killed and, after the rest had fled, the Hagana blew up the building.

Not long after that event an Arab gang attacked the Jewish nightclub Gan Hawaii on the bank of the Yarkon River near Tel Aviv. The patrons of the club were robbed, and when some of them moved, the Arabs started shooting and lobbed a hand grenade at the people. Four Jews lost their lives and several were wounded.

Once more the Hagana found the meeting place of the gang, a two-storied building in an orange grove about half an hour from Tel Aviv. A few nights later a group of Jewish men showed up at the house. They found none of the gang members present, and the Arab guard who lived there with his family said the gang had warned him that he would be killed if he disclosed anything to outsiders.

He was instructed by the Hagana to leave with his family for the house was to be mined. The family left the building, but returned after the Hagana men had departed, for they did not believe that the house would blow up. The explosive charge destroyed half the building and killed the Arab family.

This incident created trouble on the Tel Aviv-Jaffa border with loss of life on the Jewish and Arab sides. In spite of occasional violence in the country, the situation in the double city, Tel Aviv-Jaffa, returned to almost normalcy once more. Jews began to visit Arab Jaffa and Arabs came to Jewish Tel Aviv.

Actually things have never been tranquil for me since my discharge from the army more than a year ago. For the Jewish population trouble has existed much longer. Incidents continued to happen that kept the situation tense and banner headlines in newspapers. At first it was the back-and-forth strikes of the right-wing underground and the British; then the British turned on the Hagana as well, and when the Arabs got into the act, everybody was involved.

A news item a few days ago read: "With the help of a mechanical device a barrel filled with explosives was hurled at the Police Headquarters in Haifa killing several British and Arab policemen."

Though it is still unknown who the perpetrators were, I strongly believe the action to have the characteristics of the right-wing underground. They don't hesitate to reply violently to hostile actions by the British authorities and Arabs. It has become a way of life for the Jewish population – especially in rural areas – never completely to relax their guard. When serious trouble is expected, readiness changes to high alert. This time, however, I was under the impression that the increased security preparations for Friday, the day after tomorrow, will turn out to be unnecessary. It is the anniversary of the day when the British, authorized by the League of Nations in 1922, took over Palestine. It became the "Day of the Mandate," a term both Arabs and Jews dislike. Though Arabs have used less momentous occasions like the anniversary of British rule in Palestine or the loss of an Arab life in Haifa a few days ago, to riot, attack, and kill Jews, I still believe, or rather hope, that at least our area will remain calm.

At supper this evening Abe quoted from the Hebrew newspaper that, starting tomorrow, the Jewish part of the country was to be in a state of emergency. Defensive arrangements are ordered as hostile acts by Arabs are expected. As if on cue, a young fellow entered the kitchen a few minutes later and had Abe sign a paper stipulating that, starting tomorrow at noon, nobody was to leave the district of Tel Mond without special permission. The restriction was to be in force until further notice.

That curfew imposed by Jews on Jews was unexpected. Perhaps the state of things was graver than I imagined, and my judgment of the situation was just wishful thinking. It bothers me that I can't visit Tel

Aviv, Ramataim, and the relations of my mother in Kfar Saba[33] on my next few days off as I had intended. But, at least, I wanted go to Tel Aviv early tomorrow morning and attend to things I had in mind.

If the situation here becomes troublesome, and the district has to depend on the few rifles I have seen, then we are in trouble. It is known that Arabs have a great arsenal of weapons at their disposal, supplied to them by Arab countries surrounding Palestine. The Arab village of Tira and its several thousand inhabitants is less than a mile across fields from Kfar Hess and the sizable Arab city, Kalkilia, a mere three miles beyond that. $----$

Friday passed without trouble. But when, after hot discussions, the United Nations in Lake Success, New York, on November 29, 1947 decided on the partition of Palestine into a Jewish and Arab state, events progressed toward the inescapable climax. Jews were deliriously happy, Arabs talked of war. On the map the Jewish state-to-be looked like a flat piece of rubber being torn apart, the two end-pieces still clinging to each other by a narrow strip.

That night many neighbors visited Abe's house to celebrate. Laughter and song of the young sounded in the back yard while the older generation inside the house talked about the creation of a Jewish state after two millennia. The magnitude of that historical event was still difficult to believe. Ever since the Diaspora the Jews had prayed for a return to Eretz Israel: *Beshana haba'a be Jerushalaim* (next year in Jerusalem.) And now that the elusive dream was about to be realized, people rejoiced at their good fortune to be part of that momentous event.

Wine served to the guests raised the liveliness of the assembly, but with the exception of one, nobody fell victim to Bacchus. The exception was I. I cannot take much alcohol, and I became tipsy. My mind was clear enough, and when some fellows laughingly tried to convince me that I was drunk, I indignantly challenged them to give me an arithmetic problem which I, to prove my sobriety, would easily solve. They just laughed.

After the initial excitement the reaction of the Arabs had to be considered. And the Jews did not have to wait long. The very next day deadly attacks were carried out by Arabs on Jews all over the country. People hoped that this would be a temporary condition and that once the

---

[33] Survivors of the holocaust that had come to Palestine. They lived in Kfar Saba, a village five miles south of Kfar Hess as the crow flies and double the number of miles over roads.

state was officially created, unrest and riots would cease. The possibility that the Arab states surrounding Palestine would carry out their threat and attack the newly founded Jewish State was too horrendous a thought to be considered. The world would not permit this to happen, and the Arab states would hardly dare to defy the United Nations' decision. Wishful thinking again, and not only on my part. If the Jewish leadership considered aggression by Arab states likely, they did not let on. The only open warning of that possibility came from members of the right-wing underground.

For the moment quiet village life was over. Because Arab attacks were anticipated, a red alert went into effect. Extraordinary precautions were initiated to meet expected hit-and-run attacks on Jewish settlements and ambushes on vehicular traffic on roads by Arab gangs.

In our village every man was assigned three hours of guard duty for each of four consecutive nights. The fifth night was free. This arrangement was continued until the emergency was over. On three of the four duty nights we slept in a house – our guard post – on the other side of the village. The fourth night I spent at home, leaving the house only for my three hours guard stint.

A great part of the village was surrounded by orange groves, and those sections of the borders were considered higher risks than others. In some places the trees grew almost up to the houses, making them ideal places for Arabs to attempt penetration of the settlement by stealth.

The Arabs had passed from the simple robberies by gangs to murderous hit-and-ran attacks on Jews. Their final undertaking was to come later with the help of neighboring countries. After all, everybody wanted a piece of the expected pie. It was to be an all-out assault on Jewish lives, their properties and the motto: "Drive the Jews into the sea," was the slogan.

In the house near the orange grove the owner had put a small room at our disposal, and here, when not on patrol, we slept on straw mattresses on the floor. On my first night on duty I was handed a short Italian carbine that stayed with me throughout the night. No doubt, it had been coated in some kind of water-repellent and unearthed recently for the present emergency. I wondered when it had been fired last and if I could depend on it in case of need. But keeping it close to my body while I slept on the mattress gave me a feeling of security. In the corner of the same room stood a bucket filled with British Mills hand grenades for unexpected contingencies. Those hand grenades had also been buried in the ground for an extended period of time, making them unsafe. For more reasons than one we were lucky not to have had to use them. They probably were unstable, and might have exploded from just being handled.

Up until then, arrangements were well organized, yet I was bothered by one thing. The tract of land my partner – a young Russian immigrant – and I were assigned to traverse that night was unfamiliar to both of us. It made our duty so much more hazardous, for not only had we to watch out for Arabs, but the unknown, and uneven terrain tripped us in the dark many times. Had I been informed during the day of the sector to be patrolled I would have familiarized myself with the ground.

I must assume that the failure to inform us earlier of the region to be covered was because the responsible person was unaware of who was to guard the stretch. I have no doubt that people who grew up in the area were familiar with the territory and it was unfortunate that two men like us, who were relatively new to the district, had to be picked for the assigned tract.

That circumstance, as well as the midnight-to-3A.M. shift (a time that completely disrupts one's rest) makes me remember that night quite well. A few minutes before 12, several of the sleepers in the room were awakened by the man in charge. As we had slept in our clothes we were immediately ready to take over the duty of the guardsmen who filed into the room in twos. The pair we replaced described the terrain to be covered.

Then we stepped out into the night. Although our eyes adjusted quickly to the surrounding darkness, the ground below our feet was difficult to make out. Rifles at the ready, we walked softly but often tripped over rocks and uneven earth. Under the circumstances it was difficult to say which was the safest way to advance, but though the orange grove on our right looked dark and forbidding, we kept close to its trees. It seemed less menacing than the open ground to our left where I could not shake the feeling of being watched by unseen eyes. Depending not altogether on sight, we stopped often and listened into the night. In line with the little adventure booklets I used to read as a youngster, I found it prudent to walk a few steps ahead of my partner. This way I hoped that both of us would not get surprised by adversaries at the same instant.

After some time and with the trees behind us, we crossed an extensive area of cultivated ground followed by another orange grove on our left. At the end of it we came to a dry creek on whose other side was a short, but steep incline. Our instructions were to climb the slope, remain for five minutes on its crest, and listen for anything suspicious. If nothing out of the ordinary could be detected, we were to return the way we had come.

The night was not silent. In certain fields a slight breeze rustled stalks, small animals scurried by, and crickets filled the air with their uninterrupted chirping. For some reason the occasional howl of a jackal pleased me. It may have been its seeming indifference to the danger his cry might attract.

When we crossed the fields on our return trip, my partner whispered: "Let's lie down. You in one direction and I alongside you in the other. That way we have a better chance of noticing anything unusual and can't be surprised from either side." I was impressed. "Where did you learn this?" I asked in a low voice while I lowered myself to the ground. "In the Red Army," he said. I was even more impressed. They sure had more down-to-earth training than we had in the British Army. But then, I had not belonged to a fighting unit.

It was difficult to work all day and then do three hours of guard duty at different times during the night. It was also difficult to abstain from smoking during those hours and, as most people smoked at the time, we found a way to light and enjoy a cigarette in what we hoped was a concealed manner. The one that struck a match bent low to the ground while his partner hovered over him to cover the little light that might escape from the flame. Once the cigarette was lit, the glowing point was held hidden in cupped hands as we occasionally did while on guard duty in the British army. For the time of the smoke we sat on the ground, our backs against a tree trunk, listening in silence into the night. If we rested a few more minutes after the cigarettes had been put out, my partner, often an elderly farmer, might in some cases fall asleep on me.

Diary notes: The three-day strike called by the Arab High Executive on December 2, 1947, resulted in riots, the death of eight Jews, and eight Arabs. In Jerusalem an Arab mob of 200 youths between the ages of 10 and 20 looted and burned places and stabbed Jews. December 7, 1947. The British decided to surrender the mandate of Palestine on May 15 the following year. − − − −

The decision by the U.N. to create a Jewish State unleashed anti-Jewish riots in most Moslem states. The native firebrands, as the colonial powers called them, found it easy to arouse the masses against the Jews in their midst[34]. It made little difference to the local population that the Jews in those sections of Arab cities were as poor and lived in the same squalor as the rest of them. They answered the venom of rabble-rousers with the cry of: *"Alehum"*[35] not because they cared what was to happen in

---

[34] During my many years in Palestine and Israel I met Jewish people from Iraq, Yemen, Syria, and other Moslem countries. They told me that Jews often suffered abuse and degradation by Arabs in those countries even in quiet times.

[35] Alehum," translated from the Arabic, means "onto them." The definition of the word, however, was: kill the Jews. Arabs also used the cry when attacking Jews in Palestine.

Palestine, a place many, in all probability, had little or nothing heard of before, but because it was directed against *"Yahudie,"* the Jew, people who lived among them, yet were not Moslems.[36]

Riots in Aden. (Aden, in Yemen, was still under British control at the time.) *Fifty Jews, 25 Arabs dead after five days of Arab rioting. Arabs approached the Jewish settlement in the (Arab) native area, set buildings afire. Curfew imposed by the British to check murder, looting and arson. Nine hundred Jews from native settlement evacuated while 14 who remained behind were killed.*

Conscription in Syria.

December 8, 1947. Jews killed in Persia and Pakistan. And of all places in Ulm, Germany, one Jew was stabbed to death, and eight other Jews and one Moslem were wounded.

Girl killed in convoy attacked by Arabs in the hills between Bab el Wad and Abu Gosh (Palestine.) - *Hagana beats back Arab attack on Manshieh Quarters.* (Jaffa.) - *Five Jews, one Arab killed that day.*

Jerusalem bus coming down from Mount Scopus was attacked in the Nashashibi (Arab) *Quarter by a hand-grenade and automatic fire from both sides of the road. Two Jewish doctors badly hurt.* - *Sporadic fire was directed at the Jewish quarters in the Old City* (Jerusalem) *all Sunday night, ceasing only at dawn.*

Sniping, arson in Haifa.

Negba. An 18-year-old Jew was reported missing after an Arab gang ambushed a truck on the way to his settlement from Gath yesterday. He was found dead this morning. One other person in the truck was killed in the attack, and Arabs also killed a member of the party that set out to search for the missing.

December 9, 1947. Haifa. Arabs attack Hadar Hacarmel from Wadi Rushmieh Quarters and Ard el Yahoud. — *Jaffa. The border battle has taken nine more lives. Six Jews, two Arabs, and one British.*

December 11, 1947. The Transjordanian Arab Legion[37] *is in Ramleh* (Palestine.)

December 15, 1947. Fourteen Jews were killed and 10 were wounded when troops of the Arab Legion fired at the occupants of two trucks forming part of a convoy bringing supplies to Ben Shemen Children's Village near Ramleh this afternoon.

Holon and Safad (Jewish cities) attacked. Hagana and I.Z.L. strike back. - *Gunfire flares up in Haifa.* - *Seven Jews killed in attack on convoy.* -- *Arab Legion*

---

[36]Those incited hardly had the means to own a radio or the time to go to a café and listen to one. The poor in Arab cities, and especially in rural areas, never went to school. They were illiterates.

[37] The Arab Legion was the army of the neighboring Kingdom of Transjordan. The soldiers were Arabs, officers and the Commander in Chief, in the pay of King Abdullah, were British.

335

fires on Haifa buses. - Nathania. Daylong attack by Arabs on the Jewish settlement of Kfar Yavetz. (Though I logged events frequently, it was not on a day-to-day basis. Attacks and the murder of Jews by Arabs, however, were almost daily occurrences.)

In spite of continuous violence, the red alert in our area was modified to standard alert two weeks later, and guard duties became less frequent. It was almost a pleasure. – Actually that was not true. I never enjoyed guard duty. Not in the army and even less in civilian life, not in relatively peaceful times nor during turbulent periods. Who likes to be aroused from slumber to walk a beat with a rifle slung over his shoulder or at the ready in one's hands? Up to the beginning of the Arab unrest guard duty was just a nuisance to me, a tedious endeavor that interrupted or shortened my sleep. But by December of 1947 my view of guard duty changed. This obligation had become a peril not because I could face and judge its danger, but because it was invisible, and I did not know when I might be challenged by its threat. We were not guarding against thieving Arabs anymore, but an enemy who was out to kill.

During the preceding 10 years my life had repeatedly been in jeopardy, and life-menacing situations were easier to confront when in a group. The threat here was different. It was aimed at a few single men – I being one of them – or a pair of people who were walking along orange groves, over fields or other terrain at night. An enemy who intended a hit-and-run attack on a village would do well to eliminate a patrol before proceeding with his operation. He could hardly allow armed men at his back when entering the settlement or risk confrontation at the time of retreat.

After having worked for Abe five months I decided to be on my own again. Toward the end of December I move out of his house and rented a small wooden hut that stood in the front yard of another farmer. The dwelling consisted of a miniature anteroom, a kitchen almost as small, and a medium-sized room. The facility, though Spartan in design and furnishings, had the toilet inside the house, a feature I appreciated.

At Abe's place I had been almost part of the family, now I led a bachelor's existence. I occasionally cooked for myself, pressed some shirts and khaki trousers with an iron borrowed from the farmer's wife, read and scribbled notes in the evening, and generally felt quite bored and lonely. Life in the village lacked variety. People were busy during the day but stayed home in the evening. They did not stroll the village streets for pleasure nor were there businesses where one could window-shop for the sake of passing the time. But with the rainy season on, and the dirt roads and paths of the settlement a quagmire, who wanted to be outside of one's home anyway?

336

Scribbled in my book:

It rained hard. The orange trees of the grove shielded us from the downpour only during the first few minutes; after that we might just as well have stood under the open sky. I wore a trench coat I had recently waterproofed and dyed black in Tel Aviv. Its original color of khaki, too conspicuous for guard duty, now blended in with the night, but the rain still penetrated the seams and fabric of the coat.

Guard duty in the rain was twice as miserable as during the dry season. As on previous occasions when unpleasant conditions prevailed, my thoughts turned to more agreeable matters, though I did not relax my vigilance. Without disregarding the chance of a sneak attack by Arabs or their array of supporters from abroad, I envisioned hot coffee, and the warm bed that awaited me at the end of my guard shift. It made the misery and potential danger of the night more bearable.

We still went out in twos, following our illegal procedure of carrying identity papers and rifles of the few official guardians the British permitted in the village. As those men were actually farmers and could not stand guard every night and pursue their work during the day, their papers and arms were being handed from surrogate guard to surrogate guard. In case the British raided the village to search for hidden weapons (as they had done in other Jewish settlements), and to inspect the registered guards and their rifles, the switch of identity papers and arms from the surrogate guards to the real ones could still be accomplished in time.

Perhaps a little more relaxed because of the inaction in our area, we paid a brief visit to the district bakery if we were the last guard shift of the night. The baker started his work in the wee hours of the morning, and when we came to his place, the big mixing bowls were already kneading the dough. We stayed for a few minutes to get warm, talked about the topics on everybody's mind, and before long returned to the outside where darkness still prevailed. - - - -

Then, as if to remind us that we were still in an undeclared war with the Arabs, a newspaper headline on December 31, 1947 read: *"Six Arabs were killed in a bomb explosion at the refineries on the Haifa-Acre (Akko) road this morning. Enraged by the killing, 2,000 Arab employees ran amok, massacring 39 Jewish workmen and wounding others."*

I wrote again in my diary at greater length, making another effort to analyze my feelings and my uneasiness about the future. The following is the essence of this entry.

Kfar Hess, Thursday, January 1, 1948

Except for frequently scribbled notes on scrap paper, my last entry in the diary was three months ago. Glancing over the short notations and pages of October 1, 1947 I find my thoughts, my emotions, and writings influenced by concern, indeed anxiety. The great unknown, namely serious Arab unrest and rioting, is something one cannot look forward to without a feeling of discomfort. I'll be 25 on my next birthday, and more has happened to me during those years than has happened to other people twice or three times my age. Times are so turbulent and uncertain that it makes me wonder if I shall ever experience peace in my life or live in a world that has turned right side up once more. I cannot predict the future, but without a doubt we shall have to surmount all adverse things to come. There is no choice. The alternative to an Arab victory would be slaughter or the waters of the Mediterranean for us. The Arabs have land to retreat to, we don't. – – – –

From a daily paper: *January 2, 1948. Britain ignores Arab War Declaration, and insists on its neutrality.* – In reality Britain tried its best to relieve the Jews of their defensive weapons while they did not seriously interfere with the Arab aggressors when they brazenly looted government and army arms stores.

Same newspaper, same day: *USA wants to move its citizens out of Palestine.*

The situation was growing more ominous by the day. Syrian and Lebanese forces in the north were reinforced by Fauzi el Kaukji's army of irregulars, as well as by Palestinian villagers who co-operated as partisans under their sheiks. A 10,000-man Iraqi army joined Jordan's Arab Legion in the east, and in Jerusalem the Mufti[38], who had worked hand in glove with Hitler and organized Moslem troops from Bosnia Herzogovina against the Allies, declared a "jihad" or holy war against the Jews. Egypt had its armies, tanks, and the only real air force in the region poised at the Sinai-Negev border, ready to strike at a newly founded Jewish state.

A month later I moved from Kfar Hess to the village of Tel Mond where I rented a room from an elderly couple. Until then I had been hired to work only occasionally by the district's labor exchange. Now I was a registered member of the local work force. Wages were low, but work was relatively steady. Living here meant I could eat a warm dinner at Dror. The cost was 15 piasters, a somewhat high price, but I had no intention of joining the community again just for the sake of a warm meal in the evening.

---

[38] A Moslem official.

The Arab Lobby agitated against the partition of Palestine at the United Nations in New York, threatening war. Its member states had standing armies and a pool of 40,000.000 people to draw soldiers from against 650,000 Jews - men, women and children. We needed a miracle right out of the Bible to survive what the enemy had arrayed against us. A Jewish army was in the making, and I wanted to be part of it. I went to the head of the Hagana in our region, a sergeant in the border police, and told him of my wish to join the Jewish army. He said: "O.K. You are in the army from now on."

This strange declaration I did not question for a while. When three weeks later I received the same answer to the same request, I decided to act on my own. The following day I went to Tel Aviv where, I had heard, people were officially accepted into the as yet nonexistent Israeli Defense Force. At the end of March 1948, I volunteered in the basement of a school building on Rothschild Boulevard and was ordered to report to the induction center Kiryat Me'ir in Tel Aviv on April 5.

Back at Tel Mond I informed the sergeant of my step to which he commented: "You can't do that. You're in the army here."

"No," I said, "I haven't signed any papers with you, and on April 5 I'll be at Kiryat Me'ir."

On April 2, I moved from Tel Mond to Kfar Saba to stay with the relatives for the few days I had left before reporting to the army. I wanted to store part of my belongings in their house, but having lived for years without roots and carried my possessions with me at all times, it was difficult to decide what to leave behind and what to take with me. Every item I owned seemed indispensable for the life ahead, and in this frame of mind I eventually took most of my stuff with me on the morning I left. Two hours later I was sorry I had done so.

In the Army Again - Israel Defense Force

April 5, 1948, at 9 A.M. found suitcase, kit bag, and me in Kiryat Me'ir waiting to start army life anew. Of the many recruits on the camp's big square one could easily pick out the fellows who had left a real home. They had a little valise or handbag with them while the others, who had lived my way of life − and there were many − carried my kind of baggage. To have my hands free for the travel gear, I had worn my trench coat from the bus to the camp, but now, with the sun burning down on us, I had taken it off. By then it was superfluous ballast.

Waiting seemed the main reason for being in Kiryat Me'ir. Time meant nothing. To ignore the heat and pass the time I sat on my kit bag and wrote in my diary about the heat, the big square of the recruiting camp that lacked even the smallest spot of shade, and my observations of the many volunteers around me. Eventually we were assigned a place in a tent, which made the situation bearable.

Two days later a group of us was moved to Sarona, a short distance from Kiryat Me'ir, and here I met fellows I had served with in the British army. I belonged then to Chail Hatechna'im, later renamed Chail Chimush, Ordnance Corps, the technical branch of the army. My army number was 12531, and I belonged to Bet-Mem-Bet 681, the acronym of *Batei Mlacha Basisim* (Base Workshops 681).

Trucks drove us every morning to the premises of the Ta'arucha, (initially, International Fair Grounds) past the end of Ben Yehuda Street. The exhibition halls had been turned into workshops. On April 22 we transferred to camp Ben Ami, a large plot of sandy ground in northern Tel Aviv (today a premium real estate area) but continued to work at the Ta'arucha.

Before most of the above took place, however, I sought a change in my army life, disregarding once more the meaningful advice of the two Englishmen in Kurdani: never volunteer for anything. After four days at work, and feeling dissatisfied with my contribution to the war effort I requested from the commanding officer of our company – who happened to be my ex-sergeant major from the British army, Shimshon – a transfer to the armored car convoys going up to Jerusalem. Perhaps luckily for me, he refused[39]. He even gave me a short, angry dressing down. I had agreed to the assigned work, and that is what I was going to do. He would not turn our place into a transit camp.

Disappointed at Shimshon's decision, and quite unaware of what could happen even in a "safe" place like ours, I found it necessary to unburden my frustration in my diary. Trying to explain my position, if not to another person, then at least to blank pages, I wrote:

I had intended to chronicle army life from day one, but because things did not develop in the way I had imagined, I never did. Life in camp and at the workshop is too uneventful to warrant precise recordings, and I have little hope that things will change. To repair army vehicles in the hinterland seems to be too peaceful an occupation for the times we live in. But I am not looking for trouble. I do not seek a mental "high" in a military engagement that may get me killed or maimed. I do not want to die, and I dread getting crippled or disabled as much as ever.

---

[39]Many of those slow-moving vehicles on the steep road to Jerusalem fell victim and burned under the Arab fire directed at them from the hills flanking this vital lifeline to the capital. Many drivers and people escorting them lost their lives in those attacks. – Some of the vehicles can be seen beside the road. They were left there to remind people of the fallen.

If, in spite of my fears, I volunteered for the rather dangerous job of driving up to Jerusalem, it was not boredom that made me ask for the transfer. The reason can rather be found in that intoxicating feeling of being part of that momentous occasion, the creation of a Jewish state.

Some groups of Chail Hatechna'im are stationed well within danger areas — places that may become front lines in the near future. The two bases nearest to us are Chulda, on the way to Jerusalem, and Nir Am, a kibbutz at the beginning of the Negev. Nir Am is an important station. Army vehicles, armored cars and all materiel necessary for the war effort in this southern part of the country are repaired there. After my commander's outburst, however, I won't even try to ask for a transfer. Clearly every officer in charge of a base like ours needs to have as many men under his command as possible.

I fail to recollect, nor do I have a note to remind me when things started to change from the busy life we had lived until then to the hectic activities that followed. It must have happened shortly before May 15, 1948, the day the State of Israel came into being. Suddenly we had much-used American trucks of World War II vintage needing overhauls in our workshops, as well as several half-tracks[40] whose bodies, engines, and movable parts seemed rusted into an almost solid state. Those half-tracks had to be taken apart, piece by piece, almost down to the last bolt and nut. They had to be cleaned, repaired, parts replaced, oiled, and reassembled to be useful for their purpose. When those fighting vehicles were ready and being tried out in the streets of northern Tel Aviv near the Ta'arucha, people stopped and gazed elated at them. Some applauded enthusiastically. It was so reassuring to see "new" weapons.

From then on we worked to exhaustion. Reveille was at 5:30 A.M. our job officially was over by 5:30 P.M. When tasks required completion, work hours were extended to 7:30 or 9:30 P.M. It was also taken for granted that when additional means of transportation were needed for military actions, and we had unfinished vehicles in our workshops, we continued to work until 6 A.M. next morning. After that many hours of toil, interrupted only by four half-hour breaks for rest and food, we had to sleep. Twice a month we enjoyed a day off, otherwise we worked also on Saturdays and holidays. Shimshon declared: "Fellows spill their blood on the battle field, you are going to spill yours here." His prophecy

---

[40] An armored fighting vehicle without top cover. It had wheels in front and caterpillar tracks in the rear. Trucks and half-tracks of World War II, parked in open areas and exposed to the elements had been bought and shipped from Europe. Useless relics until then, they became an essential addition to Israel's fledgling army after overhaul.

almost came true. Demanding from us our last drop of strength, he worked furiously himself.

When May 15, 1948 dawned, and the last British had left the country, and Jews, after a 2,000-year wait had their own state again. As on preceding mornings the annoying sound of the wake-up call penetrated the flimsy walls of the tent to arouse me. My eyelids rose slightly only to close again. Sleep was gone, but at least I wanted to relax for a few more minutes. It was Saturday, the day of the week that used to be a day of rest, and I felt so tired.

The scare almost threw me out of bed. Two heavy explosions nearby and the distinct sound of aircraft engines had me wide-awake in a second. I was still too shocked by what had occurred to tell if the plane or planes I heard were climbing away from us or coming down to unload more deadly cargo.

It was the dawn of the first day in the new State of Israel.

Until then the only danger had come from Palestinian Arabs. In acts of terror they had ambushed Jewish vehicular traffic on highways or driving through Arab villages or cities. They had killed drivers and passengers. They had attacked Jewish settlements, and carried out random murders. Our workshop base was hardly the place where any of this was likely to happen. I had considered the danger of enemy air power but not expected an Egyptian air strike on the first day of conflict in an undeclared war[41]. A naive assumption considering past historic events[42].

But attack they did. The area of the torn-up land that was to be Israel appeared indefensible and the weaponry of the new-founded state inadequate. Each of the surrounding countries wanted a piece of this easily available pie.

And it was just the beginning.

Egyptian Spitfires reached Tel Aviv daily. They flew over the city in what seemed an almost leisurely manner, and then dove to rid themselves of their lethal cargo. To add to the terror, they sometimes strafed streets with machine-gun fire. We had no anti-aircraft equipment, and Israel's

---

[41] The nearest Arab state with a recognizable air force was Egypt. Also on the same morning the Egyptian, Jordanian, Iraqi, Syrian, and Lebanese armies penetrated the border of what had been Palestine. The Arab League stated that Syrian and Iraqi aircraft bombed Jewish communications and cities in northern Palestine.

[42] I was still in Vienna when German planes, without declaration of war, launched a surprise attack on Poland in 1939 and the USSR in 1941. Japan's imperial air force struck Pearl Harbor in the same year; also without warning.

"air force," consisting of a few Piper planes, was no match for the enemy's fighter aircraft. Frustrated by the inability to counter the attacks, fellows on the base and at the workshops fired their rifles at the enemy planes in futile attempts to bring them down. The Egyptians came at any hour of the day, clearly unafraid of the defense we could put up.

Sometimes air raids went on for days, interrupted only by short "all clear" lulls. As the Egyptians did not always show up, our commanding officer found a way to handle the situation. When sirens urged Tel Avivians to take shelter, the air-raid alarm was not for us. Shimshon stationed a soldier on a roof to act as a lookout for enemy aircraft. Only when the man sighted planes, was he permitted to activate a hand-cranked siren, and so we never had enough time to reach the open trenches we had dug for our protection.

Actually our area was a tempting target. The eastern corner of our workshop was close to the harbor. To the north of us, a short distance away and across the narrow Yarkon River, lay the large Reading Power Station.

Then came the first *hafugah* (cease-fire) in June 1948 and everyone breathed a sigh of relief. When the war started again a month later things had changed in our favor. Weapons bought in Europe had arrived, and we, as well as other locations in the city, had machine guns atop buildings. Ours, placed on the flat roof of a workshop, was handled by Shimshon personally when enemy planes appeared.

With machine guns in the city, the Egyptians changed their tactics. Spitfires still came to bomb, yet they flew high, making the machine gun defense ineffectual. Their dives had become less frequent, but an additional menace had been added to their visits – twin-engine bombers. They, like the fighter aircraft, found safety in height which resulted in indiscriminate bombings of the city. When Spitfires dove, one knew more or less where bombs would fall. When they released their loads at high altitudes, it was uncertain where calamity would strike. The only indication of an arriving bomb was a dull swish of air seconds before impact.

In addition to flying high, the enemy approached the coast in the afternoon when the setting sun in the west blinded Jewish defenses. Enemy aircraft also made their visits as short as possible. They came over the city, dropped their bombs, and immediately circled south and east which took them back over the Mediterranean Sea and away from the potential dangers of the land.

At one time the deferred air-raid alarm could have had serious consequences. The alert had been given in Tel Aviv and, adhering to our commander's standing order, we continued to work. A Hungarian fellow and I were taking air out of the brakes of a half-track when suddenly the wail of our own siren indicated the approach of the enemy. The warning had come especially late this time, for an Egyptian Spitfire was not just close to the coast or cruising at high altitude, but diving in our general direction.

I grabbed my steel helmet, and hopping off the vehicle, sprinted toward the nearest trench. My response, taking less than 15 seconds, had gone as smoothly as if I had practiced the moves beforehand. In that short time it took me to move, however, the plane had advanced considerably toward the ground, bringing back for a crazy moment the memory of the spiraling Spitfire in Haifa. Had there been a reason to fear for my life then, how much more so at this very moment! Don't drop your bomb yet, don't use your machine gun, my thoughts implored the pilot of the Spitfire as I rushed across an open space to reach the trench.

Desperate for safety, I was stunned to find the narrow confine of the trench filled with squatting soldiers. Having worked close to the shelter at the time of the alarm they had reached it before me. An instant later I saw a small opening between two men, and earnestly considered diving into the dugout headfirst. It seemed so much faster than jumping. But jump I did.

During those moves, and in spite of my anxiety, I was aware of the encouraging sound of our machine gun in action. As it turned out, Shimshon had gone to the roof right after the alert in the city, and started firing at the descending enemy almost simultaneously with our belated alarm. I admired the man who, exposed on the open roof to the peril of the advancing Spitfire, never stopped firing even for a second. Disappointingly, though, without success.

In the trench I crouched opposite a fellow who had come to our country from Iraq. We looked at each other in worried anticipation, and shook our heads, as the Egyptian plane seemed to hurtle straight toward our refuge. A few seconds later and for the same amount of time, a ffffft sound was heard followed by a deafening explosion that made us cringe even more. The walls of our trench shook, and appeared on the brink of collapse. Then there was silence. Or rather it just seemed so. Our machine gun was still in action, yet, with the frightening scream of the diving plane gone, the relief I felt made the moment almost tranquil.

I had not heard the plane depart, but assuming that it had done so, I dared to peek over the rim of our shelter. The western part of our workshop base was hidden behind a wall of dust, but the damage was not within our perimeter. A factory building, perhaps a 100 feet beyond our border, had been hit. We had been just plain lucky that the Egyptians seemed to store mostly 50 and 100 kg. [220 lbs.] bombs. They must have had a shortage of the 500 kg ones, for they rarely used them.

We had one light casualty that could have been avoided. With unforgivable stupidity one fellow walked about instead of seeking shelter or laying flat on the ground when the diving spitfire had us scrambling for cover. He was hit by a piece of flying steel yet, fortunately, only slightly wounded.

Moslem states, other than those of the Arab League, sent volunteers to fight against the Jews in Palestine. Pakistani men were sent in groups to reinforce the invading Arab armies.

To supply beleaguered Jewish Jerusalem with food and weapons and avoid the original, dangerous main road to the capital, Jewish engineers and infantrymen built a narrow alternate way through the hills of Judea. Appropriately named "Burma Road," it more or less paralleled the main road in the Arab Legion's hands, and remained undetected by the enemy.

A dramatic affair with potentially disastrous consequences shocked the Jewish population: the incident of the SS Altalena on June 20, 1948. The vessel loaded with weapons and munitions had attempted to land near Kfar Vitkin. Purchased with money from Jewish-American supporters of the IZL (Irgun Zvai Leumi) the ship's hold contained much-needed arms. Ben Gurion insisted that the ship's cargo had to go to the Israeli army, but Begin, the leader of the IZL, refused. When Irgunists tried to unload the contents of the boat, Ben Gurion, worried about a forced right-wing take-over of the country and the threat of civil war, ordered the Hagana to fire on the men of the IZL. Several members of the IZL were killed. During the night the Altalena moved south to Tel Aviv where she was beached not far from the shore. Again refusing to surrender to the Israeli government, she was fired upon and set ablaze. More of Begin's men were killed.

While this was taking place, we were working temporarily at Arditi's garage on Petach Tikwa Road in Tel Aviv. The garage, a civilian enterprise, assembled new trucks for the Israeli army. Though the burning ship was about a mile from the shop and the houses of the city were between us, we saw her smoke in the sky. Shocked by the developments, we also learned that members of the IZL had taken a few men of our company prisoner. Our fellows had refused to fire their rifles at the other men, and talking among ourselves then, we supported our comrades' conduct. We too decided never to fire a weapon at another Jew whatever the consequences. In the end Begin gave in and all his men – most of them already in the Israeli army – became regular soldiers.

How I yearned to see one of those Egyptian planes shot down, and a few days before the second cease-fire (July 17, 1948) went into effect, my wish came true. The enemy continued to bomb Tel Aviv, and to fly high and out of reach leaving us bitterly disappointed about our impotence. His pattern never varied, and with the long days of summer his deadly game kept us too often from getting work done. Yet, depending on the workload, those summer days gave us also a chance to enjoy a little bit of camp life during daylight hours. On the above-mentioned day we had returned to Ben Ami "on time," and as was our habit, most of us went straight to the showers. The noise of aircraft engines chased us from our stimulating bath though, and by the time we arrived outside, the enemy was already dropping his bombs on the built-up area of the city. We returned to the showers only to be alerted by the drone of a single bomber a short while later. As one never knew where bombs of an approaching plane would land we ran outside once more to seek shelter in a trench. By then the aircraft was straight overhead, and as no bombs had fallen, we felt safe. Bombs released by a plane directly overhead hit targets some distance away.

As we stood in the open air, partly clothed and towel-wrapped, the bomber released his load over the buildings of Tel Aviv. Suddenly a small dot appeared near the enemy that we assumed to be his fighter escort. But that little speck acted in a peculiar way. It flew circles around the big aircraft, always coming in from below and behind, and suddenly everybody screamed: "It's ours!" The hunter, like an angry wasp, circled its prey, and soon a flame shot out from underneath the bomber. From that moment on the enemy descended like a glider, the Jewish plane circling above it as if to prevent an escape. Relieved of our fears for our flier's welfare, happiness about this unexpected turn of events made us scream and dance, throwing things into the air, some of which were needed to cover ourselves. Falsely assuming the Egyptian plane would land nearby we started to run in that direction. It set down, however, in the sand dunes near Bat Yam, a little coastal city, just south of Tel Aviv.

During the second cease-fire most of our men and equipment were transferred to Sarafand (Tzrifin). It was the big camp where I had tasted military life for the first time as a recruit in the British Army. I did not mind the move, and felt right at home in the place. The camp, almost a medium-sized city, had a movie theater, a large canteen, and a network of roads that could be walked in the evening for exercise. If one wished to visit a big city, one could easily reach Tel Aviv. The closeness of our living quarters to the workshops in Sarafand eliminated commuting and provided us with a little extra time off after work.

At the end of the day Sarafand's *merkas*, or center, became a promenade for male and female soldiers. Our technical company was only a small part of the garrison of Sarafand, and many other units of different military groups were stationed here as well. It never came as a surprise to recognize a person in the crowd one had not seen in a great while.

Some friends of mine and I were strolling near the center one evening when we saw a stream of people moving in the same direction. In response to our inquiry we were told that Shertok[43] was speaking to the Palmach[44]. We followed out of curiosity and came upon a large circle of young men, sitting several rows deep on the ground. A man standing in the center of the circle spoke to them. The man was Moshe Shertok.

Two points he made I have never forgotten, and I see him clearly in my mind as he said: "You know, the weapons coming to our country are from Czechoslovakia[45] (then communist), but the dollars that bought them came from America." He then intoned: "You will go out tomorrow to fight in the Negev..."

It sounded rhetorical, but perhaps something was in the making.

Shortly before the high holidays (*Rosh Hashana*, Jewish New Year, and *Yom Kippur*, Day of Atonement) we started to work extended hours. We worked on Rosh Hashana, and when Yom Kippur arrived 10 days later, we were told that the chief rabbi of the country had given permission to work on that holiest of the holidays, too. Whoever wanted to fast could fast, but he was not excused from work. As an accommodating gesture, soldiers who fasted were sent to their barracks at noon.

With the exception of a few Jewish settlements in the south, the Egyptian army ruled the Negev. Egypt refused to let Israeli convoys supply those settlements, and after another attempt by trucks to get through the enemy lines and the loss of two vehicles due to Egyptian fire, the Israelis attacked in this sector. By October 18 the Israelis had broken through the Egyptian lines, eliminating and scattering most of the enemy's army. On October 21 the Israelis entered and captured Beersheba.

The Egyptian planes came now after dark. They flew over our camp almost nightly in their effort to strike Ludd airport (today Ben Gurion airport). Their sorties seemed hardly designed to arouse sentimental feelings, and yet the combination of enemy action and the partly solemn, partly joyous occasion of lighting Hanukkah candles on that particular

---

[43] Moshe Shertok, later Moshe Sharett, was, in succession, Israel's Foreign and Prime Minister.

[44] Members of the Palmach had been absorbed into the Israeli army by then.

[45] The rifles we received were made in Czechoslovakia when it was still occupied by the Germans. The rifle barrels were cast with the German eagle holding a swastika in its claws.

evening did just that to me. I wrote:

"Hanukkah, 1948. A mixed group of male and female soldiers has assembled in the recreation hut to celebrate the holiday. No light escapes through the darkened windows of the room into the blackness outside, for we are at war again. Almost every night the soft rumble of high flying enemy planes is heard as they cross over our camp on their way to Ludd airport, a mere three miles away from us. Sounds of explosions reach us, but the enemy's attempt to damage their target seems ineffective. They have not attacked our position, yet their presence above us is troublesome.

When Major Joe Creuden (the American who was also our commander in the British army) spoke to the assembled soldiers that evening, the whine of air-raid sirens, sounding like discordant incidental music, began to accompany his words. The warning signal, barely over, was followed again by the distant sound of enemy planes in the sky. When latecomers continued to arrive, and the illumination of the room escaped through the opened door to the outside, the lights inside the hut were turned off during alarms. The exception was a single candle and the Shamash[46] on the Hanukkah candlestick on the table near Creuden. The major did not interrupt his address. He spoke of the holiday of lights, the Maccabean revolt, and in the faint light of the candles his words were deeply impressive. Two explosions shook the hut, but they seemed to have come from larger sized bombs dropped in the distance. Nobody moved, and our major fell silent for a moment. Then, as if nothing out of the ordinary had transpired, he proceeded with his speech. The room was quiet and Creuden spoke." – – – –

Though Kfar Saba was quite close to the border of the Arab Triangle, one felt relatively safe in the village. Varda, Hanka's niece, worked in the only pharmacy in the village, and on my visits to Kfar Saba I enjoyed picking her up after work and walking her home. When calling on her one day I found a bullet hole in the plate glass window in front of which it was my habit to wait for her. I was told that the single rifle bullet, fired from across the border, had hit the window shortly before my arrival at the spot.

On another of my short leaves to Kfar Saba I hitchhiked from Sarafand to Tel Aviv in the afternoon, and from there caught a ride in a tiny Peugeot north-bound. Beside the officer who drove the car, we were three more soldiers inside the vehicle. We had gone through Petach Tikva and reached the city's edge when two civilian policemen stopped

---

[46] Shamash (Servant). In this case the extra candle with which additional candles during the week of the holiday are lit.

us. We were informed that the Jordanians, their positions a mere 3 to 4 miles to the east of the road, had fired on it with cannons. Had we been civilians we would not have been permitted to continue on our way. Military vehicles, however, could not be refused passage, but had to be warned of the danger. As this highway at the time was the only link between the north and the south of the country, there was little choice. The officer turned to us: "Do we go?" We all agreed we should continue and, putting our steel helmets on our heads, we went on. We were lucky and nothing happened. Perhaps the Jordanians of the Arab Legion were busy by then with a 5 o'clock tea in the company of their British officers.

Hanka's Bad Dream

I pulled second guard duty, the one I disliked most. It was duty from 8 P.M. to 10 P.M. and from 2 A.M. to 4 A.M. As few of us getting off at 10 were sleepy, we'd sit around talking, smoking, and drinking coffee for an hour or two, and when we finally bedded down, we had a scant two or three hours to rest until our next watch came up. This time, however, I did not mind the short time of rest. I had in my pocket a two-day weekend pass, which I wanted to spend relaxing in Kfar Saba. It rained intermittently when I hitchhiked toward my objective the next day, yet the knowledge that a warm house and an agreeable atmosphere awaited me at my journey's end offset the unpleasantness of the weather.

At the Ra'anana-Kfar Saba road crossing I jumped off the military truck and walked the mile and half to Hanka's house. She received me in her friendly manner that this time lacked conviction. Assuming it had to do with her immediate family, I found it best to ignore her mood. I was about to make myself comfortable when she suddenly blurted out: "I had a bad dream about Milek[47]." Her face had taken on the suffering expression of a worried mother, and no doubt, she really felt that way.

"You don't believe in dreams?" I asked incredulously. – "No, but..." – "If you really feel that way why don't you phone Milek's kibbutz?"

She said she had tried but had not gotten through.

I received the distinct feeling that I was the missing link in an awkward request and, figuring that if I hitchhiked to kibbutz Dan right then, I might be able to make it there and back in the 48 hours' leave I had been given from the army.

"I'll go to Dan," I said, "just to prove to you that dreams are just mental images of something one is either afraid of or wishes for, but not warnings of any kind." Her effort to dissuade me from my decision was so transparently insincere that I felt embarrassed. I did not want to blame

---

[47] Varda's brother.

349

her. Her nephew Milek, next to Varda and her own brother Shulko, was so close to her heart that anything else was of secondary importance.

I left the house without even having a cup of coffee, knowing quite well that every minute would count to get me back to Sarafand on time. Israel's highways then were narrow two-lane roads, and kibbutz Dan was nearly a 130 miles north of Kfar Saba. A lot depended on how long I would have to wait between hikes, and on possible mishaps on rain-slick roads.

It was drizzling when I returned to the Ra'anana-Kfar Saba crossing, and it rained on and off while I caught different kinds of transportation on my way to Dan. The Beit Lid junction, Hadera, Afula, through Nazareth to Tiberias on Lake Kinneret (Sea of Galilee), and on to Kiryat Shmone in the far north. Here I caught a civilian pick-up that went to Metulla, the northernmost Israeli settlement on the Lebanese border. But a few miles out of Kiryat Shmone I got off the vehicle, for here began the side road that led to the kibbutzim Dafna and Dan 5 miles away. No vehicle passed me as I walked along the unfamiliar road that led through undeveloped and uncultivated tracts of land. It was pitch dark when I finally reached Dan, just a few miles west of the Syrian border and below the Golan Heights.

In the kibbutz's office I learned that Milek was on night patrol in an armored-vehicle in the mountains along the Lebanese border.

That was bad news for me. I dreaded the thought of confronting Hanka with this kind of report, and especially after not having been able to talk to Milek. Upon my request I was taken to an underground bunker where a girl, the phone and wireless operator, got in touch with a kibbutz west of the main road, the base of the armored vehicle. The answer from there was disappointing. In no way could Milek be reached. We had to wait until he returned from his tour in the morning.

In the kibbutz's dining room I had my first bite to eat since my breakfast in Sarafand this morning, and after the meal requested the office to wake me at 5 A.M. I had to talk to Milek, and then get under way as early as possible. I slept in a pleasant little guestroom that bigger kibbutzim kept for visitors and awakened still tired in the morning.

The girl in the bunker called the armored car base again, and we were informed that Milek was safely asleep in their kibbutz. I had hoped to talk to my cousin, but under the circumstances I had to be satisfied with the outcome of my effort. If I wanted to return to my unit on time I just could not wait for him until he woke up. With Milek unharmed I could at least prove to Hanka that her dreams were just dreams.

I caught a truck loaded with milk cans from Dan to Rosh Pina and then another open truck filled with cows to be delivered to Haifa. There were about a dozen hitchhikers of mixed company aboard, and every time the driver braked the vehicle, animals and people were thrown forward. It felt so absurdly comical that we all had to laugh. Most of the way it rained, and long before we reached Haifa, men and beasts alike were soaked. Once a mishap of a more serious consequence interrupted our travel. On a curve taken at too high a speed the truck slid off the road and got stuck in the mud. All of us got off and with the engine racing we pushed the vehicle back onto the road. Very tired I reached Kfar Saba, told Hanka what I knew, then walked back to the highway to look for a ride to Sarafand.

Even while still living in Kfar Hess I liked to drop in on the relatives in Kfar Saba. Their house gave me the feeling of home, an experience I sorely missed. Later, when food items were rationed during the War of Independence, and I did not want my visits to be a burden on their household, I helped out with provisions from the military canteen.

A 10-day "rest vacation" in Jerusalem for some men of our company came as a surprise. When several fellows and I arrived at the designated building in the city, we found that 250 soldiers had been mistakenly invited instead of 150. Adding to the discomfort of six to a room, it rained for eight days, and a cold spell that rivaled Europe's winter had taken hold of Jerusalem. Water, still in short supply at the time, was shut off at 8 A.M. Whoever was late in the morning had to scoop water from a large, not too clean barrel to finish his wash and shave. Because of the disagreeable circumstances we reluctantly accepted our stay here as a rest period, but not a vacation.

In early spring of 1949 our workshops received 41 brand new Jeeps that had to be examined and, if necessary, adjusted and repaired prior to their transfer to military units. Before releasing them, however, a little project was undertaken for the benefit of a kibbutz in the *Emek Beit Sha'an*, the Beisan Valley. It was like a holiday trip when jeeps and a bus, loaded with the musicians of our company's orchestra, left the camp one early morning. The captain in charge was Shmuel, the commanding officer of my workshop. I had been with Shmuel for four years in the British Army and was, as with several other officers, on a first-name basis with him.

Whenever a lengthy army convoy traveled the roads of the country, the population proudly watched it. It was the affection of a people who had been subject to ridicule and worse in many countries for the past two millennia. The strength of the armed forces gave them the self-confidence they had so sorely lacked in past centuries. But the purpose of our convoy surely was misjudged if viewers interpreted our mission as anything but peaceful. Onlookers could not see that the four men in each vehicle had only one rifle between them. The official reason for our trip was to test the jeeps' performance and give a concert in one of the kibbutzim on the way. Most likely only a few men of rank in our group knew the second and perhaps the real reason behind our excursion.

Army convoys travel relatively slow and we reached kibbutz Afikim in the Jordan Valley in the late afternoon.

I remembered a visit to Afikim with a friend some years back while we were soldiers in the British army. We did not see much of the settlement then, except their rather noted dining room, but now we were taken on a get-acquainted tour of the kibbutz. Following the walk, most of Afikim's members who were off work or could get away from their tasks assembled on a big lawn to listen to our band perform popular and Israeli country songs. After a late dinner in the dining room we expected to end the day in some sleeping facility of the kibbutz. To our surprise we were told not to get comfortable; we were to move again.

At about 11 P.M. we mounted the Jeeps and leaving Afikim our convoy traveled slowly south toward the religious kibbutz of Tirat Tzvi, the last Jewish community in this corner of Israel.

Flanked by Jordan in the east and the prewar territory of Palestine[48] in the south, the kibbutz had been the target of Arab bands' forays even before the birth of Israel. Since the creation of the state and the outbreak of war, it had successfully withstood repeated attacks by Arab armies and irregular Arab forces. And they still were having trouble on their border.

In a string of lights that must have gotten the attention of Jordanian legionnaires and other Arabs across the border, our convoy snaked its way over slightly elevated terrain toward its objective. Without incident we arrived at Tirat Tzvi, apparently expected. A man at the entrance held the gate ajar while we drove into the settlement. With headlights on and engines running our convoy stopped. Leaving our vehicles we milled about in the lights that illuminated the Jeeps and us, and then lights and motors were shut off. We sat half an hour in our cars in silence when the orders came to start engines again, but to leave the headlights turned off. We left Tirat Tzvi at a leisurely pace driving slowly on the dark road. At a safe distance from the kibbutz headlights were turned on again, and driving became less hazardous.

The purpose of the maneuver had been to trick the enemy into believing that Tirat Tzvi had received a contingent of soldiers to strengthen its position in this exposed sector of the country. It may seem that the departing noise of the Jeeps should have alerted the enemy to the deception but apparently they believed that only the Jeeps had left

---

[48] Then under Jordanian rule.

while the soldiers had remained. We were later told that our trick had been successful, for Tirat Tzvi had no more trouble with Arabs.

Back in Afikim we spent the night on the floor of a barn and on the next day our convoy returned to our base in Sarafand.

Wadi Giraffi and the Red Sea

"Are you sick?" Shmuel, my commanding officer, inquired when I asked for a month's duty in Wadi Giraffi. His was almost a fair question.

Few soldiers wanted to be stationed in Wadi Giraffi for a month - especially in summer - or were daffy enough to volunteer for the job at any other time. But it was not entirely the fidgets that made me ask for the assignment this time, but rather the hope to see the Red Sea which, I worried, I may never see otherwise. Duty in Wadi Giraffi, however, guaranteed no visit to the Gulf of Aqaba (Eilat), as one northern end of the Red Sea was called, and to volunteer for this reason was just taking a fool's gamble. A month in a desolate place with heat of up to 115 degrees Fahrenheit was not to everybody's taste.

On Wednesday afternoon of August 13, 1949 a few fellows and I were informed that we would replace mechanics stationed in the Negev. We received a 24-hour pass, the time of which I spent in Kfar Saba. 4:40 A.M. Friday found five of us traveling south in a command car. It was still dark and the wind sweeping over the uncovered vehicle made us shiver with cold. The rising sun a while later provided relief. We passed stretches of terrain where bitter fighting had taken place during the War of Independence, but except for staked out areas along the road displaying warning signs: Danger – Mines, little else pointed to the armed conflict. For a moment I caught sight on my left of the Iraq Suidan police station, the Teggart fortress the Egyptian army had so fiercely defended before Israeli soldiers took it.

At 8 A.M. we breakfasted in a military camp, and under way once more, we reached Beersheba a short time later. I wanted to pinch myself to make certain that I really was in Beersheba. Not that there was much to see, but the name had been made famous for me by the daily column "From Dan to Beersheba" in the Palestine Post. We passed a mosque and a Teggart police station at the edge of town, and rode down a short road flanked by low, yellowish, white houses. We were through the dusty, little place before I had taken 10 puffs on my cigarette.

Most Arabs had long left the town, and about 70 Jewish families had found a home here. Even a café and an outdoor movie theater had opened their doors; their customers being mostly army personnel.

As we left Beersheba, we were stopped by military police. With the exception of Bedouins who lived in the Negev and two kibbutzim about

20 miles south of Beersheba, civilians were not permitted beyond this point. Even military personnel needed a special permit to pass the check post. The necessary papers were obtained at the military governor's office that had jurisdiction over the area. He had been informed of our arrival. We filled the gas tank of the car and two Jerry-cans with gasoline and checked the canister of drinking water for its contents, for the next military post would be 90 kilometers (55 miles) away.

The weather had turned warm and promised to become hot long before we were half way to our objective. We passed the check post and traveled south over a highway that used to lead to Egypt before the war. It was a good road and we progressed swiftly. In the distance to our left a range of sharp-pointed mountains stretched south, and to our right wavy contours of rock desert rolled along and away from the route we traveled. We were looking for a road off to the left, and one appeared after 25 kilometers. A wooden sign just above ground proclaimed *Sdom*, Sodom, in Hebrew letters. It seemed the wrong turn off and we continued straight on. Half an hour later we stopped again.

We had found no other turns, had seen no other vehicle, nor met a human being we could have asked for directions. Considering our options we returned to the first turn-off. By that time an almost forgotten conversation came to my mind. Quite a while back a friend had told me: the sign of an arrow and palm tree pointed the way south.

Back at the junction we turned off the highway and a little further on I saw a sign none of us had paid attention to. On a small wooden board low over the ground was a primitively painted palm tree and arrow. That's the right way, I declared, repeating my friend's information. The sergeant, apparently having received no specific instruction at our camp, agreed.

The way was a rock strewn, pot-holed dirt track. The command car jumped and hopped like a bucking mule while we got thrown about if we loosened our grip on something solid. At first we could not help but laugh at the comical expressions each of us made when thrown into the air and landing painfully back on the wooden benches, but after a while the fun went out of the acrobatics. Luckily, the way improved occasionally. After an especially bad passage we sarcastically congratulated ourselves of having just another six hours or more of driving ahead of us before reaching Wadi Giraffi.

We moved in a southeasterly direction. The mountains came closer, and the region got wilder. Rocks and more rocks, hills everywhere. We had not met a living soul yet and we might just as well have traveled on the moon. Before we entered the mountainous region, the sergeant told us to load our rifles. The area was not particularly dangerous, and though

Bedouins roaming the Negev were supposedly peaceful, we did not know what other kind of Arabs we might meet.

After three hours out of Beer Sheba nothing like civilization had been sighted. The only living things we met were camels that seemed to freely be roaming. Occasional arrow and palm tree markings confirmed that we were on course. Later we met a very old Arab with a child, at another time a group of Bedouins with a herd of about 30 camels.

A short while after the encounter with the Bedouins we found three big army trucks, two of which were stuck in sand. We had driven over small areas of sand without a problem, not being aware that it was a thin layer of sand blown onto solid ground. If one left the road, which was easily done, as there was no real track, one could get stuck in loose sand that worked like quicksand. I did not know how deep a vehicle could sink but, as we had seen, it was easy enough to get mired.

We pulled one of the trucks from the sand but failed to extract the other one. We promised the soldiers to inform the next army station, which was still almost two hours away, of their plight.

An hour later we were atop the notorious *Ma'ale Aqrabim* (Scorpion Hill) where the biblical Samson slew his enemies with the jawbone of an ass. A narrow serpentine dirt road descended 300 meters (1,000 feet) down a steep incline. The turns of the road were so narrow and sharp, that trucks could not navigate them without backing up at least once. Peering down the mountain, especially seeing rolls of barbed wires strewn down its side, we were awed. A few days ago a truck had plunged to its doom, but the roadway had been cleared of obstacles in the meantime.

The bird's-eye view of the enormous valley below us was spellbinding. Far to the east the sharply pointed, gray mountains of Jordan hemmed the region that again brought the picture of a moonscape to mind. The contours of the depression, however, were not the pale yellow of the moon but rather colored like pastel tints. An impressive and beautiful panorama in spite of its ghost-like appearance.

The bottom of the mountain was reached without trouble, and half an hour later the green vegetation of the oasis Ein Chusub soothed our eyes. This station, if only miniature in size, was the only military canteen between Beer Sheba and the Red Sea, still 120 kilometers (80 miles) away. We reported the troubled trucks to the officer in charge, and then had lunch with provisions brought along. Warm beer, bought at the canteen, supplemented our meal.

Beyond Ein Chusub parts of the way seemed worse than what we had encountered until then. Up, down, and around hills, through wadis (dry waterbeds) of different sizes the command car rumbled. Passing the well at Bir Menucha we headed down into low country, the wide rift of the Arava, the valley between Israel and Jordan. On we went until finally we came upon a primitive sign that directed us off the road we had traveled, toward Wadi Giraffi. At four in the afternoon the car climbed over a steep hill and behind it our destination spread out before us.

The mechanics to be relieved expressed their happiness at our arrival by yelling and hopping about as if they had ants in their pants. When they quieted down, they were full of questions. After the excitement I viewed the location that was to be home for the next month.

Wadi Giraffi is a wide and extended depression in the southern mountains of the Negev. One narrow finger of the wadi, stretching south, ends at a water well named Bir Malicha. The Egyptian border is 10 miles to the west, and the Red Sea about 20 miles south of the well. But distances measured in miles had little meaning when it came to travel through this kind of terrain. Uncharted ways leading up and down rocky rises often seemed impassable.

The living quarters for the twelve of us, soldiers and NCOs alike, were two tents. A third tent stored auto parts. A staked out area, roofed by thin fabric, was the repair shop. The cover kept the sun away but little else. Our motor pool consisted of a command car, two trucks and one tow truck.

Because of the heat, especially after midday, we worked from 9 to 12 in the morning and from 3:30 to 6 in the afternoon. The great amount of free time was spent reading, writing, playing chess or cards, or kicking a ball around after the heat had abated. A noisy generator atop a grounded pickup truck produced electricity for our needs in the garage while car batteries illuminated our tents in the evening. A number of spare batteries were kept for the use of army vehicles traveling the Negev.

A few hundred feet away from our tents were two small units of other army branches. Once or twice a day a small plane set down on a short landing strip, the wadi's surface cleared of rocks. I never tried to find out the aircraft's purpose; it always landed during our working hours. Because of the plane's loud engine we named it in jest "primus," after the noisy, open flame pressure stove that was used in every household in the Middle East at the time.

Two connected tents without walls were the mess-room for soldiers of all units, and as no military protocol was observed, all ranks ate under the same roof. A can of orange juice at lunch improved the rather monotonous food, and twice a week a ration of bread, instead of the usual zwieback, was a welcome change in our diet.

Conditions were actually better than we expected. Drinking water came from a distant well and was not rationed. We even had a shower. A pipe connected two large oil barrels on a small hill to a stall down below that contained the shower. The water smelled slightly of sulfur and was used for bathing and laundry only. It came from Bir Malicha. The water was exposed to the burning sun during the day and could only be used later in the evening when it had cooled down.

Once a week an outfit with a movie projector came to the wadi. It apparently also visited other army posts in the mountains, places I had been unaware of.

The wilds of the Negev had their beauty but I missed the pleasing greenness of the north. The flora of the south, an occasional tree or bush, was as gray as the surroundings in which it grew. At close range they turned out to be a prickly vegetation with needles for leaves. Animals were rare. Occasionally a gazelle or a small group of them would speed across the landscape, flocks of beige colored birds – looking like quails – congregated near a small oasis, and lonely vultures circled the sky. Flies were in the air and bugs crawled along the ground. Happily, we had no mosquitoes. The Negev harbors poisonous snakes and scorpions though we did not encounter any of those creatures. I killed a rather disgusting, spider-like insect the size of a man's fist in our tent, but opinions as to whether it was poisonous differed. It's called Akrabut – I have no term for it in German or English – and should not be mistaken for *Akrab*, which is scorpion in Hebrew.

In the hot, dry air occasional small whirlwinds, carrying sand with them, danced over the landscape. A surprise visit by one of those miniature twisters to our kitchen or the mess-tent during mealtime was of disgusting consequence. The food became "peppered" with sand, a condition reminiscent to me of my early days in Kurdani. On the other hand, the heat had its advantages. Our wash dried in minutes.

In the course of time soldiers stationed in the valley came to visit. One steady caller was the transportation officer. He was as portly as a barrel, deeply tanned, and always dressed the same way: shorts and sandals. The man was very friendly and greeted other soldiers with a slap to the shoulder that gave the impression he wanted to smash them to the ground.

A *gingi*, a red head, who did not belong with our group but nonetheless spent all his free time in our open-air repair shop, worked hard at any job handed him. He wanted to learn the trade and was permitted to drive a truck for a little while each day for his effort. For entertainment, actually more for his own sake than ours, he tirelessly belted out Russian songs in a stentorian voice all day long.

An officer, whose job was unclear to me, rushed into our place every few days and insisted that his life depended on our keeping his Jeep in perfect condition. He was probably right. He was called *Shoded*, which means bandit or robber in Hebrew, but his nickname derived from his outward appearance and his unexpected comings and goings. His bearded face was shaded by a wide-brimmed Australian hat, his shirt and pants were the perfection of sloppiness, and his boots seemed not to have tasted shoe cream since the capture of the Negev. A revolver stuck in a holster from his belt. At first I thought he was called Shoded behind his back but, mild mannered, he answered to the nickname.

The first week passed quickly. The newcomers were promised a sightseeing tour to the Red Sea, but our departure was always postponed because of work. Then a radio message ordered several mechanics to the Gulf of Eilat. On an outing to the mountains near Ras en Nakeb, an undefined border with Egypt, an open Israeli army truck filled with soldiers had missed a turn in the road and driven over a high cliff. Some male and female passengers had lost their lives, others were badly hurt. The victims had been taken away, and our job was to disassemble the wrecked truck in the canyon.

At 11:30 on the following morning an officer in a Jeep who was to take us to the gulf picked up a corporal, another soldier and me. Trailing us was our tow-truck. Beyond Bir Malicha our trip became wretched. There was almost no sign on the ground that other vehicles had traveled here before us, and only after our car had surmounted an elevation of almost 2,000 feet and descended into the Arava rift did the way improve.

An hour later, beyond a spot called Girandal (the name of a place in the middle of nowhere as far as I know) we stopped for lunch. We also had to wait for the tow-truck that, because of the terrain, drove much slower than we did. Far behind, on the way we had come, a tall, mobile dust column announced its progress.

When the truck arrived, the Yemenite driver and his companion, a young man from Benghazi, Libya, exited the cabin in different moods. The Yemenite could not stop laughing as he told how his partner had closed his eyes and had held on to his seat every time the truck waggled and shook when it hit a hole or rumbled over a rock. The Libyan angrily countered: "He is crazy. He tried to keep up with you and drove like a maniac." The way over the mountain range was really bad, and the tow-truck's heavy springs hardly provided a soft ride.

Our lunch took nearly an hour as we boiled tea over a low gasoline fire.

Before we reached the gulf at 4:30 P.M., we passed two green spots where a few palm trees grew. To embellish the encounter I scribbled in my notes: Two oases seen.

Eilat, previously Um Rashrash, consisted in 1949 of five tiny mud houses deserted by Arab fishermen and a few scattered army tents. The Transjordanian border was three miles to the east, Egypt a scant five miles to the south, and Saudi Arabia only 15 miles across the water. Not many isolated outposts could be closer to three enemies than this spot was. Five miles across the water from Eilat is the little Jordanian harbor city of Aqaba. A British warship, anchored just outside its port, made me wonder if it was there to guard the Arabs or us.

We placed our personal gear in a tent, and as it was too late to start work, we snooped around the neighborhood. A few steps over a sandy beach took me to the water's edge. The Red Sea. It was no different from any other large body of water I had seen, and yet, romantic that I am, I was as impressed by it as I had been when I first entered Beersheba. The famous water conjured up the Exodus story of Passover. It brought to my mind the worries I had felt as a kid when the Israelites were chased by the armies of Pharaoh and the relief that came with the destruction of evil king's soldiers in the waters of the Red Sea.

As I stood at this lonely stretch of desert along the water, the time of the Exodus was as remote as the thought that this spot was destined to become a large city and a celebrated tourist attraction?

The heat of the day had hardly abated on this late afternoon and even the closeness of the water brought no relief. I stretched out in the sand and closed my eyes. The world beyond my lids became as unreal as a dream, leaving my mind floating in a void bare of thoughts. When I opened my eyes it was early evening. The southernmost tip of Israel had somewhat cooled off while I had slept and it took me a few moments to adjust to my surroundings. I gazed across the water at the tall, rugged mountains of Jordan that, with the approaching evening, had lost their ugly brown and gray. The sinking sun painted the rocky range a vivid red that changed in the ensuing minutes into a symphony of colors. Hues of ever darker crimson became purple and finally black, making sky and mountains a single entity. A short while later sparkling stars dotted the heavens like glow-worms, and mountains and sky were again two separate creations. In the distance the lights of the British ship twinkled over the water.

On the following morning and during the next few days we traveled to the place of the accident, climbed down into the valley, and dismantled the truck. The individual parts were pulled to the top by the long steel cable of the winch on our tow truck. Loaded onto another vehicle for transportation to the north, they would be delivered to workshops for repair and reassembly.

While still in Eilat, I liked to spend time after work on that long stretch of beautiful beach. I was mostly a lone individual who lay in the sand or swam near the shore. The fish in the water seemed unafraid of me, and I could see multitudes of seahorses clinging to miniature trees of coral with their tails.

After less than a week at our job we were recalled to Wadi Giraffi. On the Saturday before our return from the gulf we drove to Ras en Nageb, high in the mountains of the southern Negev. For all I knew we might have been in Egyptian territory since no sign or post indicated a border. The mountains of Sinai and ours are equally rugged and all look like petrified waves in a storm.

From the top of our mountain and looking into the Sinai peninsular we saw at the distance of a few kilometers a fortified building which we assumed to be an Egyptian police station. Observing the place for a while through binoculars we detected no movement and judged it to be deserted. In this general direction was a site we wanted to visit. It was a deep valley whose walls have layers of differently colored sandstone. This sediment rock was easily ground into sand and, when filled into clear bottles, it could create manifold patterns.

At one spot several of us climbed down the side of the mountain, leaving our rifles with fellows that shied away from the descent. I found the excursion exciting, more for its exploratory aspect than because of the few small rocks I collected at the bottom of the canyon. The pulverized stones eventually ended up in different designs in a small bottle that I gave to Hanka as a gift.

In the side of the cliff we found a small cavity where water, dripping from a crack had hollowed out and filled a small basin. The water was sweet and very cold.

Back in Wadi Giraffi another week passed and on the following Saturday we arranged for a trip to Sodom on the Dead Sea. The chief cook who participated in the journey provided provisions.

Before the first rays of the sun sneaked over the rocky crests to the east, a group of 13 male and two female soldiers were under way. On the previously traveled track we drove north, had breakfast in Ein Chusub, and rumbled on over parched rock-desert dotted here and there by those dusty thistle bushes and withered looking trees. We felt no downward slope of the way, and yet the ground we traveled got imperceptibly lower; the Dead Sea, nearly 400 meters (1,300 feet) below sea level, is the lowest inhabited spot in the world.

We traversed a flat-bottomed wadi, hemmed in by steep walls. The walls' formation clearly displayed signs of levels of water that had been here perhaps millions of years ago. A perfect spot for an ambush. Sitting on both sides of the command car our rifles were trained on the opposite rims of the walls. But we had no trouble.

Once out of the canyon we entered a big valley that, to my surprise, had stretches of green vegetation. It was a true part of the variety and beauty the Negev has to offer.

Less than two hours beyond Ein Chusub we drove through the gate of the salt and potash factory in Sodom. Sodom, at the southernmost point of the Dead Sea, was neither city nor town. It consisted of the factory, the workers' housing settlement, and a small military garrison. Druse, an Israeli-friendly religious sect thought to be of Kurdish, Persian, and Arab lineage, guarded the entrance to the compound. They were soldiers in the Israeli army.

The blistering heat felt almost like a solid substance. In a military canteen we bought cold beer that, temporarily, alleviated the discomfort of the high temperature outside. The most pleasant and interesting event, however, came on an excursion led by a soldier of the local post.

He took us to a natural tunnel leading into a mountain. In places the underground passage became so low we had to bend over to advance. Our goal was a natural chimney of about 60 feet in diameter that opened out at a height of perhaps 200 feet. The strange blue light illuminating this vertical shaft was called the real daylight by the soldier. Wonderful was the coolness of the place.

Four weeks were up and our relief arrived on time. When our command car rumbled north toward civilization again, I contemplated the many new things I had seen and the emotions experienced. Foolish though it might have seemed to others and in spite what my intellect tried to tell me, I still found pleasure in life that was a little unusual, a wee bit adventurous. The short spell in Wadi Giraffi, the miniature sandstorms and the wilds of the Negev were exciting. Titillating the travel over untamed terrain and even the danger that may have lurked near the stretches traversed. And the trip to Sodom and the Dead Sea was an experience I would have been sorry to have missed.

Once up north and all too soon, the vividness of extensive rock deserts, hills and mountains began to fade ever so slightly as time progressed. Impressions lost their power and some seemed again like parts of a dream.

Shortly after my return from the Negev two soldiers and I received permission to take a military truck to Tel Aviv to take the test for a civilian driver's license. I drove the truck; the other two had no military driver's licenses. We passed the test though examiners at times tried to fail candidates by trickery, we were told. A tester might move the rear view mirror and, if the prospective candidate for a license continued to drive without being aware of it, he failed the exam. Another way to flunk one was the order: "Turn right." It would be the wrong way into a one-way street.

In the times we lived it was not unusual to encounter danger in places and situations one would least expect it. An officer's pickup had broken down at his home in Bat Yam, and another soldier and I were sent out in a GMC truck to bring the vehicle back to Sarafand. We found the pickup at the Bat Yam address, and on our return trip my partner, driving the GMC, towed me in the disabled car. On the main highway to Jerusalem, and halfway to our camp, a loud explosion in front of me made me jump in my seat. I hit the brakes of at the same moment; a fortunate reaction. Though the back of the truck ahead of me had disappeared in black smoke, it too had stopped abruptly and rear-ending it could have had serious consequences for me.

Jumping from my car to check what had caused this unexpected blast, I found the air heavy with the smell of burned rubber. The other driver and I met where we believed a tire of his truck had had a blowout, but what we found was unexpected. The American-made GMC had four double sets of wheels in the rear and, on closer inspection, we saw that the four tires on the right side of the truck were half torn away. We also noticed that both rear axles had holes in them and were losing oil. It was obvious that this had not been an ordinary blow-out, and searching the area between and around the tires we found pieces of shrapnel that had come from a Mills hand-grenade which had exploded on the road between the two sets of wheels.

This discovery made me look at my vehicle and I found several shrapnel holes in the hood of my pickup. It was the closest I had come in my life to an exploding hand-grenade. A disturbing feeling.

Someone had carelessly lost this grenade, and we had had the misfortune to drive over it. We were lucky not to be hurt, but had people in a small car driven over this explosive device they may not have been as lucky as we.

Our company had undergone a change in this summer of 1949. "Older" men with a specific length of service in the army were being discharged. Being only 26 years of age, but believing that my four years in the British army would be taken into account, I felt certain that I too was about to become a civilian. I was excited and restless, but my discharge did not take place. It was not envy that made me feel depressed to see so many acquaintances disappear. The young arrivals that replaced them failed to generate the camaraderie that had existed before. Feelings of dejection prompted me to turn to my security blanket: putting thoughts and emotions to paper:

I entered the recreation hut in the late afternoon. It had not been my objective when I had started my stroll, but arriving here may have had to do with my subconscious desire to bring back happy memories of the past. Yet glancing through the room I only felt sadness. How things had changed! What a difference the last few months had brought to the place! Gone were the single candle of the last Hanukah party, the bright illumination of many lamps, the entertaining and funny sketches of our men on the primitive stage, the steady sound of conversations, the rustle of newspapers, and the clicking of games. Now the room was heavy with silence. The feeling that this world of life, sound, and light had existed eons ago and not just a few weeks or months in the past was overwhelming. I advanced into this world of silence and was alone in its solitude. My steps on rubber-soled shoes were inaudible, and I felt like a ghost of times past.

Things were familiar. Hand-drawn cartoons on walls, decorative fir twigs near the ceiling, and isolated flowerpots on windowsills. Decorations that ended at the empty stage. I walked forward and memories began to appear like the flickering lights of a will-o'-the-wisp. I sat down in an easy chair near the piano and my eyes traveled over the room. In each object I saw a period of my army time and an era in the life of our military unit.

The room, bare of humans now, was cold and cheerless. But pictures of past events found form in my mind. More than a year had passed since it all started and so much had happened in the interim. Times had been difficult, especially in the beginning. But looking back I found them beautiful. The hard times had united us, had made us feel that a job had to be done whose proportion we can only perceive today. The formidable undertaking of creating a state was accomplished because we were One.

The hut is empty and I stare after the smoke of my cigarette that curls toward the ceiling. My dreams, like the smoke, fuse with the rays of the sinking sun that comes through the window. As its last golden gleam pierces the settling dusk, my memories flicker and then disappear too.

I get off the chair and wander through the room. I look again at the pictures on the walls, the empty benches, chairs, and tables, and the three locked bookcases containing games, newspapers, and books. They, too, seem to belong to the past. But perhaps not. There has to come a time when this room will again be filled with light, laughter, and life. When others will be here who don't know its past. And perhaps one of the soldiers will be sitting in this very easy chair I had just vacated and wonder: "It would be interesting to know what it looked like in the beginning. Who were the people who started it all?"

And perhaps the walls and corners will answer, and whisper: "Es war einmal..." "*Once upon a time...*" — — — —

Following the patriotic trend of many foreign born I changed my German first name of Gustav to the Hebrew name of Gershon. It brought me closer to the name by which I go today. Born Gustav Ziegler, I was forced with the advent of the Nazis in Austria to call myself Gustav Israel Pimselstein and, by hebrewizing my first name now I became Gershon Pimselstein. The metamorphosis of the name came full circle when, granted American citizenship in later years, I changed our names to Evan. Having gone through so many tribulations since I became Pimselstein and being sentimental about it, I retained the last part of my name, stein (stone) which is evan (pronounced avan) in Hebrew. Even though that my first and last name are Hebrew now, I receive occasionally letters from research companies who, because of the name Evan, want to put together a family tree of my ancestors in Ireland.

In July of 1949 my sister and her husband emigrated from Austria to New York, increasing the distance between us more than threefold. In October of '49 grandma died in New York, and I had hoped so very much to see her again. She was my closest relative next to my sister.

One day a directive transferred most of the soldiers of our unit to workshops in other camps. The few of us who remained, received odd jobs. Several of us were made "policemen" whose job it was to guard our campsite and workshops. The assignment, though not to my taste, enabled me to work occasionally in the city on my days off and earn money. This in turn made it possible for me to realize a wish I had had for years: own a typewriter, and may it only be a small and used one.

Shortly before the end of the year, the remaining soldiers were moved to a new location. The site was a short distance off Beit Dagon Junction, a crossroads half way between Tel Aviv and Sarafand.
In this winter of 1949/50 snow was on the ground not only in Jerusalem but also in the central lowlands of Israel. When almost half a century later this rare precipitation occurred, I happened to be on a visit near Tel Aviv.
On March 13, 1950, I was discharged from the Israeli army.
Growing up in Vienna I had never thought that I would witness and participate in the creation of a Jewish state. My part in that great event may have been small, but it is something that I am proud of.

I could have ended my story right here and written: "Now I was a civilian once more and, at age 27, no longer buffeted by the events of this cruel century. Was allowed to lead a normal life. But normal would have meant a job eight hours a day, leisure on weekends and life in a peaceful environment. Two factors stood in the way of this kind of life. First, the work I chose rarely permitted an eight-hour workday with a weekend at home, and the second element was the very *existence* of Israel, a Jewish State in the Middle East. I had dreamed of adventures, experienced more than my share of them, yet never had they been the kind I had imagined. My life continued to have its adventurous periods, and often lacked peace and quiet. A 30 day service in the army every year was a requirement and in times of trouble duty also called. An even less agreeable scenario would have been an encounter with an enemy from across the border in a non-military capacity.

Shortly after my release from the army, and at the recommendation of Hanka's brother, Shulko, Water Works, a water (later also oil) drilling company in Yasur, hired me. To his question of whether I wanted to work in northern Israel or in the south, I inquired about the difference. "In the south the pay is higher," he said, " but it is more dangerous down there." Short of money, I choose the south.

Being aware that subsequent drill sites would often be along borders and in remote places, I bought a revolver and received a permit from the government to carry the weapon in all of Israel.

At Hanka's insistence I made my home in her house and again kept my personal belongings there. In her two room and kitchen apartment lived, next to herself, Shulko, Varda and her father, Shloime. Actually I was happy with the offer. I had no place to go, and knew, of course, that most of my time would be spent working in places away from Kfar Saba. The same arrangement was extended to Mundek, a nephew of hers, who was a second cousin of mine. As Mundek also began working for Water Works, he too would rarely be home.

To travel south of Beersheba in the early 1950s, civilians were still required to have a valid purpose for passing the army checkpost at the end of town. Furthermore, they also needed a special document to cross this point.

On my first job in the south I drove a command car that was part of a fourteen vehicle convoy. The riders in those conveyances were crew-members of several drilling companies, and though we were a fair number of people, one permit to pass the military post covered all of us. The crew I belonged to consisted of Herr Engelhardt, in charge of the drilling, and whom I addressed in German because he only spoke Polish and German. Then there was Ari, the first assistant, and I, the man Friday of the trio, second assistant, driver, mechanic and executer of a variety of other tasks. We also had two middle-aged guards (newcomers to the country) who carried rifles, but whose fighting skills I seriously doubted.

Our destination, Bir Hindis, an oasis in the geological depression of the Arava, was about 120 road miles south of Beersheba. I drove last in the convoy, for my command car had a problem. The engine leaked oil badly and every so often I had to stop and check its level. If needed I added a quart of oil and then raced on to catch up with the already distant tail end of the convoy. When the road described a half circle, the vehicles of the convoy ahead of me looked like a huge crawling caterpillar blanketed in a cloud of dust.

From our assembly point on Dizengoff Circle in Tel Aviv early in the morning it took us 13 hours to reach our destination. The journey over the miserable terrain beyond Beersheba seemed, in some respects, like a deja vue. But numerous stretches had been improved and though many were still in poor condition, they could not be compared to those of my trip to Wadi Giraffi in the army. Even the narrow serpentine dirt road of Ma'ale Aqrabim, the steep Scorpion Hill, had been widened, and yet it remained one of the worst spots on the trip to negotiate.

Our assignments were of three weeks duration, 12-hour workdays, and a week at leisure in the north. I worked with this arrangement till the end of the year, and then I had enough. Because of the extended stays in Bir Hindis the area became my home away from home. After all, I spent more time in the hard ground desert of the Arava than with my relatives in Kfar Saba.

In time for the second trip my command car had been repaired.

Eventually travel time became shorter, and not only did I begin to feel familiar with the hills and mountains and every bend of the way, but almost seemed to know the potholes and rocks that still could damage my car and its passengers.

The regular shift changes were made by convoy. On two different occasions, when something was urgently needed, I did the round-trip to Tel Aviv and back alone. During my time in the south I always drove the Dodge command car and the vehicle almost became a part of me. It had a four-wheel drive, and in front of the radiator grill was a drum with a long steel cable coiled around it. That winch was a versatile tool to have, especially in the lonely stretches of the Arava. It moved heavy equipment at the drill site and on one of my individual trips, I was happy to pull another army truck from a sand trap it had got stuck in. Not far from that spot stood a cannibalized GMC civilian truck which had hit a mine.

During my work in the south it only happened in isolated cases that cars, traveling individually, were fired on. Two had their windshields pierced by a bullet but I, lucky as always, never had any trouble. In spite of that fact something occurred that could have turned out differently, and which I later chronicled...

KM 74

Bir Hindis, or Be'er Ora as it is called today, was about 3 miles off the dirt road that started in the northern Negev and ended at the southernmost point of the Arava valley where it disappeared into the sands of the Red Sea shore. The quality of that most important route can be compared only with the tracks the wagon trains of the old American West had to traverse to reach their Promised Land.

"Bir" in Arabic and "Be'er" in Hebrew, mean water well, equally important in both languages. Water, the synonym for life, was especially vital in the barren regions of the Negev and Arava. We came here in search of water.

After two or three trips, travel and assignment in this southern desert became routine, and timely moves of the steering wheel prevented potential break-downs of my command car. Life in camp was dull. A single generator supplied the light for the walking areas of our small compound and the big tent that alternated as our dining room and recreation center. On moonless nights, when the splendor of the stars was not at its full strength yet, the terrain surrounding the illuminated camp disappeared into deep blackness. One could easily have surrendered to the feeling of being on an island suspended in the dark regions of outer space. After dinner, the big tent became packed with "roughnecks" (drillers), helpers, guards, and assorted other people who, for lack of better entertainment and to pass the time in this forsaken place, spent their evenings playing cards, sometimes chess, or reading. The air in the tent hung heavy with the smoke of innumerable cigarettes, while the constant bubble of voices blended into a steady hum, similar to the sound inside an airborne plane. Once in a while the irate outcry of a sore loser or the self-satisfied laughter of a winner interrupted the monotonous noise.

I never played cards in the tent and if I did not read one of the books I always brought with me from the north, I became an avid kibitzer at the game tables. However, not everybody found their pleasure in the above mentioned diversions. It was the men who love to argue politics, a favored Jewish pastime.

This particular evening was running its usual course, when suddenly a fellow burst into the tent and declared the Jordanian army had taken Bir Menucha. If this was true we were cut off from the north, as surely as a guillotine severs the head from the body.

The tent became silent. Standing next to the fellow, I admonished him: "Don't joke."

"No joke," he said.

I went to bed as usual and was awakened by a dark figure shaking my shoulder. It felt as if I had just closed my eyes.

"Get up, and stand guard," I was told.

Sleepily I raised the leather cover off my wristwatch and gazed at its luminous dial. It read midnight. I looked at the dim shape hovering over me and asked if he was crazy. I worked twelve hours during the day. Was the third in a three-man crew at our rig, which meant I had to do the dirtiest jobs, act as the provisional cook at our drill site, and did all the mechanical things the other two guys did not know how to do. And he wanted me to stand guard? Besides, we had our own guards.

The dark figure left, and I fell asleep again.

But the man came back. This time, however, he did not relent. "Get up," he said. "It's four o' clock in the morning, and your boss and first mate have stood guard already. It's your turn."

I got up and went outside. I had no rifle and was freezing miserably. I went back into the tent and picked up a blanket, which I wrapped around my shoulders. I also took the revolver from its holster and slipped it into my trousers pocket. Together with a guard, who carried a rifle, I watched the sun come up over the high mountains of Jordan on the other side of the Arava valley and wondered what the day had in store for us.

Breakfast developed into a rambling discussion. Everybody hotly pursued his ideas of what was to be done. We had a government representative in charge of the camp and our convoys, but it appeared the drillers had the right to decide on their own what they did or did not want to do.

As our camp lacked the implements of communication with the outside world, in our case the government office at the Kirya[49] in Tel Aviv, I told my boss, Herr Engelhardt, that I intended to drive our command car to Eilat where the Israeli army had an outpost. At that northernmost point of the Red Sea I hoped to find clarification of our situation and then decide on the next step.

Herr Engelhardt, an elderly gentleman, had drilled many years ago in the oil fields of Galicia, in the then Austro-Hungarian monarchy. I don't think though that his experiences, outside of drilling, prepared him for

---

[49] The Kirya, until the State of Israel, was called Sarona. It was then a settlement of German Templars, a Christian Order, just outside a small sized Tel Aviv. For security reasons the British, at the outbreak of World War II, deported the Templars.

anything like the Israeli Arava in the early 1950s. My boss liked to play it safe, and I definitely had no disagreement with that. However, one could overemphasize some risks. Admittedly, we were in the dark about the developments north of us, but Eilat lay in the south, and there was no visible reason to fear a drive in this direction. Still, Herr Engelhardt opposed my idea. It was surprising that he worked here at all, and it could only have been the relatively good pay that helped him overcome his fears. I was no hero, but the last thing I wanted was to be trapped in the Arava should war break out with Jordan. Israel tapers in the south to a narrow point that leaves little leeway to the east or west. The Egyptian border was 4 miles and the Jordanian a mere two and one half miles away from today's Eilat. That left little space to maneuver. I finally convinced my boss of the usefulness of my idea and, to my surprise, he suddenly decided to accompany me.

A few more men jumped on my command car when my objective became known and we drove the 25 kilometers to Eilat. Eventually I found out Engelhardt's reason for joining us. He had hoped to get on the Dakota aircraft that departed Eilat for Lod airport once a day. But the plane had left and none was expected for the time being.

Not much had changed since I had been here last with the army the year before. Perhaps a few more tents had gone up. At the army command post they knew little about the situation and only that there had been fighting with the Jordanians. The trouble spot, however, was not Bir Menucha but the stretch of road between kilometer 74 and 78. Actually, it made little difference which of the two areas had been occupied by the Jordanian army. We were south of both location and trapped in either case.

At our request the army got in touch by wireless with the people in the Kirya who were in charge of our operations. We asked for instructions, expecting, because of the uncertainty in the region, to be recalled to the north. The answer of the Kirya officials was unsatisfactory to me. I did not know how informed they were about the situation in the south, but they told us to stay put and not to worry. Should it become "necessary," (a euphemism for dangerous) we would be instructed what to do.

I did not like their attitude. It was simple for them to keep us here while they were safely in Tel Aviv. Assuming the Jordanians had really occupied that four kilometers stretch of road and had expanded their territory further to the west, it was clear that the Israelis would try to retake this section of land. Nobody could predict developments arising from that incident, especially in a region like the Middle East. For all I knew, the Jordanians might decide to strike next in the south, and that's where we were.

369

I had no intention to wait in Bir Hindis for instructions from the Kirya or for the next move of the Jordanians. I decided that if I found a partner to accompany me, I would leave very early the next morning and drive north. It was not a heroic decision; rather, I was certain that in case of danger, Israeli soldiers would, at some point, prevent me from continuing the journey.

My boss shared none of my convictions. He had missed the last plane out of Eilat, and as none was expected until the situation cleared, he was in no mood for adventure.

Back in camp another fierce verbal battle took place. More men than I had anticipated were ready to take the chance and drive north, and eventually all the drillers and their mates chose to go back to Tel Aviv. It was decided, however, that every crew should drive to its respective drill site[50], pick up as many tools as they could, and bury the rest in the vicinity. Everyone was aware that marauding Bedouins from Jordan would not miss the opportunity to plunder an abandoned drill site if the chance arose.

Thinking back, the burial of equipment seemed a ludicrous waste of time and energy. Bedouins were famous for their tracking ability and their skills in reading the ground. We certainly left enough signs to lead them straight to the hiding places.

Still in the dark about what was going on, we watched our surroundings apprehensively while loading the command car at the drill site. The two guards and their rifles did little to alleviate the feeling of insecurity, and the little Webley revolver I carried in the holster again was no protection should the Jordanians try to take over the south as well. At best, our weapons were useful against rambling Bedouins.

We worked in a hurry, and felt relieved when we were on our way back to the camp.

At dinner that night, I got into another hassle with Engelhardt. He vehemently rejected my request to be the lead car of our convoy. "We can hit a mine," he argued, and he was right, of course. It had happened in relatively peaceful times that Arabs planted mines. My boss obviously had no stomach to sit up front with me on that trip, but probably was ashamed to ask to travel in one of the vehicles behind me. Yet again, it was not heroism that made me volunteer to lead the convoy. Long stretches of that primitive way were made up of very fine, powdery sand, and only the driver of the lead car saw the road clearly ahead of him. The second vehicle in a convoy perceived its surroundings through a veil of dust, while the third in line could just make out the rear of the car in

---

[50] We drilled at several different locations, usually within a fifteen-mile radius north of Bir Hindis.

front of him. After a while everybody in such a convoy, with the exception of the driver of the first car and the man beside him, looked as if they had been dunked into a barrel of flour. In their clown-like faces only the eyes retained their original shine and color.

Engelhardt was the lone objector to my wish. Others probably thought I had lost my senses, but were only too willing to let me drive at the head of the column. Trying to ease my boss's fear with reasoning even I found a little ambiguous, I told him that cars did not always drive in the ruts created by the ones ahead. In which case I might miss a mine had one been planted while one of the following vehicles could be the unfortunate one to activate it by driving over the device.

Hardly convinced, but with little choice, my boss reluctantly gave in.

The camp had been blacked out, and we cleaned our plates and silverware outside in the dark. While I rinsed my utensils, I unintentionally overheard two men talking about me. They voiced their feelings, unaware of my presence.

"If there is trouble on the way tomorrow, the *Yekke* will take off," one said.

"What can you do?" the other one asked. "Nobody wants to be first."

"Yekke" is a rather derogatory word for a German Jew. Though I was not from Germany, I was included in this classification because German was my mother tongue. If somebody was called Yekke, it sometimes meant a person so straight, square, and overly honest, as to be considered stupid. To me those traits were something to be proud of. But they certainly did not fit every German Jew.

"If there is trouble on the way," I interrupted them, "I shall take off all right, but I am not running away. I'll just run and you can follow me."

Early next morning our convoy snaked its way out of the camp. Ari, the first assistant to the boss and the two guards sat in the back of our command car. Engelhardt, in spite of his misgivings about being in the first car of the convoy, sat beside me. He looked worried, and I too awaited the next few hours with mixed feelings.

But nothing happened. Kilometer after kilometer rolled by without any interference or interruption. The wide valley of the Arava lay peaceful in the simmering heat of the day, and yet the tranquillity of the scene seemed deceptive. The Jordanian mountain range to our right distanced itself as we progressed to the north. Notwithstanding the distance it appeared ominous. The Israeli hills to our left were reassuring.

Whenever I drove the unpaved roads of the Negev and the Arava, I scanned the ground just ahead of the moving vehicle. It helped me avoid cracks, potholes and rocks. My traveling speed was around the usual 25-mph. On many occasions I reduced the speed to avoid damaging the springs or tires of our vehicle. Some sections of the way were of a rough, but evenly contoured surface, while others became as torturous to a person in a car as an ice cube might be in a cocktail shaker. The uneven terrain on both sides of the road appeared like waves of an ocean frozen into immobility. The area was dotted with short trees whose gnarled branches sprouted thorns instead of leaves.

We passed Ain Radian on our right, a place of several water holes and a few slanted palm trees standing guard over them. I had dubbed the spot "little oasis" the first time I had seen it, but it had nothing in common with the romanticism of a Hollywood oasis of the same size. During the rainy season of winter Bedouins let their camels roam freely to look for food. Several of those animals were usually seen near the water holes as they move about with their swaying gait. Today the place lay deserted.

Depending on the surface composition of the road, the car behind me was sometimes seen clearly in my rear-view mirror, at other times it rumbled along in a dusty haze. Its driver and co-rider had their heads swathed in Arab headgear, the best protection against the fine powdery sand stirred up by the wheels of my command car. At those times the rest of our convoy was invisible in the murkiness of the whirling dust.

With my *kefie* (Arab shawl) just rolled around my neck, I forgot for a moment the purpose of our journey. It seemed so pleasant to view the open spaces ahead of me, especially with "home" as the tantalizing goal of the journey. As always when I felt good I fished for a cigarette. I steadied the steering wheel with my left hand, while my right went to my shirt pocket. Engelhardt gave me a disapproving look but held his tongue. It was not the smoke he minded or the worry about my health, but his own safety. As he once told me, I could lose control of the car while lighting a cigarette. It never happened and, as any smoker, I believed in the relaxing effect of a cigarette in moments of stress and pleasure.

More kilometers disappeared under our wheels as we passed the small rocks on the side of the way that displayed the primitively painted numbers of 70, 71, 72, 73. Anxiously, I awaited kilometer 74, glancing more frequently to the right where the invisible border with Jordan lay. I saw nothing unusual – no Israelis and, with relief, no Jordanians. But before we reached the 74th kilometer, I spotted barbed wire concertinas pushed to the left side of the way. Still, nothing and nobody. – Kilometer 75 rolled by, and the next kilometer was about due when I beheld "it."

Like the iron body of a warship at sea the tank on my right appeared to be plowing right through the wavy contours of the barren waste. It seemed intent on reaching a point ahead of us, ready to cut short our progress toward freedom. But the direction of the cannon in its turret seemed strange. It pointed straight ahead. We could have been easy prey for the tank commander had he turned the cannon our way. I hoped he had not spotted us though it seemed stupid to believe that. The dust we raised could be seen for miles.

The moment I became aware of the tank, I leaned over the steering wheel and pushed the accelerator down as far as it would go. The car lurched forward, my passengers hung on for all they were worth, and the speedometer needle climbed to 50 mph, an untenable speed for long in this terrain. I worried a bit about the springs of my Dodge but hoped that the drivers in the cars behind me would nonetheless heed the advice I had given them. Match my speed.

Before I could check a mischievous impulse I cried out, half mockingly, to my boss: "Look to your right, Herr Engelhardt."

I knew that the road a little further up angled to the left, which would get me deeper into Israeli territory, and I breathed a sigh of relief when it happened. The rest of the cars had followed me faithfully, and on we went until we finally ascended into the hills with Bir Menucha just ahead of us.

We found the well and its surroundings occupied by the Israeli army. It was a reassuring feeling to see the soldiers and I wanted to continue on our way. A soldier, guarding the road, stopped us.

"You can't pass through here," he said. – "Why?" – "My orders are to let nobody through," he said. – "We have to go through. We are on our way to Tel Aviv." – "Nobody gets through", he insisted. – "I want to see the officer in charge," I told the man, and he directed me to the temporary camp just off the road.

The other cars had stopped behind me when I went in search of the officer in command. I found a very young lieutenant in overalls, a typical Sabra[51].

"Look," I told him, "we are several cars that want to pass through here, but your guard refuses to let us continue." – "Where do you come from and where do you want to go?" – "We come from Bir Hindis, and are on our way to Tel Aviv." – "You're lucky," he said. "Didn't you know that there was fighting on that road yesterday? The Jordanians had to be dislodged from the stretch of ground they had occupied."

No, we didn't, and I told him about the tank. Nothing to worry about, he explained. The Jordanian lead tank had been hit by Israeli artillery fire yesterday and was burned out. The other enemy tanks then retreated.

He gave me permission to continue on our way.

---

[51] An Israeli born.

I wished I had known that the tank was a mere shell. Nobody likes to be in the sights of an anxious tank commander half a mile away, especially while traveling in an open vehicle like ours with no cover around.

When I got back to our convoy, the other fellows had found out about our artillery sitting on top of the Israeli hills to the left. They still were there when we had passed through, and I was glad they did not mistake us for Jordanians in our *kefies*. I gave the news to Engelhardt. "See," I said, "we had nothing to worry about. The Jordanian army may have been on our right; but the Israeli cannons were in the hills to our left."

"Yes," he commented dryly, "and we were right between them."

We reached Tel Aviv that evening without further complications, and spent a few extra days in civilization. Three days later, we drove south once more.

That short stretch, ostensibly, did belong to Jordan. The UN awarded it to them. The Israelis eventually pioneered a road just to the west of the old one and it was there that our convoys traveled from then on. I never knew the difference. The surface of this area, two hundred yards either way, was little different to the eye and just as rough.

I worked eight years for Water Works. In time, through the relentless effort of Mr. Novak, a director in the company, he successfully convinced the proper authorities in the Israeli government that big drill rigs from the United States were needed for the search of water and oil. His dream and belief was that oil can be found in Israel.

With those rigs came a superintendent from Texas who was to teach us how to run them. As almost none of the drillers and their assistants spoke English, a few others and I translated his instructions into Hebrew. When work on those IDECO rigs started, I was made shift leader with a crew of four.

Our first job on an IDECO rigs was to deep-drill for water in Revivim, a kibbutz in the desert south of Beersheba.

As mentioned earlier in my narration, many developments in one's life depended on IFs and BECAUSEs. Sometimes these words are used for excuses, at other times they really make the difference.

At this point in my life, the if of a promise and the because of a coincidence changed my future forever.

Mundek, my second cousin, and I met infrequently on our days off in Kfar Saba. On one occasion he told me of his upcoming wedding to Ruti, a girl from Bulgaria, whom he had met while a member at Kibbutz Dan. He asked if I would come to his wedding at the *Waad Hakehilah*, the committee for religious community matters in Tel Aviv, and the following social gathering. I agreed to be at both affairs if our crew was off duty. And because we were up north I attended the wedding. It was a simple ceremony in line with their financial standing, and at the subsequent get-together of relatives and friends, cakes, soft drinks and wine were served.

The newlyweds had rented a small apartment in Shchunat Hatikwa, the majority of whose residents, though Jewish, came mostly from Arabian countries.

Another cake had to be picked up at Ruti's home, a small hut in an immigrant camp a few miles up the road, and I was chosen to get it. I used Shulko's pickup truck, and my guide was Ruti's younger sister, a beautiful young woman by the name of Rina. We talked little on the way and returned speedily.

I had learned earlier from Mundek that Ruti's closest family consisted of her mother and two younger sisters, Rina being the girl in the middle. The father had died during the war.

I would have liked to invite Rina to a movie but felt certain that with her looks she doubtlessly had lots of fellows interested in her. Besides, my irregular shifts at work, and my frequent absence from the Tel Aviv area, made my chance to meet her slim. Nonetheless, in the course of the afternoon I asked her if she would go with me to a movie. I found her answer strange. She had to ask her mother. When we eventually did go to a movie, her younger sister, Esther, accompanied us.

Three weeks later Rina informed me that her mother would not permit her to go out with me unless we were engaged. This declaration came as a shock. Engagements usually became marriages and I did not think that I was ready for married life yet. In all honesty, however, I feared the responsibility of starting a family, uncertain whether my income would suffice for this kind of commitment.

Luckily, the sense and fear of losing that beautiful girl got the better of me and I agreed to the condition. To seal the engagement I bought a gold ring with an aquamarine stone; all that I could afford.

I had expected Rina to stay home after we were married, but she too had worked since she was 14, and she would not hear of it. With her by my side, all of life's tribulations were always overcome.

At Ruti's wedding Rina had been ten days shy of her nineteenth birthday and I was twenty-nine. We were married on December 11, 1952, also at the Waad Hakehila and had a wedding as "elaborate" as Ruti and Mundek's.

On October 29, 1953 our son, Shabtai was born in Tel Aviv.

My sister in the United States appealed to me in each of her letters to move to America. She wrote that we were the only two survivors of our family and should live closer to each other. Her stated reason was of course only part of the motive, and it was the concern for my safety that influenced her writing.

For years my replies to Betty, as she is called now, were always the same. I liked my life in Israel and there was little chance that I would change my mind. But again, there was this expression "never say never," and one day, with the consent of Rina, I gave in to my sister's entreaties and began to take the necessary steps for a move to the USA.

In early 1958 my wife and small son left for the United States and I followed two months later. After my plane had landed in New York and I stepped outside the big airport building, it felt as if I had entered one of my childhood fantasies. There were cars and people, but what characterized America most for me was a man in a policeman's uniform, the kind I had seen so often in movies, and an American flag fluttering in a breeze high on a pole.

Despite the visual effects, my mind had to adjust to the thought that I was really in America. The truth was that I could not help but feel this situation was improbable. And yet, it was true. My yearning for adventure seemed to have been satisfied with my arrival here, but just being here was an adventure again.

My dreams had come full circle.

Israel will always be close to my heart and so will my experiences in Palestine and Egypt. The 18 years spent in the Middle East and Egypt provided all emotions a human being is capable of, as well as decisions, wise and foolish, times secure and times of danger. But throughout all of my experiences a major factor to my well-being was always with me, luck.

The British government awarded British soldiers who had served in North Africa during the time of Rommel and his Afrika Korps the Africa Star. Having served in this theater of war in 1942, I received in 1953 a little box from England that contained the Africa Star (the bar of that medal had been worn before by soldiers), the War Medal 1939-45 and a 4x5½" paper that said: The Under-Secretary of State for War presents his compliments and by Command of the Army Council has the honour to transmit the enclosed Awards granted for service during the war of 1939-45. – Handwritten beneath it is, Pal 6585 Gustav Pimselstein.

Less elaborate is the acknowledgment of the Israeli government for its servicemen. I received two little bars in different colors, one representing my service in the War of Independence 1948-50, the other for the 1956 Sinai Campaign.

376

I had left my sister in Vienna, a young teenager, I met her again, a "lifetime" later, a married woman and mother of two daughters.

In the USA we first lived in Denver, where our daughter Clara was born October 29 1962. In 1964 we moved to San Francisco where we have resided ever since.